The Marquis

CHARLES WATSON–WENTWORTH
SECOND MARQUIS OF ROCKINGHAM

Studio of Sir Joshua Reynolds
National Portrait Gallery
London

The Marquis

A Study of
Lord Rockingham,
1730–1782

ROSS J. S. HOFFMAN

New York
Fordham University Press
1973

Printed in the United States of America

To my Daughter

Mary Ellen Flinn

Contents

Illustrations

Preface

THE MARQUIS OF ROCKINGHAM (1730–1782) headed the ministry of King George III which carried the repeal of the Stamp Act and redressed the commercial grievances of the American colonies in 1766. Sixteen years later he returned to office at the head of another administration resolved to end the American war even at the price of surrendering British sovereignty over the colonies. During the intervening years he was head of the whig party and of the principal part of the parliamentary minority which had from the beginning opposed the resort to arms in America. He sagaciously foresaw that this was an impractical undertaking, and he had condemned all the rash and imprudent policies and measures which culminated in provoking the American rebellion. This is not to say that he was in any sense "pro-American," or that he agreed with ideas and opinions in the colonies which were inconsistent with British constitutional principles. He was simply a peace-loving whig brought up in the political school of Walpole, Hardwicke, and Newcastle. To him it was axiomatic that maintaining a balanced equilibrium of power in continental Europe was the first principle of British national security; and since he judged that military coercion of America was too big an undertaking for British forces, the contest would be drawn out and the Bourbon monarchies of France and Spain would combine decisively against Great Britain. The colonies would be lost in the general disaster. Rockingham was no imperialist but he prized these overseas plantations and rejoiced in their healthy growth because they nourished the commerce, industry, and naval strength of Great Britain: which was why, as it seemed so obvious to him, they ought not to be vexed and irritated but held on whatever terms of indulgence were necessary to prosper their interests and conserve their natural loyalty to British community.

The Marquis was one of the foremost men of politics in the age of Chatham and Shelburne, of North, Burke, and Charles Fox—all of whom have been closely studied by historians and biographers during two centuries. But Rockingham has been neglected, regarded as not very interesting or even historically important: a virtuous but rather sickly Georgian nobleman managed by a talented secretary, Edmund Burke. In 1852 the Earl of Albemarle, enjoying privileged access to Rockingham's papers in Wentworth Woodhouse, drew him out from the shadow of Burke in *Memoirs of the Marquis of Rockingham,* a selective edition in two volumes of his letters and papers with a discursive historical commentary linking them in more or less chronological order. One could hardly suspect from this work alone that Burke had an important part in Rockingham's life. This exclusion may be explained by the publication eight years before of a select edition of Burke's correspondence, which contained many of Rockingham's letters to him. The materials of this work were drawn from the same muniments. Albemarle's *Memoirs* did not arrest the trend among historians to look upon the Marquis as a sort of background figure on the political stage. All have accepted the opinion of his contemporaries (without exception) that his character was good, his honor high, his reputation unblemished by a hint of corruption or scandal—extraordinary homage paid to a politician who practiced politics in an age of very great political corruption—yet he was allowed to remain in comparative obscurity.

The prime reason for this was that nineteenth-century historians and whig leaders, reading the ways of their time back into Rockingham's, missed much that they might not have missed if they had perceived fully the revolutionary influence of Charles Fox upon the whig party. Rockingham was succeeded as "head of the whigs" by the Duke of Portland who yielded the active party leadership to Fox, a man of glittering talents but no principled consistency, whose political conduct would assuredly have been reprobated by the Marquis. He carried on a bitter, even personal, contest against the King, desiring to reduce the monarchy to complete subjection to the House of Commons. He saw kings as a greater menace to liberty than the Jacobin revolutionaries of France, alienated Burke, and then almost all other whigs who had long been attached to Rockingham; all the while courting reformers, radicals, and republicans, stirring public passions, and promoting party activity far beyond the halls of Parliament. Without intending what in reality he was doing he undermined the equipoise of the monarchic-aristocratic-representative constitution so venerated in the eighteenth century. Foxite whiggism is the bridge over the abyss between the age of Newcastle and Rockingham and the age of Grey, Melbourne, and Russell. The Marquis to be sure engaged in a contest against George III but only for the purpose of reducing what he conceived to be the *excessive* influence of the crown over the other parts of the legislature, an influence tending to disturb the equipoise. For this effort he of course wished all possible support from the real interests and sober opinion in the country, that is, from men capable of forming genuine opinions on public business; but he was ever shy of "hot" and "wild" politicians and consistently tried to restrain his friends from fomenting and exploiting public passions. Although Fox may be regarded as a Rockingham whig in the last years of the American war, a great contrast may be drawn between their purposes. To whigs of the Victorian age who adored the memory of Fox and did not fully perceive the gulf of difference between their own times and the early decades of the reign of George III it was inevitable that Rockingham should seem a rather timidly mild and temperate man, wanting in energy, a leader too cautious and slow-witted or too lazy to lead a great party.

Not until a more realistic understanding was gained of the way politics were practiced in the eighteenth century could it seem worthwhile to focus close attention upon Rockingham. Many historians have wrought this advance during the last fifty-odd years. Great have been the achievements and influence of the late Sir Lewis Namier and his so-called school, although they too have rather deprecated Rockingham, largely, it may be, because of his connection with Burke whom they blamed for misleading several generations of historians who used his partisan political pamphlets as mirrors of political history. In 1949 the Fitzwilliam family, proprietors of Wentworth Woodhouse and Milton Park, removed their muniments to libraries open to all scholars, thus opening the previously inaccessible corpus of the papers of Burke, Rockingham, and his heir Earl Fitzwilliam (to whom Burke owed his seat in Parliament after the Marquis' death). Scores of fresh studies of Burke have resulted from the opening of his private papers, inevitably shedding new light upon the leader he followed for seventeen years. The new nine-volume *Correspondence of Edmund Burke* (1958–1971), masterfully edited, contains all of his letters to Rockingham and nearly all of the latter's to him. All historians of eighteenth-century politics have explored in the Fitzwilliam mine, and it may be said that a more realistic picture of Rockingham shows in the works of such historians as Sir Herbert Butterfield, John Brooke, Ian Christie, Bernard Donoughmore, and John Cannon. Cedric Collyer has written several valuable articles illuminating Rockingham's commanding role in the local politics of the county and city of York. The late Professor George H. Guttridge used the fresh sources to write his pamphlet-study *The Early Career of Lord Rockingham* (1952). It did not go beyond 1765.

My interest in Rockingham was stirred while working on Burke. Why did the latter, after gaining considerable stature in Parliament, refuse tempting ministerial offers and adhere so faithfully to the Marquis through all those years of futile opposition against the administrations of Chatham, Grafton, and North? What was the attractive force which engaged so deeply the loyalty of that most reputable country gentleman William Dowdeswell, county member for Worcestershire and former tory, who led the main body of the whigs in the House of Commons from 1767 to his death in 1775? Why the universal esteem for the Marquis as a man of unblemished character? Were there indeed no stains? Why did George III who from the early 'sixties to 1782 judged his lights as dim yet come to see him as the most formidable opponent of Majesty's preferred way of recruiting and sustaining administrations? Why did this nobleman of great wealth who always preferred private to public life continue as a politician for so long after the King was resolved against employing him again as minister? To these and other questions I attempted to find some answers, and the result is this book; which is not a biography but a piece of political history, a story which seemed worth trying to tell in one short book.

I wish to express gratitude to the Earl Fitzwilliam, proprietor of the Wentworth Woodhouse Muniments, and to the staff of the Sheffield Central Library (where these are on deposit), especially Miss Rosamund Meredith, archivist; to the Duke of Portland and the Uni-

versity of Nottingham for permission to quote from the papers of
the third Duke of Portland; to the staff of the British Museum,
especially the ever-helpful custodians of the manuscripts division; to
the William Salt Library at Stafford for providing photocopies of
certain manuscripts of the second Earl of Dartmouth; to Sir William
Pennington-Ramsden for permission to quote from the Ramsden MSS
on deposit in the Central Library of Leeds; to Mr. Thomas Wragg,
librarian at Chatsworth, for allowing me to explore and quote from
the papers of the fourth Duke of Devonshire; to the William L.
Clements Library, University of Michigan, at Ann Arbor, for permission to study and quote from letters of William Dowdeswell,
Charles Townshend, John Lee, and Lord Shelburne; to the University of Chicago Press for permission to quote from *The Correspondence of Edmund Burke*; to Professor James E. Bunce of St.
John's University for help on a certain problem; to Professor
Cornelius Foster of Providence College for enabling me to read
various documents collected in the course of his study of Charles
Townshend; to Mr. John Brooke, most erudite scholar of Rocking-
ham's age, for many wise and friendly counsels; to Sir Herbert
Butterfield and Professor Henry Steele Commager for their en-
couraging interest in my study; to my wife, Hannah McCruden
Hoffman, for working side by side with me in libraries, and our
granddaughter Margaret M. S. Flinn, a graduate in history from
Barnard College, for checking some references and quotations. When
I started the first explorations of my subject the American Philosophical Society generously provided a grant-in-aid.

Ross J. S. HOFFMAN

Rye, New York

1

The Inheritance

IN THE WEST RIDING OF YORKSHIRE there were Wentworths from time immemorial. The first to gain great fame was Sir Thomas (of Wentworth Park) whom Charles I created Earl of Strafford. He governed Ireland in a masterful way for his sovereign and might have governed England too if an infuriated Puritan Parliament had not forced Majesty to sacrifice him on the block. From this great man Charles Watson-Wentworth second Marquis of Rockingham traced his descent. He lived in Strafford's "wood house" (by then encased in palatial stone), possessed his property, read his private papers, and revered his name. Strafford's son and heir, William Wentworth, died without issue in 1694; the peerage passed collaterally but the properties were inherited by Thomas Watson, son of Strafford's daughter Anne and Edward Watson second Baron Rockingham of Rockingham Castle (Northants). Thus Thomas Watson became master at Wentworth Park and appropriately assumed his grandfather's name; while his older brother Lewis became third Baron Rockingham. Thomas

Watson-Wentworth married a baronet's daughter, Alice Proby, who bore him one son, his namesake. Thomas Watson-Wentworth II (1693–1750) took for wife Mary Finch, daughter of Daniel seventh Earl of Winchelsea and Earl of Nottingham. Their son Charles was born at Wentworth Park on May 13, 1730.[1]

At that time Thomas Watson-Wentworth II was one of the most politically influential men in Yorkshire. He had sat as member for Malton (where his property enabled him to nominate both representatives) in George I's two parliaments and was an ally of the whigs in administration. Following his election as a county member in 1728 he was raised to the peerage as Baron Malton. Since before his time the prevailing interests in the county had been "independent" or unfriendly to the ministerial whigs, Lord Malton was instrumental in opening what has been called the "great whig age" in Yorkshire. Perhaps the Finch family with its ancestral toryism was helpful to him in turning tories into whigs—two of his Finch brothers-in-law owed their seats in Parliament to his nomination. In 1733–1734 he was created Earl of Malton and appointed lord lieutenant and custos rotulorum (chief magistrate) of the West, East, and North Ridings—all Yorkshire, England's greatest county. This was his meridian, as it was Sir Robert Walpole's. Eight years later his loss of an expensive election contest as Sir Robert's grip on the House of Commons failed shows how closely Malton's fortunes were linked with those of the great Minister.[2] Respect and admiration for Walpole prevailed in Malton's family along with a detestation of the "patriots" whose opposition had undermined him. Charles's aunt and godmother, Lady Isabella Finch, wrote to Malton on December 13, 1744: ". . . if that Great Man was to be dissected, there would be found more true patriotism in his Gutts, than in all those who bellowed so much and so long for their dear Country." [3]

The death of older brothers left Charles by 1739 an only son with four sisters. He wore the courtesy title of Viscount Higham and was entered at Westminster School, a fact probably related to his father's purchase (in 1741) of the Grosvenor Square house (number 4) which in later years would be the scene of great whig conclaves. A few slight glimpses can be had of the young lord at Westminster, where he relished bold pranks and the dramatics fashionable among young gentlemen.[4] His uncle, Lord Winchelsea, noticed him in a letter to Lord Malton in 1741: "I told him I think he never will be safe if he continues the practice of overheating himself and then drinking cold water. . . . the young man is of a pretty healthy strong constitution." In 1745 he comes into clear historical daylight and with some éclat. His father organized volunteers to help defend the country against the Pretender and made Higham a colonel. As the Scotch army of Prince Charles Stuart marched into the heart of England (putting the Wentworth household in flight to Doncaster), Higham maneuvered with his regiment. His sister Mary wrote from London that the King "did not doubt but that you was as good a colonel as he has in his army"; and sister Charlotte told him "you have gained immortal honour and I have every day the satisfaction of hearing twenty handsome things said of the Blues and their Collonel." When the rebels retreated, Malton was directed to dissolve his volunteers and urge them to enlist in the regular forces of the King; whereupon Higham, with one servant, rode from Wakefield over the Pennines and through the robber-infested country of Westmoreland and Cumberland to the headquarters of the Duke of Cumberland's army at Carlisle. The royal Duke, admiring the young lord's courage, kept him safe and notified the anxiety-ridden Malton, saying that Higham's "zeal on this occasion shows the same principles fix't that you yourself have given such strong proofs of." Having run off without parental permission Higham wrote a proudly penitent letter to his father, saying that the Duke "blamed me for my disobedience, yet as I came with a design of saving my King and country . . . it greatly palliated my offence." His brother-in-law Lord Fitzwilliam applauded the boy's "courage and spirit." Sister Mary said that everyone was saying "it will always be remembered to his honour," but she feared "Papa's anger"; that however was smothered by parental pride and High- am's only punishment was being required to write a de- tailed account of his adventure. "Though I hope you won't tell it him," Lady Malton counseled her husband from Grosvenor Square, "never any thing met with such general applause, in short he is the hero of these times, and his Majesty talks of this young Subject, in such terms, as must please you to hear . . . in the Drawing Room no two peo- ple talk together, but he makes part of the discourse." Mal- ton's family relished this honorable attention marking a darling son and brother as an outstanding member of his generation—one who had been signally distinguished by the King's brother Cumberland.[5]

No doubt Malton felt that all this added some weight to the argument for his own further elevation in the peerage. In February, 1746, Thomas Watson Earl of Rockingham died without issue and that peerage, which antedated Mal- ton's earldom, passed to the Watson-Wentworth family. Two months later the new Lord Rockingham was made a marquis, an honor of singular distinction in view of the fact that then and for long afterward there was no other mar- quis in the British peerage. The new Marquis seems to have owed his elevation to the restored ascendancy in administra- tion of Walpole whigs under the lead of Henry Pelham. Lord Higham too got a step-up in courtesy rank, and from this time was known as Earl of Malton. On April 24 his father wrote to him:

> It is a great Joy to me that in the first Letter I write to you by your new Stile I can congratulate upon the glorious Victory obtained by the Duke over the Rebells. . . . I take my Place as Marquess in the House of Lords to day introduced by the Duke of Devonshire & Earl of Pembroke. His Grace of New- castle & Mr. Pelham dined with me yesterday.[6]

Young Malton had by this time gone abroad. Although his father had been at Cambridge a decision appears to have been taken against sending the son there. He went to Geneva under the tutorship of George Quarme, a cultivated young Yorkshireman who had served as an officer in the West Riding volunteers. Sending their last and only living son to the heart of Europe while war with France continued suggests that the Watson-Wentworths had a hearty confidence in both the boy's character and Quarme's. Watched over by agents of the British and Hanoverian governments, the young gentlemen traveled via The Hague through Germany—avoiding war zones—and reached Geneva toward the end of May. The Marquis on June 11 was "very glad to hear you got safe to Geneva, hope you like the Place & have begun Your Study & Exercises in a Regular manner, want to know what they are, the French Language should be industriously regarded—I think you might write oftener & take care to form the Characters large, for your present Hand is much too small." [7] There are no extant letters from Malton during his stay at Geneva (which lasted almost two years), but letters to him from members of the family survive. "I heard from other hands," wrote Mary on October 13, "that you apply yourself to French and every thing else a Man of Quality ought to know." That Malton soon heard the siren call of Italy is evidenced by a letter from his mother the next month. She would not believe that he had gained such a mastery of French that he could so soon "give room" to learning Italian:

> I should be verry Sorry to see you finish with only Smatterings of different Languages which can only serve to make a Coxcomb of you and tempt you frequently to expose yourself when a totall Ignorance might have secured you. Of those Sorts of Animals the present Age is Sufficiently furnished with and I hope in a few years you will have as great a contempt for them as they justly deserve.[8]

Quarme was naturally shy of pulling the reins too hard on one to whom he would look in the future for favor and preference, but he did confide to Lord Rockingham that his son spent more time amusing himself with English friends of his own generation than at his studies. A relative in England wrote to Malton that "keeping a table" was a "very wild scheme" which his parents would not approve. By the end of 1747 the Marquis decided: "The Geneva letters are not agreeable as to the Oeconomy carried on there, and I think his coming home for a small time may be agreeable." [9] Early the next year the young Lord returned.

The parental plan was for Malton to make "a progress to see the most considerable places in England," to enlarge his acquaintance with the class to which he belonged, and to spend some time at Wentworth before going abroad again. About this time the Marquis made a comprehensive survey of his properties and revenues, which were in much disorder, and took counsel from his brother-in-law, Solicitor General William Murray, who advised a more exact and methodical administration of these affairs. A total income of £20,500 was derived mainly from estates in Yorkshire, Northamptonshire, and County Wicklow in Ireland. Malton probably was made acquainted with the nature and state of his prospective inheritance before setting off upon the grand continental tour. Nearing sixty and in uncertain health Lord Rockingham redrafted his will in May, 1748, so that all might be in order, and Murray was named a trustee to administer the estates if the Marquis died before Malton came of age.[10]

Late that summer, the war being over, Malton crossed to France in the company of Major James Forrester. The officer's leave had been attained through Lord Rockingham's intercession with Secretary of State Newcastle and the Duke of Cumberland.[11] The travelers made their way leisurely through France intent on spending the winter in Italy. Somewhere along the way Lady Isabella Finch met her nephew and reported to his father: "Lord Malton . . . is a most charming youth in every body's opinion, as well as in mine, and you have sent him abroad in so handsome a manner, that one may expect at his Return to see him a very accomplished & valuable man." [12] In November Malton and Forrester reached Turin where they were presented to King Charles Emmanuel and the Duke of Savoy. They went on

to Parma, Placentia, and Bologna, and by January were
lodged for the winter in Florence. The young lord fell in
love with Italy and according to his companion this love was
not unrequited. The Major wrote to the Marquis "how
much every body of distinguished rank" was pleased by his
son "whose heart makes him as amiable as his Head makes
him useful to the world."

> As all Strangers of Distinction keep a house in this place, my
> Lord Malton has got the best that was to be hired here & the
> Company he frequents & who come to him, are such only, as I
> flatter myself, Your Lordship & My Lady Marchioness would
> chuse for him.

No doubt the Marquis suspected that the Major wrote with
greater partiality than candor, but in replying said of his
son:

> God has given him a good Bodily Constitution & I hope a mind
> capable of improvement . . . to which end Literature & a po-
> lite Knowledge of Men & Books will greatly contribute & if
> built upon the solid Body of true Religion cannot fail of suc-
> cess.[13]

More interested in people than in pictures or books, Malton
moved gracefully in Florentine society. The ladies pronounced him a *garbatissimo Signore*.[14] He listed in a small
book the notable persons (mostly women) with whom he
became acquainted wherever he went, and devised a system
of numbered dots to distinguish "been in their house"–
"dined"–"supped"–"handsomest." After spending a good
deal of money he and Forrester went to Siena for the summer of 1749 and there he showed some inclination "to give
more time to books than was compatible with the diversions
& numerous visits at Florence." He wrote jejune notes on
various topics and even composed a short sketch of the civil
government of Siena: trivialities displaying no trace of any
sort of talent. He bought some yellow marble tables, a
picture by Andrea del Sarto, some brass figures by Giovanni

da Bologna, and executed a commission from his father to
purchase marble statuary for Wentworth House. The travelers were at Lucca in September and then journeyed to
Rome and Naples. At Rome there were many English, and
Malton was delighted to find that the whigs outnumbered
the Jacobites four to one, that there were "no Persons of
rank about the Pretender," and that "the vile spirit of
Jacobitism" was in great decline. Among his countrymen he
found two sons of the Duke of Devonshire and the Irish
peer Lord Charlemont—all destined to be his lifelong
friends. Malton was received by the heads of the Roman
nobility and became acquainted with such high ecclesiastics
as Cardinals Albani, Spinelli, Portocarrara, and Colonna.
At Naples he formed an attachment to an interesting lady,
the Principessa Francavilla. In mid-March 1750 he answered an appeal from his father to start for home by saying that he would set out in a month or six weeks, make haste
through Italy, and get into France, "that in case you should
think my return proper earlier in the winter, I shall be nearer
to England." Soon the Marquis directed him so to arrange
his course as to attend the King at Hanover in September.
Before starting north at the end of April Malton bought a
harpsichord for his prospective bride because "Miss Bright
is no small proficient in Musick." [15]

Mary Bright was the daughter of Lady Ramsden (relict
of Thomas Bright of Badsworth, Yorkshire) and step-
daughter to Sir John Ramsden of Byrom who was a friend
of the Watson-Wentworth family and had commanded a
regiment in the volunteers of '45. Nothing but the fact is
known of her betrothal to Malton. He was at Padua when
he received news that her smallpox inoculation had gone
well and that their engagement, hitherto unpublished, had
been announced; which rather startled him, although he
wrote to his sister Mary that "nothing could be more wished
for by me," and that "all my Friends greatly approve of the
match." [16]

After a stay at Venice he and Forrester made their way
to Vienna and were received at the court of Maria Theresa

and the Emperor Francis. Attending military maneuvers in Bohemia they were signally noticed by the sovereigns: "We dined with their Majesties & the Emperor order'd me to set next him & conversed as familiarly as if I had been his sworn friend many years." Very different was the reception at Berlin and Potsdam where Frederick the Great snubbed him. In a letter to his father Malton described the Prussian King as an officious and odious tyrant without whose approval not even a prop could go on the stage of the opera: ". . . his overbearing Vanity & the perfidies he is capable of makes him detestable." The lower class of people were "extravagantly fond of him" but he was "not so much loved as feared among his principal subjects." After quitting that despot's domain Malton spent ten days at the court of Brunswick where "it was the Study of the Court how to make us pass our time with Pleasure." In mid-September he presented himself to his sovereign at Herrenhausen. The Duke of Newcastle was there and showed every attention to the Marquis of Rockingham's son. George II told uncle Henry Finch that he never had seen a finer or more promising youth. After a short visit to Hamburg Malton went to Paris where in December 1750 news reached him of his father's death.[17]

While Malton lived in Europe the Marquis appears to have busied himself primarily with family interests. The work of raising the great stone pile Wentworth House (later known as Wentworth Woodhouse) was still going on, and its master built in the park a monument in the form of a pyramid to commemorate the whig glories of his age. Although consulted by Henry Pelham and William Murray on the choice of a candidate to fill a vacant county seat in 1749, he declined an active part and preferred another man to the one administration supported. He had the bulk of his correspondence since 1734 copied into a large folio volume, presumably for his son. On October 3, 1750, he wrote to Malton rejoicing in "that cultivation I hope you will never suffer to be defaced by the temptations of wicked courses allways remembering that Vitious Pleasures ever destroy the

Bodily Constitution & cloak the Intellectual Spirit." He considered bringing Malton into the House of Commons, and asked the King to make the young man an Irish peer; which request was granted. Shortly before his death (December 14) with his own hand he copied into his letter-book the sage and virtuous advice written by Sir William Wentworth to his son Thomas, Earl of Strafford; and then, after the fashion of fathers, addressed his son in a similar letter, noble and deeply Christian.[18]

II

On May 13, 1751—a festive day at Wentworth Park[19]— the young Marquis of Rockingham came into his inheritance: landed estates in Yorkshire, Northamptonshire, and Ireland (with rent rolls of about £20,000 a year); a parliamentary "interest" consisting of both seats for the borough of Malton and one for the single-member borough of Higham Ferrers (Northants); and the nomination to 23 livings and five chaplaincies in the church.[20] The Duke of Newcastle had already written to assure him of the King's "greatest regard and affection . . . and desire to shew it upon all occasions." In July he was named lord lieutenant and custos rotulorum of the West Riding, lord lieutenant of the city of York, and custos rotulorum of the city and county of York. These county honors too were in a sense a part of the inheritance. A request that the deceased Marquis had made in vain for Major Forrester was now granted by Newcastle, and indeed the young lord was in a position to get whatever he wanted from ministers disposed to court him. "I have the honour & pleasure of your most kind letter," wrote the Duke on August 28, "and tho' your commands are various, I will endeavor to obey them all as soon as I can." During 1751–1752 he joined White's, the Jockey Club, and the Royal Society.[21]

Right from the start Rockingham showed a lively and practical interest in his business affairs, in ways and means for making technical and agricultural improvements. As

early as September 17, 1751, his uncle William Murray
(Solicitor General) complimented him: "You could not en-
tertain me with a more uncommon sight, than a man of your
age, surrounded by all the baits & instruments of folly,
daring to be wise; in the season of dissatisfaction, daring to
think." [22] On March 17, 1752, he spoke in the House of
Lords (for the first time) in support of a bill disposing of
Scotch lands confiscated from the rebels of '45. He wished
the lands to be occupied by people "employed in husbandry
& handicrafts" who dreaded "plunder, rapine & rebellion."
What had become, he asked, of "those swarms of fighting
men, which overspread all Europe after the destruction of
the Roman Empire?" The northern nations were as prolific
as ever but had found work at home in agriculture and manufactures, "whereas the Highlanders have remained in their
ancient state, prolific, bold, idle, & consequently hives of
rebellion." He likened the measure he supported to the policy of his ancestor Strafford in Ireland: "If it were proper
I could show his opinion & way of thinking more at large
on this matter from the Ms papers which I have." Horace
Walpole ridiculed him for entering "a debate so much above
his force." [23] Probably his was a poor performance, since
afterward he rarely opened his mouth in Parliament and it
even came to be believed that he dared not. Nevertheless,
the chiefs of Pelhamite whiggery saw him as a man to be
groomed for political leadership. Murray undertook to be
mentor. Deeming his protégé insufficiently educated, the
Solicitor General laid out a course of study for him under
the direction of George Quarme. The young lord was to
learn Demosthenes for oratory and be instructed in the history of the Assyrian, Persian, Greek, and Roman empires,
after which a course was to be taken in modern history. The
Marquis should model himself upon that wit, scholar, courtier, statesman, soldier, Sir Walter Raleigh—"Let Quarme
tell you who Sir Raleigh was." The plan of study should
continue for four months and would be "a tryal whether you
have genius & resolution enough to persevere." Six weeks

later Murray was "mortified" at hearing that the young lord had not even started on the course:

> Looking into your own estate is a very good employment, but need not interfere. Pardon me, my dear Lord, your many good qualities make me wish you great accomplishments & manly force, I love you so well that I am impatient to see you laying in earnest the foundation of a character, my imagination fain would draw for you. Now is the time or never.[24]

It was hardly in nature that a peer of the realm who had frequented the courts of Europe, moved in society with Roman cardinals, and made love in Naples, would go back to school under George Quarme. Murray was more successful in what might be called, in the modern language of public relations, the "build-up" of the Marquis as a public figure. "Old" Horace Walpole was writing a pamphlet expressive of the complaints of woolen manufacturers, and Murray persuaded him to address it to the young lord of the West Riding where the industry was concentrated.

> It would give you [he told the Marquis] credit both above & below as interesting yourself in matters of this sort & endeavouring to understand them. . . . I think it will spread thro' the kingdom a favourable impression of you, they who don't know must judge from their ear & most who have the opportunity of knowing are incapable of judging for themselves. They follow the cry. You see my dear Lord I do what I can to get you talked into high reputation but you must not yourself be deceived by it.

Rockingham chose to read the pamphlet in manuscript before agreeing to this scheme and took such a serious and informed interest in it as to suggest several material points which had not occurred to the author.[25]

One may recognize here something durably characteristic. Whatever pertained to his interests he wished to be done exactly as he thought right. Uncreative, he was a practical improver of other men's work and had the kind of critical

eye which makes a man a good judge of a horse. As master
of one of the largest houses in England and landlord over
many and diversified estates he was head of a big business
which called for laborious attention. The great east portico
of Wentworth House remained to be built, as did the massive stables. He opened a coal mine at Wentworth in 1752,
and for many years he busied himself with breeding horses,
extracting tar from coal, draining, fertilizing, baking bricks
and tiles, and even devising agricultural instruments. In
1769 Arthur Young was lost in admiration at the fruits of
Rockingham's work, saying that he "never saw the advan-
tages of a great fortune applied so nobly to the improvement
of a country."

> Every discovery of other counties—every successful experiment
> in agriculture—every new implement (and many of his Lord-
> ship's own invention) introduced at a great expence—Draining,
> the general management of grassland, and manure . . . are, at
> Wentworth, carried to the utmost perfection.[26]

Rockingham loved his home and county and spent little time
in the metropolis, even though he had been made a lord of
the bedchamber in 1752, which required periodic attendance
at court. Yorkshire politics and county magisterial duties he
neither could nor wished to avoid; they went with the great
station in life which he had inherited. Connection with the
administration whigs was hardly less a part of that inheritance.

He was married now. Mary Bright became Marchioness
of Rockingham early in 1752. She was a witty, spirited, religious woman who believed that she loved her husband
more than he loved her. She constantly urged him to act on
right principles with high moral purpose, reminded him of
his religious duties (sometimes sowing little homilies into
her letters to him), and when his health was uncertain she
endlessly worried, fussed, warned, and prescribed. She detested all gambling except on horses and could write to her
husband at Newmarket: "Pray do take the utmost care of

yourself & don't keep late hours nor agitate yourself with any sort of gaming but just upon *the turf*, for there is always a possibility of some pleasure in that; but not the smallest in any other sorts, therefore let neither the *great* nor the little ones engage you in it." Lady Rockingham would develop a lively interest in politics and play a part in charting the course of those whigs who one day acknowledged her husband's leadership. She copied letters for him, wrote when he was too busy to write, and sometimes conducted political business for him. She once declared that she liked much better the company of her lord and his friends than "the croaking of my female intimates." As early as 1753 a friend of the Marquis wrote of her as "your fair secretary." [27] After Rockingham's death Edmund Burke told her: "Your names ought to go down together; for it is no mean part you have had in the great services which that great and good man has done this country." [28]

III

In 1753 Rockingham had his first fling in election politics. The Duke of Newcastle and his aides and agents were busy preparing constituencies for the return of a new parliament the next year, and wide over the counties of England men were caucusing to balance rival interests and settle upon candidates so as to avoid election contests. The new master of Wentworth, although a member of the court and treasury party, resolved to throw his weight about by backing a candidate of his own. The county members in the parliament of 1747 were Viscount Downe and Sir Conyers Darcy. The latter, nearing seventy, had been in Parliament for more than forty years. He held the court place of comptroller of the household and was an uncle of the Earl of Holderness, Newcastle's colleague as secretary of state. When rumor said that he would not stand again, a movement got under way to make Sir George Savile his successor. The Saviles of Rufford Abbey (Notts) and the Watson-Wentworths were friends of long standing. Sir George owned large property in the West Riding and was a widely respected man. He was 27 and had been lieutenant colonel in the Marquis' (Lord Higham's) regiment of the volunteers of 1745. These men were warm friends and the union of Rockingham's hereditary rank with Savile's honorable reputation and popularity made a strong political alliance. The candidacy was to be launched at York Races in August. Hearing of this, Lord Holderness, head of the Darcy family in the North Riding, advised his friends that Sir Conyers did not intend to retire, that "many considerable persons" wished to choose again the present members, and that York Races was not a proper occasion for a political meeting "more especially as I myself should not be able to attend." Darcy's supporters induced the high sheriff to summon a county meeting in July. It was clear to Savile that the administration whigs "were against us," but he was convinced that the sense of the county would show in his favor and he told Rockingham that "if I find myself founded there, by all that's good, I will not be bambouzled." The Marquis was not less resolute.[29]

At the county meeting at York on July 16, Rockingham, Holderness, and other peers were present.[30] The prudent rule for such men was to avoid a conspicuous part, since a prejudice existed against lords' meddling in the business of nominating candidates for the House of Commons. Very rashly the Marquis made a speech for Savile and compounded the folly by contrasting Darcy's age with Savile's youth. An "old staunch whig," he said, "could not do any thing more to his honour than sacrifice his private ambition, when he secured by it the present & future peace of the county." [31] Such words not only affronted Darcy but hinted a contested election—awful thought—if Savile were not nominated. Appearances turned against Sir George who then withdrew his name after receiving assurance from Darcy's friends that he would have their support at the next vacancy for the county. Later in the day Rockingham discovered to his "inexpressible horror" that "the foolishest thing, that ever can be within my reach" had been done. He had listened to certain peers, who had duped him, when he ought to have persuaded Sir George to ask the gentry to put up their hands: he had "let slip an opportunity of showing my interest to the utmost advantage that could have been wished" since Savile would have been chosen by a great majority. The master of Wentworth was in "such a confounded passion" that he could not trust himself "to write cooly on the subject." [32] Murray, whose leash he had slipped, saw that he had made a fool of himself and told him so: he should not have opposed Darcy in the first place but having backed Savile should have carried the business through. Murray agreed that Savile was the real favorite of the county but Rockingham ought not to have interfered so openly; his friends among the gentry should have done the business at least in appearance. "The language I find in the country," Murray told him, "is that you fancy to give yourself the air of nominating." That would never do. Moreover, the young lord should beware of saying now what he could have done since such bragging carried with it "a degree of ridicule." He ought now to bring Sir George into Parliament for Higham Ferrers. The old member was dying and Savile's coming in there under Rockingham's patronage would be to the latter's honor.

> Such a man appearing to be & I suppose really being strongly attached to you will give you credit & support in the career you may have to run. . . . It will mark him particularly as your friend when he comes in for the county & at present it will give some air of private freindship to the part you have taken for him. When he is in parliament, he may soon get to be more considered.[33]

But Savile waited for the county seat, not wishing to come into Parliament from any man's nomination borough.

A few days after the York meeting the Marquis, convinced that Holderness had been guilty of an "inexcusable breach of faith" by altering a statement for the newspaper after they had agreed upon the text, wrote to tell him plainly what he thought of such trickery. The Earl showed the letter to Murray and Newcastle. The Duke said that Lord Rockingham "might write warm" but could not mean a serious affront. Murray rebuked his nephew: "Is a provincial personal contest with Lord H. to be the object of your ambition? . . . I conjure you most earnestly not to be led away by narrow hot provincial prejudice which will . . . undo your credit reputation & figure in the opinion of the King & your best friends & all sober thinking men." The Marquis remained stung. Subsequent letters from Murray show that it was not easy to smooth the ruffled feathers; but the Solicitor General did manage to extract from him a civil letter to Holderness. "Dont look upon the County of Y[ork] as your only scene of action," Murray counseled; "You are born to figure in a larger & nobler sphere."

The Marquis' rub with a secretary of state disturbed the center of political influence. When the Duke of Grafton, Lord Chamberlain, heard of his speech at York he exclaimed: "God, Lord R. declares against men because they are old, I don't like that." [34] David Garrick lampooned him in verse:

> When Rock–g–m met with the County to cavil
>   To down with Sir Darcy, & up with Sir Savile.
> He urged that the first, was unfit for his age,
>   In the Business & Bustle of State to Engage;
> Quoth *Darcy,* my Lord, that I'm old is the Truth;
>   But old as I am, I can still cope with Youth;
> Shall Age & Experience be counted demerit,
>   Tho' Time has not yet blited the Flesh or the Spirit?
> To prove that my powers can support the old Member,
>   Let us try if your May can outdo my December,
> While thus my Lord Marquis I'm *hearty* & strong,
>   'Tis better so *old,* than be always too young. [35]

Another tiff between Rockingham and Holderness occurred when they met in August at York Races, and once again Murray told his pupil that he was in the wrong and ought not to stay that way till his "hat was shot thro'." Murray and Newcastle now thought that he might raise his stature and lift his eyes to the national level by inducing him to

move the address in the Lords when Parliament was opened.
He declined the honor. "I am sorry for it," the Duke said;
"he should push himself." He pleased the whig chiefs in
October, however, by offering Lord Chancellor Hardwicke
the nomination for Higham Ferrers as an opening for his
son, John Yorke, to come into Parliament.[36]

Soon afterward he won a feather for his shot-through
hat in the city of York. A joint whig–tory interest there had
sent William Thornton and Robert Fox-Lane to Parliament.
Now the former did not wish to stand again and confided to
Dr. John Fountayne, Dean of York Minster, that he would
like to give his support to one of Rockingham's friends,
preferably Sir George Savile. Fountayne passed the word to
the Marquis, saying: "I wish to see your Lordship's interest
perfectly established here & this may be a time for doing it
at an easy rate." Rockingham fixed upon his distant cousin,
Frederick Wentworth, and Thornton, not much pleased, undertook to find how this would go down with the whigs of
the city. Murray counseled: "If you think there will be no
contest I would propose or recommend him with such parade
as should mark the compliment being made to you & that it
is your doing." Henry Pelham, head of the Treasury and
the King's principal minister, expressed hope that Rockingham would meet with "all the respect and encouragement he
deserves," and "endeavoured to turn every thing his way."
Among the York city whigs so great was the enthusiasm for
so promising a noble patron with so large a purse that many
were for a contest to win both seats. But Wentworth, reputedly close with money, had no local popularity; there
were other whig aspirants; and Dr. Fountayne not only advised Rockingham against trying for both seats but even
urged him to be present at the caucus as "nothing less than
your Lordship's interest" could secure the naming of Wentworth. Before the caucus Wentworth disconcerted everyone
by declining to stand. Rockingham knew that Henry Pelham
would be pleased to have a Mr. Dawnay chosen but weighty
local advisers thought that he would not please the people.[37]
Wherefore did the Marquis opt for his old friend Sir John

Armytage, but did not name him openly until Fountayne had artfully prepared the way.

> We gave out [wrote the reverend Dean] that Lord R. had once prevailed upon Mr. W[entworth] to stand but having been informed that a report had been industriously propagated (tho' but by a few) as if his Lordship had attempted to force a person upon the City, he has consented that Mr. W. shall decline, but if his friends of the Whig Interest will call a general meeting, & at that meeting to desire Lord R. to nominate another person, his Lordship had one in his eye at the time he named Mr. W. who he believes will be much more agreeable to them & who he will at their request name & support, as finding Mr. W. indifferent to the thing & that he is not so acceptable to his Lordship's friends as he had once hoped to have found him.[38]

Advancing rapidly now in the craft of an electioneering politician, Rockingham wrote to Lord Downe, brother of Dawnay, that the latter would have had his support if this had been agreeable to the city whigs. Since it was not, and since "the proposing of a candidate is again insisted on to come from me . . . I shall propose Sir John Armytage to be nominated on Monday [December 3] as I have already had the approbation of the principal people of York on his behalf." There was perhaps more artfulness than candor in what Rockingham told Lord Downe. How far he was actually bending to local opinion is suggested by Dr. Fountayne's telling him that not even Armytage would be accepted without his lordship's plain-spoken recommendation. He went to York for the caucus. A delegation of more than a hundred waited upon him at the Dean's house and upon their asking him to name a candidate he gave them Sir John. The noble patron of the city whigs gave a ball and sponsored other public entertainments. Armytage was chosen. The local whig club contributed fifty pounds toward building the Marquis' stand at the Races. His father had never cut such a figure in this place and his mother wrote: "So extraordinary a compliment from yͤ City of York to yͤ House of Wentworth

was one of ye last things y^t I sh[oul]d have imagined
w[oul]d have happen'd in my days." [39]

This time the Solicitor General congratulated the young
lord on having acted with whiggish sagacity. He had avoided
all appearance of trying to dictate, had let the whigs come
to him. He had withdrawn—such was the pretense—a candidate not pleasing to the electors and not named another
until so requested. He had neither gone with the hot elements who would have contested for the whole city representation nor slapped the heads of party at court. Newcastle
wrote to him:

> His Majesty was most extremely pleased with it; and ap-
> proved your very prudent conduct on this occasion. It is a very
> great pleasure to me, that so considerable a town, and such a
> number of loyal gentlemen have put themselves under your
> Lordship's protection.[40]

So eager indeed were these "loyal gentlemen" to please
their patron that their club was now named the Rockingham
Club. Fountayne told him that "nothing will go down for
the name of the club, but Rockingham." Gratified, the Marquis engaged James Stuart to paint portraits of William III
and George II for the club rooms where monthly meetings
were held and innumerable toasts drunk. A list dated June
3, 1754, shows 133 members. Savile belonged and one may
recognize the names of many leading gentry and men who
would be known later as Rockingham's political agents. The
members of the club were the first "Rockingham whigs." [41]

Newcastle, who succeeded his brother as First Lord of
the Treasury in 1754, looked upon Rockingham as the main
pillar in Yorkshire of the court and treasury party. In June
the Lord Chancellor answered the Marquis' solicitation for
a church appointment in York with the assurance that "no
obstacle shall obstruct my ready compliance with your request." Soon afterward, at the young lord's request, the
Duke stopped the appointment of an objectionable man as
collector of customs at Hull. More and more, Yorkshiremen

learned to look to the master of Wentworth to get favors from government. Early in 1755 the crown conferred on him the ancient and honorary office of vice admiral of the north.[42]

IV

The country was now drifting into a new war with France. Much fumbling by administration and the raising of Henry Fox as leader in the House of Commons, against the claims of the popular William Pitt, provoked a formidable new parliamentary opposition. Headed by Pitt and backed by politicians connected with the Dowager Princess of Wales, it swelled as administration blundered in war. Rockingham adhered to the Duke. Fears of a French invasion moved him, early in 1756, to act in the manner of his father by raising a volunteer militia. He, Savile, and others did this without official authorization and at their own expense, at a moment when ministry in panic was preparing to bring over Hessian mercenaries to protect the country. Fox paid Rockingham a handsome compliment in Parliament for this conduct, and Murray (now Attorney General) wrote that it "set you in a very advantageous light." That summer widespread rioting broke out against army enlistments. Without the use of military force the Lord Lieutenant of the West Riding overcame disorders at Sheffield. War Secretary Barrington wrote to the Marquis: "You are the only instance of a Lord lieutenant's exerting the civil authority upon these occasions." [43]

In the autumn of 1756 Rockingham almost joined the court of the Prince of Wales. The latter having come of age, the King desired to separate him from his mother and from the political hopefuls gathered about her and her principal confidant, the Scotch Earl of Bute, to whom the young Prince was deeply attached. The heir to the throne of an aged king asked permission to remain with his mother at Leicester House, and Newcastle with an eye to detaching the Prince from the opposition advised George II to appease him. The Duke wished to place trusted friends about him, and for this reason Rockingham was designated to be his master of the horse. The King, who liked the Marquis as much as he disliked the treaty with Leicester House, grudgingly consented to part with a favorite bedchamber lord. Rockingham confided to his wife October 5:

> . . . there are many reasons to make it acceptable, yet there are almost as many to make it hazardous to accept. The K[in]g I believe, is so kind, as rather to be unwilling to part with me & that weighs much with me. At the same time, it will be odd not to accept & perhaps that reason may not be proper to give, because it will be no compliment to the P[rince]. . . . If I see any prospects of affairs in the royal Family going on cordially with his M[ajesty]'s intentions, I shall certainly accept, but if I see any appearance of diffidence among them, I shall keep myself to myself, & making him the compliment of not chusing to quit him, which I will do in the closet.

Soon afterward he chose to accept, only to change his mind because of the ministerial crisis which the Leicester House treaty brought on. Fox, who had not been consulted in it, read it as meaning Newcastle's intention to give him up for Pitt, and resigned, confident that the King who abhorred Pitt would not accept him as secretary of state and minister of the House of Commons. Newcastle then treated with Pitt who refused to serve under him; whereupon the Duke resigned, and Pitt supported by popularity in effect imposed himself upon the King, to direct the war, with the Duke of Devonshire at the head of the Treasury. Rockingham clung to Newcastle and stayed at the court of George II. This was not an unimportant decision since it kept him from becoming associated in interest or sympathy with persons close to the young man who in a few years became George III.[44]

Strong was the Marquis' loyalty to Newcastle. When Pitt gave up his seat for the Duke's borough of Aldborough in Yorkshire, Rockingham helped to find a man to fill it who would "shew his zeal for his Majesty, his love for his country & his personal regard to your Grace." He resented the attacks and threats of inquiry suffered by the fallen ministers, avowing to Newcastle (February 13, 1757) : "I don't at all doubt, but your Grace & your former confederates will now soon triumph over all the scandalous insinuations. . . . I shall rejoice exceedingly in the ample justification of persons for whom I profess so great private regard & the more so as the publick good will ensue from it." In June when the King, after turning out Pitt, tried to float a Fox administration with Lord Waldegrave as nominal head, Newcastle organized a revolt of friends at court. Rockingham resolved to resign his place, and the Duke was so grateful that he said it would be the study of his life to show "the regard, esteem, and respect which is due to your zeal for the King, and the publick, and to those great and amiable qualities which adorn your character." Soon Newcastle and Pitt composed their differences, allied and took office together, the former returning to the Treasury, the latter deserting Leicester House. The Duke supported the Marquis' candidate for a parliamentary vacancy at Hull, found places for his friends in the customs service, and fortified the master of Wentworth as a regional dispenser of patronage. "You see, I do all your jobs as far as I can. Nobody has more right to demand of me than yourself." [45]

Meanwhile Rockingham was performing services of great importance to the country. It was the duty of lords lieutenant under the Militia Act of 1757 to raise troops for home defense. Fears arose that militia men might be sent out of their counties or brigaded into the army and shipped abroad, so that something like insurrection appeared. A total collapse of magisterial authority occurred in the East Riding, and riots to destroy lists of eligible men burst forth in the city of York and in the West Riding.[46] Wentworth House was menaced.

I am persuaded [wrote Rockingham to Newcastle in September] with the assistance of my own workmen & neighbouring farmers I shall be an over-match for any sudden riot, but my dear Lord my own private security is not sufficient, I want a plan for the security & quiet of the West Riding & some thing to restore power & respect to the civil authority, which indeed in every instance is sinking most lamentably.

He managed to have a Yorkshire regiment of regular troops which he and Savile had recruited the previous year sent into Derby and Nottingham "with a power to remove them into Yorkshire if necessary." This, he thought, would serve the further purpose of contradicting "those false reports which had been raised & malitiously fomented of the hardships etc. which that regiment had suffered." [47] The plan worked and order was restored without setting Yorkshiremen upon Yorkshiremen. Rockingham raised three militia regiments under the command of his friends, Savile, Thornton, and Lord Downe. He was their "general" and thought of himself as bearing responsibility for directing the defense of a considerable part of the country. Murray (now Baron Mansfield) urged him to exert himself "so as may in a manner demand the garter." With time out for business affairs, horses, and bouts of illness he directed his regiments through the war. In October 1759 the war secretary ordered him to send two West Riding regiments to Hull and Beverley in the East Riding where a French landing was feared. He complained to Newcastle that the order had been delayed by its being relayed through an army general: "I must desire that Lord Barrington would give orders that copys of the orders for this militia may be also sent directly to me as events may happen which will make it necessary for no time to be lost." With great confidence in his troops he wished to direct them with wide discretionary powers, so that if the French landed he might, instead of waiting for orders, act quickly as he thought best. His officers were "all men of large fortune," "calm and determined," and the "private men . . . a fine body." Like a great territorial feudal lord he wished to captain them as his own.[48]

During the summer of '59, on the eve of the great British successes of that year, Newcastle worried over the costs of the war and asked the Marquis for the sentiments of reliable friends on going on with it or seeking peace. He answered that the general wish was for peace but that would be hard to make on satisfactory terms; that the public was so enamored of the King of Prussia that it would not approve a desertion of that ally. His own view was that Great Britain and Prussia ought to seek peace when "the intended encroachments" of their enemies had been repulsed, but

> If once we get over the danger & expectations of the invasion & if things take a favourable turn on the continent, I fear the generality of people's minds will be so elated that tho' our finances may make peace necessary yet it will add to the difficulty of concluding a peace agreeable to the expectations that will then be raised.[49]

V

In 1758 Sir John Armytage was killed in battle and a by-election was ordered at York. The city tories, controlling the corporation, chose to contest for the seat, and the Rockingham whigs were thrown into confusion by the behavior of William Thornton. Although a member of the club it gave him some misgivings: he caviled at the name and came to think that it represented the interest of a great peer more than the whig party. An admirer of Savile, Thornton was every inch an independent and disliked the influence of peers in choosing members of the House of Commons. He was far from hostile to Rockingham but in offering himself again as a candidate he preferred to be supported rather than adopted by the Rockingham Club.[50] The Marquis was willing to support him if that was the general desire even though his personal preference was for a brother of the late Sir John. On arriving in York, Rockingham found "every thing in confusion" with Thornton holding an edge; but presently a compromise was arranged whereby Thornton would be supported in this election and then make way for Sir George Armytage at the general election in 1761. So did the whigs close ranks. Writing to Newcastle while the hot contest was on, Rockingham said:

> We have had some disadvantages & some advantages. The unfairness of the [tory] attempt has divided the Corporation so that they are not totally nor so warmly against us as they otherwise would have been. We have a noble spirit among our whig friends in the City & the whigs in the County are very strenuous upon this occasion. . . . Numbers of whig gentlemen are come, many have subscribed largely to the *cause,* tho' Thornton himself does not support with money sufficiently. As to myself, win or lose, I shall be soused but shall have money's worth for the money. . . . The mobs have been furious.[51]

Defeat in this contest would have been a serious reverse for Lord Rockingham, damaging his prestige in Yorkshire and Newcastle's in the country at large. Pitt was now the idol of the nation, inspiring whig and tory alike with a patriotism not easily submissive either to ministerial management or to the influence of great territorial lords. Contests like that at York were rare in the age of the whig supremacy and their results had national significance. Lady Rockingham took the liveliest interest, telling her husband:

> I can't help being delighted that the *whig interest* is as dependent upon this event as your private interest & that in Yorkshire it takes that note & rouses all, for then the more éclat you conquer with, double the victory for you, as you gain it for the publick advantage of your country, which will give you endless applause. Without the whig motive, you would only have continued by your success what you are, & I hope ever will be, the first man in Yorkshire, & (entre nous) by MERIT ALONE the first man *everywhere.*[52]

When the poll ended December 7 Thornton had prevailed, 1239 to 994, over the tory (Robert Fox-Lane), and the Marquis had spent about £12,000 of his own money.[53]

Easy success in the county followed the hard-fought city contest. The death of Sir Conyers Darcy about this time meant that the time had come for the popular Savile to be sent to Parliament. At the caucus on January 3 a vague threat of candidacy by Charles Turner, whose uncle had once sat for the county, failed to materialize. Nor did Robert Fox-Lane make good an uttered threat to stand for the county if defeated in the city. Newcastle seconded Rockingham's support of Savile, who was elected without opposition.[54]

Sir George was not the Marquis' "man" but his friend and would have been chosen if Rockingham had not existed. He was nevertheless a tremendous asset to Rockingham, screening the latter against the prejudicial enmity of "independent" men; and this asset would grow in value as Savile gained in the House of Commons the same kind of respect and admiration he enjoyed in Yorkshire.

At the turn of the decade Rockingham was, at thirty, one of the pillars of the ruling system of politics in the kingdom. No sign was given, however, that he ever would be a minister of the crown. Away from Yorkshire he was known chiefly as a sportsman of the Jockey Club, a great figure at Newmarket. Horace Walpole said of him, "This Lord loves only horses." [55] He was given the court's highest honor, the Garter; he wanted it and asked for it;[56] and political circumstances were ripe for his receiving it. When in 1759 that honor was promised to Earl Temple, Lord Privy Seal and brother-in-law of Pitt, the Duke of Newcastle demanded the same for the Marquis. A royal message (April 10, 1760) delivered by the Lord Chamberlain summoned "Our Right Trusty and entirely beloved Cousin" to Windsor Castle for installation as "one of the Companions of Our Most Noble Order of the Garter." [57] Another fine feather for the master of Wentworth Park, but no indication of his moving to the center of national politics. Only a threat— now not far off—to his interest in Yorkshire could provoke that. Besides he had, or thought that he had, precarious health. There was some chronic disorder productive of recurrent pain in side and breast. He never got rid of it. He was always doctoring himself for his "old complaint," and his letters are studded with reports on the state of his health. Since, however, he spent no small part of his life in the saddle his most serious malady may well have been hypochondria. Early in 1761 Savile told him:

> I cannot help mentioning a little seriously what we have so often laughed about, your having recourse so continuously to medicine with hardly any reason. . . . I am not speaking my own thoughts only but those of 9 in 10 of your Lordship's friends and yet I have no great hopes of your minding us, for I do not believe that any habit is more unalterable, not even the confirmed avarice of old age is more incorrigible than this game of quacking.[58]

NOTES

1. For Rockingham's early life I am much indebted to the pioneer pamphlet by the late G. H. Guttridge, *The Early Career of Lord Rockingham,* University of California Publications in History (Berkeley and Los Angeles, 1962).

2. Arthur Gooder, *The Parliamentary Representation of the County of York* (2 vols.; Wakefield, 1938), II 105–106 *et passim*; Cedric Collyer, "The Yorkshire Election of 1734," *Proceedings of the Leeds Philosophical and Literary Society,* 3, Pt. 1 (1952), 53–81, and "The Rockinghams and Yorkshire Politics," *Publications of the Thoresby Soc.* (Leeds), 12, Pt. 4 (1954), 352–382; J. H. Plumb, *Sir Robert Walpole* (London, 1960), II 179, 319–320.

3. Wentworth Woodhouse Muniments in the Sheffield Central Library (cited hereafter as WWM) M 2 ff. 182–183.

4. G. F. R. Baker and A. B. Stenning, *The Record of Old Westminsters* (2 vols.; London, 1928) II *passim*; A. M. W. Stirling, *The Hothams* (2 vols.; London, 1918), II 15–16.

5. WWM M 2 ff. 291–293, 338–352; R 169 (unnumbered MSS).

6. *Ibid.*

7. *Ibid.*

8. *Ibid.*

9. WWM M 2 f. 453.

10. *Ibid.,* ff. 461, 464–466.

11. *Ibid.,* f. 489.

12. *Ibid.,* ff. 494–495.

13. *Ibid.,* ff. 508, 510.

14. "And indeed my dear Lord you must give me leave to say that if you have not some regard for this place, you are a little ungrateful, for I

believe never any Stranger was so universally loved & esteemed."—Lord Stormont to Rockingham, Florence, 5 Nov. 1761, WWM R 1: 8.

15. WWM M 2 ff. 515, 536; R 170 (unnumbered MSS).

16. WWM M 2 ff. 531, 537, 539. It was said that the Princess Francavilla held herself responsible for impairing Malton's health.—W. N. Wraxall, *Historical and Posthumous Memoirs* (4 vols.; New York, 1884), II 349–350. Malton's notebook shows that he "dined" and "supped" with her. Several years later he promised a friend a letter to her.—WWM R 1: 64. In the spring of 1768 Lord Carlyle wrote from Naples: "The Princess Francavilla is extremely civil to us, but I lay it a little to the account of Lord Fitzwilliam, whom she found to be very like his uncle, Lord Rockingham."—J. R. Jesse, *George Selwyn and His Contemporaries* (4 vols.; London, 1843–1844), II 298.

17. WWM R 170.

18. WWM M 2 ff. 528–529, 550–551, 573–576, 589–594; British Museum Additional Manuscript[s] (cited hereafter as Add. MS[s]) 32723, f. 389.

19. There were refreshments for 5000 people.—York Minster Library MS BB53.

20. WWM R 170.

21. Add. MS 32723, f. 397; WWM R 1: 5; W. B. Boulton, *History of White's* (2 vols.; London, 1892), II 25–32; Robert Black, *The Jockey Club* (London, 1891), 12, 63–64.

22. WWM R 1: 6; W. H. G. Armytage, "Charles Watson-Wentworth, second Marquis of Rockingham: Some Aspects of his Scientific Interests," *Notes and Records of the Royal Society of London,* 12, No. 1 (1956), 64–96.

23. WWM R 1: 2130; Horace Walpole, *Memoirs of the Reign of George the Second* (3 vols.; London, 1846) I 272.

24. WWM R 1: 11, 12.

25. *Ibid.,* 13–15, 17, 18; Herbert Heaton, *Yorkshire Woolen and Worsted Industries* (Oxford, 1920), Ch. 8.

26. *A Six Months Tour through the North of England* (London, 1771), 201.

27. WWM R 159: 1–5; R 168: 60; F 35 (Godfrey Wentworth to Rockingham 2 Dec. 1752).

28. *Correspondence of Edmund Burke,* cited hereafter as *Corr. Burke* (9 vols.; Cambridge and Chicago, 1958–1970), V 46.

29. Add. MS 32732, ff. 313–314; *Various Collections* (Royal Commission on Historical Manuscripts [cited hereafter as Hist. MSS Comm.]) 8 (London, 1913), 176. Nine of Sir George's ancestors had been county members for Yorkshire since the early-sixteenth century.—Gooder, *Parliamentary Representation, passim.*

30. WWM R 1: 24, 27. The King was said to have been as anxious over the York election as over the election of a Holy Roman emperor, and Newcastle groaned that "the Tories will take advantage from our divisions . . . in the first and most zealous County in England."—Add. MS 32732, f. 158.

31. WWM R 1: 24.

32. *Ibid.,* 27.

33. *Ibid.,* 30.

34. *Ibid.,* 24, 28, 31, 32, 34, 36.

35. Devonshire MS (at Chatsworth) 3544.

36. WWM R 1: 40, 44, 46.

37. WWM F 35(a); R 1: 47, 50.

38. Fountayne to Rockingham, 22 Nov.—WWM F 35(b).

39. WWM R 145: 5, 6.

40. WWM R 1: 52; Add. MS 32735, ff. 375, 403.

41. WWM F 35; R 1: 68, 70; R 95; R 75: 31.

42. WWM R 1: 71; Add. MSS 32855, f. 304; 32856, ff. 82, 573; 35592, f. 369.

43. Add. MS 32863, ff. 225–227; WWM R 1: 22, 80.

44. WWM R 1: 82–84; R 160: 1; Add. MS 35594, f. 258.

45. Add. MSS 32869, f. 217; 32870, f. 178; 32871, ff. 228, 278; George Harris, *Life of Lord Chancellor Hardwicke* (3 vols.; London, 1841), III 131.

46. WWM R 1: 102; Walpole, *Memoirs* (George II), III 40; Add. MS 32875, f. 155

47. WWM R 1: 105

48. Add. MS 32897, ff. 296, 361.

49. Add. MSS 38893, f. 435; 32856, f. 281.

50. WWM R 145: 4; F 35(d)

51. Add. MS 32856, ff. 138–139

52. *Ibid.,* f. 237.

53. Collyer, "The Rockinghams and Yorkshire Politics," 255.

54. Add. MS 32887, f. 49

55. "Taste for the satisfactions of aristocratic independence in the country rather than Court politics combined with his personal friendships to make Rockingham a great Country Whig."—Cedric Collyer, "The Rockingham Connections and Country Opinion in the Early Years of George III," *Proceedings of the Leeds Philosophical and Literary Society,* 3, Pt. 4 (1955), 252.

56. Rockingham to the Duke of Portland, 25 Nov. 1766.—Portland MSS (University of Nottingham library).

57. WWM R 1: 120, 156, 161; *The Grenville Papers* ed. W. J. Smith (4 vols.; London, 1852–1853), I 330–332 (cited hereafter as *Grenville*); *The Correspondence of William Pitt, Earl of Chatham* (4 vols.; London, 1838–1840), I 438–439 (cited hereafter as *Chatham*).

58. WWM R 1: 190. Eleven years later the Duke of Richmond wrote to the Marquis: "You are so often ill without being dangerously so, and are so often doctoring yourself that when I first heard you were not well I concluded it was only a surfeit of Physic, and I am told that it might possibly be owing to your not letting yourself alone when you have been ill."—*Ibid.,* 1403.

2

The Whip of Whiggery

THE OPENING OF A NEW REIGN (October 1760) and the resultant ascendancy of Lord Bute over all other politicians produced a jarring effect upon Lord Rockingham's great interest. Newcastle's influence sank, which was a loss for the Marquis, and there seemed to be at the court of King George III a spirit of vague hostility toward that sort of great territorial influence which he enjoyed in Yorkshire. An ill omen was the removal (early December) of his uncle Henry Finch from the office of surveyor-general of the Board of Works in favor of Bute's friend Thomas Worsley, a North Riding tory. Although Finch was an old man near to dying and his office was not part of Rockingham's patronage, he owed his seat in Parliament to his nephew who therefore felt a little stung. Newcastle tried to stop the removal, and Finch in telling the story to Rockingham said that "no mention was made of any thing to make *you easy,* which is the technical term now in use." [1] This soon began to look like the detail of a pattern, for the Marquis proved unable to get the support of administration for his friend Hugh

Bethel's candidacy for a parliamentary seat for Beverley. By the turn of the year enough unfriendly signs were showing to make Rockingham apprehensive lest his county honors be "divided against me." [2]

The unwarming wind from the south was felt in the choosing of a whig candidate for the county in the impending election of a new parliament. Lord Downe died in December and almost immediately Charles Turner, a North Riding squire, announced that he would put himself forward at the county meeting on January 19. His uncle had sat for Yorkshire, 1742–1747, and been a thorn in the side of Rockingham's father. Unconnected with the Rockingham Club, Turner was for rallying "independents" biased against the influence of peers in selecting candidates for the House of Commons. Rockingham was for naming Edwin Lascelles if the latter could gather sufficient support. With this recommendation Lascelles hurried to Westminster to "canvas the grandees" who had influence in Yorkshire. He found Newcastle willing to help all he could and avowing himself "Lord Rockingham's friend, only." The Duke of Devonshire, titular head of the whigs, was "zealous" for Lascelles but warned against any attempt by Rockingham's friends "to dictate." On the other hand Secretary of State Holderness, now in Bute's pocket, declined to help Lascelles, saying that he wished to remain with "those who had distinguished themselves on a particular occasion [i.e. in 1753] in support of his uncle," the late Sir Conyers Darcy. Thus some roles were curiously reversed: eight years before Holderness had been a creature of the Pelhamite system which Rockingham and Savile had gone against, but now the Marquis represented an establishment against which the Bute–Holderness interest promoted "independency." Four days before the county meeting one of Rockingham's agents reported that "the Cry of Freedom & Independency is in many Mouths, and what say they have Lords to do with Elections?" Newcastle worried over hearing that Turner had gained all the tories and some considerable whig interests: "The Yorkshire election makes a great noise here," he wrote to the Marquis.[3]

Among the numerous peers at the York meeting were two who had made a significant journey: Holderness[4] and the King's master of the horse, the Earl of Huntingdon. Between them and Rockingham there had for long been no cordiality. After the names of Turner and Lascelles were put forward Sir George Savile, whose own renomination was assured, announced that he would join whichever candidate the majority of his friends favored. Turner's father spoke a denunciation of peers' influence and said that his son stood on "independent principles." Both Holderness and Huntingdon blundered by making speeches for Turner, which gave Rockingham his opportunity to say that men of such fortunes as Turner and Lascelles possessed were assuredly independent but that it was strange to hear a candidate called independent who was supported by a secretary of state and a master of the horse. "Whereupon [wrote one who was there] some few strokes of good humour passed amongst these Noble Lords, with respect to the influence of the two former, from the High Posts they held under the Government and the long Journey they had taken to support their Friends." The upshot of the day was produced by Savile's asking the candidates to show him their lists of promised supporters. Lascelles agreed but Turner declined, whereupon Sir George declared for the former, who was then chosen; and Rockingham thought that "nothing could happen better or more agreeably." Holderness, much vexed, considered pressing for a contest at the poll with Turner calling for single votes, but soon gave it up.[5] Thus a court-backed attempt against the stronghold of a whig magnate allied with Newcastle was repulsed. Mary Wentworth wrote to her brother from Westminster: "Lord Holdernesse's journey to York was, it's now said, to persuade Mr. Turner to withdraw." Newcastle gleefully took the news of the York meeting to the King, who made no comment. Replying to the Duke's congratulations Rocking-

ham said: "I rejoice that I was not deceived in the part
which I recommended to your Grace as it has appeared very
plain that I knew the sentiments of the generality & indeed
the leading gentlemen of Yorkshire." Reflecting that
Thomas Worsley had been one of Turner's supporters, the
Marquis added: "I fancy the event at York must have been
matter of surprize in a Certain Closet." [6]

The Rockinghamites might have tried for both seats for
the city of York had not their county strategy required an
agreement not to set up a candidate against Fox-Lane. They
settled for one, Sir George Armytage, and all went well in
spite of some murmurs against great men dividing the city.
Except for his abortive attempt at Beverley, the Marquis
suffered no reverse in the elections of 1761. At Malton
where his sway was incontestable he gave his interest to the
old members, John Mostyn and Henry Finch, but the latter
died and his place was filled by another Finch. At Higham
Ferrers Rockingham again secured the return of John
Yorke. An incident at Malton showed how resolute he
could be in maintaining his "right." Some voters petitioned
for his interest in behalf of a Mr. St. Quintin as a candidate
in succession to the deceased Finch, and the father of the
would-be candidate appealed by letter to Rockingham but
got no answer. "I wonder at their assurance to pretend to
nominate a representative themselves," wrote a Rockingham agent; "I think if this request were granted, at another
time they may be so insolent as to petition for to recommend
two representatives." When Rockingham designated Savile
Finch as his man St. Quintin sent an apology: "Not having
had the Honour of hearing from Your Lordship, I greatly
fear that my Request has given Offence, if so, I heartily ask
Pardon for having been so impertinent in asking for so great
a Favour." Such were the ways of the lowly with the great. [7]

February 1761 found Rockingham in Grosvenor Square.
He came to town at Newcastle's summons. Alterations impended in administration: Pitt was at odds with Bute who
was for negotiating an early end to the war, while Newcastle was seeking a fruitful union of his own friends with

Bute. "You must come," he had urged upon the Marquis,
"for the conjunction will be so critical, that I hope I shall be
countenanced & assisted by all my great & considerable
friends." When Rockingham learned that Newcastle, Devonshire, and Hardwicke—the great whig trinity—favored
Bute's coming into ministerial office, he protested that this
was unwise; but it was done, Holderness making way for
the royal Favorite to become Pitt's colleague as secretary of
state. Pitt disliked this and also other changes made at the
same time, which however were pleasing to Newcastle. Lord
Barrington, a reputed dependent of the latter, replaced
H. B. Legge at the Exchequer, and Charles Townshend, a
nephew of the old Duke, replaced Barrington as war secretary. But Bute was master now and his intrusive influence
was felt in all spheres of government; although his tactic
was rather to smooth than to bully. Thus, the illusory prospect of an Irish dukedom was at this time dangled before
Rockingham.[8]

From March to August the Marquis was at Bath treating
an attack of gallstones. On returning to town he got into a
quarrel over some obscure point with Holderness who was
now groom of the stole. Newcastle sought to assuage his
anger: "I am not imposed upon, I assure you, and I know
my Lord Bute is for you, that is, that what you fear, should
not happen." [9] In September Rockingham attended the marriage of the King and supported the royal arm at the corona-
tion. In October he was lamenting the administration's "in-
justice & inhumanity." His old friend and traveling companion, Major Forrester, had been promised a continuance
as commandant in Jersey and the promise was broken.
Charles Townshend had given the promise and "some one"
had interfered. Forrester complained to Rockingham who
quoted the scriptural "Ye do not gather figs from thistles."
This, he said, was a "Thistle Administration." [10] However,
on Pitt's resignation that month he joined Newcastle's
friends in painting the Great Man's going out as petulant
desertion.[11]

At the opening of Parliament in November George Grenville, successor to Pitt as minister of the House of Commons, offered the comptrollership of the household to Sir George Savile. Sir George refused it, well knowing that his Yorkshire constituents would not like to see him a courtier or placeman. But the offer was a compliment and pleased Rockingham, as did the giving of the place subsequently to Lord George Cavendish, Devonshire's brother. Such dispositions, said the duped Newcastle, "shew a regard to Whigs and old friends." The Marquis, less deluded, was not ready to bend the knee to the rising sun, as was shown in a disputed election. His friend James Murray petitioned against the return of a Bute man for a Scotch constituency and the Marquis sought Newcastle's help in this cause. Bute rebuffed the Duke who then told Rockingham that a way ought to be found to make Bute "easy." Instead of asking Murray to drop his petition the Marquis urged him "to spare no pains or costs" because his case was "founded on strict right and justice." Bute then said he would not interfere, whereupon Rockingham confided to Devonshire: "Your Grace knows how far that goes, & I believe Mr. Murray is prepared to find Mr. G[eorge] G[renville] & all those who are particularly connected with it, will accidentally all be against him." In the end, however, Murray was seated.[12]

During the winter of 1761–1762 Bute, employing Grenville and Lord Egremont as his instruments, progressively nullified Newcastle's weight in administration. In May, after suffering the ignominy of being overruled at his own board, the old Duke decided to leave office. Informed of this intention Rockingham wrote from Wentworth that he had long been convinced that Bute and his followers meant to take "the whole Administration & Government of this country into their hands." This would be "a national misfortune" but since Newcastle was certain to be pushed out sooner or later now was the time to resign. It would be hard to exaggerate the dismay with which this revolution in politics was viewed by the Marquis, whose mind was filled with all the assumptions and myths of his rank. He believed

that the tranquillity of society, the security of property and
liberty, the growth of material well-being—all the ingredi-
ents of the good life he knew—had been nourished and
strengthened by the whig party: a long-continuing connection of men who had a large sense of public responsibility,
who had settled the constitution perfectly, secured the
Hanoverian dynasty, and understood the politics of Europe:
men sagacious and temperate, natural leaders of the public,
the wisest possible counselors of the throne. In association
with them Rockingham's father had gained the first honors
in his county and risen high in the peerage. By inheritance
and choice the Marquis was of their body, and toward the
Duke of Newcastle who had for so long managed their political business he felt the strongest ties of loyalty and gratitude:

> . . . without flattery to your Grace, I must look and ever
> shall upon you and your connections as the solid foundations
> on which every good which has happened to this country since
> the Revolution, have been erected. . . . What a medley of
> government is probably soon to take place & when it does what
> an alarm will ensue!

When Newcastle described to him how Bute expressed indifference toward his exit from the Treasury and talked
about "the loaves and fishes" and how a young King "would
find friends, and would be supported," Rockingham answered:

> His Lordship may perhaps find, that tho' a young King (ac-
> cording to his remark) will not want support, yet it may be
> difficult to fix his Lordship at the head of government, adopting
> plans and measures the reverse of what has been the policy of
> the present Royal Family since it came to the throne. I entirely
> approve that your Grace should not be shy of apprizing the
> Ministers that you are entirely free to oppose or support ac-
> cording to the measures which are adopted, for indeed your
> country will expect that you will not be a tacit spectator of
> its ruin.[13]

The old Duke hated giving up the Treasury and was hurt when the King did not coax him to stay. He dared not yet think of throwing royal affairs into confusion by calling on friends to resign, since he must have known that few were prepared to do that; and he had no idea of starting an opposition, which he had always reprobated as factional. The strategy he hit on was to advise all his friends to remain in their employments and to let everyone know "that what I do is with their approbation . . . and that they shall continue to act with me, in the same conduct, as when I was in business." That is to say, he elected to pretend that he had given over the party to Lord Bute on loan recoverable if the royal Favorite failed in his effort "to intimidate the whole world." [14]

II

"If that clamour arises which in my mind most certainly will, Your Grace will be called on & your assistance expected by all the old whigs." So wrote Rockingham to Newcastle on May 26 from Yorkshire where he saw many signs of uneasiness over the new direction of politics. Among Newcastle's friends the Marquis appears to have been alone in urging that something be done to thwart Lord Bute. He came to town, conferred with Devonshire, visited Newcastle at Claremont, and then went on to his old friend and admirer, His Royal Highness the Duke of Cumberland at Windsor Lodge whom he attended at Ascot Races.[15] H.R.H. had not concealed his displeasure at Bute's assuming full powers, and had offended the King by "sulky" demeanor at Bute's installation as Knight of the Garter on May 27. He was the only man alive who could by patronizing an opposition give it the color of loyalty to the house of Hanover, and any clustering of anti-Bute whig magnates around him was bound to worry a court which had offended both Pitt and Newcastle. On June 14 one of Bute's agents reported that an association had been formed consisting of the dukes of Newcastle, Cumberland, Devonshire, and Richmond, Lord Hardwicke, Lord Rockingham, and Pitt. The King, jumping at shadows, described this "league of Dukes" as "most contemptible," refused to believe that it existed yet feared that Lord Mansfield might have joined it, and told Bute that "as to Lord Rockingham etc. I think they ought to be question'd and if their answers are dubious ought to lose their employments." [16] Returned to Wentworth, the Marquis was advised by a friend: "Send not your letters to the D[uke] of N[ewcastle] with his directions on the outside, all his letters are opened." On July 2 Rockingham described himself to Devonshire "as hot as ever," [17] and when in mid-August he went to court to congratulate the King on the birth of a prince Newcastle found him

> possessed against my Lord B[ute] and says the whole Kingdom is so much so, that whoever endeavours to support him, or should join with him (which he hopes I will never do in any shape) will ruin themselves & lose their own reputation without being able to do any real service, either to my Lord B[ute] or to the publick; and that the people (the mob) will pull him down, if others do not attempt it.[18]

With respect to attempting that, the only foreseeable point of attack when Parliament met again was the prospective peace treaty. But Newcastle's friends were ill-positioned for that. The old Duke had long wished for peace at almost any price except giving up the balance of power on the continent, and looked upon the North American conquests by Pitt's generals as negotiable. Devonshire, still Lord Chamberlain and titular head of the whigs, told the King in July that he did not doubt he could induce all his friends, Newcastle included, to support the peace; and in September when the Duke of Bedford went to Paris to negotiate it the King found Newcastle "in good humour," a little fearful that returning the French island of St. Lucia would be attacked, but convinced that "the state of our finances requir'd peace." A few days later Devonshire opined to Majesty that giving back this island was "very proper." Cumberland too deprecated the importance of St. Lucia to the King but hoped that the French would be "well bounded off from Canada." [19] These great persons plainly had no concert of opinion on the peace in early September; nor had the court any hint that the specter of a "league of dukes" would rise against the pending treaty. At Wentworth, however, Lord Rockingham was thinking of how to employ the treaty to bludgeon Bute. He wrote to Newcastle on September 6:

> A strong administration backed with national confidence would have found it a difficult task, after the great successes we have had, to make a peace in any degree adequate to the expectation. The general opinion in their favour would make many trust & rely, that what was done, was the best that could be. In the present case, the contrary will be experienced & indeed if even a *Good* peace was made under this administration it would not be unreasonable to suppose that a better might be made, had the administration had the appearance of being strong enough to have carried on the war.[20]

Holding that a good argument could be made in favor of the proposition that a more strongly supported government was needed to secure satisfactory terms of peace, Rockingham wished to compound Bute's difficulties in order to show the King why he ought to place his affairs in the hands of better-supported men. He was very eager for "good news" from the expedition which had gone to attack Havana. It was commanded by the Duke of Cumberland's close friends, George Keppel Earl of Albemarle and his brother Admiral Augustus Keppel. Success at Havana would be a feather for Cumberland, who had been allowed to choose these officers, and could hardly fail to complicate the negotiations at Paris.

On coming to town (September 20) the Marquis received from Newcastle a mass of papers for him to "read with the greatest attention" in order "to judge what conduct we should hold upon the appearance of things, as they now are." Bute was certainly "in distress" and hints were being thrown out of an inclination at court "to have us return to Council" to help him, but nothing should be determined until "we see what their peace is." [21] Events were developing much as Rockingham had predicted and desired. In the last days of September Bedford's preliminary treaty arrived almost simultaneously with news of the capture of Havana —to the court an embarrassing victory. The secretaries of state, Grenville and Egremont, balked at approving a peace without compensation for restoring Havana. Willing if necessary to sack both of these obstructionists Bute engaged Henry Fox, Paymaster and long connected with Cumberland, to mediate with H.R.H. for the return of Newcastle to administration and the support of his friends. Cumberland not only declined to be so used but went to the King (September 30) and stated a series of objections to the treaty.[22] Battle lines began forming. Rockingham went to rally supporters at Newmarket for dishing Bute, and reported to Newcastle (October 20) : "All the *conversations* I have had *here* have been in good stile, & I am in great hopes that the proof will be as good as the appearance." [23]

Thus arose the first opposition in George III's reign. It was signaled by Cumberland, who could not lead it; nor could Devonshire who had promised the King to support the peace. Newcastle was the unwilling, half-hearted organizing promoter who hardly knew what he was doing since he had always looked upon an opposition as reprobate factionalism. Rockingham provided the spur and relished his role as a sort of whip. His hope for success was fortified by the reaction of many to Fox's taking over from Grenville the management of the House of Commons, and by the report going about that Pitt thought no man "fit to be at the head of affairs, but the Duke of Cumberland." While Newcastle was seeing failure as certain and groaning that he could "scarce be sure of any body," Rockingham carried his campaign from Newmarket into Yorkshire. From Wentworth he wrote (October 26) : "I have reason to believe that some who I thought doubtful, or indeed reckoned inclined to the present administration, are very adverse to it & I must add that in return I have not found any to take off from those who I thought early were not inclined towards the present administration." He was back at Newmarket with Cumberland by the end of the month and there heard the exciting news that the King had counterattacked from strength: had fired the Duke of Devonshire. Many proud tempers smarted at that. "I like the looks of the politicians here," wrote the Marquis in sending the news to his wife. Then he hastened to town where Newcastle said that people were "very much enraged." As expectation now became general that Bute would become lord chamberlain and the long-unpopular Fox would take the Treasury, even the old Duke was momentarily almost convinced that the country would prevail over the court: "If we show spirit & *have a system* these gentlemen cannot go on." [24]

Meanwhile, Lord George Cavendish in order to show a proper feeling for his ducal brother resigned his place at court, and Rockingham resolved to do the same although on a different principle. "Stress may be laid by the family connections of the Duke of Devonshire on the *personal* ill usage," the Marquis told Newcastle (November 1), "but in my opinion it should be looked on in general as only in consequence of the *same advice* prevailing which has influenced all the late domestic measures." [25] He knew then that other resignations were imminent but declined to join Newcastle and Cumberland on the following day when a general plan was adopted for calling on faithful Pelhamite whigs to throw up their places in administration—to prove to the King that Bute and Fox could not go on. Electing to be ignorant of what was brewing Rockingham went to the King on November 3 to resign his place at court.

I had an audience this morning of the King [he confided to Lady Rockingham that night] in which I acquainted him, with how much uneasiness & regret I had seen the tendency of all the late domestic measures, that I looked upon the last event of the Duke of Devonshire, as a further explanation & illustration of all the foregoing, that I was grieved to see that all persons, who had long been steadily attached to his Majesty's family etc. were now more the objects of his Majesty's displeasure than of his favour, that the pursuit of such counsels had given much alarm, & that as I felt the whole so strongly in my mind I beg'd leave not to continue a Lord of the Bed-chamber, least my continuance should carry with it the appearance of approbation.[26]

Since Rockingham confidently expected other resignations to follow, his solo performance which the King heard with cold indifference had more pretense than reality. There is no doubt that he wished to set a lofty example. Old dependents of Newcastle might go out in answer to a summons but a great peer had to act a great part. Before Lady Rockingham understood fully what was going on she had expressed the wish to her husband "that your conduct may always *take* the *lead* & give the *example* rather than follow it. . . . I should be miserable if you gave up in a string of resignations." The Duke of Cumberland complimented his young friend upon his conduct and deplored that "we live in such times that a man of your rank and steady attachment to the King and his family should find himself necessitated to take the step you have taken." All the kingdom, he said, would be convinced that the Marquis had acted solely for the King's service; and he hoped that "we shall soon see these clouds nay storms well over & you and others of your principles at court again." [27]

As Rockingham headed for Yorkshire, stopping en route at Chatsworth to see Devonshire, the Newcastle–Cumberland plan of mass resignations went into operation. One by one, slowly and reluctantly, about half the men on the list answered the call of their old chief. Rockingham said that there was "something awful in this slow firing" and tried to make himself believe that it might make "more impression than a hurry of fire & sudden passion"; while Devonshire flattered himself that "a properly spaced series would keep up the attention of the public better and be more effectual in the end." [28] But it daily became plain that the scheme was fizzling, as the few places vacated were easily filled to give new strength to the administration. Newcastle lost all hope. When Rockingham returned to town the old Duke told him sadly, "things certainly do not mend, Mr. Pitt is awkward." A few days before, Pitt had met with Cumberland and urged that the peace terms be attacked but flatly declined all concert with men whose purpose he believed to be a mere restoration of Newcastle at the Treasury. When Parliament was opened (November 25) there were perhaps 180 men in the House of Commons angry enough to divide against administration if a good popular motion were put and Pitt led them; but he would not lead an opposition and they had no one else. Pitt did not even appear in Parliament. Rockingham said, worthlessly, that something "must be done & soon," but nothing better was thought of than to oppose the peace and attempt to exploit Pitt's known intention of criticizing it.[29] A worse front on which to fight could hardly have been chosen. When the address on the peace was moved (December 9) Pitt appeared, spoke some detailed criticism of it, and went away without voting. The address passed with only 65 dividing against it and in the Lords there was no division.

The new opposition's defeat was ignominious and well deserved. Professional politicians, trying what was strange to them, got out of touch with reality and bungled like amateurs. Pitt judged them not unfairly. His own objections to the peace terms became well enough the architect of victory robbed of his direction of the concluding phase of the war; but objections issuing from Newcastle and company could not fail to appear captious and uncandid, mere pretexts in a struggle for power. After more than six years of war an attempt to obstruct the peace for the purpose of showing George III that Bute and Fox were bad ministers was a wretchedly desperate expedient; and Rockingham's argument that the Bute administration was not strong enough to make a good peace was hollow, since in the circumstances any minister firmly supported by the King could have done it. Much responsibility for the fiasco must be laid to the Marquis, hotspur among the "great whigs." He enjoyed a special and perhaps influential intimacy with Cumberland, who gave the signal which started Newcastle on the rash course; and his beating up for supporters at Newmarket injected the spirit of a sort of Jockey Club *fronde*. Thus his first plunge into high politics ended rather like his initial fling in county politics. It had seemed in 1753 as right and natural that the master of Wentworth should have his way in nominating a whig member for Yorkshire, as in 1762 it seemed right and natural to him that he and his friends should bar men disagreeable to themselves from being ministers of a king of the house of Hanover. His uncle Lord Mansfield might again have read him a sobering lesson but the Lord Chief Justice was now separated from old allies and became a friend of the court. The former mentor and pupil had parted forever in politics.

As might have been expected after their great success the King and his ministers meted out punishments and rewards. The remains of the pre-Bute political machinery were extinguished and an abundance of places was opened for supporters and friends of supporters of the court. The purge was carried even into the counties, so that Rockingham was informed by a secretary of state on December 23:

> The King has commanded me to acquaint Your Lordship that His Majesty has no further Occasion for your Service as Lord Lieutenant of the West Riding of the County of York, of the City of York, and County of the same City; as Custos Rotulorum of the North and West Ridings of the County of York; for the City of York and County of the same City and Ainsty, otherwise Ainstie of York; and as Vice Admiral of the County of York, City of York and County of the same City.[30]

His tilt with the court thus cost the Marquis a part of his inheritance; and his honors were divided between his political enemies, Holderness and Huntingdon. Newcastle was similarly struck at and also the young Duke of Grafton. Devonshire was excepted from this treatment but he resigned the honors of Derbyshire in protest against the court's attack upon his friends. Contemporary opinion seems to have regarded the "slaughter of the Pelhamites" as an

extreme abuse of the spoils system, and Rockingham found
a little cold comfort in reflecting: "Every act of violence
justified the opinion we had formed of the temper & intention of this administration & will help to open the people's
eyes." [31] His county friends evinced both sympathy and
fidelity. A number of justices of the peace wished to show
their feelings by throwing up their commissions until Rockingham advised that "it should not be in that way, that they
should show their dislike to what happened." Sir George
Armytage hoped that "a true British spirit" would rise up
and "wrench the reigns of government out of the hands of
a man who I believe endeavours to instill Despotism in the
Heart of the Sovereign." The Rockingham Club sent its
president an address of congratulation "for that Steadiness
and Uniformity of Conduct; that distinguished Zeal; which
has constantly animated your Lordship (even from the early
part of life) for the public Good; and the Support of our
Happiness under the illustrious House of Hanover." [32] The
lost honors would not be recovered by the Marquis until he
became the King's minister in 1765.

III

The new opposition did not yet wither away. Rockingham
made one with a small party on December 23 at the house
of Newcastle's nephew George Onslow. According to the
Duke, who was there, almost all were "violent for a Club."
He reported to Devonshire:

> . . . I think, at last the Marquess gave in to them. They said,
> there was nothing to do without it; that they must collect their
> friends, and they seem'd much elated with the effect, which the
> violence and persecutions have had everywhere.[33]

The old Duke was against forming a political club; it would
carry "the air of faction." Devonshire was hardly less disinclined and thought that they should first find out whom
they could "really depend on." Great whig magnates could

hardly allow an angry minority in Parliament to chart their political course. They needed an able leader, one of their own, in the House of Commons to give dignity and effect to the whig cause. They would stretch far to get Pitt but he loftily disclaimed all connection with them. Hardwicke's son, Charles Yorke, gifted and respectable, might have served them had he not preferred to remain the King's attorney general in hope of being the next lord chancellor. Rockingham was sanguine about his friend and neighbor, the sparkling Charles Townshend, who had resigned office at his uncle Newcastle's bidding; but Townshend was re-penting that folly and would soon re-enter administration. Henry Bilson Legge was thought of; son of an Earl of Dartmouth, he had been formed under Sir Robert Walpole and had held the Exchequer at Newcastle's Treasury board, but he was growing old and was a poor speaker. There was no one else deemed worthy of consideration; nor could any-one think of a good popular point to contend for; so that whiggery divorced from government cut a sorry figure. Horace Walpole said that "this opposition died at birth," and Richard Rigby, the Duke of Bedford's hireling who held a joint vice-treasurership for Ireland, sneered: "These turned out gentlemen are surprized that all the world are not as angry at their removals as they are, whereas nobody cares a farthing about them." Lord Bute saw them limited to "little despicable arts of sewing lies, perverting well-intentioned people, and tearing away from me any little merit I can acquire." Impotence bred dismay and despair in them and brought out a tendency to blame one another. According to Rigby there was "nothing more curious in the formation of this opposition, if it can be called one, than to hear the Duke of Cumberland's friends cursing the Duke of Newcastle for drawing their master into this scrap, and all the Duke of Newcastle's turned-out friends damning the Duke of Cumberland for making them lose their places." [34]

In February a small sign of hope was given that some-thing might be done when Pitt's brother-in-law Earl Temple made an overture to Devonshire and Rockingham, giving to the latter explicit declarations "both for himself & Mr. Pitt" that they never would act with or support Bute. Pitt confirmed this declaration to Devonshire but declined any engagement with the opposition; although he would, health permitting, attend Parliament upon "any national or constitutional points." To discover such points became the aim of the chiefs of whiggery. In March one emerged: ministry's bill to extend the excise to the production of cider (even to a producer's domestic consumption). The measure was hated by country gentlemen, notably in the western counties where most cider was made. Its inquisitorial provisions offended generally and many who usually supported administration voted with the minority against the bill. Pitt appeared and spoke in condemnation of it. When it reached the Lords Newcastle was at first little inclined to contest it, Cumberland doubted the propriety of opposing a revenue measure, and Devonshire was out of town. Rockingham, however, was for battle and went to consult Pitt, reporting afterward: "I found every thing as I could wish. He thought the opportunity a good one especially as the Cyder Lords continued warm." [35] On March 28 forty-eight peers divided against committing the bill. Newcastle did his part; Devonshire appeared to do his; Lord Hardwicke spoke against the bill; and Rockingham appears to have acted again as the whip of the whigs. A better issue for them to exploit could hardly have been imagined. Nothing in the land was more disliked than the excise. The cider bill stirred a new hate wave against Bute which convinced him that he should cease to be the prime minister. The act, moreover, was to remain a grievance to many, and those who were most affected were tory squires in western England whose most effective spokesman was a member for Worcestershire, William Dowdeswell.[36] His pamphlet against the act charged a "Machiavellian Plan for *Power* not for *Revenue*" and breathed the same passion for justice and liberty which animated the breasts of whigs like Sir George Savile.[37] A stream of country toryism was flowing into the whiggish pool of discontent, and Dowdeswell in a few years would be leading the "Rockingham whigs" in the House of Commons.

George Grenville succeeded Bute at the Treasury in early April and took over from Fox the leadership of Commons. Instead of one all-powerful minister there was formed a triumvirate consisting of Grenville and the secretaries of state, Egremont and Halifax. The arrangement, shaped largely by Bute, aimed at recruiting from various groups so that new strength might be gained in Parliament. Some lucrative places were reserved for special friends of Bute. Several reputed friends of Pitt were provided for. The friends of the Duke of Bedford, who had held the privy seal since 1761, got more places than they had ever had before, although Bedford himself withdrew from a system in which he believed that Bute's influence was still overriding. The new ministry was designed to be more acceptable to the public, hence harder for an opposition to attack effectively. Grenville was a respected House of Commons man whose honesty and competence at public business were recognized. Lord Mansfield esteemed him highly, as did Charles Yorke. Grenville's brother Temple and brother-in-law Pitt had been separated from him in politics since 1761, but neither could feel toward him as they had toward Bute. Egremont too was of this family connection and Halifax stirred no great animosities. Both secretaries of state had remained on amicable terms with Newcastle. No overtures at this time of ministerial change were made to proscribed whigs. Rockingham looked upon the new system as a continuation of all that he disliked and found some satisfaction in Charles Townshend's forming no part of it. Perhaps this brilliant nephew of Newcastle would lead the opposition in the next session of Parliament.

Hard upon the rising of Parliament in April the Wilkes case exploded to the great embarrassment of the new administration. A general warrant signed by a secretary of state was issued for the arrest of author, publisher, printer of Number 45 of the *North Briton,* a scurrilous weekly sheet got out by John Wilkes and Charles Churchill. The charge was seditious libel of crown and ministers. Wilkes was a member of Parliament politically connected with Lord Temple. He was taken up, interrogated, and lodged in the Tower until Temple's suit for a writ of habeas corpus brought him before Chief Justice Pratt of the Court of Common Pleas, a long-time friend of Temple and Pitt. The arrest of an M.P. on such a charge, Pratt ruled, breached the privilege of Parliament, and he also condemned general warrants as illegal. Overnight Wilkes, Pratt, and Temple became heroes to the metropolitan populace which abounded with various unnamed grievances against established power. The King stripped Temple of his county honors in Buckinghamshire and struck his name from the Privy Council, which fanned the fire. Repeated prosecutions for libel failed that summer because juries refused to convict; so that one aggravating event after another kept tempers on the boil. Thus more good "constitutional points" were in prospect for the opposition to exploit when Parliament met again.

Cumberland–Newcastle whigs had no sympathy with Wilkes but they hoped that the tempest centering on his name would show the King that his ministers knew not how to quiet the country: ergo, that the Pelhamites should be restored. Nor were they prepared to assert the rightness of Pratt's legal views which clashed with the opinions of their friend Attorney General Yorke, who had approved the warrant in the *North Briton* case. No doubt they would have liked Yorke to resign his office and join the opposition, but he was more lawyer than politician and in any event much could be forgiven the son of Lord Hardwicke. Pitt and Temple of course agreed with Pratt's law; and in this situation Rockingham appointed himself to the role of go-between to form a united front. He kept up friendly contacts with Pitt and Temple while trying to "manage" Yorke toward the end of stopping or delaying a further prosecution of Wilkes in the Court of King's Bench. Artfully, on May 19, he took Sir George Savile with him to consult with Pitt, Temple, and the latter's brother James Grenville, and then reported to Newcastle that "the stile of conversation & all that was dropped seemed to indicate good humour &

moderation in Mr. Pitt." Savile was exactly the right man to bring into such a consultation, since he had much influence with country gentlemen in Parliament and had long been an almost worshipful admirer of the Great Commoner. A few days later Savile accompanied the Marquis to Claremont to meet with the old Duke, the young Duke of Portland, and Charles Yorke. Newcastle pronounced Sir George "a most valuable man." Rockingham also induced Charles Town-shend to join political councils at Claremont, so that one may get a few glimpses of him at this time practicing his art of getting men together. He told Newcastle (June 2) of "my determined plan . . . to preserve & cement harmony and understanding between His Lordship [Temple] Mr. Pitt & us." It was he who arranged a Pitt–Yorke meeting five days later, when Pitt avowed union with "the great Whig Lords" and an intention to act on whig principles taking along such tories as were willing to act with him and his friends. Pitt even professed neutrality with respect to the known competitive aspirations of Yorke and Justice Pratt to the Great Seal, and hoped that questions rising out of the Wilkes affair would not have the consequences which some feared. The Attorney General soon hinted to Grenville that he might resign. While Pitt and Yorke conferred Rocking-ham was with Cumberland at Windsor Lodge for a five-day visit during which he "liked much the stile of the conversa-tion." It appears that the Marquis was becoming the pivotal man among the heads of the minority. The faithful friend of Newcastle and apparent favorite of H.R.H., he was also their most effective contact man with the Pitt–Temple peo-ple. Another sign of his key position was shown in the fact that Lord Bute, troubled by the situation of the triumvirate ministry, made an oblique approach to Rockingham to learn whether his friends were disposed to come into administra-tion. His answer was that Bute was not a proper person to treat with and that the friends of the Duke of Cumberland would act *en corps* with the Great Commoner.[38]

Late in June Rockingham returned to Yorkshire where he found that the county sheriffs had advertised a meeting of freeholders to adopt an address complimenting the King on the peace of Paris. Similar moves were under way wide over the country by partisans of the court, and the ministers were eager for these addresses as proof of general contentment with administration. Rockingham wished to prevent a York address but quietly and without offending the King or showing "personal picque & resentment." He passed the word to friends and political agents that although he would not oppose an address he did not favor one. Yorkshire did not address. The Cavendishes smothered an address in Derbyshire, as did Savile and the Duke of Portland in Nottingham. Newcastle sent word of similar success in Sussex and Surrey: "As you go on triumphantly in the North, we, in the South, are not behind you." As if to celebrate the supremacy of his friends in their counties the Duke of Cumberland on July 26 visited Devonshire at Chatsworth. A great company gathered: the Earl of Albemarle and Admiral Keppel, the latter's inseparable friend Admiral Sir Charles Saunders, the Earl of Bessborough, the dukes of Portland and Grafton, the Marquis, and others including even Lord Mansfield.[39] The event was social rather than political but a royal duke could hardly visit a peer lately turned out of office who was looked up to as "head of the whigs" without some political repercussions. From Chatsworth H.R.H. and many of the party went on to Wentworth and this indeed was a counterstroke for the prestige of the whig magnate lately punished by the crown. The Marquis wrote to Newcastle:

. . . the conversations I had with his Royal Highness on the subject of politicks were perfectly agreeable & indeed there seems to be amongst us such a demonstration of union & steadiness, that I think will find its weight sooner or later.[40]

Meanwhile, partly from an opinion of weakness in the ministry and partly to hold fast to Charles Yorke, the King sent Lord Egremont early in August to offer the vacant lord presidency of the council to Hardwicke. If necessary for

gaining him, a great state office would be opened for Newcastle too. Hardwicke declined to accept on any terms, saying that for forty years he had acted with the great whig
lords and their families and that to separate from them
would tarnish his character "in the opinion of the world"
and thus incapacitate him from useful service to the crown.
A few weeks later Egremont died and the King sought to
make Pitt again a secretary of state. For three hours on
August 26 Pitt was in the closet exposing to Majesty his
views of men and measures, explaining the conditions in
which he would serve, and went away believing that he
would soon head a new administration. His plan would put
Temple at the Treasury and make Charles Townshend the
second secretary of state and deputy leader in Commons.
Newcastle would have the privy seal, Hardwicke the lord
presidency, Rockingham the admiralty; Devonshire would
be restored as lord chamberlain, Grafton brought into cabinet council, and Pratt raised to the peerage. Pitt went to
Claremont (where Newcastle thought his attitude toward
the whigs "proper & very honourable") and sent off expresses summoning prospective ministers to town.[41] Rockingham arrived to find a mare's nest. The King refused to make
such extensive changes and Pitt declined to take office without them. Whereupon enlarged powers were given to Grenville, the Duke of Bedford was induced to take the vacant
lord presidency, and his friend Lord Sandwich was raised to
be a secretary of state. The better to please his ministers
the King agreed to keep Bute away from court and out of
town. Grenville was now the principal or "prime" minister
—in the language of the age "the Minister"—and he was
no less determined than Lord Bute to prevent great politicians from forcing the hand of Majesty; yet he too was a
politician in alliance with Bedford, who headed a well-
known faction often called the "Bloomsbury gang"; so that
George III was far from certain that ministry was as well
settled as he wished it to be and continued to look to Bute
for advice.

    If the Cumberland–Newcastle whigs were gratified by the

show Pitt had made of union with them, Pitt fancied that he had laid them under some obligations to himself. His choice of their representative to treat with was the Marquis. The two conferred at Hayes (Pitt's home) on September 5 when Rockingham never saw "more appearance of good humour and union." They talked like party chiefs of an administration they might form. "The necessity of many removals was talked over & assented to," the Marquis told Newcastle, making it clear however that all was "with the idea that it should appear as it ought in truth not only the opinions of R[ockingham] and P[itt]." [42] On his way back to Yorkshire the Marquis did not fail to pay a visit to Temple.

While Rockingham was courting Pitt the Duke of Newcastle was engaged in a political business aimed at honoring his noble young friend and giving Grenville a black eye. He lined up enough promised votes to elect the Marquis a governor of Charterhouse in succession to the late Egremont. To be a governor of this greatest of charitable foundations was a high honor and provided opportunities for conferring obligations. Including the Head Master there were fifteen governors always chosen from the most eminent ranks and they elected their successors. At the time they were the Archbishop of Canterbury, the Bishop of London, the dukes of Bedford, Devonshire, Dorset, Rutland, and Newcastle, the Lord Chancellor, and the earls of Holderness, Hardwicke, Sandwich, Mansfield, and Bute. Since the Treasury minister was usually a governor, Grenville was shocked at learning that he would be opposed by "a young Nobleman that has never filled any public post" and was in "open and declared opposition" to the King's administration. This was nothing less than "an affront upon one whom the King has called to so high an office in his Government." The election was held October 11 but two weeks earlier the Duke of Rutland broke the news to Grenville that Rockingham had the necessary votes, and this the Duke attributed to "a most unjustifiable and unprecedented behaviour of the Duke of Newcastle and his Associates." [43] While this stroke was preparing the old

Duke busied himself too in an effort to get some plan of parliamentary operations concerted by the whig chiefs and Pitt. The latter was shy of anything which looked like a formed opposition and perhaps resented Newcastle's taking it upon himself to press the business. The latter appealed to Rockingham to come to see Pitt but the Marquis at Newmarket was disabled by a cut foot. In mid-October it appears to have dawned on Pitt for the first time that Charles Yorke differed from Justice Pratt's decision respecting parliamentary privilege. Had he known that earlier, Pitt told Newcastle, he "might not have proceeded in the vain dream, that some solid union, on Revolution principles, and an assertion of the freedom of the constitution, was possible." He asked how Yorke's "lingering on in a court situation, under a rash and odious ministry" could be squared "with the conduct of those, who are openly resisting the dangerous power of it?" [44]

The whig prescription now was for the Attorney General's friends to get him out of office and for Rockingham, the old Duke's superior in the art of smoothing Pitt, to reopen conversations with the indispensable man. Unable to leave his couch, the Marquis received Pitt in Grosvenor Square (October 31) and told him that Yorke would resign; whereupon Pitt, "very cordial," avowed anew his union with the whigs; although when Cumberland later that day pressed him for specifics he shied off them as having "an air of faction." He hardly seemed the same man to H.R.H. and to the Marquis; the former now despaired of him, but the latter did not. A few days later Yorke resigned, telling the King that it was to please his father who was under the influence of Newcastle.[45] On November 7 Rockingham was with Temple who would see Pitt the next day, and he recorded:

I recommended that if Mr. Pitt & Mr. Yorke did differ in opinion, that it might not be with warmth, etc. & that if it was possible it should be contrived that the House should see that if

they disagreed upon the point of privilege that there were other
points in that affair on which they did agree & how inclined
& determined they were to act together.[46]

Further evidence of the "right" disposition of the Yorke
family was shown soon after by the resignation from the
Board of Trade of John Yorke who owed his seat in Parliament to Rockingham. How far the Marquis' blandishments
and the conduct of the Yorkes may have conciliated Pitt's
temper cannot be said, but he was on hand to play a great
part when Parliament was opened.

If Rockingham had formed an opinion of his own on
Pratt's ruling with respect to parliamentary privilege it
would probably have squared with Yorke's, as did Lord
Mansfield's; but when great lawyers differed he saw the
question as political, and Pitt being indispensable to the
whigs Rockingham was ready to support his views. On the
day before Parliament opened he wrote to Yorke that
"the times make the necessity." [47] On the first day (November 15) of the session a ministerial motion to condemn Number 45 of the *North Briton* as a seditious and traitorous libel
was made and carried. Pitt's motion to strike out the word
traitorous failed by 273 to 111. The following night he met
with leading whigs (Rockingham was not well enough to be
there) and they agreed to support the doctrine that privilege
screened a member of the House of Commons against prosecution for seditious libel. This question came on a week later.
Charles Yorke's resignation could not release him from the
honorable duty of giving the same opinion in the House
which he had given as a law officer of the crown; hence he
and Pitt were opponents in debate, at the end of which the
House voted (255 to 133) to deny privilege. In the Lords
35 opposed, concurring with the Commons' resolution. A
convalescent Marquis regretted to Newcastle that they had
not done better, "but that is now over & we must look forward." [48] The minority, especially in Commons, was numerous and growing. The young Earl of Shelburne, who had recently resigned the Board of Trade, was dismissed as aide-

de-camp to the King for his vote on the question of privilege, and for the same offense General William A'Court had his regiment taken away. The city rioted against the hangman's burning of Number 45. Charles Townshend was acting as Rockingham hoped ardently that he would: "I am so *willing* to think, that he will be steady [which Townshend alas never was] that I own, I was thoroughly pleased. . . . He seems to be quite determined." Since Pitt professed physical inability to attend the House often, the Marquis resolved to try to get Yorke, Townshend, and Legge to form a triumvirate leadership in Commons, taking " 'the imprimatur' from Mr. Pitt." Looking forward to a yet larger and more active minority after Christmas holidays, he told Cumberland that surely all military officers who had ever voted with the Pelhamite whigs would now be "clinched." Other great whigs were less optimistic. Newcastle saw "a good many *If's* in our way" and thought all depended on a firm Yorke–Pitt reconciliation; while Devonshire talked of retirement if Pitt stayed away. None of these lords knew that Yorke had already regretted to Grenville the resignation which he said had been forced upon him by his friends.[49]

During the Christmas parliamentary recess, opposition whigs drew some capital from the presence in England of Charles, Hereditary Prince of Brunswick, who came to marry the King's sister Augusta. His father, Prince Ferdinand, was a whiggish hero of the late war. "The people, enchanted by novelty, and a hero," wrote Horace Walpole, "were unbounded in their exultations wherever he appeared." On the eve of his arrival it was reported to Grenville that "great doings" were "preparing at Lord Rockingham's for the Prince's reception." He was rather coolly received by the King, dined twice with H.R.H., and went to visit Pitt at Hayes.[50]

Only a fraction of the minority in Commons opposed the motion expelling Wilkes (January 19) from the House, but this removal of his person and conduct from all consideration opened the way for opposition to launch a formidable attack upon the arbitrary manner of his arrest and the seizure of his private papers. The business was started with a motion for inquiry concerted by Sir George Savile and Sir William Meredith.[51] Knowing that there was massive opposition to the doctrine that general warrants were legal, Grenville chose not to oppose the inquiry and when he tried to bring it on a few days later in order to dispose of the business quickly the House balked. According to James Grenville's report of the debate (January 23), Meredith and Savile dominated "by the irresistible weight of the natural and striking justice of their demand." [52] Pitt was not present, and it seemed as if the minority were casting up its own natural leaders. That Savile was Rockingham's close friend was of course well-known. Meredith, who sat for Liverpool, was a baronet of tory background but hot against the administration and eager for a well-formed opposition. The next day William Dowdeswell obtained the consent of the House to go into committee to consider the Cider Act, and a week later his motion to modify it swelled the minority to 152. According to Horace Walpole, seven for the motion were shut out when the question was put—"so near was the Court run by the minority, though without leaders, and frequently obstructed and distressed by the family of Yorke and the duplicity of Charles Townshend, who oftener spoke against than for them." [53] Nor was Pitt present at this time to lend his weight. Dowdeswell joined in the debate for the minority on February 6 when Meredith moved for the information on which the general warrant in the *North Briton* case had been issued. Prominent too for the minority in that and previous debates of the session was General Henry Seymour Conway, a man who ever voted according to the dictates of his conscience. Already in middle age, Conway had been in Parliament since 1741, although his career had been largely military. He had been aide-de-camp to Cumberland in the defeat of the Scottish rebellion and the last commander of British forces in Germany in the last war. He was close to the Duke of Devonshire's family, a cousin of Horace Walpole, and sat in Parliament for his friend the Duke of Grafton's borough of Thetford. A lieutenant-general in rank, he possessed a valuable regiment and at court was a groom of the bedchamber. His brother the Earl of Hertford was the King's ambassador at the court of France. Conway hated "faction" and never dreamed of going to systematic opposition, but he had opposed the ministry on the question of privilege and even voted against the expulsion of Wilkes. The King would have taken away his regiment and dismissed him from the court if Grenville had not advised against striking in such a way at such a man. Conway's was a strong and influential voice in the minority of 1763–1764.[54] Moreover, an opposition club, merely talked of the year before, had come into being. It met at Wildman's Tavern. A list dated February 6 shows 106 members including peers and commoners. Rockingham, Grafton, Devonshire, Newcastle, Portland, Temple, Albemarle all belonged although the great majority were House of Commons men.[55] A parliamentary minority sparked by a political club and drawing support from such reputable independents as Dowdeswell and Conway was formidable, as the events of mid-February were to prove.

In the great debates (February 13–17) on general warrants Meredith and Savile, Townshend, Yorke, Legge, the Duke of Devonshire's brothers (Lord John, Lord George, and Lord Frederick Cavendish), Dowdeswell, Conway, Isaac Barré, and the Great Commoner himself came near to overwhelming Grenville's ranks. The crucial resolution to condemn the use of general warrants in libel cases was lost by only 14 in a House swollen to 450. At almost the same time Rockingham instigated the condemnation by the Lords of a royalist tract (Brecknock's *Droit de Roi*) as a libel upon the constitution not less heinous than Number 45 of the *North Briton*.[56] It was widely expected, after Grenville's near-defeat, that the King would change the administration. Newcastle told Pitt that so great a minority "must have its weight, and produce the most happy consequences to the public." But nothing happened.

While mankind expected [wrote Horace Walpole] that the Opposition would vigourously pursue the advantage of so large an increase in their numbers, day after day, and week after week slipped away without their exerting one symptom of spirit or activity. . . . At first they seemed to expect the Ministers would come and lay their places at their feet. The dream was over before an effort was made to realise it.[57]

The explanation is simple enough: no one could think of any more great and stirring popular questions to raise. The opposition—far less numerous than the 214 who had voted to damn general warrants—had no program, no purpose but to dish the administration, and could only wait until government did something to make a lot of people angry. Pitt went away to nurse his gout until another great national and constitutional point might arise. The Duke of Cumberland had a stroke and the deaths of their fathers took Charles Townshend and Charles Yorke into temporary seclusion from politics. An election contest for the high stewardship at Cambridge University diverted whiggery's energies. The new Earl of Hardwicke sought the honor in succession to his father and was opposed by Secretary of State Sandwich who would be narrowly defeated. But in Parliament nothing of consequence was moved by the minority, and Grenville's American Revenue Act, big with consequences, passed almost as routine. One day Lord Rockingham, his successor at the Treasury, would have to revise this measure, but there is no evidence to show that he saw its importance in the spring of 1764.

At the close of the session (April 19) Conway was stripped of his regiment and dismissed from the court for having followed his conscience instead of Grenville's direction in voting. A sense of outrage spread. No more reputable man lived in the knigdom; if he was not an ornament of George III's court who could be? The issue of punishing military officers for votes in Parliament looked like a hot one for minority exploitation in the next session. That Rockingham intended to press it is evidenced by his extant notes for a speech about it.[58] Horace Walpole addressed the public with a pamphlet in defense of his great cousin.

During the summer Rockingham did something for political education in the interest of the opposition by promoting distribution of pamphlets—Walpole's, Charles Townshend's *Defence of the Minority,* and David Hartley's *The Budget*—which not only attacked Grenville's financial policy but probed the sore inflicted by the Cider Act. By summer's end the Marquis was confident that political dispositions in Yorkshire were much as he wished them to be, and from his frequent contacts with the Cavendishes, Savile, and the Duke of Portland he gathered that the same good appearances were showing in Derby and Nottingham. He wrote to Newcastle on September 15:

> What may be the general wish when Parliament meets I know not, but so far I am sure that the general wish is, extirpation to the present administration & that an administration may be formed among those, whereof many enjoy your Grace's friendship & all who are now connected & acting in concert with you & your friends.[59]

This was all very well, Newcastle thought, "But we want hands; & in one sense, I may say heads." Where were the leaders in the House of Commons who could weld opposition into a revived whig party? Legge was dead, Townshend demonstratively unreliable, and Yorke too much the lawyer. Meredith and Dowdeswell were looked upon as tories. Savile could shine in debate but had little sense of party. Pitt signified that he did not even wish to enter into consultations.[60] During October a series of events sank Rockingham's spirits. Devonshire died, Cumberland's precarious health took a turn for the worse, and the Marquis' youngest sister disgraced the family by eloping with a footman. On November 3 he lamented to Newcastle:

> I fear there is no very pleasing subject to write on either in regard to public matters or private concerns. . . . If nothing is to be done, there is no one will lament it more than I shall, but I am sure there is no one at present more ready to submit to the lot of retirement than I am.[61]

Before Parliament met again in January he heard many opinions on what to do and not to do in politics. Meredith visited Wentworth during November and the Marquis found him "very strenuous." No doubt he expressed the same views which he later gave to Portland, namely that it was futile to place faith in such whig favorites as Townshend and Yorke or to place any reliance upon courting Pitt, and that backing should be given to the men who came naturally to the front in the minority.[62] About the same time (November 14) Newcastle sent a packet of political correspondence and told Rockingham that H.R.H. and many friends thought that the whigs should support repeal of the Cider Act but without entering into any engagements with tory members who had proposed a treaty for this purpose; that a "middle way" between support of the administration and opposition should be followed to avoid offending Pitt; and that Grafton and Conway agreed to this line. On the other hand, said the old Duke, many of "our young and zealous friends" were for an active opposition and the Cavendishes felt that if such appeared "we owe it to those, who sacrificed themselves for us, to support it." [63] The Cavendish brothers it would seem were nearer to agreeing with Meredith than with Newcastle and Cumberland. Rockingham answered (November 23) that he did not like the "middle way," that he agreed with the Cavendishes that a bad administration should always be opposed, and that "none was ever more deserving of opposition than the present." On the other hand he rejected Meredith's opinion that no reliance should be placed on Yorke and Townshend and that Pitt should be treated as if he no longer existed. He kept faith in his long-standing friendship with the former two and declined to despair of enlisting help from Pitt, with whom it was expedient to keep on good terms and "where we can carry him with us, ever availing ourselves of the idea of his connection with us." In other words, if Pitt would not be with them they ought to encourage the world to think that he was. The Marquis was to make effective use of this trick in recruiting men for a new administration the following year. Stepping now by a sort of natural succession to Devonshire as the titular head of whiggery, he resolved to try to bring all opponents of ministry to a common agreement. He promised Newcastle to come to town well in advance of the opening of Parliament, and to urge all his friends to do the same "that some thing might be agreed on to act early with spirit & I hope efficacy."

> I am convinced that there is matter enough of various sorts which would be sufficient if properly handled to get the better of this administration. . . . I only wish to see the whole acting upon a plan & *two* or *three* good leaders in the H[ouse] of C[ommons].[64]

In December Rockingham's hopes that two of these leaders might be Townshend and Yorke were dashed. The former decided that opposition was futile and put himself at Grenville's service. Yorke too compromised himself by accepting the royal favor of a patent of precedency in the courts, something much prized by lawyers. Newcastle described it as a "retaining fee" from administration and Portland judged that Yorke committed a breach of political friendship at exactly the moment he could hurt his friends most; while Meredith was provoked to denounce "men, who have no regard for the party they are bound to, but as it is the ladder to their ambition & interest." In a letter to the Marquis, Yorke pleaded that his acceptance of the patent had no political significance, and Rockingham, incapable of believing such a friend capable of treachery, refused to condemn him. Ensuing circumstances were to preclude a separation of these men, but Yorke, hardly less than Townshend, had rendered himself useless to Rockingham's plan for an opposition led in Commons by men of great whig families.[65]

On returning to town in early January the Marquis went with Savile, the Cavendish brothers, Lord Bessborough, and Portland to Wildman's Tavern where the club of the minority met. A little earlier it had been observed that "such a murrain among the factions" existed there that "the hand of God seems stretched out against them." [66] To bring all to agreement the Marquis urged an early resumption of the great popular question of general warrants, and pressed such men as Sir William Baker (influential city merchant long connected with Newcastle), Sir Anthony Abdy (a lawyer who sat for a Cavendish-owned borough), together with Meredith and Savile and a few others, to have frequent communications. He hoped to have "some eight ten or a doz. of our good steady & able friends" meet often and concert "plans of operation." Included in such a steering committee as he envisaged it would be General Conway and two western county tory members zealous against the Cider Act, Dowdeswell and Thomas Prowse. The Marquis' tactic was thus to encourage men who came naturally to the front in the House of Commons to take the lead and fashion the minority into an opposition party which would engage the support of great whig peers. He was in a sense trying to introduce among the minority the political arts and methods he had learned in Yorkshire.[67]

This effort proved unproductive in 1765. The general-warrants question was, to be sure, fought over again hotly (January 29), Meredith leading with the motion to condemn and Savile and Conway sharing with him the main burden of the debate; but Pitt did not appear in the House and the minority divided only 185—twenty-nine fewer than in the previous year. A motion of complaint against the dismissal of officers for their votes was dropped because Conway dreaded putting his military brothers in the awkward position of either letting him down or incurring the anger of the court, and because Pitt, when consulted by Lord John Cavendish, warned that defeat of such a motion might be interpreted as parliamentary approval of the practice. Only 49 voted against Grenville's American stamp tax, repeal of which was to become the hotly contested question of the next session; but none could foresee that, and there was nothing about this measure in February 1765 which could alert and mobilize the minority. While it was in legislative process Rockingham visited Pitt who would

within twelve months discover in the Stamp Act another
great "national and constitutional point." There is no evidence that anything passed between them on this subject.
The conversation, the Marquis said afterward, "did not
edify or indeed give me much satisfaction" since his host had
displayed "more appearance of a determined inactivity than
I had before met with." Other than general warrants there
was no question which could unite and alert that minority
out of which Rockingham had hoped to form a revitalized
whig party. It could not have been otherwise. The times
were not right; the public had grown quiet; men lost interest
and went away. On March 28 the Marquis pronounced that
politics were at a "standstill." Newcastle judged that "opposition has dwindled away to nothing." [68]

NOTES

1. WWM R 1: 171. It was said that Rockingham considered resigning
from court if Finch received no compensation.—Sir Lewis Namier and John
Brooke, *The History of Parliament: The House of Commons, 1754–1790,*
(3 vols.; New York: Oxford University Press, 1964), II 425; cited hereafter
as *Hist. Parl.*
2. Add. MSS 32916, ff. 158, 223, 228; 32917, f. 187.
3. WWM R 1: 160, 174, 180; Add. MS 32917, f. 355.
4. "Lord Holdernesse is gone into Yorkshire to support Turner against
Lord Rockingham which will make a good deal of provincial discord I
believe."—Richard Rigby to the Duke of Bedford, 16 Jan., *Correspondence
of John Fourth Duke of Bedford,* ed. Lord John Russell (3 vols.; London,
1842–1846), III 4; cited hereafter as *Bedford.*
5. WWM R 1: 186; Devonshire MS 443.3; Add. MS 32917, f. 449.
6. WWM R 189; Add. MS 32915, f. 47.
7. Collyer, "The Rockingham Connections," 255–256; WWM R 82.
8. Add. MS 32917, f. 355; Harris, *Life . . . Hardwicke* III 242; WWM R
1: 136.
9. When the point was settled Rockingham acknowledged that Bute "ac-
quitted himself very well."—Add. MS 32924, ff. 221, 392.
10. WWM R 1: 203, 204.
11. Add. MS 32930, f. 158; Savile declined to aid this tactic and probably
reflected Yorkshire sentiments more accurately than Rockingham.—WWM
R 1: 200.
12. Add. MSS 32931, ff. 51, 147, 248, 317; 32932, f. 306; WWM R 1: 208;
Devonshire MS 434.4.
13. Add. MS 32938, ff. 124–125, 262.

14. Quoted by George Thomas, Earl of Albemarle, *Memoirs of the Marquis of Rockingham and his Contemporaries* (2 vols.; London, 1852), I 109; cited hereafter as Albemarle.

15. Add. MS 32939, ff. 15, 136, 137; Devonshire MS 443.5.

16. Romney Sedgwick, ed., *Letters from George III to Lord Bute* (London, 1939), Nos. 149, 160, 161.

17. WWM R 1: 258; Devonshire MS 443.6.

18. Add. MS 35422, ff. 14–15.

19. Sedgwick, *Letters*, Nos. 179, 180, 183–185.

20. Add. MS 32942, ff. 181–182.

21. *Ibid.* 307.

22. Albemarle I 128–133; Devonshire MS 260.388; Sedgwick, *Letters*, No. 192; Add. MS 32943, f. 3.

23. Add. MS 32943, f. 146.

24. *Ibid.*, f. 430; 32944, ff. 10, 170.

25. *Ibid.*, f. 196.

26. WWM R 160: 3.

27. WWM R 168: 234; R 1: 324.

28. Devonshire MS 443.8; WWM R 1: 330.

29. Add. MS 32945, f. 106; the estimate of strength was made by Newcastle's nephew George Onslow.—*Ibid.*, f. 200. On the eve of the session William Burke, who was working for Fox, wrote: "There are certainly seeds of discontent in quantity, but they are fallen on rocky soil. In one word the opposition is made up of men whose nature and habit are not simply unfit, they are repugnant to all opposition."—R. J. S. Hoffman, *Edmund Burke, New York Agent* (Philadelphia, 1956), 292.

30. WWM R 1: 336.

31. Devonshire MS 443.12. The experienced Hardwicke's judgment was: "I never was more offended & provoked at ministerial wantonness in my life. . . . It will turn at last upon the authors."—Add. MS 32946, f. 367.

32. WWM R 1: 344, 346, 347–352, 355, 357, 358, 360.

33. Add. MS 32945, f. 341.

34. WWM R 1: 341; *Bedford* III 186; *Lonsdale Manuscripts* (Hist. MSS Comm. 13th *Report* App. VII), 132.

35. Add. MSS 32946, f. 347; 32947, f. 21; 35422, f. 226.

36. William Dowdeswell (1725–1775), a country gentleman who had been elected member for Worcestershire in 1761 as a tory and the next year opposed the peace. He had long been a friend of Charles Townshend but there is no evidence that he and Rockingham were acquainted in 1763. —*Hist. Parl.* II 333–335. His later connection with the Marquis has been depicted by M. Francis de Sales Boran in "William Dowdeswell and the Rockingham Whigs" (Fordham University dissertation, 1954).

37. *An Address to Such of the Electors of Great Britain as are Makers of Cyder and Perry* (London: W. Nicoll, October 1763).

38. Add. MSS 32948, ff. 246, 263, 273, 341; 32949, ff. 29, 122; Philip Yorke, *Life and Correspondence of Philip Yorke, Earl of Hardwicke* (3 vols.; London, 1913) III 503.

39. WWM R 1: 376, 380; Devonshire to Portland, 24 July.—Portland MSS; Add. MS 32949, ff. 406, 438.

40. Add. MS 32950, f. 196.

41. *Chatham* II 237–245; Albemarle I 171; *Grenville* II 197–200; Add. MS 35422, ff. 323–324.

42. Add. MS 32950, f. 329.

43. J. R. G. Tomlinson, ed., *Additional Grenville Papers* (Manchester, 1962), 31–42; *Life and Letters of Lady Sarah Lennox,* edd. Countess of Ilchester and Lord Stavordale (2 vols.; London, 1901–1902), I 134–135.

44. Add. MS 32951, ff. 101–107, 174, 192–204, 249–255, 329, 331; WWM R 146: 4; *Chatham* II 260–263.

45. Add. MS 32952, ff. 143, 166. John Yorke told Rockingham that he resigned "for the sake of those friends, with whom I ever wish to act & to some of whom I am highly obliged. Among these your Lordship stands one of the foremost."—WWM R 146: 14.

46. Add. MS 32952, f. 285.

47. Add. MS 35430, f. 8.

48. Add. MS 32953, f. 115.

49. Devonshire MS 443.18; Add. MS 32954, ff. 95, 150; *Grenville* II 229, 239.

50. *Ibid.,* 251–252; Horace Walpole, *Memoirs of the Reign of King George the Third,* ed. G. R. Barker (4 vols.; London–New York, 1894), I 275–277 (cited hereafter as *Memoirs*) ; *Chatham* II 277.

51. Sir William Meredith (1725–1790) had been in Parliament since 1754, at which time he was reputed to be not only tory but Jacobite. He voted for the peace in 1762 and was a supporter of Grenville until the persecution of Wilkes.—*Hist. Parl.* III 130–131. By 1764 he had entered into connection with the Duke of Portland and his letters to the latter (in the Portland MSS) show great zeal for forming the minority into a party backed by the Duke, Lord Rockingham, and their friends.

52. *Chatham* II 284.

53. *Memoirs* I 281–282.

54. Vide John Brooke's short history of Conway in Parliament.—*Hist. Parl.* II 244–247.

55. Add. MS 32955, ff. 409–410.

56. Walpole, *Memoirs* I 304–306. The motion was made by Lord Lyttelton but after a Rockingham–Pitt concert; the Marquis summoned peers to support it.—Add. MS 32956, f. 1.

57. *Memoirs* I 303.

58. WWM R 61: 36. The Cumberland–Newcastle whigs talked idly of an opposition plan of action before the next session. Rockingham and Devonshire met with Charles Townshend on April 29 and heard from him of a plan he then spelled out to Newcastle: a nation-wide system of clubs, a daily paper, and the setting the City of London in motion. The great whigs judged the plan impractical.—*Townshend Manuscripts* (Hist. MSS Comm. 11th *Report* App. IV 398–400).

59. Add. MS 32962, f. 113.

60. *Ibid.,* ff. 166, 347–349.

61. Add. MS 32963, f. 195. Lady Harriet Watson-Wentworth married one Sturgeon. The shock to the family is reflected in WWM R 143: 13–15: "The Marquis supped last night at White's, and blushed at Willis's request to be helped to some sturgeon."—Gilly William to George Selwyn 4 Jan. (Jesse, *George Selwyn* I 340).

62. Meredith to Portland, 24 Dec.—Portland MSS.

63. Add. MS 32963, ff. 375–378.

64. Add. MS 32964, ff. 93–96. A copy of this letter (23 Nov.) exists in Lady Rockingham's hand.—WWM R 1: 441. It now became a practice for her to make copies of letters the Marquis regarded as documents of record.

65. *Grenville* II 461–462, 525–532; Add. MS 32964, ff. 239, 257; Meredith to Portland, 21 Dec.—Portland MSS; WWM R 1: 443.

66. Jesse, *George Selwyn* I 311.

67. Add. MS 32965, ff. 10–12, 28–29, 40–41.

68. Walpole, *Memoirs* II 47–48; Add. MS 32966, ff. 91, 110, 127.

3

The Minister

DURING THE WINTER OF 1765 George III found his Minister, George Grenville, an irksome servant. Bent on protecting the independence of the crown against the pressure of political factions, Grenville demanded too insistently the right to be sole agent for dispensing the favors of the crown. Early in April he and his principal colleagues looked askance at a regency bill which the King, who had been alarmingly ill, desired to have enacted into law. The bill reserved to his Majesty the right secretly to name a regent and four other persons who with the principal officers of state would compose a regency council. The ministers feared that such a bill would arouse fresh suspicion of Lord Bute's influence, and induced the King to agree that the right to be regent should be restricted to the Queen and members of the royal family resident in England. While the bill was preparing the King summoned his uncle, the Duke of Cumberland, to inform him of it. H.R.H. received the impression that his Majesty had intended to say something else too. Soon afterward Cumberland was approached by the

Earl of Northumberland who said that a change of ministers was desired by the King and proposed a negotiation. Northumberland was to be named for the Treasury; Temple, Pitt, Charles Townshend, Newcastle, and Rockingham were envisaged as ministers. H.R.H. was not prepared to engage with Northumberland, whose family was linked with Bute's and who was regarded as a renegade Pelhamite and agent of the Favorite. Nor did H.R.H. like a regency bill creating a council to which he might or might not be appointed.

After more painful sessions with Grenville, the King resolved to have his royal brothers and the Duke of Cumberland named in the bill and sent Northumberland to discuss again with H.R.H. the recruitment of a new slate of ministers.[1] Rockingham wrote to Newcastle at 2 A.M. on April 23: "When I came home about 11 o'clock I found Lord Albemarle, who was just come from Cumberland House to desire me to go to his R.H. . . . Lord Northumberland has been again with his R.H. . . . there is still a probability of the negociation taking effect. Don't be too sanguine."[2] The negotiation was broken off but it was clear that Cumberland and Rockingham were zealous to help the King. H.R.H. at this time believed that Majesty's first intention had been to name the Queen regent and that certain complications started by lawyers had caused him to decide for secret reserved nomination. It was probably with the idea of pleasing their sovereign that Rockingham and some other friends of H.R.H. began to rally support for an amendment to name the Queen in the bill.[3]

Meanwhile, the ministers introduced and carried in the Lords a regency bill so phrased as to exclude his Majesty's mother, the Dowager Princess of Wales, from eligibility, thus showing to the world that her friend Lord Bute had no influence with them. Whereupon the King charged Grenville with the embarrassing task of correcting the offensive clause in the House of Commons. The Minister would assent to no more than accepting such a motion to amend. So it was done and the bill was passed in the lower House without a division, the Lords quickly concurring. Immediately afterward the King attempted to get rid of ministers he thought had served him ill. A careful watcher of the scene of politics, his Majesty saw little danger of delivering himself into the hands of the late opposition. He knew that Cumberland wished to help him. Only 67 in Commons had supported an opposition motion to name the Queen regent, and none had divided against the bill when it passed. Pitt had not appeared the whole session. Rockingham had followed Cumberland in accepting the bill when it came back to the Lords, although Newcastle and Portland had spoken objections to restoring the name of the King's mother.[4] From such a disunited corps of minority men it seemed probable that a ministry might be recruited which would be more deferential to the wishes of Majesty.

Designating the Earl of Northumberland for the Treasury, the King sent him to ask for the help of the Duke of Cumberland in forming a slate of ministers which would not include Grenville, Bedford, Sandwich, and Halifax. H.R.H. accepted the commission, conferred first with Rockingham and Newcastle, summoned Grafton and Temple, and sent Lord Albemarle to open the plan to Pitt. An administration was envisaged in which the Great Commoner, as secretary of state and minister of the House of Commons, would be the principal figure. According to Cumberland, such a system the King "had been pleased to chalk out for all our joint consideration"; and H.R.H.'s assignment had been "to see whether Mr. Pitt and Lord Temple, with the other great Whig families, could be brought to form him a strong and lasting administration." [5] No doubt Cumberland's effort would have succeeded if Pitt and Temple had proved co-operative; but they objected to Northumberland at the Treasury (suspecting the hand of Lord Bute) and stated terms to which the King would have to assent before they were willing to come into his service. Cumberland thought it very improper for men to demand commitments from Majesty before engaging to serve, and saw an end of the negotiation. Of this moment he recorded:

. . . I had no difficulties with our friends, but a little too much caution, not caring to engage without Mr. Pitt. Of this number I must except the Marquis of Rockingham, who from private reasons and inclinations, prefers a private life . . . yet when he saw the shyness of our friends he shook off his natural dislike and was ready to kiss the King's hand in whatever shape was most for the service in general. To this resolution I flatter myself his personal friendship for me had some share, seeing the distressed situation my friends had left me in, from their fears of stirring hand or foot without Mr. Pitt at their head.[6]

On May 19 H.R.H. himself went to Hayes and talked with Pitt, whose attitude remained unchanged. During the next few days Cumberland attempted to float an administration with Lord Lyttelton—Temple's cousin—at the Treasury instead of Northumberland, but he too declined. So ended George III's first effort to get rid of the men who had displeased him. However abortive, it yielded something of value: the dispositions of minority chiefs had been tested. And it may be assumed that Cumberland did not fail to tell the King of Rockingham's zeal for his service.

During the following three weeks the King sullenly went on with his ministers, who exacted *their* terms for staying. Moreover, George Grenville had a complete personal and political reconciliation with his brother Temple, and even closed a four-year-old breach with Pitt. "I have been told," wrote Rockingham, "that the D[uke] of Bedford *now* says that Mr. Pitt is the only man who can or should govern this country." [7] Belief was general that Pitt's return to office was imminent; the court and the Cumberland–Newcastle whigs had sought him, and ministers were prepared to make way for him. The King, hating his servants, was harried by fear that foreign courts would take advantage of his situation, and by fear of having to submit to a Grenville "family" administration. In mid-June he appealed directly to Cumberland to recruit new ministers. His message crossed one from H.R.H. relating that Bedford meditated resignation to make way for Lord Temple, whom Cumberland advised against because "we can treat better with Mr.

Pitt." [8] The King, however, was envisaging a junction of Cumberland–Newcastle whigs with the remains of administration after Grenville, Bedford, Halifax, and Sandwich had been turned out:

> I shall rather be surprized [the King told H.R.H.] if Mr. Pitt can be persuaded to accept Office on terms not entirely to my dishonour & to that of those worthy men, Lord Rockingham, the Dukes of Grafton, Newcastle & others; for they are men who have principles & therefore cannot approve of seeing the Crown dictated to by low men; if Mr. Pitt should again decline I hope the Parliament being prorogued they & their friends will join amicably the few persons that have zealously stood by me & that the World will see that this Country is not at that low Ebb that no Administration can be formed without the Grenville family. [9]

The men whom the court had struck at in 1762 were now become "worthy" in the eyes of Majesty.

II

Ascot Races were running when Cumberland received his royal nephew's appeal. Rockingham was there, staying with H.R.H. and Lord Albemarle at nearby Windsor Lodge. The Duke of Grafton too was of the company. The day was Wednesday, June 12. The royal Duke answered the King that "no stone shall be left unturned by me for the Honour and Dignity of Your Crown," and rejoiced that there were "some as faithful Subjects as any Prince can have . . . who feel for Your Majesty as well as for the Support of the Crown." What happened during the next few days is obscure except for the dispatch on June 16 of Albemarle to confer with Newcastle and Rockingham's going to town to rest in preparation for a bustle the following week; but it seems probable that a good deal of canvassing of whig views began at Ascot right after H.R.H. received the King's request. From Windsor Lodge on June 13 Rockingham wrote to Newcastle: *"Everything at present*

seems to denote that next week will be a busy one. . . . I
know nothing new *which might enable one* to form any
Guess what may be the event of all the Bustle." [10] By June
17 Cumberland saw that so many friends were unwilling to
enlist without Pitt that he advised the King to make a direct
appeal in the closet to the Great Man. Grafton carried the
royal message to Pitt who was with his Majesty two days
later. It was generally assumed by the Cumberland–Newcastle whigs that Pitt would head an administration in
alliance with the leading men of the minority. The Duke
of Portland was sure that "we may be very sanguine" and
congratulated Newcastle on "the pleasing prospect of affairs." [11] The old Duke too was confident that Pitt would
accept office and was eager to lay out plans and lists, although perplexed and a little uneasy because no one had
asked him to do that. Were the young men around H.R.H.
going ahead without his advice? To Rockingham he complained on June 19: "your total silence ever since the re-
newal of the negotiations . . . gives me great uneasiness.
. . . I should think, the Heads of the Party would use me
very ungratefully, if they did not desire, that I should be
consulted, *in every step to be taken,* in the forming a new
Administration." The Marquis answered that he was not
in Pitt's confidence and could not foresee how matters would
end, that he had been "astonished" when H.R.H. told him
that Pitt was likely to accept, and that he was "not very
sanguine in the expectation that things will go quite as your
Grace & others & myself wish." [12]

A week later this skepticism was vindicated. Temple
sabotaged Pitt's plan of administration by refusing to cooperate, and then gave out to the world that Bute had inspired the negotiation. Cumberland faced the alternative
of confessing failure again or trying to recruit enough men
willing to risk taking office without Pitt. In one respect such
an attempt had been made harder. Temple's language, so
H.R.H. told the King on June 30, "does but too much
harm & the *Person* to whose name they have tack'd so much
odium, is so frightful in the eyes of weak men, and so con-

venient in the hands of knaves that they over-turn as fast as honest men can build." [13] However, the King, after Pitt's withdrawal, had requested H.R.H. to persist in seeking such men as would serve, and the latter had laid an outline of administration before Rockingham, Newcastle, Grafton, and Albemarle. It specified Grafton and Charles Townshend or General Conway as secretaries of state, Townshend or Conway as Chancellor of the Exchequer, Rockingham as first lord of the Treasury, and the Marquis' uncle, Lord Winchilsea, as lord president.[14] Such were the offices in which the King desired to make changes, but it was assumed that new ministers would expect to bring many of their friends into administration. Next, Newcastle gathered a group of eighteen at his home (Claremont) to confer on the practicality of taking office without Pitt. There were six peers (Rockingham, Portland, Albemarle, Ashburnham, Bessborough, Newcastle) and twelve commoners including Conway and the three Cavendish brothers. All agreed that they could not assist in forming an administration without the King's agreement to terms calculated to stifle a cry against them as being tools of Lord Bute; which meant that certain reputed friends of Bute should be dismissed "as proof to the world" that the hated Favorite exerted no influence. To the question whether—this anti-Bute gesture conceded—the minority whigs should assist in forming a ministry without Pitt, there were twelve affirmatives and six negatives. Albemarle was disgusted and without hope, as was H.R.H. until Newcastle went to him the next day to urge that the plan go forward. According to the old Duke, "General Conway was present the whole time; and the Marquis of Rockingham came in at last. . . . they supported my opinion as strongly as possible." Although Cumberland knew that it was not less decent to lay the Claremont terms than Pitt's and Temple's before Majesty, he was sure that the King would not refuse to part with some men reputedly connected with Bute.[15] And so the attempt at forming a new administration went forward.

Rockingham remained doubtful of success until July 4.

That day he pressed Charles Townshend to be Chancellor of the Exchequer or secretary of state. That Townshend should be so eagerly sought for a principal office in the new system calls for some explanation. Barely a month before, he had accepted the Pay Office on Grenville's nomination, as a reward for deserting the minority and supporting administration in the previous session. The removal of Lord Holland from that office and the giving it to Townshend had been exacted (though Townshend seems not to have known the fact) from an angry and reluctant sovereign. In spite of a well-earned reputation for fickleness in politics, Townshend was a man of great charm, large knowledge, expert parliamentary ability, and long friendship with Rockingham who saw him now as indispensable to a new administration's business in the House of Commons and especially as spokesman there for the Treasury. The Marquis found him in a state of doubt and uncertainty, unconvinced that a new system was viable without Pitt. He refused the Exchequer but when Rockingham countered with the offer of secretary of state he vacillated. He lamented the coolness of the court toward him because it was said that he had been forced upon the King. Rockingham urged that it would not be wise to offend again by refusing now, and probably said that his acceptance would have Pitt's "private approbation." Half-persuaded, Townshend pleaded that he would have to consult his brother, Viscount Townshend, from whom he could not separate, and wrote to the latter immediately saying that it would be "delicate to disobey the Crown in such a minute of distraction." Rockingham let it be known that night that "with some previous steps" Townshend would accept office as secretary of state. Confident prediction was quickly blown up to a bubble of certainty, which process was aided by rapid dissemination of an inaccurate report that Pitt approved and would support the prospective new administration.[16] Another favorable sign appeared on July 4 to promise the cooperation of the Yorkes. Charles Yorke, who had balked at returning to the office of attorney general, was pressed by the King personally with a promise of the Great Seal within a year;[17] he could hardly resist such a demand and Rockingham would keep up the pressure by appealing to Yorke's duty to act with his friends. The Great Seal, goal of Yorke's ambition, could not be given to him at this time without offending Pitt, who wished Pratt to have it; nor could it have been offered to Pratt without totally alienating the Yorkes.

On July 5 Rockingham, Newcastle, Portland, Winchilsea, Conway, and Albemarle met with H.R.H. A list, in the Marquis' hand, of removals and nominations to be laid before Majesty, memorializes the occasion.[18] Townshend was designated as successor to Secretary of State Sandwich and Grafton was named to replace Halifax; Conway appeared as prospective Chancellor of the Exchequer, an office he did not want and for which Dowdeswell was being considered. The General's preference was the War Office. About thirty changes in the boards, lesser ministerial places, and at court were indicated on the list which would undergo later alterations. Both Rockingham and Newcastle, still smarting under the wounds of whiggery, desired more extensive removals than Cumberland believed proper. "Upon the whole [the Marquis reflected] I think the plan good in parts but too many of those who have suffered heretofore are left to trust to time & I think unnecessarily as room may be found immediately." [19] All agreed that if Charles Townshend declined the secretaryship of state Conway must take it; otherwise the General was needed for the Exchequer, which he agreed on July 7 to accept under pressure from Cumberland and Rockingham, who could argue that Conway would be no less a novice at the Treasury board than the prospective first lord. To Newcastle the latter said, "surely no first Commissioner nor no Chancelor of the Exchequer ever went into these great offices with so much concern & unwillingness." [20] Conway then changed his mind and Dowdeswell was put down for the Exchequer on the list laid before the King on July 9, which designated Townshend and Grafton as the secretaries.[21] In the end Townshend chose to keep the Pay Office and Conway assented to taking the seals. On July 10 Rockingham, Grafton, Conway, and Dowdeswell kissed hands. Some days later Newcastle received the privy seal.

So began what later historians (but no one in 1765) called the Rockingham administration. Many offices remained to be filled, and some important men of the previous system—notably Lord Chancellor Northington, and the First Lord of the Admiralty, Lord Egmont—were to continue in office. Common opinion held that Newcastle would be the principal dispenser of employment, since the secretaries of state and first lord of the Treasury were ministerial novices. Lord Mansfield told Grenville that

> in the new Ministry, he neither saw the man capable of directing the foreign business, nor of managing the revenue, nor what relates to the interior of the kingdom; that he had great personal regard for Lord Rockingham, who he thought was a man of sense, but unequal to the task he had undertaken from want of ability, experience, and health.[22]

The smear that the new ministers were pawns of Lord Bute, who had been repudiated by Grenville and Bedford, was made from the start of the negotiation. Temple called it "Butal-Ducal" and Bedford expressed amazement "that any people will be hardy enough to undertake an Administration, which is constructed on no better foundation than the support of Lord Bute's favouritism." [23]

The state of mind in which Lord Rockingham assumed office is revealed in what he wrote to Meredith, for whom a seat on the Admiralty Board would soon be provided, and who was at the time in Ireland:

> It must surprize you to hear that I am at the head of the Treasury. . . . but indeed the necessity here made it necessary that some thing should be done, & therefore howsoever unsuitable I might be for that office from my health & inexperience in the sort of business, yet I thought it incumbent on me to acquiesce in the attempting it, rather than throw any fresh

confusion into the negociation, which had but too many difficulties without my adding to them by a refusal which my own
private ease & comfort would no doubt have strongly inclined
me to; I am sure you will do me the justice to believe that I
shall be very anxious in every circumstance to do my best endeavours for the publick service, how the success & event of
our undertaking will turn out is difficult to guess.[24]

Why the Marquis at the head of the Treasury? Few
could have thought him suitable as the first minister of the
crown, and certainly he did not so assess himself. His
steady desire since 1762 to see the whig old corps restored
to administration had not meant that he wanted a place of
great responsibility for himself. The Earl of Dartmouth,
who was to head the Board of Trade in the administration
now forming, has testified that the Marquis "was pitched
upon to be first lord of the Treasury, which he strenuously
resisted, for some time, but being told that the scheme must
[otherwise] be abandoned, he willingly consented to take
that part & the other arrangements ensued." [25] It is not
improbable that he saw himself at first as a mere *locum
tenens* until a better arrangement could be made.[26] Horace
Walpole wrote that Rockingham "having been only known
. . . by his passion for horse races, men could not be cured
of their surprise at seeing him First Minister";[27] yet it
must be remembered that Pitt in 1763 had envisaged him
at the Admiralty and in June 1765 intended to offer him
the viceroyalty of Ireland.[28] Among whigs the idea of the
Marquis at the Treasury was hardly a novelty. When Newcastle and Devonshire talked political strategy in the mid-
summer of 1762, the latter recorded in his diary: "We
talked of what was to be done if Lord Bute should come to
treat with his Grace, he [Newcastle] said he would not go
again into the Treasury, that if I would not take it, Lord
Rockingham must go there with Mr. Legge for his Chancellor of the Exchequer." [29] The Marquis had cultivated a
host of friends in the House of Commons, enjoyed amicable
relations with Pitt (who was averse to Newcastle's return

to the Treasury), and enjoyed great popularity and influence in Yorkshire which had more than twice as many freehold electors as any other county in England. No politician in the land had greater influence derivative naturally from his station in life, and none was so close to the Duke of Cumberland who sponsored the new ministers. The King had a low opinion of his ability, but the willingness he had shown to help Majesty in an hour of difficulty must have created a favorable impression. However central and important the Treasury was in administration, the King had no thought of finding a prime minister in Rockingham. Longing to be free of those who offended him, George III was ready to accept at the Treasury anyone Cumberland proposed. He aimed at bringing in the Cumberland–Newcastle whigs to share office with men such as Lord Chancellor Northington and Lord Egmont in whom he placed his confidence, so that it was the old story of dropping one set of men to bring in another to help the court to carry on its business. H.R.H. had no other choice for the Treasury than the Marquis, since Grafton, his only conceivable rival, had publicly appeared with a mistress and was even unwilling to join the new ministry without assurance of Pitt's approval and of the readiness of colleagues to make way for Pitt at any time; whereas Rockingham stood foremost among those who were willing to undertake without the Great Commoner.

The primacy of the Marquis was shown at the beginning of the negotiations. The naming of his uncle[30] to the lord presidency was a badge attesting it; and his strong wish for Charles Townshend to take a leading part suggests that Rockingham's was the influence which put Townshend's name on Cumberland's original slate. It was Rockingham who first spoke to Yorke about returning as attorney general, who opened negotiations with Townshend, Dartmouth, Portland, Shelburne, and many others. It was to the Marquis that Conway addressed his decision against going to the Exchequer. On July 2 George Grenville noted: "The report of this day is that the Ministry is forming with the

Duke of Cumberland and the Duke of Newcastle, with Lord Rockingham at the head of the Treasury." On July 6 he informed Temple, "Lord Rockingham takes the lead and speaks to everybody with what encouragement I know not," and on July 7 he added, "Lord Rockingham . . . takes the lead entirely." [31]

Newcastle very early began to sense that he had been eclipsed. To him it was one thing and proper enough for Rockingham to act as Cumberland's agent in recruiting ministers, but something else and most improper for the old party manager to be kept uninformed and unemployed in that business. On July 2 he scolded Rockingham for not informing him "of what passed, last night, either with the King, or Charles Yorke, or what measures are taking place about Charles Townshend." The next day he pleaded to Albemarle that he could be of more use to H.R.H. "in telling the character & consequence of those, that must make the Object of his plan of administration, than all the young men he can consult."

> I love & honour my Lord Rockingham & think he is a most valuable man & deserves the first consideration & attention from the King & the Duke; but I think he can not know men as well as I do.[32]

It seemed so right and natural to the old working manager of whig politics upon whom applications for restoration to many places were pouring, that he should guide in forming a new administration. He was vexed too over Cumberland's not presenting to the King the "terms" agreed upon at the Claremont meeting on June 3, and fearful of anything being done which might displease Pitt. Not Grafton himself was more persistent than the old Duke in stressing the latter consideration.[33] And surely, he thought, Rockingham would be guided by him in staffing the Treasury board and office. On July 7 Newcastle requested that James West be made either a lord commissioner or secretary of the Treasury. West was a long-standing dependent of the old

Duke, had been a joint secretary of the Treasury under him, gone out with him in 1762, and headed a long list of men whom Newcastle wished to see restored. Five days later, after kissing hands, the Marquis declined to have West in the Treasury even though he "could scarce refrain from doing it when Your Grace expressed your wishes." Newcastle wrote back very fretfully, lamenting this refusal, asking the treasurership of the navy for West, making still other demands, and complaining that an imperfect plan for filling various offices was being carried precipitately into execution: "I must beg, and indeed insist, that you would not do it, till it is finally adjusted with me. . . . I think, from long experience, that I have a better nack at these sort of adjustments than any body." [34] In the same communication Newcastle suggested that one Royer, who had served him as private secretary, be taken in the same capacity by Rockingham, who had already appointed Edmund Burke to the place. The Marquis tried hard to accommodate the old Duke but lacked both authority and means to meet all his demands. The whole situation distressed Newcastle sorely:

> I do think [he wrote on July 14] that, at my age, and in my situation, when a Ministry was to have been formed, out of what is shortly called the *Opposition,* after Mr. Pitt, whose consequence to be sure was greater than any body's, I had the first right to be consulted & my recommendations to have been prefer'd to any body's; *and there is my Grievance.*[35]

The following day he kissed hands for the privy seal, received the acclamation of friends, and was invited by Rockingham to dine with the other ministers and "go forward in adjusting to your Grace's & to all our minds the offices etc. now vacant or which will soon be made so by our act." He was somewhat mollified and when Rockingham told him a few days later that a spate of his desired restitutions had been executed, he burst into joy. Soon, however, he was sending more lists of dependents who had been turned out by Bute and Fox and must now be restored to their places.

When Rockingham explained that delays were necessitated by proper civilities to persons of rank, he fell to groaning over James West, complaining about "very worthless" men retained in offices, and protesting church appointments made without consulting him.[36] Tiring of the old Duke's repeated demands in behalf of dependents, Rockingham fell to ignoring them until at length he was provoked to read him a lecture:

> I am satisfied if a stand is not made to the warmth of friends in different parts of England, who desire dismission in low offices, in order to make room for persons to serve their interests, I doubt not but that all who have been put in for the last two or three years would be turned out & we might suffer the vindictive spirit of retaliation to prevail so far that we should surpass in severity the example of 1763 & be equally odious.[37]

With the Yorkes the new Treasury Minister had other difficulties. Philip second Earl of Hardwicke received the first offer of the presidency of the Board of Trade and declined it. Charles proved hard to get in spite of the King's personal promise of the Great Seal within twelve months. His Majesty was as eager as Rockingham for Yorke's services and avowed that he would "on no account lose that able & I think honest man." Despite his family link with the historic whig connection, Yorke was a poor party man, had a single-purposed ambition, and feared the proclivity of incoming ministers toward appeasing the desires of Pitt; he had deserted the late opposition and actually preferred Grenville to Rockingham at the Treasury. If the hard core of his resistance had been broken by the royal promise, he continued to think return to his former office not very becoming and remained reluctant, setting the condition that Sir Fletcher Norton—the Attorney General who was to be turned out as a "Bute"—should have a proper provision. When he learned that Pratt, whose legal views he abhorred, was to be made a peer, reluctance hardened again into refusal. At Rockingham's request, Newcastle engaged the Archbishop of Canterbury to exert suasion on Yorke. On

July 19 the Marquis wrote to him: "This morning Sir
Fletcher Norton's fate was decided. . . . I am sure that
if you would lay aside your personal delicacies you can not
be sorry." Yorke told Grenville that same day he would
accept, then talked anew with Rockingham and Newcastle,
and found another ground for holding back in the fear that
ministers would seek a reversal of Wilkes's outlawry. On
July 25 the Marquis found him still cold but reported: "I
still think he will take the office." On August 8 Rockingham
advised him of the King's desire to see him the next day,
saying that his Majesty was "very intent upon your returning to the office." Yorke surrendered in the closet.[38] His
brother John, who was obliged to Rockingham for his seat
in the House, had in the meantime accepted a place on the
Board of Trade.

What with the suspicion of Bute's influence and want of
certainty as to Pitt's approval, doubt of the ministry's duration held back many from accepting office. The Earl of Shelburne, who had quit as head of the Board of Trade in 1763
and attached himself to Pitt, followed Hardwicke in declining to resume that office. Lord Dartmouth required much
persuasion before accepting it, and at one time Rockingham
considered offering it to Sir William Baker.[39] James Grenville, who was rather Pittite than attached politically to
his brother George, refused a vice-treasurership of Ireland.
Lord Lyttelton, too, pressed by Conway to take a part in
administration, declined to serve without Temple and Pitt;
and Thomas Pitt, his nephew, although asked to remain on
the Admiralty board, chose to resign. The shyness of the
Temple–Pitt connection toward the new administration now
became obvious and ominous.[40]

Dowdeswell's appointment to the Exchequer, which
brought him into close official relations with Rockingham,
has never been satisfactorily explained. No doubt the standing he had acquired in Parliament since 1763 partly accounts
for it, and there was nothing novel in whigs' taking into
office tories who acted on whig principles; but it was unusual for a county member to become a minister—Savile,

for example, refused office. Dowdeswell's identification with
the cause of repealing the cider tax made him appear as a
specialist in revenue business, and bringing him to the Treasury board clearly was a bid for support from the western
counties; but the offer was not made to him until Townshend and Conway had refused it.[41] Nothing is known of
Dowdeswell's previous relationship with Rockingham, but
he was a long-standing friend of Charles Townshend and
this fact may also help to account for his appointment,[42]
since the Marquis left nothing undone which might win
over the latter to supporting administration actively. Early
in August Rockingham hinted of an earldom for Viscount
Townshend [43] whose enmity to the Duke of Cumberland was
believed to be a reason for Charles's shyness. A little later
a joint-secretaryship of the Treasury was offered to Townshend's friend Grey Cooper who, after some doubts and the
promise of a pension if turned out, accepted the place.[44]
Rockingham's strategy in courting Townshend may even
have influenced his taking Edmund Burke as private secretary.

Townshend attracted knowing men and Burke had gotten
into his entourage about two months before the Rockingham administration was formed, although the nature of the
connection is obscure. Henry Flood alluded to Townshend
in a letter to Burke of May 30, saying "If I could envy a
man I love, I should envy your intercourse with this latter
bright genius." [45] An exchange of letters between Townshend and Burke in the latter part of June indicates that it
was part of a more extensive mutual communication and
that a personal and political intimacy existed. It shows too
that Burke was in contact with high sources of information.
His letter of July 4 to Charles O'Hara attests that he knew
of the intention to offer Townshend the Exchequer and of
Rockingham's going to Adderbury to seek his acceptance.
Burke wished him to accept and said that the refusal drew
"tears of indignation and grief from me"; which suggests
that Burke, who was eager for a place, saw his own prospects of fortune dashed. If O'Hara had not lost a letter

which Burke wrote after engaging to be Rockingham's secretary, more might be learned of his connection with Townshend, since O'Hara wrote in reply: "I understand from yours that you still go on with him tho' you belong to Lord Rockingham. This may prove a nice card to play; and the opinion people have of Charles will make it more so." There is, however, no direct evidence that Townshend recommended Burke to Rockingham. Edmund and his kinsman Will Burke, another clever and ambitious man, were applicants for employment; but neither had any political connection with the new ministers.

Will had formerly been attached to Henry Fox and had sought to serve Grenville, while Edmund had been on the rim of Halifax' entourage, perhaps even of Bute's. They were befriended now by William Fitzherbert who was connected with the Cavendish interest. Edmund recorded on July 4 that Fitzherbert made "well managed and eloquent recommendations of us, to all this batch of people"; and Will attested at the same time that Lord John Cavendish "mentioned us both as fit men to be employed to Lord Rockingham." Charles O'Hara, friend of General Conway, may also have served the interest of the Burkes whom he knew intimately and loved. Will became Conway's undersecretary. Edmund wrote to O'Hara on July 11: "I have got an employment of a kind humble enough; but which may be worked into some sort of consideration, or at least advantage: private secretary to Lord Rockingham; who has the reputation of a man of honour and integrity; and with whom, they say, it is not difficult to live." O'Hara thought that Will had got the better place and advised Edmund: "You have pride to deal with, but much softened by manner; and exceeding good sense, but you must feed it, for it can't feed itself." [46]

III

"The Ministry is at last upon its legs," observed the new Earl of Camden on August 7, ". . . but I can't yet tell who is that Prometheus that is to give it animation, or will undertake to steal fire from heaven for that purpose." [47] Only Pitt could have played such a role. His absence greatly disappointed the public, and the gradual dissipation of the illusion that he approved and supported the new administration was a serious embarrassment to ministers. Lord Chesterfield saw a "manifest interregnum" at the Treasury. Nothing was more remarkable than the extent of changes: a completely new Treasury board, five new members of the Admiralty board, four new members of the Board of Trade including the head, a new lord chamberlain, new secretary of war, new treasurer of the navy, new joint postmasters, plus major alteration in court places. The door to office was opened wide to whiggery, and what with the refusals on the part of the Temple–Pitt people and so much resultant doubt and timidity, Rockingham was able to provide for many friends who might otherwise have gotten nothing. The King raised no objections and wore an appearance of being pleased. No vendetta was carried on against men reputed as Bute's friends; there was no abusing of the King's necessity. Lord Holland observed on August 26 that the King "resists nothing, and seems satisfy'd with his deliverers from Gr[enville] etc. He speaks of and to his new ministers as his deliverers." [48]

Men such as Pitt and Shelburne, knowing nothing of Newcastle's complaints within administration, assumed that his influence was overriding. Far more dangerous to the new ministry, however, was the suspicion, nay the belief, that Lord Bute's was the hidden operative hand which had turned out one set of men and brought in another who must be either his creatures or his dupes. Allegations to this effect were political stock-in-trade among outgoing ministers; and in the absence of any other rationale such a theory gained plausibility with the public. According to Beaumont Hotham (a friend and supporter of the new administration), in all the northern parts of the country there was "not a man who is not persuaded that Mr. Pitt was as averse to making part of the ministry as Lord Tem-

ple, that you have submitted to terms which they rejected
jointly, and that Lord Bute is with your concurrence in
possession of absolute power." [49] The press abounded with
suspicion of this secret influence and a spate of pamphlets
spread the slander. One writer described the ministry as "a
perfect emblem of the Bartholomewfair Monster, an old
fellow's head, puling and sputtering on a pair of children's
shoulders." [50] The friends of the ministers, wrote another,
"do not scruple to say, that they do not dare to turn out his
partizans." [51] A third warned that if ministers' professed
opposition to Bute was genuine, then he who had turned
out the previous men would soon turn out their successors.[52]

Efforts were made in the press to counter and crush allegations of Bute's influence. *A Short, Reasonable, and Plain
Address, From an Honest Old Man to the Good People of
England* [53] sketched the life and drew the character of the
Marquis: "Give asses and sycophants leave to rail and talk,
but for God's sake let them never persuade you, that such a
man will ever be the instrument or tool of any *favourite*
on earth." Grey Cooper wrote several tracts for ministry.
In *The Merits of the New Administration*[54] he contended
that the incoming men "if their offices were elective, would,
upon Mr. Pitt's declension, have been chosen by the independent part of the nation," and that it required "some
ignorance of the value of good character, as well as much
credulity, and prejudice against them, to be persuaded, that
they would abruptly plunge into odium and contempt, by
descending to be the creatures of one, whose power they
had manfully resisted at a time, when it was of more consequence than now, to defy his resentment." In the *Gentleman's Magazine*[55] the author of "The Conduct of the Late
Minority" struck with force and brilliance in repelling attacks made by partisans of the previous administration. This
pamphlet war was kept up until American resistance to the
Stamp Act temporarily superseded the bogey of Lord Bute
in the public consciousness. Rumors of a ministerial approach to Lord Holland, Bute's erstwhile ally, and of fur-

ther courting of Charles Townshend (an erstwhile bene-
ficiary of the Favorite) gave nourishment to the myth of
Bute's secret influence. As late as November 16 a satirical
print was published, depicting a nursery with a cradle sur-
mounted by a marquis' coronet. Newcastle stands with a pan
of gruel while Rockingham rides a hobby horse and cries
"Ge up, to the Treasury." Charles Townshend has a
weathervane on his head and spins a whirlygig to amuse
the baby; Dowdeswell howls with pain from cutting his
finger while peeling an apple; and Lord Holland wearing a
fox's head rides whip in hand on Lord Bute's back.[56]

Within administration all appeared very different. No
doubt there were some who believed that Bute's advice had
induced the King to turn to H.R.H. for a fresh slate of
servants; but there is no evidence that this was so. Bute
offered the King a sacrifice of his own interest, and his
Majesty thought it necessary to request support for the
new system from some "Butes" who were suffered to keep
their places; when others were turned out.[57] Newcastle believed that not enough was done to show aversion to Bute
and favor to Pitt; while Charles Yorke saw the ministers
leaning too much to the latter, "the shadow of whose name,
whose nods, and whose frowns they have respected, and to
whom they have sacrificed their friends, and their opinions,
and their dignity." [58] The only basis for the rumor of Lord
Holland's influence was his application to Rockingham for
reinstatement of a man who had been turned out of the
land tax office by Grenville; the Marquis referred the matter
to H.R.H. who advised granting the favor, saying that
Holland ought to be neither courted nor repulsed. Rockingham actually feared Holland's appearance as a supporter of
administration, thinking that it would "not tend to the
general credit with the publick, on which this administration
founded their reliance of support." [59] As for Charles Townshend, inconclusive evidence suggests persistent efforts of
Rockingham to induce him to undertake the management of
the House of Commons.[60] During September and October a

number of negotiations were opened to enlist active support from a variety of reluctant men; none was successful and none was with reputed friends of Bute.

Meanwhile, the business of government was carried on. Rockingham, Grafton, and Conway constituted a triumvirate after the fashion of Grenville, Halifax, and Egremont in 1763. This was the *conciliabulum,* or inner cabinet, as distinguished from the outer cabinet or cabinet council. There was no definable cabinet system then existing, no group of ministers acknowledging collective responsibility; no business was brought before a cabinet without prior direction from the King, who dealt individually with ministers. Little is known of the early inner history of this administration. The Duke of Cumberland attended its councils. There is Grafton's testimony that "We proceeded in business with great zeal and perfect concord, and we had every reason to be satisfied with the conduct of our new friends Lords Northington and Egmont in all our meetings." [61] The pressure of business was not great enough to prevent Rockingham from going north in August to Wentworth and to York Races.

Not until early autumn did the stupendous economic and political crisis growing out of the colonial legislation of the previous administration confront the ministers and test their ability to act together. And then, suddenly on October 31, the Duke of Cumberland died. The prop of the July system was removed. Rockingham's immediate reaction may be read in what he wrote that night to his wife at Bath:

> Howsoever I feel this stroke in regard to the private sensations of my own mind, it must not be suffered to depress us in that publick situation which we are now in. . . . I hope the same zeal & spirit with which we undertook, will & must carry us through.[62]

All through that month there had been reports of discord among ministers and likely alterations of the system. Conway and Egmont were said to have quarreled; rumor said

that Grafton was discontented.[63] "Pray let me know if there
are any bustles among you," wrote Lady Rockingham to
her husband on October 19, "because I have heard such a
rumour." [64] The Lord Chancellor was uneasy over what the
Treasury was preparing for an easing of colonial trade. The
Grenvillite Hans Stanley and Isaac Barré, who belonged to
Shelburne, refused offers of office. Charles Townshend was
standing off fresh approaches to enlist him for active service
when Parliament convened. Now, with Cumberland gone,
few believed that so strange a ministry could survive, and it
was generally believed that Pitt would be called to remodel
and direct administration. Grafton desired that, and the
Duke of Newcastle took it upon himself so to advise the
King:

> His Majesty [wrote Newcastle to Grafton on November 6]
> seem'd entirely to agree in that opinion; & said, the Duke of
> Grafton was the person to be employed in it. Upon my ac-
> quainting your Grace, my Lord Rockingham & General Con-
> way, with what had passed with the King, I had the pleasure
> to find you all zealously in that opinion. I cannot but hope
> that your Grace has already wrote or will soon write to Mr.
> Pitt, in the very proper manner your Grace proposed.[65]

The triumvirate, however, were not prepared to be directed
by Newcastle. The matter was considered at a meeting that
night,[66] and it is evident that a decision was made against
Grafton's writing to Pitt. The King, although willing to
allow ministers to seek Pitt's counsel, was utterly averse to
summoning the man who had so recently thrice refused to
come into his service.[67] Rockingham, Grafton, and Conway
had so far not displeased George III who always believed
that any ministers could manage his affairs if he firmly supported them. Late that night, the Marquis wrote to Lady
Rockingham: "Every thing here goes well. . . . It seems
like vanity to puff that we are well in the Closet, and therefore on that subject it may be decent to be silent. Events and
circumstances will fully evince that we are so." And having
heard that Pitt was going soon to Bath, where Lady Rock-

ingham then was, the Marquis added: "If a *Real Great Man* comes there, I would have you consider him etc. as such." [68] Confident in the firmness of the closet, Rockingham, Grafton, and Conway chose to go on without appealing to Pitt, while Lady Rockingham undertook a sort of good-will mission to him. Her own advice to the Marquis at this critical moment is of interest in view of the weight which he habitually gave to her counsels:

> I think all political success will greatly turn upon the channel his [the King's] confidence now falls into & therefore I would hasten as soon as possible to draw his mind to a right decision. . . . I would tell him this, that . . . every real friend to his *M[ajes]ty* must deeply lament the loss he sustains in his Uncle, whose abilities & judgment were of so superior a sort as to be irreparable, that the only attempt to any degree of equivalent must be the superadded assiduity of his Administration . . . that his Ministers can only be enabled so to do by the concurrence of his Majesty's firm & unreserved confidence; that therefore you humbly presume to submit it to his consideration whether he was so far satisfied with the conduct of his present Ministers as to think they merit the continuance of that full & *undivided* confidence they must expect to enjoy in order to serve him well . . . that on the other hand you should be ready with the greatest submission to resign the trust to his better choice. . . . Some thing to this effect, in y[ou]r words, I mean, & would have said at first, to show him that the confidence he placed in the Duke must now in its full scope be transferr'd to all of you; & instantly, for I think now w[oul]d be the time for *certain past influences* to try to revive . . . for when the mind is again on flote for a repositary it is more liable to sink back into old habits; you are all in a manner strangers to the King. My politicks are to fix him now or give him up forever. [69]

Soon Lady Rockingham was buying a pair of Pitt's coach horses and "many obliging messages" were exchanged at Bath. Then Rockingham directed his lady to present his respects to the Great Man, "to return him many thanks for his politeness to you & to convey to him the enclosed Minute of the Treasury which I believe is in itself correct & may be serviceable." The Minute recorded the first important step taken to relieve distress of colonial trade, and sending it to Pitt was a gesture signifying ministerial desire to keep him informed and have his advice. Pitt thanked Lady Rockingham warmly and begged her to tell her husband that he "highly" applauded the "contents of the paper." Whereupon the Marquis directed his wife to tell Pitt "that his approving the Minute is to me as strong confirmation of the Minute's being right & proper as any of the letters of thanks with which some of the great manufacturing & trade towns have honoured us at the Board of Treasury on this occasion." [70]

Probably Grafton and Conway knew of this studied attempt to ingratiate Pitt, but Newcastle was kept in the dark, probably from apprehension that he might say or do something awkward. The Old Duke repeatedly complained to Rockingham over the laying aside of an application to Pitt, and groaned:

> The truth is that my Lord Rockingham and the Duke of Grafton think themselves so sure of the closet, that they neglect every other consideration. . . . they think no other opinion necessary, but that of themselves, viz., Lord Rockingham, the Duke of Grafton, and Genl. Conway.[71]

The allowing Newcastle to give the triumvirate's invitation to Pitt's admirer, George Cooke, to second the address on the opening of Parliament showed how little the real state of ministry was known to outsiders and how easily this could be misunderstood. Before answering, Cooke consulted Pitt, who cautioned him against being "held out to the world as connected with the Duke of Newcastle." That Pitt held a completely mistaken view is shown by his reference to "his Grace's Ministry," and his saying that there could be "no solid system for the settlement of this distracted country, as long as his Grace's influence predominates." [72] The death of Cumberland must have appeared to many as creating a vacancy which must be filled, if not by Pitt for the public, or by Bute for the crown, then by the old master of political management. But the vacancy was filled by the King.

That George III should entrust the business of kingdom and empire, in the greatest crisis since the 1740s, to a triumvirate of amateurs in state affairs, seemed hard to believe. But it was so.

Like all his predecessors on the throne since the crown became dependent upon frequently meeting parliaments, George III could not carry on government merely with professional royal servants indifferent to any interest but the King's personal pleasure. Government had to be shared with leaders of parties. Bute had tried to act without these, but had soon to turn to Henry Fox. Grenville tried the same thing but was forced to ally with the Duke of Bedford. Now, however, something different had appeared. The Treasury was in the hands of a party leader who had been a zealous enemy of the Bute–Grenville system and there was no potent minister enjoying the royal confidence to overshadow him in administration; yet the principle of party was not asserted against the court because the whigs who had come into the principal offices were not acting as a party—despite the open door to whiggery—but as a group of men willing and eager to serve their King. They too became "King's men." Naturally, the Marquis of Rockingham, who seems to have been animated by a simple, virtuous desire to do his best for his sovereign, regarded his friends as hereditarily qualified to promote the true interests of a sovereign of the House of Hanover. The grand aim of the Cumberland–Newcastle whigs had never been to force themselves on the King, but to convince him that they were the true guardians of the royal interest; so that, without ceasing to be whigs—men of party, partisans of "the good cause"—they became royalists when their sovereign made them ministers.

NOTES

1. Cumberland's statement, printed in Albemarle I 185–208; *A Narrative of the Changes in the Ministry, 1765–1767, as Told by the Duke of Newcastle* etc., ed. Mary Bateson (London, 1898), 4–6. A memorandum prepared for the King at this time shows that he was meditating a change.—*Correspondence of George the Third,* ed. Sir John Fortescue (6 vols.; London, 1927–1928), No. 100; cited hereafter as *Corr. George III.* The dating of this document is corrected by L. B. Namier in *Additions and Corrections* (Manchester, 1937), 32–33.

2. Add. MS 32966, f. 274.

3. *Ibid.,* f. 236; W. R. Anson, ed., *Autobiography and Political Correspondence of the Duke of Grafton* (London, 1898), 32–33 (cited hereafter as *Grafton*); Rockingham to the Duke of Portland [23 April].—Portland MSS.

4. *Grenville* III 25–29; Walpole, *Memoirs* II 109.

5. Cumberland's statement (n. 1).

6. *Ibid.*

7. Add. MS 32966, f. 429.

8. *Corr. George III,* Nos. 117, 118, 119.

9. *Ibid.,* No. 118.

10. Add. MS 32967, f. 36. Newcastle, mystified, answered: "I am quite out of your secret & therefore cannot reason about it."—*Ibid.,* f. 42. Not until Albemarle was at Claremont several days later did Newcastle learn of Cumberland's assignment from the King.

11. *Ibid.,* f. 73.

12. *Ibid.,* ff. 69, 71.

13. *Corr. George III,* No. 113 (correctly dated by Namier in *Additions,* 35).

14. Newcastle, *Narrative* (n. 1), 25.

15. *Ibid.,* 26–28, 30–31; Albemarle I 218–220; Newcastle would have laid the Claremont terms before the King, but was overruled.—Add. MS 32967, f. 208. According to the *Narrative,* everybody was assured by Cumberland that the King would not allow Bute to interfere in any way, that he (H.R.H.) had told the King that he would give up all part in the royal affairs if the event proved otherwise.

16. Charles Townshend to Lord Townshend, 3, 4 July.—*Grenville* III 65–68; Add. MS 32967, ff. 234, 245.

17. Yorke's memorandum of 4 July audience.—Add. MS 35428, ff. 94–102.

18. Add. MS 32967, ff. 240, 241.

19. WWM R 14: 2.

20. Add. MS 32967, f. 278.

21. WWM R 1: 457, 462.

22. *Grenville* III 208

23. *Ibid.,* 14, 70.

24. WWM R 1: 473 (copy by Lady Rockingham).

25. Dartmouth MS (William Salt Library, Stafford): D.1448.v.221.B.

26. The Governors of the Bank told George Grenville that "they under-

stood Lord Rockingham gave it out that he did not mean to continue in the situation, and only held it for a time."—*Grenville* III 220. Lord Lyttelton wrote 28 July that "Lord Rockingham . . . is so infirm in his health, that it hardly seems possible to stand" parliamentary business.—R. J. Phillimore, *Memoirs and Correspondence of George, Lord Lyttelton* (2 vols.; London, 1845), II 684.

27. *Memoirs* II 140.

28. WWM R 1: 468.

29. Devonshire MS 260.384.

30. Daniel Finch eighth Earl of Winchilsea (1688–1769), brother of first Marchioness of Rockingham, had headed the Admiralty in 1742–1744, but held no ministerial office thereafter.

31. *Grenville* III 205; Tomlinson, ed., *Add. Grenville Papers,* Nos. 315, 317.

32. Add. MS 32967, ff. 208, 209, 220.

33. To Albemarle, 3 July.—WWM R 1: 445a; Add. MS 32967, f. 253. In a long memorandum to Rockingham on 6 July (*ibid.* ff. 455 *et seq.*), the Duke said that the plan of administration "should in general, be as palatable to Mr. Pitt & as agreeable, as is possible, to his notions & ideas." On 12 July he wrote again: "I see the world is running mad again about Mr. Pitt. Pray, my dear Lord, for your own sake, as well as for the sake of the whole, don't despise it."—*Ibid.,* f. 356.

34. WWM R 14: 6; Add. MS 32967, ff. 303, 315.

35. WWM R 1: 474.

36. Add. MSS 32967, ff. 389, 392; 32968, ff. 80–82, 264.

37. Add. MS 32970, ff. 198–200.

38. *Corr. George III,* Nos. 126, 139; Add. MSS 32967, f. 315; 32968, f. 240; 35428, ff. 76–80; 35430, ff. 14, 163; WWM R 1: 463; *Grenville* III 219.

39. WWM R 14: 2.

40. *Grenville* III 71–72; Walpole, *Memoirs* II 140. Shelburne's letter of refusal to Rockingham (12 July) was shown to Pitt who "highly applauded it."—Pitt to Calcraft, 19 July (Shelburne–Lacaita papers, W. L. Clements Library, Ann Arbor).

41. But his claims were considered well before that.—Charles Townshend to Dowdeswell, 27 June (Dowdeswell MSS, Clements Library).

42. Townshend to Dowdeswell, 28 Oct. 1766.

43. WWM R 1: 477, 478.

44. *Ibid.,* 493, 495; N. S. Jucker, ed., *The Jenkinson Papers* (London, 1949), 387; Sackville to Irwin (Hist. MSS Comm. 4th *Report* App. III 21).

45. WWM Burke papers.

46. *Corr. Burke* I 204–211, 214; Hoffman, *Edmund Burke,* 7–10, 26, 320–322.

47. *Grenville* III 77.

48. Lord Ilchester, *Henry Fox, First Lord Holland* (2 vols.; London, 1920), I 300–301.

49. Hotham to Duke of Portland, 1 Aug.—Portland MSS.

50. *A Letter to the Earl of B—— Relative to the Late Changes That Have Happened in the Administration* (London: Richardson & Urquehart, 1765).

51. *The Political Apology; or Candid Reasons for Not Taking Part in the Present System* (London: Wilkie, 1765).

52. *An Honest Man's Reason for Declining to Take Any Part in the New Administration* (London: Wilkie, 1765).

53. London: Wilkie, 1765.

54. London: J. Williams, 1765.

55. November 1765.

56. "The State Nursery," British Museum prints and drawings No. 4133. Cf. *The Public Advertiser* for Nov. 16.

57. *Corr. George III*, Nos. 120, 121, 124.

58. Add. MS 35428, ff. 73–75.

59. WWM R 1: 506; Albemarle I 240–244; Ilchester, *Henry Fox*, II 298–299.

60. Charles Townshend to Dr. Richard Brocklesby [?], 27, 30 Oct.—Letters of Charles Townshend (Clements Library).

61. *Grafton*, 55; WWM R 2: 21, 27.

62. WWM R 156: 1.

63. *Grenville* III 88.

64. WWM R 168: 191.

65. Add. MS 32971, ff. 289–290.

66. *Ibid.*, f. 287.

67. ". . . the Ministers from the hour of the Duke of Cumberland's death wanted to approach Mr. Pitt; I constantly told them I had three times in vain attempted that measure, that it could never again arise from me.—George III to Bute, 10 Jan. 1766 (Sedgwick, *Letters*, No. 243).

68. WWM R 156: 4.

69. WWM R 168: 177.

70. WWM R 168: 17; 156: 5; 151: 1; 168: 175; 156: 6.

71. Newcastle, *Narrative*, 37–38.

72. *Chatham* II 342–343.

4

The Conciliator

ALTHOUGH MANY SIGNS of a disposition in the American colonies to protest the Stamp Act were reported to ministers during August–September, Rockingham and his colleagues were unable to foresee that the execution of that law would be violently resisted. When the crisis revealed alarming dimensions they knew that physical means of enforcement did not exist in North America, and their instinct was to maintain authority while trying through mollifying measures to bring about a better disposition toward the law. As early as October 18 the state of the American colonies was judged in Privy Council as "a Matter of the Utmost Importance . . . proper only for the Consideration of Parliament," [1] but Parliament remained prorogued to December 17. The death of H.R.H., the uncertainties over prospective support, slow-traveling intelligence from over the Atlantic, and timidities born of inexperience rendered ministers unwilling to hurry the Houses into session.

Meanwhile, Rockingham's Treasury board applied a remedy to one colonial commercial grievance. Numerous memorials were being presented from merchants, manufacturers, and magistrates in the Midlands complaining of a stagnation in exports due "to the late orders & commissions . . . given to the Commanders of his Majesty's ships stationed in the West Indies & America." Florida and the West Indian colonies had suffered since 1763 from the suppression of commercial relations with the bullion-exporting colonies of Spain. The navy had stopped foreign ships from entering British ports merely to purchase refreshments. Although the laws of Spain forbade the export of bullion to British colonies and British laws forbade the entry into the colonies of foreign goods in foreign ships, an illicit but bullion-producing trade with Spanish colonies had formerly been connived at by British government. The Treasury acted now to restore the connivance. Dowdeswell on October 9 suggested that foreign ships be allowed to bring bullion into the colonies in exchange for British manufactures; thus, he said, "the three great objects of the Laws of Trade are perfectly secured, as by the vent of our manufactures imported by your own ships into the Colonies the British shipping is increased, the British sailors are employed and the British Manufactures find a purchase." Rockingham agreed. A study was made of Anglo-Spanish treaties to ascertain whether they allowed the King to indulge the liberty of his ports to the subjects of Spain and the conclusion was that the treaties did so allow. By October 22 the Marquis was circulating papers on this subject among ministers. Lord Chancellor Northington, perhaps interested in saving George Grenville's reputation, advised that "where the law is against opinion . . . the Relief must await the judgment of the Legislature," but the other law officers of the crown offered no arguments against the Treasury project. On November 15 the Treasury directed the customs commissioners to send the necessary directions for a return to connivance. Conway so advised the governors and the Admiralty. The Treasury minute recording this decision was the one which Rockingham, as we have already noticed, sent to Pitt, who applauded it. The King read and approved it, and afterward gave a cold reception at court to Grenville who was widely blamed for the ill condition new ministers were correcting. Newcastle was sure the minute would do the Marquis credit: "It is as strong an article of impeachment against G. Grenville as can be formed. And it will show, you have been doing something." John Roberts of the Board of Trade expressed admiration for Rockingham's "spirit in determining to do what is manifestly right, not by *halves,* but *boldly* and *completely*." [2]

This initial step toward liberalizing a too-restrictive commercial system was a prelude to the revision of the 1764 Revenue Act and the enactment of a bill to open free ports in the British West Indies. It marked the line which Rockingham wished to walk toward a healing of the discontents of the colonies. Although a modification of the Stamp Act was under ministerial consideration, a memorandum in Rockingham's hand dated November 27 shows that he wished "consideration of N[orth] A[merica] in the Commercial to be brought on and to avoid the discussion of the Stamp Act till good principles are laid down for easing & assisting N. A., the high importance of the Commerce to N. A. respectively to the Mother Country." [3] He was naturally more concerned over the plight into which American non-importation and non-payment of debts had thrown British merchants and manufacturers than over riots and breaches of law three thousand miles away. He was in contact with London merchants in the North American trade, a committee of whom, headed by Barlow Trecothick, in early December wrote to the principal mercantile and manufacturing interests of the country, asking for their "support of a regular application to parliament." Without mentioning the Stamp Act the circular letter stated: "we mean to take for our Sole Object, the Interests of these Kingdoms, it being our opinion, that Conclusive Arguments for granting every Ease or Advantage the North Americans can with a propriety desire, may be deduced from that Principle only." According to Burke's testimony some years later, the sending out of this letter was concerted with the Treasury

Minister and was "the principal instrument in the happy repeal of the Stamp Act." [4] Burke meant that it started many petitions to Parliament for whatever measures might be necessary to induce the Americans to resume buying and paying, and that ultimately Parliament decided that repeal was necessary to that end. But in December Rockingham was not envisaging repeal of the Stamp Act, but hoping to delay or obviate that question by restoring prosperity to the whole empire and getting the colonists into a better temper. He hoped too for less-alarming reports from America, so that tempers might cool in England, and it was not until five days before the opening of Parliament that he admitted the necessity of mentioning North America in the King's speech.[5] Even then a low key was struck, the speech referring to the American disorders in the colorless words "matters of importance." The address in reply emphasized the common interests of imperial community, and committed Parliament to "most zealous endeavours for the honour of your Majesty's government, and the true interests of all your people, in all parts of your extended empire." To avoid inflaming tempers on both sides of the Atlantic, to treat a malady of empire rather than indict disobedience, was the motivation in Rockingham as Parliament convened.

Belief was widespread that ministers were not agreed on what to propose, that they lacked firm closet support and the experience necessary to carry on the King's business in Parliament, that they must soon make way for another set of men. All negotiations for additional support had failed except one with Lord George Sackville, but if he came into office great offense would be given to Pitt. Sackville was a friend whom Charles Townshend desired to oblige and Rockingham still hoped to gain Townshend's active service in Parliament. Moreover, the ministry's small prestige was at stake in an election contest at Rochester where Grey Cooper was opposed by John Calcraft who was connected with Pitt's friend Shelburne. Four close friends of Rockingham—his uncle Winchilsea and three Admiralty lords—

went down to help Cooper, who was aided too by secret-service money.[6] The poll was expected to be close and a reverse would be damaging to administration.

A hostile amendment condemning "outrageous tumults and insurrections" in North America was moved in the debate on the address in both Houses, but was easily defeated. George Grenville showed his teeth, and the Marquis heard Temple speak for the amendment in the Lords and also avow his connection with Pitt. On the other hand, Shelburne's speech on that occasion pleased Rockingham. According to his own account, Shelburne had

> endeavoured to distinguish the real ties by which America might
> be supposed to hold to this country, in order to obviate objections
> arising from a thousand false lights thrown out on the subject;
> acknowledging the power of parliament to be supreme, but pre-
> ferring the expediency of the [Stamp] act to be considered in a
> commercial view, regard being had to the abilities of the Ameri-
> cans to pay this tax, and likewise to the consequences likely to
> proceed, in any event, from the late violences.

Rockingham at once offered Shelburne any opening he might choose for coming into administration, with an Irish vice-treasureship for his friend Colonel Isaac Barré. Shelburne answered that no durable system was possible without Pitt as its directing head. Immediately after this rebuff Lord George Sackville was given the vice-treasureship, and a few days later Cooper beat Calcraft at Rochester by a narrow majority. The King called this success "very commendable" and assured the Marquis that "steady perseverance unattended by heats" would overturn "all other oppositions even in Parliament." Parliament had now risen for the Christmas holiday and Burke, who was elected member for Wendover on December 24, observed that "this Administration, which could not stand an hour, appears to have pretty strong stamina." [7]

Breathing a little easier in what Burke called "this narrow but dreadful interval," Rockingham spent the recess working for a ministerial consensus on measures for quieting

America. By January 2 he could tell Newcastle that on one point opinion was general: that the legislative right of Great Britain over the colonies should be declared after the fashion of the 1720 Declaratory Act for Ireland. Further he said:

> I think it also seems the general opinion, that in the King's & in all the parliamentary proceedings the intentions of giving the Colonies every possible relief in trade & convenience should go hand in hand with declarations of authority or censures of the riots and tumults. The main matter in which as yet I cannot see exactly where & how the different opinions can be brought to agree is, what must finally be done upon the Stamp Act.[8]

Secretary of State Grafton had demanded, with Conway's concurrence, that Pitt be applied to for his views on the great question and they had so advised the King on the day before Rockingham wrote the words just quoted. His Majesty had answered that ministers might consult whom they pleased but that he personally would not ask anything of the man who had three times in three years refused royal offers of office. The Marquis did not relish sending an embassy to the Great Man who was off in Somerset, but feared the secretaries would resign and break up administration if he opposed their wishes. Hence Thomas Townshend, a junior lord of the Treasury known to be *persona grata* with Pitt, was dispatched to him. According to Grafton, Townshend was authorized not only to seek Pitt's counsel but to express the desire of ministers to receive him at their head—empty words from anyone but the King. Pitt told Townshend that he would give his views on America only to the King in the closet or from his seat in the House; but he also said enough to suggest that he differed from Temple (who nevertheless would have to be offered the Treasury if Pitt ever became the Minister) and to imply that the present set of men in office, Newcastle excepted, were the only ones he would act with. He said too that all the late acts relating to the colonies were wrong. Rockingham told all this to the King on January 5 and to a full cabinet council on January 7.[9] Grafton interpreted Pitt's response as an offer to treat with administration. Newcastle declared himself willing to be sacrificed, but Rockingham objected, as did the King who told the Marquis on January 8:

> I am of opinion that so loose a conversation as that of Mr. Pitt with Mr. Townshend is not sufficient to risk either my dignity or the continuance of my Administration by a fresh treaty with that Gentleman, for if it should miscarry all public opinion of this Ministry would be destroy'd. . . . I shall therefore undoubtedly tomorrow decline authorizing the D. of Grafton to say any thing to Mr. Pitt, & don't doubt that when I set the example of steadiness most of you will see the propriety of that conduct & will follow it also; I wish therefore you would be at St. James's by one tomorrow that I may talk this affair over with you previous to my seeing the two Secretarys of State.[10]

On the morrow, when the King refused to allow the secretaries "to form me a ministry," they urged that Grafton, who seemed on the brink of resigning, be authorized to write to Pitt in Majesty's name asking him to give his views in the closet when he came to town. According to Grafton the King did not refuse this advice "until after he had seen Lord Rockingham." On January 10 the Marquis reported to the King that this idea was laid aside, and the latter answered: "You have very properly put an end to the idea of writing to Mr. Pitt; if you continue firm I don't doubt of success but if you in the least seem to hesitate the inferiors will fly off." [11]

The Marquis, however, was unconvinced that being "firm" was likely to prevent the secretaries from breaking up the administration. No doubt he would have been glad to be free of his burden, to transfer it to Pitt if that could be done without betraying such friends as Newcastle and the Yorkes; but only the King, whom the Marquis could not govern, could make Pitt the Minister. In deep anxiety Rockingham confided to Charles Yorke on January 11: "The continual hurry from the late occasion occupied my mind so much that I can hardly remember any thing. . . . No Message or Note will be sent to Bath but whether, if the Person comes to Town, it may not be pressed, that he should have an audience, is still matter of doubt to me." [12] If only Pitt could be induced to help ministry without coming in— so that Grafton could be at ease and Conway assured of not having to face the formidable man as an opponent in the House—and if that help could be gained without disgusting the King by an obsequious pursuit of it, then the system would hold. The closet ground on which it stood was firm enough. The King on January 10 warned Bute against any attempt by his friends to overturn the ministers, who had not "rose in any one term they made at first attempting"; he had promised them ample support and his honor obliged him to keep faith with them; he would neither give Pitt "carte blanche" nor allow them to bring him in to direct them. "I mean to support these men if they can go on, if not I am free to do what I think best." [13]

With internal differences unresolved, ministers met Parliament on January 14. The royal speech showed that they had not advanced beyond assertion of authority and redress of American commercial grievances. It stated that orders had been given "for the exertion of all the powers of government in the suppression of riots and tumults," and that whatever remained to be done was committed to the wisdom of Parliament: "If any alterations should be wanting in the commercial economy of the plantations which may tend to enlarge and secure the mutual and beneficial intercourse of my kingdom and colonies, they will deserve your most serious consideration." The Stamp Act was not mentioned. Pitt was present and in the debate on the address made his famous speech denouncing the act as unconstitutional and calling for its repeal. He clashed bitterly with Grenville and showed himself as differing from Temple. Among the ministers he professed to discern traces of an overruling influence—presumably meaning Newcastle's—and because of their youth and inexperience he could not yet declare his confidence in them. Dramatically, he revealed himself ready to save the country again. Conway complimented him, and declared himself ready to yield the lead. And the next day Rockingham wrote to the King that administration would be shaken to the greatest degree if no further attempt were made "to get Mr. Pitt to take a cordial part."

> His personal altercations with Mr. G. Greenville & the Conduct of L[or]d Temple in the House of Commons who was present & who dissented to every assertion of Mr. Pitt's has made very many believe that Mr. Pitt is more separated from G. Greenville & L[or]d Temple than could have been relied on some days ago & in that light strengthened the D. of Grafton's & General Conway's ideas that Mr. Pitt might be separated from them.[14]

The King was much displeased at Rockingham's apparent going over to the secretaries' opinion and began to cast about for another ministry without either Pitt or the Grenville brothers—that is, for a set of men more confident in the efficacy of closet support.[15] He did not understand the crafty game which the Marquis now began to play. The latter could not have been so slow-witted as not to see that, Pitt having openly committed himself, the ministers had only to decide for repeal of the Stamp Act in order to avail themselves of his support without his coming into office. Therefore, a negotiation could safely be opened with him. The King, temporizing, was induced to allow Grafton to go to Pitt to ascertain the terms on which he would come into administration; but no royal message was sent and the Duke was forbidden to make any declaration in the King's name. Grafton was with Pitt the night of January 16 and afterward dictated a memoir stating that the latter had not only disavowed Temple but said that if he were to form a new system it would be with Rockingham, Conway, and Grafton, although Newcastle would have to leave the cabinet and Lord George Sackville would be turned out. Pitt conveyed to Grafton the impression that he had come up to Parliament for the American affair in which he had feared the ministers would be "borne down": *ergo,* he had come to help them. On hearing Grafton's report, the King, who had not found an alternative slate of ministers, sent the Duke with the Marquis to ask Pitt in Majesty's name, (1) whether he was disposed at this time to come into office, and (2) whether Lord Temple's coming in, or having an offer to come in, was a necessary condition. There are two accounts of the meeting with Pitt the night of January 18, Grafton's which was written some years later and Rockingham's which was written that night. According to the former, Pitt lamented that he could not have the assistance of Temple because of differing opinions, was willing to act with the present ministers, but would turn out Sackville and effect a "transposition of offices." This last point, Grafton stated, was "ill received" by Rockingham.[16] The Marquis' statement is a short report written to Newcastle after he and Grafton had communicated their story to the King:

> We were with him [Pitt] above two hours & have been again with his Majesty tonight. It is impossible to enter into detail in writing, but in short I think there will not be much more to pass upon this subject. The variety of matters which arose rather increases than decreases the difficulties & yet I am glad on the whole that this affair has gone as far as it has, because it will prevent the differences amongst *us* which was the thing I most dreaded.[17]

Two days later Newcastle recorded a fuller statement from the Marquis which testifies that Pitt had again named Newcastle as objectionable; that he wished to form a new administration including Rockingham, Grafton, and Conway but in which many new arrangements would be required; and that Temple must be offered the Treasury. This statement shows too that the Marquis had asked Pitt what he meant by saying in the House of Commons that the ministry was subject to an "over-riding influence," and that Pitt disavowed meaning either Newcastle or Bute but named Mansfield; to which Rockingham replied, "That, I suppose, is directed to me," and denied it. The statement shows further that the Marquis refused to serve in the system which Pitt projected, saying that "having entered into connections with those, with whom he always acted . . . he could not give up any of them, or remain in the Administration if that were done." [18] The King's memoir[19] of what he was told by Rockingham and Grafton in general corroborates what Newcastle heard from the Marquis. Grafton, who saw nothing objectionable in Pitt's attitude and was eager to serve under him, recorded in later years that he "never was able to make out how the business dropt after having had so favourable an appearance." The fact was that the King sent Rockingham alone to bear the royal answer to Pitt, which was that his taking office was "not practicable at present." The Marquis was instructed "to avoid a long Conversation, by saying that your business only permits You to call for a few minutes; be extrem'ly civil but firm in what you say." Disappointed, Pitt presaged "melancholy things for this country." The necessary overture had been made and the divisive strains within administration had been relieved.[20]

Moreover, ministers had by this time agreed upon a plan of measures likely to engage the support of Pitt, who in his great speech of January 14 had not only called for repeal of the Stamp Act but urged alterations in the regulation of the colonies' trade. The plan settled at a meeting on January 17 of Rockingham, Conway, Grafton, Dowdeswell, and Charles Townshend was, in the Marquis' words: "a declaratory Act, in general terms, afterwards to *Consideration of Trade* etc. & finally *determination on the Stamp Act,* i.e., a *Repeal* & which its own demerits & inconveniences *felt here* will justify." [21] That a repeal gained the King's support is shown by his writing to the Marquis a few days later that Lord Talbot, Treasurer of the Household, "is as right as I can desire on the Stamp Act; strong for our declaring the right but willing to repeal." [22] New differences among ministers broke out in drafting the parliamentary resolutions to condemn lawless conduct in the colonies and to affirm the supreme authority of the British legislature. Some, notably Charles Yorke, desired stronger language than the Marquis and the secretaries of state preferred; while Newcastle

dreaded that stern resolutions would prevent the repeal
from having the desired effect of restoring a proper temper
in America. Yorke, too, wished to have the *right of taxation*
spelled out in the declaratory act and warned of the danger
likely to arise if an amendment to insert it were moved by
an enemy of administration since, if ministers resisted a
motion, it might be carried against them.[23] But Rockingham
would not agree to insert words which were certain to displease Pitt, who held that the colonies were constitutionally
exempt from taxation by Parliament. The upshot was that
the *right of taxation* was not mentioned in the declaratory
act; that was to be, in the Marquis' words, "like the Act of
Parliament for Ireland," which provided a precedent of
British legislative supremacy without imposing taxes on the
dependent country.

What with having to maintain subservience to the King
and sufficient harmony among ministers while guarding
against the displeasure of the Great Commoner, Rockingham groaned to Newcastle that "the continual hurry &
anxiety almost overpowers my constitution." But by January
25 he could say:

> The Resolutions in general exceed in spirit what the generality
> of our Friends wish, but in expectation that coming into them
> will pave the way for the *actual repeal of the Stamp Act,* I
> think they will be agreed to. . . . I see more and more the
> difficulties that surround us, and therefore feel the necessity of
> not *temporizing.* Convinced as I am that the Confusion at
> home will be much too great (if the Repeal is not obtained)
> for us to have withstood, either as private or public men, my
> opinion being entirely for Repeal, I shall certainly persist in
> that Measure; and although many in the House of Commons
> may be against us, and particularly some who have lately called
> themselves under the denomination of Lord B[ute]'s friends;
> yet I am persuaded that the House will repeal the Stamp Act
> by a Great Majority. *If it does,* we shall show them *how* we
> stand as an Administration. If it does not, I wish no man so
> great a curse as to desire him to be the person to take Ad-
> ministration, and be obliged to enforce the Act.[24]

The woods were still thick on all sides. Conway seems to have been in perfect accord with Rockingham's views, but was susceptible of being influenced by Grafton to go too far to accommodate Pitt. Newcastle was for quick repeal, cared nothing about a declaratory act, and feared angry words in parliamentary resolutions; whereas Charles Yorke held the old Duke's American opinions to be "insanity" and was pressed daily by his brother Hardwicke to hold to a strong line. The advice of many men in and out of administration had to be listened to, and a music of confused chorus beat in the Marquis' ears. "I hope they will come *soon* to repeal," wrote Newcastle to him on January 28, "or, believe me, my Dear Lord, you will see great confusion amongst your own friends." [25]

II

The Treasury Minister's persuasion that the House of Commons would vote to repeal was the result of the course of proceedings there. The many petitions for relief from distress caused by American non-importation and non-payment of accounts were being heard and witnesses were being examined on evidence in committee of the whole House. Opinion of the inexpediency of the Stamp Act, in the existing state of circumstances, was growing before any ministerial resolutions were moved.

On January 27 the member for Middlesex, George Cooke, devoté of Pitt, moved for receiving the petition of the American Stamp Act Congress. Rockingham thought this premature and likely to offend a majority and divide his own friends. Pitt spoke for the motion as did Sir William Meredith and two junior lords of the Treasury (Tommy Townshend and George Onslow), while Conway, Dowdeswell, and Lord John Cavendish opposed it, along with Grenville and such "Bute's" as Charles Jenkinson, Jeremiah Dyson, and Fletcher Norton. An embarrassing division was avoided by Conway's inducing Cooke to withdraw the motion, but not until after Pitt had inflamed many tempers. According to Conway, the Great Commoner said "some imprudent things" which "indisposed the House much to the Petition; particularly that he thought *the Original Compact with the Americans was broke, by the Stamp Act*—on which words he was strongly attack'd by the late Attorney Gen[eral] who rais'd a strong cry against him & intimated he shou'd have been call'd to the Bar for them." [26]

Afterward it was reported about that the King was angry with Pitt, disgusted by the deference ministers showed to him, and meditated a change. On January 31 administration was nearly defeated on an election petition. Many desertions were noticed among members holding employments from the crown and Conway explained this to the King as due to rumors of an impending change of administration.[27] The Duke of Newcastle and lords Bessborough, Grantham, and Albemarle feared that this event would swell an already formidable opposition in the House of Lords and jeopardize the repeal; hence they urged Rockingham to press the King for a show of support. What passed at the Marquis' audience, February 1, remains undisclosed. No punitive dismissals of deserters followed, and there is no proof that Rockingham asked for any. It is certain that the King read no significance in the narrow vote of the day before, certain too that the Marquis was—or at least pretended to be— entirely satisfied, since he wrote afterward "that in perfect reliance on His Majesty's gracious support, His Majesty's Servants will do their utmost to carry on the business to the utmost of their abilities"; to which the King answered that "the resolution of standing firmly by the fate of the American question" would govern his language to the Lord Chancellor.[28] Doubts that the ministry could continue remained widespread, however, and after a very narrow division in the Lords on February 4 Newcastle went into the closet to ask Majesty pointblank if a change was intended. The King answered that he sincerely wished the ministers to go on if they could. The Duke asked too if the King was for repealing the Stamp Act, and was told: "I am; I was always against enforcing it, I have thought some middle way might be taken, but I am convinced that nothing but repeal will do." [29] On February 7 Rockingham obtained royal permission to tell it abroad that Majesty was for the repeal, and that night a smashing triumph was won in Commons. On the first division, testing sentiments on the great question soon to be put, supporters of administration prevailed by a majority of 140. Rockingham instantly sent the news to the King, who replied: "I just take up my pen to thank you for your attention in sending me a few particulars of this days debate in the House of Commons, which by the great Majority must be reckon'd a very favourable appearance for the Repeal of the Stamp Act in that House." After an audience on the following day, the Marquis recorded:

> He [the King] was very desirous of knowing who voted in the minority & seemed pleased & surprized at the number of the majority. He asked me if I expected so great a majority. I told him that a month or more ago I was sanguine that it would be so, but that I really had doubted much of late, from the fluctuating situation in which administration stood. . . . I pressed his Majesty to express his own wishes about the Repeal & to take opportunities of doing it among his Lords & Gentlemen of the Bedchamber, which I hope & believe he will do.[30]

Instead, George III pulled the rug out from under his Minister. On February 10 he authorized Lord Strange, Chancellor of the Duchy of Lancashire and a reputed "Bute," to go among members of Parliament with the word that Majesty favored modification instead of repeal of the Stamp Act. Why the royal change of mind? No one can say for certain. Bute, who was very active against repeal and was attempting a concert with Grenville and the Duke of Bedford, may have employed the Dowager Princess of Wales to enforce upon her son's mind the belief that repeal would not be concurred in by the House of Lords; but the King hardly needed to be told of the formidable opposition among the peers. The most probable explanation of his shift was fear of a deadlock between the two Houses of Parliament. Even so, it was shabby treatment of the First Lord of the Treasury and seemed to say that closet confidence was withdrawn from administration.[31] After hearing Rockingham's expostulations, the King cleared him of all imputation of misrepresentation, and in a few days Newcastle thought that the explanations had come out "tolerably well." [32] A week later the House of Commons approved the repeal resolution 275 to 167. After seeing the King, who was impressed by the size of the majority, Rockingham told Newcastle:

> I remarked to his Majesty how strong the torrent of opinion in favour of Repeal was & is . . . notwithstanding the checks of seeing so many persons in his Majestie's Service voting against it, notwithstanding the great combinations there were in the House of Commons against it & ultimately the knowledge that had lately been given of his Majestie's own sentiments being for Modification.

If repeal moved from resolution in committee of the whole through the House and up to the peers, Rockingham dared to hope

> that his Majestie may be inclined to adopt the opinion that the House of Lords should not disagree with the Commons & I think if this can be done, it will be right for his Majestie to begin early to talk that idea to *all* Lords who frequent his Closet.[33]

But much uncertainty was felt by the Minister. So great was his apprehension of being thwarted by a combination of the forces of Bute, Grenville, Temple, and Bedford—plus the Duke of York's known opposition to repeal—that he turned anew to Pitt, who had been showing a querulous attitude toward the ministry and disapproving Rockingham's "tone" as a "Minister master of the court and of the public." The Marquis invited him to join with the present heads of administration to prepare a plan for carrying on with himself at the head, and promised to advise the King to send for him to present the plan. The overture revealed more desperation than wisdom. As might be expected, Pitt declined all treaty without the King's express command.[34] The rebuff worsened relations with the Great Commoner and darkened Rockingham's hope of getting safely through the great business. On March 3—the day Commons sent up the repeal bill to the peers—his secretary Burke observed: "We are in an odd way . . . in the road of being the strongest ministry ever known in England, are our superiors now: in the road of being none at all." [35] Even Newcastle half-deserted at this time, blaming Rockingham with grotesque inconsistency for refusing to treat for additional support from the friends of Bute. The Marquis was now acting, said the old Duke, "as the sole Minister." [36]

Because the King elected to await the decision of Parliament on the Stamp Act, Rockingham was able to carry on. In mid-March the Lords, despite a stiff opposition, concurred in the repeal. That the Lord Chancellor spoke and voted for concurrence showed that Majesty did not try to thwart it; although more than seventy holders of office under the crown in both Houses voted against the repeal, and the Duke of York opposed to the end. When the Lords had decided, the King expressed his satisfaction to Rockingham, who said to Charles Yorke, "this has been a good day, the King pleased etc." [37]

During the previous few weeks nothing seems to have clouded relations between the King and the Marquis, and not until May did the former show the slightest intention of changing administration. No royal reason for a change existed: ministers gave Majesty no offense, and the principal Minister was serving with fidelity, deference, and courtesy. The business of government was proceeding well in Parliament where a total alteration of the unpopular Cider Act was already under way. Rockingham had written on March 14:

In the House of Commons I hardly expect any great difficulty in this matter & I think we shall scarce be violently opposed in the House of Lords. The correcting of the Trade Acts of the late Administration are preparing & by the temper which now prevails, both among those concerned for the West India Islands & those concerned for America I think we shall be able to do some good service.[38]

That liberalization of Grenville's Revenue Act of 1764 was the measure which Rockingham, the previous autumn, had envisaged as the primary means of quieting American discontents. Hearings on it in committee were to begin after the Easter recess, and as late as April 8 Burke, who was in a good situation to judge, observed:

I do not look for much opposition; the spirit of the adverse faction begins to evaporate; even Mr. Grenville begins to slacken his attendance. . . . In short, if some foolish measure of those at the head does not precipitate them from their situations, or if some court earthquake (the thing most to be dreaded in this climate) does not shake the ground under them, I see nothing in the union, the ability, or the spirit of the opposition, which is able to move them. So much popularity never was possessed by any set of people who possessed great offices. Yet all is in an odd way.[39]

III

The Great Commoner had been at once a potent ally in the contest for repeal of the Stamp Act and an embarrassment to administration, which could not (as Parliament would not) accept his doctrine of the unconstitutionality of that Act or his Lockian doctrine of an original compact between crown and colonies. He withheld his confidence from the ministers, yet expected to be consulted in advance on their measures. He flicked them in debate even while siding with them. On the famous night of February 21, when the House voted for leave to bring in the repeal bill, he took a strenuous part yet complained that ministers were under ill influences;[40] and soon afterward he rebuffed the Marquis' desperate overture. In the final debate in Commons on the declaratory and repeal bills, he moved to strike from the former the words that could be interpreted as meaning that the authority of the British legislature over the colonies did not stop short of taxation; and according to Horace Walpole, he said that night that he would like to see "such an administration as the King should like and the people approve." [41] In April he struck the blow which started the undoing of the Rockingham administration.

Early that month petitions came into Parliament from various mercantile interests asking for the opening of free ports in the West Indies. The Treasury saw the project as integral with the policy of benefiting the colonies by enlarging commercial opportunities throughout the empire, which was the central aim in revising the Revenue Act of 1764. A free port bill was about to be considered in cabinet when Rockingham remembered that no word of it had been communicated to Pitt; hence Edmund Burke was sent to him to explain what was intended. Burke found the Great Commoner "peevish and perverse" and determined to be "out of humour." There is indirect evidence that Pitt complained of being slighted by administration, and was angered by Burke's telling him of Rockingham's wish for him to state the conditions on which he would come into the King's service. Burke blundered, perhaps from politeness, since it is incredible that the Marquis would have authorized such a mode of overture to Pitt; but in any event, the latter was disposed to take offense even where none was intended.[42] In cabinet the following day Grafton opposed bringing in the free port bill, as did Egmont and Northington. Conway was ill in the country. Rockingham submitted to putting off the bill to the next session but insisted that in the present session an address to the crown be moved for the opinion of government boards on the subject.[43] Burke had visited Pitt on Friday, April 11. On the following Monday the latter appeared in the House and captiously seized upon a routine motion touching the militia to declare open hostility toward the administration.

This event was an elixir for opposition in Commons at

the same time that it caused a rift in the ministry. The revision of the 1764 Revenue Act was stalled until the next month. Grafton decided that he could not stay in an administration which alienated Pitt; he had always understood that the door should be open to the Great Commoner whenever he chose to come in, and now believed that the loss of Pitt's support would force Rockingham to a negotiation with the Butes. Grafton on April 21 urged upon the Marquis that the ministers give collective advice to the King to summon Pitt to head administration. Rockingham answered that he never would advise the King to do any such thing, and added, according to Grafton, "that he saw no reason why the present Administration, (if they received assurances from the king that people in office were to hold their posts at the good will of the ministers) should not carry on very well and with honour to themselves the king's business." [44] Whatever reason the Marquis may have had for entertaining the slightest hope that George III would give such assurances does not appear. On that very day, however, ministerial forces in Commons showed a surprising recovery, carrying the window tax 169 to 85 after opposition had three days before swelled to 112 against it in committee. On April 22 Sir William Meredith and Sir George Savile, with ministerial support, brought forward the question of general warrants, and reversed the defeats of 1764 and 1765 by carrying a resolution condemning the use made of them in the *North Briton* case as illegal and a breach of parliamentary privilege. Pitt tried without success to have all general warrants declared illegal, and on April 24 made what Richard Rigby called

a kind of farewell speech, in which he told us . . . that he wished, for the sake of his dear country, that all our factions might cease; that there might be a ministry fixed, such as the King should appoint, and the public approve; that the men might be properly adapted to the employments they were appointed to, and whose names were known in Europe, to convey an idea of dignity to this government both at home and abroad; that if ever he was again admitted, as he had been,

into the Royal presence, it should be independent of any personal connections whatsoever; with plenty of recommendations
to unanimity, virtue, etc.[45]

Burke called it a "fine flaming patriotick speech against any
sort of personal connections; he means with any besides
himself . . . a speech too virtuous to be honest." [46] The
following day the King in a note to Rockingham characterized rumors of a change of administration as "gross
falsehoods." [47] And then, on April 28, Grafton asked for
the King's permission to resign because his colleagues had
set Pitt at defiance.

His Majesty was naturally surprised at hearing Grafton
say that it had been the unanimous understanding among
the ministers from their coming in that whenever Pitt chose
to come forth they would put themselves at his disposition.
Obviously, the young Duke had deluded himself or been
duped; and he was deluded now in fancying that his going
out must immediately disrupt the administration. The King
recorded that "we parted civilly, all the ground I could gain
was that he would give me as much time to form a Government as his honour would admit." But the King preferred
to keep his ministers and, believing that Pitt now would ally
with his Grenville brothers-in-law, saw the way opened for
strengthening government with those men he most esteemed,
the so-called friends of Lord Bute. His Majesty on May 1
told Lord Egmont: "I am hourly of the opinion that if the
present Ministry can possibly go on it is the most prudent
mode for me; else the absurdity of Men will force me into
accepting *the Family,* than which there is nothing I would
not rather submit to." [48]

Nothing had occurred in his relations with Rockingham
to make George III suspect that his Treasury Minister
would balk at treating with the Butes. He had seemed the
most deferential of servants, had done the royal bidding in
warding off Pitt, had swallowed his pride and anger when
Majesty embarrassed him on the question of repealing the
Stamp Act, had accepted the refusal of punitive action

against placemen who did not support ministerial measures, and never had bedeviled the King for proofs of hostility to Lord Bute. It must have seemed to the King that the proud hotspur who quit the court four years before had been tamed to an obedient servant. Moreover, the parliamentary situation facing ministers had taken such a turn for the worse that they must bid for fresh support, which they could do only by drawing the Bedford faction away from the Grenvilles or by gaining the Butes. On April 29 George Grenville, supported by Pitt, moved and carried without a division a motion for leave to bring in a bill declaring the seizure of papers illegal in all cases but treason and felonies. On the same day administration saved its window tax bill from postponement by the slender majority of 40 in a House of 314. On the next day Dowdeswell moved the resolutions preparatory to revising colonial trade laws, including the free port proposal, and met with such opposition, especially from Grenville and Pitt, that Rockingham feared his measures would founder.[49] Such was the state of things when the Marquis, instead of showing a pliant disposition to the sovereign, resolved to get the necessary closet support or to resign. He not only rejected treating with Bute, which would have appeared to all the world as if ministers "were acting their parts only under his patronage," but said that they could not go on unless the King ordered men holding places to speak and vote regularly for the government. In a cabinet meeting on May 1 ministers failed to agree on the person whom they would advise the King to name as Grafton's successor, and Rockingham explicitly rejected Egmont's argument—recognized as from the King—for a thorough coalition with the Butes. He would go so far as to restore to office Bute's brother, James Mackenzie Stuart, who had been forced out by the Grenville–Bedford set in the previous year to the great displeasure of the King. That would be consistent with reversing the measures of blundering predecessors, but he would offer nothing to other Butes save on terms of strict loyalty to the administration.[50]

With his closet support slipping, the Marquis in despair

and disgust threatened in cabinet that he would resign not later than May 6 when he expected such desertions as would defeat the free port resolution. Newcastle was shocked at this threat and cautioned Rockingham that resignation in such circumstances—throwing the King's affairs into confusion—might be disrespectful to Majesty, "be blamed by the nation, and more particularly, by all our own friends." [51] The manner of the compliant king's servant had given way, however, to the pride and passion of the whig grandee. Egmont saw him the day after the unhappy cabinet and reported to the King that he "was disposed to resign immediately, or at least by Tuesday next, when he apprehends a debate in the House of Commons in which he expects to be beat"; that he was "obstinately resolved not to admit into employment any more of those who are called my Lord Bute's friends besides Mr. Mackenzie," and "much exasperated against those of the same description who now continue in place"; that these must be required to support "absolutely & actively on all occasions without any Reserve"; and that this was "the sine qua non of his holding his Employment an hour longer." [52]

The King was in such a state of panic at the prospect of losing a ministry before another could be put together that he wrote to Bute for counsel and assistance, saying that he would "take any but the men that us'd me so infamously last year." [53] Meanwhile, it was observed that Rockingham and Dowdeswell were "caressed by the King at court beyond any expression." By May 4 Egmont had learned from Mackenzie and the Earl of Northumberland, acting as spokesmen for the Bute group, that they would not embarrass the King's business in Parliament.[54] Bute was unable to show the King any alternative but a ministry headed by Pitt or Grenville. In two audiences on May 4 and May 5 Rockingham recalled to the King assurances the late Duke of Cumberland had given ministers that all Butes staying in office would support the administration. According to Newcastle, who appears to have been present, "His Majesty admitted the truth of that & seem'd not displeased with my Lord Rockingham for having remember'd it." The old Duke now praised the Marquis' "wise and steddy way of acting" and recorded: "No man could have talked better, more wisely or stronger than he did both Sunday and Monday to the King." [55]

In the meantime, Pitt gave up opposing the Dowdeswell measures and went off to Bath—perhaps to quiet the rumor that he was in league with Grenville—and, what with the resolution of the Butes to stop opposition, the way was cleared for the new colonial regulations and even the bill to open West Indian free ports. They were carried easily in mid-May, and the Rockingham legislative program for ending colonial discontents was fully enacted into law.

There persisted much discord among ministers, however, and the King meant to effect a change whenever that became practicable. His resolution would be fortified by subsequent events in the month of May.

IV

Finding a successor to Grafton was left by the King to the ministers. The problem was not merely filling the office of Secretary of State for the Northern Department, but making another ministerial leader in the Lords. Grafton had led there because he was an able speaker, which Rockingham, who is known to have spoken but twice that session, was not.[56] Lord Hardwicke was first pitched upon for the place, and Rockingham tried to make the whole Yorke family happy by inducing Northington to take the lord presidency (which Winchilsea was prepared to vacate) in order that Charles Yorke might have the Great Seal, as the King had promised.[57] The Lord Chancellor angrily refused to change his office. Then Hardwicke, who at heart had little regard for the administration, declined to be secretary of state unless the King personally pressed him; which the latter would not do. Rockingham then proposed that Egmont take the seals, with Lord Hillsborough replacing him at the Admiralty. The King interpreted this nomination as designed to make "an appearance to the world" that he meant to stand by his ministers. Egmont was willing to accept if Majesty wished it, but was told that whatever he elected to do would give no displeasure; whereupon he too shied off. Then it was that Rockingham and Conway, acting together, elected to back the nomination of the Duke of Richmond, a man the King regarded as not qualified for the great office.

Charles Lennox, third Duke of Richmond, had—like Grafton—the blood of Charles II in his veins.[58] One of the great peers of the realm, he possessed a famous estate in Sussex, which county the Duke of Newcastle thought of as his own political domain wherein he wished no rival influence. Hard upon George III's accession Richmond had been named to the bedchamber and quickly resigned in protest against a slight to his brother. He had not joined the opposition to the Bute and Grenville ministries, but was devoted to Conway with whom he had a family connection. He had served as ambassador to the French court during the winter of 1765–1766, and returning on leave had supported the Rockingham administration's measures. He was a good speaker and perhaps no worse qualified for great office than any other available peer. Given the nature of the place to be filled, the choice of a man was narrowly restricted. The plan was for Conway to move to the northern office, for Richmond to take the southern, and for colonial affairs to be separated under a third secretaryship of state to which Lord Dartmouth, head of the Board of Trade, would be raised.

When the Marquis, on May 16, asked for the Richmond nomination, the King balked and told him that Newcastle had suggested that Charles Yorke might be willing to take the seals and afterward be made Lord Chancellor "whenever there was an opening." Rockingham said that if neither of the Yorkes could be induced to accept he would not remain in office unless Richmond was appointed. According to the King he said that "many of his friends wished him rather to decline continuing but He thought it owed it to me to go on if He could, tho' his own private wish was to retire." [59] To Newcastle, who did not like the Richmond nomination, the Marquis said that it "would not be for the King's real service" for Yorke to take the seals, but he ought instead to be "at the Head of the Law," and that the appointment of Richmond was "the best thing to do in the present circumstances." [60] Egmont advised the King to agree as "a temporary expedient" lest Rockingham resign:

> And if he should throw up his friends and the whole Party now in administration I believe would follow; and (whatever their intentions may now be) would insensibly become a new tho' different body of malcontents.[61]

On May 18 the Marquis settled the point with the King, who afterward told Newcastle that if he had not "given in to that measure" Rockingham and Conway would have taken it "extremely ill" and probably caused a "total dissolution of this Administration." Newcastle disculpated himself, complained of the Marquis' coolness and little inclination to consult with him, and even asked for permission to withdraw from meetings with ministers.[62] Granting it, the King must have reflected that administration was in pieces. He refused to create a third secretary of state for the colonies, which disappointed Dartmouth.[63] Belief was general that the end was near. Lord Richard Howe gave up the treasurership of the navy for the same reason Grafton had gone. Lord North refused an offer. There were places available which none would take, from unwillingness to board a sinking ship. Richmond appears to have been blindly unaware that it was going down. If Rockingham was so deluded as not to know this, his delusion was honorable. He had carried all his measures and served his King well, restoring tranquillity to empire (or so it appeared) and prosperity to commerce. There was abundant evidence of public satisfaction with what had been done. Why should Majesty withdraw support from so successful an administration? Almost to the end the Marquis retained the belief that all would be well. "We shall have a rough sea to sail through," he wrote to Savile about this time, "but as I hope our bottom is sound, we may weather all storms, or, at least if we should be wrecked, we shall not suffer in honour, or as private men." [64] What the Marquis seems not to have realized was that the King was weary of too much decision in the closet, too much dependence of ministers on closet support. He had confided to Bute in early May that he could neither eat nor sleep, that "if I am to continue the life of agitation I have these three years, the next year there will be a Council of Regency." He longed for the kind of relief which Bute and Cumberland had given; and although Rockingham had not offended him as Grenville had done, royal dread of "faction" forbade finding that relief in the head of a party. By the latter part of May he ascertained that Pitt, never a man of party, was loose enough from the Grenvilles to undertake, on a comprehensive basis, to be a prime minister. A savior was in sight.

Early in the spring Rockingham and his colleagues had agreed to apply to Parliament for a grant to the King's sister who was soon to marry the King of Denmark, and to distribute the grant for the late Duke of Cumberland among three royal brothers now come of age. Dowdeswell told Rockingham on April 14 that he intended that morning to draft the royal message to Parliament requesting these grants, and that he hoped to present it three days later.[65] Somehow the business was delayed. Then Conway, who had been ill in the country, returned April 25 and raised objection to bringing it on so late in the session. Followed the ministerial crisis started by Grafton's resignation. According to the King's letter of May 3 to Bute, the ministers refused to propose the settlements for the royal brothers unless they were assured of continuing in office. For whatever reason, the measure continued to be put off, and the longer the delay the stronger became the reason for postponing at least the grants for the King's brothers until the next session. Many members had left town and might resent being deprived of an opportunity to vote on a question dear to the King's heart; or the bringing it in so near the end of the session

might suggest that a largely-attended House would not have
approved it. His Majesty, however, was insistent and on
Sunday, May 25, understood from Rockingham that it
would "without fail" be moved the following week. There
seems to have been no reluctance to move the grant for the
princess, so that the royal concern was for the satisfaction
of the brothers. At a cabinet meeting the next day a majority
(against Northington and Egmont) favored postponement
to the next session, and Rockingham explained to the King
that "objections have been made, in no respect from doubt
on the propriety of the matter, but arising from the lateness
of the Session & the thinness of Parl[iamen]t at this Junc-
ture." The King rejected all explanations and told his ministers that if administration did not move the measure the
opposition would; to which the Marquis answered, "then it
must be withstood." [66] His words angered the King.

On the night of May 28, after seeing the dukes of York
and Gloucester at the House of Lords, the Marquis sought
to break the impasse by proposing to the King: "It might
be doing some thing if the Affair was mentioned in Parliament as intended for the Consideration of the Opening of
the next Sessions." At a cabinet the next day he advocated
this step, at the same time avowing that he would resign if
the King persisted in demanding the grant to his brothers
immediately. Newcastle told him that resignation never
could be justified: "if His Majesty insists upon it, it is the
King that must take the consequences of its being brought in
at an improper time; which His Majesty says, was not his
fault. . . . I am persuaded, every real Friend & cool thinking man will be of opinion, that it cannot be avoided; & will
be stronger of opinion, that it will not be a Justifiable Cause
for leaving the Service of the King, and the Nation." The
Marquis got his way, however, without having to put his
threat to the test.[67] On June 3 the grant for the princess was
voted, but the business of the princes was put off to the next
session in spite of last-minute royal commands to both Rockingham and Richmond that it be brought on immediately.
The next day Parliament rose.

Apart from royal refusal of the Marquis' request for the creation of several peerages and for the dismissal of Jeremiah Dyson from the Board of Trade,[68] little can be reported of the relations of Majesty and Minister during the next few weeks. Pressed by Newcastle on June 18 to learn "whether the Closet continues as it was," Rockingham answered: "Matters remain much as they have been. His Majesty in good Humour easy & gracious." In this season of expectation that a change would be made, the ministers did not wish to be kept in the dark if such were intended by the King; and if no change was intended they felt that some sign ought to be given of royal confidence in them, that the King's service required it. On June 27, Rockingham, Conway, Richmond, and Newcastle met to discuss this subject and decided to ask that Jeremiah Dyson and Lord Eglintoun, two reputed "Butes," be dismissed from their places. Richmond was for declaring their inability to go on if this satisfaction were not given, but the others were not willing to give up over such a point. They went to court, found the King in equable temper, apparently satisfied with his ministers, intending to support them, and willing—in the future but not at the present—to remove placemen who acted against them.[69] That night, at a cabinet meeting, the Lord Chancellor balked at approving new instructions prepared for the Governor of Canada, complained of negligence in the circulation of relevant papers, and said that he would not attend more cabinet meetings. Rockingham now was of opinion that, if the King would make Charles Yorke chancellor and show a real intention to support, all might go on with ease, but he can hardly have had any hope that this would happen. Newcastle recorded on the following day:

My Lord Rockingham, I believe, wishes a means to get out; & flatters himself, that he shall go out with more éclat, than any men ever did; that he has done great service to the King & to the publick; that he had shew'd the King, that he could carry the Repeal of the Stamp Act, with his Majesty & my Lord Bute against him; that he could carry the Free Port Bill with Mr. Pitt against him; and had carried all the regulations that were proper, relating to the American trade.[70]

On July 4 Northington asked the King's permission to absent himself from further cabinets, explaining that he could not continue in office unless a stronger administration were formed. Thus the moment arrived for which Majesty had been waiting. Two days later he told the Marquis that administration was weak and must be stronger. The latter recalled that he and his colleagues had more than once drawn the royal attention to the fact and ascribed the weakness to want of display of royal support. "I went thro' great part of our conduct [he recorded] particularly in all the circumstances wherein I thought his Majesty might have any feelings of a degree of being dissatisfied." The King thought that the Marquis "behaved very properly," and Lady Rockingham, whose source of information was her husband, said that the King displayed "great civility & kind expressions to my L[or]d." On July 7 a summons to attend in the closet was sent to Pitt. Ministers were not told of this until two days later and then only in reply to Rockingham's asking the King if he had come to a determination. The Marquis sent off expresses to friends but offered no opinion because, as he said to Newcastle, "in fact I have none—except that of keeping quiet." [71] It was the end. He would take no part in a Pitt administration, had told the Great Man so months before, and now it was totally out of consideration.

Pitt's commission from the crown was to new-model administration and his intended mode of executing it was to turn out Newcastle, Richmond, Winchilsea, and Rockingham while retaining many of their friends in office; to place Temple at the Treasury, make Shelburne southern secretary of state, and shift Northington to the lord presidency in order to give the Great Seal to Camden. Conway was to continue as minister in the House of Commons, since Pitt elected to go to the Lords as Earl of Chatham. With the privy seal and no office of exacting business, he would serve the crown as sole Minister, having underlings but no colleagues. Lord

Temple's refusal to take the assigned part in such a system disrupted the initial plan. Until this was known Rockingham was very pessimistic for his host of whig friends, old Newcastle men and younger men more closely connected with himself, all of whom he thought of as constituting the historic whig party. He had feared that Pitt with Temple would mean Grenville too, and that a union of the court with "the Family" and the man of popularity would be disastrous for the party. Now it seemed that Pitt's breaking off with Temple meant that the Grenville–Bedford corps would withhold support, and that he must rely upon the Newcastle–Rockingham connection. So it turned out, but not to the extent that the more optimistic hoped. He found a pliant tool in Grafton for the Treasury and because the latter desired to have a Treasury representative in Commons Charles Townshend was forced to leave the Pay Office for the Exchequer. Dowdeswell was offered the Board of Trade but declined to go down the ladder and retired from office.

The Rockingham tactic while Pitt was making his arrangements was to avoid irritating him for the sake of friends who might be allowed to keep their places. All who were allowed to stay were encouraged to do so. The Marquis' position was much like that in which Newcastle had found himself on going out in 1762, and there could be no thought of a different tactic. He hoped, however, to keep alive an *esprit de corps* among friends both in and out of office; and he expected to maintain cordial relations with Conway and Grafton. Unable to serve the King as minister he was resolved to serve the public by preserving the principle of party in the ranks of whiggery. A share of the patronage of government was necessary to that end. It was, therefore, of no service to him for Dowdeswell to refuse office; nor was it at his behest that Lord John Cavendish resigned his seat on the Treasury board. Charles Yorke was the only friend the Marquis did not urge to remain. The royal promise of the Great Seal having been broken, Rockingham told Yorke that it was doubtful that "personal dignity" would allow him to take any part in the new system.[72] The retiring Minister had of course no illusions about the hostility of Pitt toward the Newcastle–Rockingham political connection. The Great Man wished to dissolve all "factions." The old corps tactic was aimed at thwarting this intention by quiet acquiescence, support, and the maintenance of influence within the new system. Among them, however, much resentment abounded, and the Marquis himself breached the rule by losing his temper over Pitt's uncommunicativeness during the long period of arranging his system. "There seems to be much anger among many at the total silence of Mr. Pitt," he wrote on July 26, ". . . neither directly or indirectly thro' either Conway or the D[uke] of Grafton any mark of civility or even desiring or wishing for their concurrence has as yet been made." [73] When Pitt called in Grosvenor Square the next day the Marquis spitefully declined to see him. Pitt had come to make the long-awaited explanations.[74] A little later they met at court and Rockingham was reported as saying to the new Earl of Chatham that on first view the refusal to see him might have appeared improper, but that he had only to recollect his inattention and disregard to see that the refusal was justified. Burke observed on July 29 that "an ill humour, very contrary to the spirit of support, and yet not vigorous enough for the spirit of opposition, got up, and grows every day." Not until November, however, was the party tactic altered. Three days after his dismissal Rockingham held a dinner at his house with a company formed of "outs" and "ins." It would have been a larger affair had the host not feared giving alarm without serving a purpose.[75]

Before leaving town the Marquis returned Chatham's call and the latter declared himself "extremely obliged to Lord Rockingham's goodness for allowing him the pleasure of kissing his hands before he sets out for Yorkshire." [76]

NOTES

1. W. L. Grant and J. Munro, edd., *Acts of the Privy Council,* Colonial Series (8 vols.; Hereford, 1908–1910), IV 732.

2. Various unnumbered papers in WWM R 34 and 35; R 1: 512, 513, 515, 519, 526, 2137; Add. MSS 32971, ff. 13–14, 85; 38717, f. 100; *Grenville* III 221. Rockingham paid his private secretary Burke £150 from the secret service fund "for obtaining various informations & materials relative to the Trade & Manufactures."—R 15: 1.

3. WWM R 49: 6.

4. WWM R 1: 535, 537. Burke's words were written, after Rockingham's death, on the back of a copy of the circular letter.

5. On 12 Dec. he wrote to Newcastle that the disorders at New York would "oblige us to mention N[orth] A[merica] by name in the Speech."— Add. MS 32972, f. 214.

6. *Hist. Parl.* I 314; II 393.

7. *Chatham* II 353–358; WWM R 1: 549; *Corr. Burke* I 224.

8. Add. MS 32973, ff. 11–12.

9. King to Bute 10 Jan.—Sedgwick, *Letters,* Nos. 243–244; Albemarle I 264–265.

10. WWM R 2: 32.

11. *Grafton,* 63; *Corr. George III,* Nos. 183, 184. At 2 A.M. 11 Jan. Rockingham wrote to Newcastle: "I think it is determined that *no* letter should be wrote to Mr. Pitt signifying that His Majesty would see him on the N[orth] A[merican] matter etc. Whether if *he* comes to town soon the King will or will not call him to his Closet after a levee, is not determined, the D. of Grafton & Conway much press it. I have but little hopes that this storm will blow over."—Add. MS 32973, f. 119.

12. Add. MS 35430, f. 29. "Mr. Pitt is expected in town every day. When he comes one thing more will arise. His Grace of Grafton continues very anxious & I fear nothing will calm his Grace. . . . My head & feelings have been so agitated."—Rockingham to Newcastle, 12 Jan., Add. MS 32973, f. 119.

13. Sedgwick, *Letters,* No. 245.

14. WWM R 2: 26.

15. *Corr. George III,* Nos. 178, 201, 202, 324 (dates corrected by Namier in *Additions*) ; Jucker, *Jenkinson Papers,* 404–408.

16. *Grafton,* 64–68.

17. Add. MS 32973, ff. 174–175. Had Pitt agreed to the only terms on which it was possible at this time for him to take office, the Yorkes would have gone into opposition.—*Ibid.,* 35639, f. 333. WWM R 1: 557 shows the strategy of approach to Pitt. The King would place direction of his affairs in Pitt's hands but not dissolve the ministry; Newcastle would stay and Pitt was to be shown that the Duke had no overriding influence; Temple must not be proposed for the Treasury even as a gesture since "it would be an unbecoming request, to desire Lord Rockingham to continue in office dependent on the option of Lord Temple." According to Grafton, he and the Marquis after starting out to see Pitt turned back to see the King who said that the Duke's understanding of the royal intention was correct; but Rockingham's testimony after meeting with Pitt suggests that the paper cited here controlled the overture.

18. "Lord R.'s account of what passed with Mr. Pitt."—Add. MS 32873, ff. 194–196.

19. *Corr. George III,* No. 209.

20. WWM R 1: 559; *Chatham* III 6. Rockingham told the King that "the whole passed in very good humour."—*Corr. George III*, No. 213.

21. Add. MS 35430, ff. 21–32.

22. *Corr. George III*, No. 212.

23. WWM R 1: 560.

24. Add. MSS 32973, f. 262; 35430, ff. 37–38 (printed in Albemarle I 287–288).

25. Add. MS 32973, f. 305.

26. *Corr. George III*, No. 216. According to Lord Charlemont who heard the debate Pitt's words gave great alarm and Sir Fletcher Norton said that he "deserved no less than the Tower . . . his conduct is in general blamed, and the cry is that whatever may hereafter happen in America, he is to be esteem'd the author of it—this Norton asserted, and seemingly with the approbation of the generality."—Add. MS 32930, ff. 12–13. Lord Hardwicke heard the debate and wrote: "The Great Commoner never laid himself so open, never asserted such absurd & pernicious doctrines."—*Ibid.*, 35361, f. 261. According to Lord George Sackville the rumor that Pitt would soon take over administration now subsided: ". . . in general his conduct in this transaction has hurt him with his warmest friends."—Hist. MSS Comm. 9th *Report* App. III 22.

27. *Grenville* III 353–356; *Bedford* III 326–327; *Corr. George III*, No. 219; WWM R 1: 566 (printed in Albemarle I 294).

28. WWM R 1: 563–565, 567; Add. MS 32973, ff. 338–339.

29. Dartmouth MS D.1448.V.221.B.

30. Add. MS 32973, ff. 383–384.

31. Lord Strange's account is given in *Grenville* III 364–366. Another and perhaps more accurate account is found in Dartmouth's diary (Dartmouth MS D.1448.V.221.B) which is in almost exact accord with the little slips of paper which passed between the King and Rockingham and are preserved in WWM R 161. For the King's account see *Corr. George III*, No. 248.

32. Add. MS 32974, ff. 5–6. It is possible that the whole episode was caused by Lord Strange's misunderstanding of the King's words.

33. *Ibid.*, ff. 65–66.

34. Lord Edmond Fitzmaurice, *Life of William, Earl of Shelburne* (2 vols.; London, 1875–1876), I 261–262, 377–383; *Chatham* II 397–402.

35. *Corr. Burke* I 241.

36. Add. MS 32974, ff. 105–107.

37. WWM R 2: 40; Add. MS 35420, f. 41.

38. To William Weddell (Ramsden MSS [Central Library, Leeds] 1: 11).

39. *Corr. Burke* I 248.

40. *Chatham* II 390.

41. *Memoirs* II 215.

42. WWM R 153: 16; *Corr. Burke* I 251; Add. MS 32974, ff. 417–423.

43. *Ibid.*, ff. 370–371; WWM R 1: 599.

44. Grafton to Conway, 22 April.—*Grafton*, 71–72.

45. *Bedford* III 333.

46. *Corr. Burke* I 252.

47. Albemarle I 322; WWM R 1: 605.

48. *Corr. George III*, No. 301; Sedgwick, *Letters*, Nos. 246–247. Rumor abounded that with the repeal question disposed of Pitt would act again

with his brothers-in-law. According to Newcastle, Conway after meeting with Pitt on 29 April told the King that Pitt thought that there should be a total change and that if he were called to form a ministry he would be against all parties or connections and would take the best and ablest men of them all.—Newcastle, *Narrative, 57–58.*

49. Add. MS 32975, ff. 52, 58–59.

50. *Corr. George III,* Nos. 301–305.

51. Add. MS 32975, f. 72.

52. *Corr. George III,* No. 307.

53. Sedgwick, *Letters,* Nos. 246–250.

54. *Chatham* II 414; *Corr. George III,* No. 307.

55. Newcastle, *Narrative,* 65.

56. Not until mid-January did he speak in the Lords. "I am pleased that Opposition has forced you to hear your own voice, which I hope will encourage you to stand forth in other debates."—The King to Rockingham 20 Jan. (WWM R 1: 559).

57. Newcastle, *Narrative,* 67.

58. His history with a selection of his letters is given by Alison Olson, *The Radical Duke* (London, 1961).

59. *Corr. George III,* No. 309.

60. Add. MS 32975, f. 195.

61. *Corr. George III,* No. 308.

62. Add. MS 32975, ff. 254–257; Newcastle, *Narrative,* 66–69.

63. *Manuscripts of the Earl of Dartmouth* (Hist. MSS Comm. 15th *Report* App. V 182).

64. Albemarle I 347.

65. WWM R 1: 589.

66. *Corr. George III,* Nos. 317, 319; WWM R 1: 622.

67. *Corr. George III,* No. 316; Add. MS 32975, ff. 287, 291; WWM R 1: 622.

68. *Corr. George III,* Nos. 330, 334, 335.

69. Add. MS 32975, ff. 440, 505. A sign to the public of their total independence of Bute seemed especially necessary at this moment because of the publication of John Almon's *History of the Late Minority,* which alleged that the Marquis and his friends had been the dupes of Bute and lacked the courage to dismiss his dependents or to oppose his influence.

70. Add. MS 32975, ff. 521–530.

71. Add. MS 32976, ff. 19–20, 48; WWM R 147 : 6.

72. Charles Yorke was asked to keep his office, but declined; his brother John resigned from the Admiralty board.

73. Add. MS 32976, f. 253.

74. Before the day was out Rockingham knew what Pitt had intended and sent him a coldly explanatory rather than apologetic letter.—WWM R 1: 659, printed in Albemarle II 5.

75. *Grenville* III 290; *Corr. Burke* I 262; Add. MS 32976, f. 346.

76. WWM R 1: 671.

5

Strategist of Party

THERE WAS A STRIKING CONTRAST between the public compliments showered upon Rockingham in the summer of 1766 and the abuse which fell upon the Great Commoner when it was known that he had quit the arena of popular representation in order to be a lord. As Earl of Chatham he was lampooned in the press and attacked scurrilously. A cry was raised that he had made himself the tool of the hated Favorite.

> To turn the Heart of P[itt] Ah! Who could do it?
> None but the Northern Thane, the mighty B[u]te.[1]

At Wentworth Rockingham observed "how universally the Torrent runs against the late Great Commoner." It sharpened his relish for the complimentary addresses he himself was receiving. The stream of these had started in the spring and swollen in the summer. The mayor and commonalty of Liverpool voted an address to him on July 6 and the freedom of the city was offered two weeks later. The London merchants trading to North America and the West Indies adopted a flattering address on August 4. The city of York gave him a public reception on August 17, and at York Races deputations came to him with addresses from Leeds, Sheffield, Hull, Halifax, and Wakefield. Typical was the thanks of the "Merchants, Traders, Manufacturers and other Inhabitants" of Sheffield

> for your unwearied and laudable Endeavours in your late high office in the Public Administration exerted in the most constitutional manner in the support of civil Liberty, and in the Advancement of the Commercial Interests of these Kingdoms by removing the Embarrassments in which Trade had been lately involved and by opening and establishing upon a firm Basis, a System of Commerce liberal and beneficial.

The merchants of Lancaster addressed in September, as did those of Liverpool, Leicester, and Manchester. The "Merchants, Gentlemen, and Citizens of York" presented an expression of gratitude signed by many members of the Rockingham Club.[2] Nor did all such expressions come from the municipal and mercantile interest. "A Plain Country Gentleman" addressed him in the *British Chronicle* as "forever distinguished by the epithets of the *good* and *virtuous Minister*" who had been turned out "by the joint Machinations of a factious Demagogue, and an ambitious and overbearing Thane."[3] Velters Cornewall (a tory) wrote: "We Country Squires, My Lord, often & boldly say that modern Ministers are Jockeys but you are called a good high-bred Racer."[4] It is probable that nearly a quarter of the county members of Parliament—representative of the gentry—were favorable (after their whig or tory manner) to the Marquis.[5] So many of the complimentary addresses and his replies got into the press that Lord Hardwicke wrote: "You are really beating the late Great C[ommoner] at his own weapons & receiving those Eulogiums which his Buffs have hitherto supposed that no-body was entitled to but himself."[6]

Rockingham relished all this. It added to the zest he felt in returning into Yorkshire which he had not seen for nearly a year. His lord lieutenancies and other county honors had

been restored to him, and none could doubt the primacy of
the Master of Wentworth in his native county. The Duke of
York attended York Races, was "all politeness," and in mid-
September visited Wentworth. Chatham's nomination of the
Marquis' close friend Sir Charles Saunders as First Lord of
the Admiralty wore the appearance of a friendly gesture,
and Rockingham continued "anxious that we & our friends
should be quiet & that our only object should be to keep up
a good humour with those parts of the present system who
are parts of ours." [7] There was much political talk at Wentworth, and the Marquis told Portland on August 29:

> My line of conversation on political subjects is, *to commend
> all those with whom I had the honour to be called into Ad-
> ministration*—to represent the D. of Grafton and Genl. Con-
> way as only differing with many of us, on the single subject
> of their opinion of the late Mr. Pitt—& I venture to abuse
> Lord Temple as the worst of men—& Mr. G. Grenville as the
> worst of ministers for this country's service.
> As to Lord Bute & the Lady [Dowager Princess] of Wales
> I give them the credit of being the secret spring of the late
> events & continue on this subject the calm contempt, by which
> it is said I gave offence when in office.[8]

He could not know that Bute had no part in the late alterations, and there was plausibility in this notion of the "secret
spring." Had not he been pressed by the court to ally with
the Butes after Pitt's support was withdrawn? George III
had shown the previous winter great aversion to giving Pitt
the full power of administration. Why had he afterward
done exactly that? What with Chatham's separation from
his Grenville brothers-in-law and the probability of opposition from them, it seemed to Rockingham that he would
have to throw himself upon the Butes or "be very much
reconciled to us." The latter course seemed less and less
likely as days and weeks passed. By mid-September Newcastle reported hearing from Conway that more removals
would be made and that some "would be very disagreeable
to us." It was said that the Duke of Portland would be asked

for his staff as lord chamberlain. Lord Monson, a cousin of the Marquis, was asked to exchange his justiceship in eyre for an elevation in the peerage. By October 7 Newcastle was groaning that "every day produces fresh instance of the sacrifice of our best friends." [9]

Rockingham spent several days at Newmarket in late September and then went to town, where he dined with Conway who had "uneasy feels" on the subject of politics. He went to court and found the King "very gracious," saw Newcastle at Claremont, and traveled to Bath where Lady Rockingham was nursing herself; returning, he stopped with Dowdeswell in Worcestershire and made "a tour ending in Newmarket's meeting." [10] Back at Wentworth, he wrote to Burke on November 1: "I reserve all political speculations till we meet. I own I think speculation is as far as the present state of politics can lead to, as I do not yet see data enough to form a direct judgment upon." [11] Ten days later Parliament was opened.

Rockingham and Newcastle urged their friends to attend, as expected supporters of administration, the meetings of commoners at Conway's house and of peers at Grafton's, to hear the speech and address before the official opening of the session. A bad harvest, resultant scarcity of food and widespread rioting, an embargo by order in council on the export of grain, were stated in the speech as the reason for an early summoning of Parliament. There seemed no catchhold for an opposition in this business. "The public talk and newspapers," observed Lord Hardwicke, "are full of harmony and accommodation." Newcastle, whose duchess was said to be enthusiastic for Chatham, by this time thought that the party had been treated "tolerably well" and could not foresee anything his friends were likely to disapprove. [12] According to Burke, Lord Rockingham intended a support of government which would be "more or less vigorous as my Lord Chatham shows himself better or worse inclined to the party." A good inclination had just been shown by Conway's telling Burke of an intention to make "offers that would be pleasing" to him. That Burke, and presumably his chief too, could envisage the possibility of a withdrawal of support from the Chatham administration, was shown in his telling Conway that he could accept only on the condition that he would "belong not to the administration, but to those who were out":

> . . . therefore if ever they should set up a standard, though spread for direct and personal opposition, I must be revocable into their party, and join it.[13]

On November 17 the event occurred which Rockingham seized upon for drawing the line between administration and party. Lord Edgecumbe, created Treasurer of the Household during the previous administration, was removed and his office given to John Shelley, a nephew of Newcastle's. Edgecumbe disposed of five seats in the House of Commons and had but recently brought a nephew of Conway's into Parliament. Conway protested sharply to Chatham, saying that he would resign rather than concur "in such repeated injuries to those with whom I have lately acted . . . as I understood that far from being objects of particular neglect or resentment, they would rather, in preference, meet the favour and protection of government under the present administration." After penning those words, the General sent a message asking Rockingham to call. Here, the Marquis judged, was a situation to exploit. There should be a rally of friends to encourage Conway to hold his ground or come out, and Rockingham suspected that the General's conduct would depend "on ours." He collected a group of friends on November 19 and all agreed that something should be done "to shew spirit, to keep our friends together, and to encourage Mr. Conway to persist in the good disposition he was in at present." Several peers holding offices, headed by Lord Chamberlain the Duke of Portland, would inform Conway of their intention to resign if satisfaction were not accorded Lord Edgecumbe. If this threat failed of the desired results a general call-out of friends was to follow, and if it came to that Rockingham's friends hoped that Conway would resign; which must either dish Chatham or force him to terms. It was generally (and correctly) believed at this time that Chatham had opened a negotiation with the Duke of Bedford, which signified more weeding-out of Rockingham–Newcastle people; so that dramatic resignations *en corps* might be better than tame submission to being turned out one by one. In addition to the peers (Portland, Bessborough, Monson, Scarborough), there were fourteen Rockingham–Newcastle followers in the House of Commons who at this moment held court and administrative offices. Half of these were of Newcastle's old corps, the rest being connected more closely with Rockingham. The old Duke feared letting this challenge to Chatham go to the point of calling for resignations because he suspected that it would fail, as his call-out had failed in 1762.[14] Dowdeswell advised Rockingham that the removal of a man from a court office was not the right occasion for the party to take up arms: "As a party plan it would certainly be ineffectual and I believe would be disavowed." [15]

On November 21 Portland gave Conway a three-day party ultimatum to lay before Chatham. The terms were: 1. Immediate satisfaction to Edgcumbe; 2. assurance of regard and respect to the party; 3. Chatham's admittance of Conway "to that confidence and those communications which could alone give us security for any promises that might be made in the present exigancy." [16] Conway agreed to take up the matter with Chatham. If satisfactory assurances could be extracted Rockingham thought (or pretended to think) that all would be well:

> I think then that we may have the opportunity of bringing the Great Man to form an honourable, firm, and lasting plan; and that we may now render our friends in administration safe, restore or compensate Lord Edgecumbe, and perhaps put administration upon the foot which has always been my desire . . . that I may *enjoy* Yorkshire, and feel the satisfaction of thinking that I have co-operated in establishing a solid, and an able, and a *prudent* Administration.[17]

It may appear that Rockingham had gotten into cloud-cuckoo-land, since no idea could have been more remote from the practical order; but it must be remembered that the King's purpose, which Chatham aimed at realizing—namely, the annihilation of all political factions by a comprehensive administration raised above party—had never been publicly avowed. The Marquis could not know that his own aims were in diametric opposition to the resolution of his sovereign. About this time he made, or had made, a sort of political census of the House of Commons. It showed 225 dependable supporters of Chatham's administration, 121 Rockingham–Newcastle whigs, 17 Grenvilles, 35 Bedfords, 86 tories, 69 doubtful, and 5 unclassified.[18] Given the lights he had, it was not wildly unrealistic for Rockingham to hope that Chatham might see that his own interest lay in standing well with the 121. Late at night on November 21 the Marquis wrote to Newcastle:

> The present reports are, that Lord Chatham's treaty with the Bedfords is over. I hear the Bedfords are enquiring whether we are growing angry & probably that surmize has stopped them from contracting with Lord Chatham & may be the occasion, that some accommodation will be proposed to keep us in good humour. We must act with firmness.[19]

The next day he learned that an act of stupidity had been done. Lord Bessborough, thinking perhaps of an easy way to resign his office of joint postmaster, had gone to Conway with the proposal that Edgecumbe take it, while he would accept the lordship of the bedchamber which had been offered as a solace to Edgecumbe. The news was the more shocking from the fact that Bessborough had mentioned this to Rockingham before proposing it to Conway and had been told that "it would not answer any one purpose." On going at once to see Conway, the Marquis was further taken aback by learning that the General, catching for a straw, "had conceived hopes that we would be satisfied by Lord Chatham's consenting to this proposal." Actually, Chatham had already rejected it, but Conway seems not to have been candid enough to say so. Rockingham made it clear that Bessborough's idea had no authorization from heads of party, that "such a plaister" could not "cure the wounds of the affronts we had received in the persons of some of our friends." He was in an indignant state, heightened still more by Conway's saying that Lord Monson would have to give up his office, although after that "nothing further would be done to make us uneasy & if there was we might resent." [20] The Marquis could hardly doubt now that Conway meant to stay in office no matter how Chatham behaved. Two days later the ultimatum expired without an answer.

Resignations were delayed a little but in the House of Commons some new signals were called. Hitherto Dowdeswell, Burke, Lord John Cavendish, and other friends of Rockingham had refrained from any gesture of opposition. Now, on November 24–25, they joined with the Grenvilles to force a modification of the ministerial bill for an indemnity which was necessitated by the embargoing of grain exports without legal authorization. They also opposed a ministry-supported motion by William Beckford for a committee to inquire into the affairs of the East India Company. Beckford, no minister, was known to be a kind of parliamentary agent for Chatham. Rockinghams, Grenvilles, and Bedfords succeeded in so amending the motion as to prevent laying of the company's papers before the House. There is no proof that Rockingham's friends were sparked into activity by party council: "You cannot think with what spirit and system our little corps went on," recorded Edmund Burke, ". . . without the least previous consultation or concert between ourselves." [21] Nevertheless, a body wounded by Chatham had struck back. That night Rockingham sent a note to Portland:

> This event makes it in my opinion very necessary, that the answer to your Grace should be received early tomorrow morning, that according to it, the step if necessary of resignation, should be carried into execution *tomorrow*.[22]

The next day (November 26) Conway transmitted to Portland Chatham's flat refusal of the terms of the ultimatum,
and left the Duke under the impression that he would not
stay long in an administration which, upon Chatham's principles, could not long **continue. Followed the** resignations of
four peers (Portland, Monson, Bessborough, Scarborough)
on November 27. "What will happen, I cannot ascertain,"
wrote Rockingham to Charles Yorke, "but as long as our
friends act with honour & spirit, I shall ever think they do
right & I am sure this step in that light is necessary." [23] The
following day Sir Charles Saunders resigned the Admiralty
along with two members of his board, Augustus Keppel and
Sir William Meredith.

That was the end of the string. Newcastle had great misgivings over this tactic of resignations and only because it
was "a measure" adopted by his friends did he support it;
but none of his six nephews in office would go out. Rockingham observed to him "how many of your Grace's friends
divide their affection & let Lord Chatham in for part." A
longer string, however, could have had no greater effect unless it had included Conway and Charles Townshend. The
Marquis was at the moment more concerned over revived
reports of an administration treaty with the Bedfords, for
it would hardly be possible to defend the tactic of resignations if it merely opened places for them. If that treaty
failed, however, it seemed that Chatham must fill up the
vacancies with reputed friends of Bute and thus damage his
system in the public eye. Although Rockingham nowhere
spelled out a strategy of throwing Chatham into an apparent
dependence on the detested Scotch peer, this may well have
been his aim. On November 29 he wrote: "The last three
days have been days of suspence, in regard to the determination what the Bedfords *would* do . . . tho' in general the
opinion is that they will accept." [24] Burke thought that they
"must be mad" to refuse the offers being made to them. At
this time Lord Lyttelton proposed to Rockingham a union
with the Grenvilles in a combined opposition drawing in the
Bedfords. The proposal was rejected, partly because the

Marquis never would ally with George Grenville against Henry Conway, partly because such a union instead of drawing in the Bedfords was more likely to deliver them to Chatham. In the end the Chatham–Bedford treaty foundered and the vacant offices were filled by men of no party ties. Some were so-called Butes.

George Grenville's view was that "all this looks so like Lord Bute and Lord Chatham having an understanding together, that it can no longer be doubted." Temple and Bedford were equally sure it was so. Newcastle wrote to Rockingham: "Lord Chatham . . . has flung himself absolutely into my Lord Bute; & from thence hopes (which he will certainly find) for protection & support at Court." [25] All but the few who were in a position to know how wildly untrue this was, appear to have believed it. Rockingham hoped that it would serve his aims: "Every day, more and more [he observed to Portland] Lord Chatham's union and dependence on Lord Bute will appear & I should hope will occasion some of our friends now in office to reconsider the propriety of remaining." [26] To Newcastle on the same day (December 4) the Marquis said:

> Every event which has since happened confirms me the more strongly in the opinion that it [the resignations] was right, necessary and indeed unavoidable. . . . I think good consequences will ensue. . . . I still hope that a little time may bring these matters to a right termination & that we shall soon be again *all* or *nearly* all together.[27]

Rockingham had no idea, however, of leading a united whig party into opposition against the existing administration. He wished to create enough difficulty to undermine the King's confidence in Chatham as prime minister, yet he desired to keep on the best terms with Grafton, Conway, and Charles Townshend who were the executive instruments of Chatham's will. The latter two ministers were personal friends of the Marquis. Conway was a vastly respected man and Townshend had great parliamentary talents. Neither was contented with the way Chatham conducted administration. Townshend had had to force his way into the cabinet, and Conway, although the King's minister in the House of Commons, actually admitted in the House on December 9 that he was a mere "passenger" in the administration. Whig ministers had an ingrained dislike of an aloof and lofty minister-master who made servants of colleagues and monopolized the influence of the crown. Rockingham hoped to exploit this dislike and somehow to support friends in office while opposing Chatham; all the while making it more uncomfortable for those friends to stay in an administration which was publicly libeled as the agency of Lord Bute. Tactical operations in such a strategy had to depend, however, on opportunities which the Marquis could not create, and it was certain to be very hard to obtain a concerted approval of that strategy by his friends. Newcastle was for an alliance with the Bedfords as an initial step toward a united opposition of whigs, Bedfords, and Grenvilles, to play the game of uniting the "outs" against the "ins." On the other hand, the Yorkes preferred an association with the Grenvilles, as did Sir William Meredith. Rockingham liked better the counsels of Dowdeswell, the Cavendish brothers, and the Duke of Portland, which were more in line with his own opinions. He told Newcastle and Bessborough on December 17 that he wished his friends to avoid the appearance of systematic opposition and to oppose only on points "that were wrong in themselves & not inconsistent with our former behaviour." A union of opposition groups would raise George Grenville to the leadership of them in the House of Commons: the whigs had no one who could dispute his claim to it. If such an opposition prevailed it might open the way for Grenville's return to the Treasury. The Marquis said that "it was not consistent with their honour & consciences, to be bringing Mr. Grenville back into that office where he had conducted himself, in a manner that had been so much blamed by them; & had produced the very contrary behaviour in the last Treasury." Rockingham conceded that, abstractly considered, an alliance with the Bedfords would be worthwhile, if they could be separated from Temple and

Grenville. He even consented to a cautious sounding of Bedford dispositions, but before this was done the Duke of Portland wrote to Newcastle that such an overture would reveal weakness and over-anxiety, that the Bedfords would demand too much, and that the "uprightness and disinterestedness" by which the party of the late administration had gained great credit would appear "warped by an eagerness after power and emoluments." Newcastle was sobered by this expression, which Rockingham said tallied "greatly with my own sentiments." On December 19, just before going north for the holiday, the Marquis wrote to the old Pelhamite chief:

> I look upon it now as fixed that we should wait for & not be the makers of overtures, which indeed *Your Grace knows has always been my opinion.* . . . I am clear that by acting on such a plan, we shall always feel happy & justified in our own minds & I think it will ensure the continuance of the publick good opinion. Perhaps adhering to such a plan will not accelerate success, but if it ever does succeed, it will be on a foundation, which will not afterwards be easily shaken.[28]

No other course was consistent with the purpose of reuniting whigs, and maintaining the kind of reputation necessary to win public and royal confidence. A day or two after writing the words just quoted, Lord Lyttelton proposed to Rockingham a union with the Grenvilles to draw into combination all who opposed the existing administration. The overture was bluntly rebuffed. Relating the story to Dowdeswell (the designated leader of the whig corps in Commons), the Marquis wrote:

> I acknowledged that I thought the state of us & our friends viewed through political glasses would appear a forlorn hope & that no immediate success could be expected, but that on the other hand we were not in an uncomfortable situation, because every dictate of honour & principle encouraged us to persevere on the same plan which we had done before.[29]

Of all his political friends Rockingham probably was best
understood by William Dowdeswell, and between these men
there was an intimacy and shared outlook which only the
death of the latter would terminate. Perhaps the Marquis
spelled out his high strategy to Dowdeswell; there is no record of his having done so to anyone else. Not even Burke, if
he knew it, believed in it since he wrote at this time that he
could not conceive that "we shall rise" by Chatham's fall.
Rockingham's method he characterized as "barren and unproductive." Its only merits were that

> the walk is certain; there are no contradictions to reconcile;
> no cross points of honour or interest to adjust; all is clear
> and open; and the wear and tear of mind, which is saved by
> keeping aloof from crooked politics, is a consideration absolutely
> inestimable.[30]

II

With the exception of Burke's *Short Account of a Late
Short Administration* Rockingham's friends had issued no
printed address of any kind to the public. The time was approaching when they would make careful use of the published
word to influence the thinking of men, but as yet they remained hardly aware of a political nation beyond the halls
of Parliament and therefore had small appreciation of the
press as a political instrument. Moreover, they had few men
capable of writing for publication. Dowdeswell during December was at work on a pamphlet to defend the late administration. "I am apt to think," he told Burke, "we suffer much
at present for want of our tale being told." He gave a portion of his manuscript to Burke for criticism and suggestion,
and when the latter traveled north with Rockingham to
Portland at Welbeck during the Christmas holiday he took
it along. The Marquis took it on to Wentworth for study.
Dowdeswell wished to have it "well-considered, examined &
corrected by others & send it forth to the press." All that is

known of Burke's advice is that he thought it would be "sufficient to damn the Stamp Act as a scheme of revenue, that it would require an army to enforce obedience to it." Rockingham, although suggesting caution on the subject of paring funds for the navy and militia, told Dowdeswell on January 7: "I like it most exceedingly & wish the publick was in possession of it." For some reason which does not appear the public never saw it.[31]

In the newspaper press, however, someone—very probably Burke—broke the proud silence of the Rockinghams. The treatment of Admiral Keppel, a naval hero and close friend of the late Duke of Cumberland, served as the provocation. After his resignation from the Admiralty board Keppel had been dismissed as a groom of the bedchamber and made the target of inspired attacks in the press. A partisan of the late administration retaliated with a letter of heavy Burkeian irony in the *Public Advertiser* after December 24:

> . . . in this Age of a large Way of thinking, private Honour and private Friendships are become public Crimes; and it was fit that a Person, who possessed both in so high a Degree, and was daring enough to avow them, should be distinguished by the Severity of his Punishment. . . . It was altogether in the Spirit of this manly Administration, that Examples should be made of People of that Cast. It was fit that every Friend of the Duke of Cumberland should be proscribed, and that every friend of the Earl of B[ut]e should be cherished and rewarded.
>
> One of the Gentlemen remarked the other Day in your Paper, and very well, that Lord C[hatham] considers nothing but Merit in the Appointment to Offices, and that he is determined to dissolve all Parties and Connections of Men.
>
> It happens very oddly, but fortunately I suppose, that these Men of Merit should be found no where but in the *Corps* of Lord B[u]te; amongst the Friends of a certain *adequate* Peace; amongst the Advocates for, and Inventors of, private Excise; the Asserters of General Warrants; the Defenders of American Stamp Acts; among Men who never gave a single Vote in concurrence with his Sentiments during their whole lives.
>
> It happens also very fortunately that the Weak, the Factious,

the Furious, the Unreasonable, should be found only among
that Set of Men, who opposed all or most of those Measures
whilst they were out, and reverted them when they came into
Power. If the Character of our illustrious and sole Minister
were not too well established, one might suspect (with some
wicked People) that it was safer to have contradicted his
Principles than not to have benefitted his Ambition; because his
Principles are only fictitious, and his Ambition real; but this is
a way of Reasoning never practised by those wrong headed
People, who would undertake to judge of a Man's Sentiments
by the most fallacious of all Standards—his Acts. . . .

On reading this Newcastle wrote to Rockingham calling it
"one of the justest, severest, & most ingenious papers I ever
read; I wish I knew the author, as well as your Lordship
does." [32]

Meanwhile, Rockingham had gone to Wentworth via
Portland's at Welbeck and Savile's at Rufford. At the former's he saw John White, an old and honorable friend of
Newcastle who had been in Parliament for more than thirty
years, thought the whigs should "stand on their own bottom," and that it made no difference how small that bottom
was, "provided the world have a good opinion of the men."
Meredith had joined the councils at Welbeck and John Hew-
ett, a member for Nottinghamshire, was at Rufford. All
these men Rockingham found to be "as right as can be . . .
in point of honour & determination, in point of spirit &
temper. Peevish opposition they will not support, neither will
they decline taking just opportunities of showing themselves." [33] Savile, an old admirer of the Great Commoner,
was perhaps a little uneasy. A political individualist with the
natural disposition of an independent county member, he
dreaded the kind of politics which ran to "a devlish stroke, a
fine topic of conversation, popular, etc." There were so many
people who did not comprehend that there was no sense in
merely "pulling down, coming in, etc., without considering
what footing they must come in upon or how long they could
last, or whether they would have it in their power to do any
one good thing." He thought that "a warm ingenious zealous

friend" had been "a little upon the slapdash," and urged
Rockingham to "put him in mind now & then of our wise &
cold deliberations & my cold hesitations in your cold room.
Pray don't keep your rooms too hot." [34] This little thrust
was at Burke who was not quite satisfied with his chief's
political course although for reasons the opposite of Savile's.
Intensely hostile to Chatham he was perhaps the most eager
of Rockingham's friends for office. Proud of their "fairness
of character," he could not but regret that this militated
against their "practicability"; and he saw their cause as
"desperate" from inability to coalesce "with any body in or
out of possession." [35]

Rockingham interpreted the circumstances of early 1767
as offering a measure of hope. Chatham had gone away with
something like a nervous breakdown, and with the reopening
of Parliament it became evident that his ministerial agents
had no relish for carrying out his vague and undefined intentions with respect to the East India Company. If his system
broke from inner strain, or if illness forced him to give up
direction of the King's affairs, the Marquis thought it not
improbable that such men as Grafton, Conway, and Townshend would exert themselves toward reconstituting the late
administration. Rockingham was on excellent personal terms
with the King, which could not be said of George Grenville,
Lord Temple, and the Duke of Bedford; and Majesty was
likely to think the better of the Marquis if the latter avoided
an unprincipled combination with these leaders for the purpose of hamstringing government and storming the closet.
Finally, he really believed that George III must ultimately
learn the wisdom of placing his affairs in the hands of whiggery's most reputable men, the natural-born advisers of the
crown and custodians of the liberties and securities of the
people.

The tactic in Parliament now was to move nothing and
avoid voting against Conway. The Rockinghams did not
even intervene in debate on January 26 when Charles Townshend was provoked by Grenville to defend parliamentary
taxation of America and to commit the Exchequer to raising

an American revenue.[36] Not until the next month was a motion concerted against administration. Designed to gratify
the "country gentlemen" in Parliament, it was for a reduction of the land tax from the war-time level of four shillings
in the pound to three. At a meeting of friends in Grosvenor
Square on February 11 Dowdeswell proposed it, arguing
that government could afford the reduction, that the ministry
was certain to move it the next year, that it would be warmly
supported, and that if they did not anticipate him George
Grenville would be the mover. All possible calls went out to
get men on hand for the day of the Chancellor of the Exchequer's budget. Not all of Rockingham's friends relished
the plan. Burke gave no opinion on it and the event was to
show that he would not vote for it. Lord Albemarle was
against it, and Admiral Keppel told Newcastle that "if Mr.
Dowdeswell moved it, he believed he should be for it; but if
Mr. Grenville moved it he should certainly be against it."
That such a motion should originate in Rockingham's councils seems hardly consistent with his general aim, but it was
always his instinct to support rather than to direct his friends
in Parliament. He must have known that so popular a motion was likely to be carried and naturally preferred that
Dowdeswell rather than Grenville should make it. White,
Baker, Meredith, and Dowdeswell met with the Marquis on
February 21 when it was settled that on the appointed day
Dowdeswell should seize the earliest moment to speak, in
order, as Rockingham told Newcastle, "to intercept the
possible popularity falling to G. Grenville." Six days later
when Townshend, minister for the Treasury in Commons,
proposed a continuation of four shillings, Dowdeswell
moved the reduction and Grenville seconded; on the division
administration was in a minority of 188 to 206. According
to Burke, "the majority of the Rockinghams, the whole Bedfords and Grenvilles, reinforced by the almost complete band
of Tories, came into the field." [37] So large a House could
hardly have surprised the ministry, yet the historian of the
Chatham administration discovered no evidence of a mobilization of their supporters.[38] The King, to be sure, expressed

surprise to Grafton on the eve of the vote "that there should be a likelihood of a numerous opposition to the land tax," and called the Duke's precautions against it "highly meritorious";[39] but there is no evidence that Conway or Townshend exerted efforts to get men to the House. Since the division was in committee the matter could have been fought over again on the report, and there seems no answer to the question why that did not happen. Perhaps there was collusion between the ministers in the House of Commons and Lord Rockingham. That cannot be proved, but Conway and Townshend were friends of the Marquis and sharply at odds with Chatham. These ministers dined with Dowdeswell and Burke at Rockingham's on February 15 when the call was going out for the day of the budget; and that night all agreed to table a New York petition which seemed to throw some doubt on the Rockingham claim of having brought the colonies to tranquillity.[40] It is hard to believe that Townshend and Conway did not know what Rockingham's friends were up to on the land-tax question. Moreover, there are two letters written by Townshend to Rockingham about this time which seem perfectly consistent with the theory of collusion.[41]

Loss of the four-shilling land tax brought Chatham from Bath to Westminster. He came to discipline or cashier his agents, and even before his arrival (March 2) the King sounded the Earl of Bristol as a possible successor to Conway as Secretary of State. Chatham then offered the Exchequer to Lord North. He was angry not only over the defeat of February 27, but over the unwillingness of these ministers to execute his will with respect to the East India Company. He desired Parliament to vest the company's territorial right in the crown; both Townshend and Conway preferred a negotiation with the company for a share of its profits. Rockingham's intimacy with them enabled him to know the exact state of the interior of administration when he confided to Newcastle on March 5:

> Where my wishes are warm, I check myself for fear of disappointment, but I can not but think this Administration will

not last many days. What may come after I know not, but if
Chs. Townshend and Conway come out & to us, I think a
good Administration with prudence and temper may be
formed.[42]

The Marquis was mistaken in his estimate of things to
come. North declined the Exchequer, Chatham went away to
nurse himself incommunicado, and the ministry did not
break. The East India business was left in the hands of
ministers who preferred negotiation to coercion. Conway
could not bring himself to throw the King's affairs into confusion by resigning, and Townshend saw the way opened for
his own ascendancy. Rockingham did not despair of these
men, however, and persisted along his course of strategy, but
was hard-pressed by friends who wanted a solid union of
parties in opposition. There was a widespread but probably
false notion—inspired by the defeat of administration on the
land tax—that such a union could prevail, and so far from
reality were Newcastle, Bedford, Temple, and Grenville that
they could talk of the arrangement of offices in a new administration—as if George III were not George III! Newcastle tried to drive the Marquis along this road, but he
maintained his stand of the previous December: he would
accept the Bedfords, without Grenville, and only on his own
terms. "I am sorry to see," groaned the old Duke, "that nothing I say has the least weight with Lord Rockingham. . . .
I think Mr. Grenville necessary; His Lordship does not.
Time will show, who is in the right." He was so vexed and
angry that Albemarle told him, "it is very fortunate the
Marquis is so cool & moderate, or you must have quarrelled
long ago." In resisting Newcastle Rockingham appealed to
the necessity of acting with trusted friends, and when pressed
to name those who supported his stand he named Portland,
Albemarle, Scarborough, Dartmouth, Saunders, Keppel,
Dowdeswell, and the Cavendish brothers as friends without
whom he would take no step.[43] He might have added Lady
Rockingham who from Bath was in constant communication
during these days. "I beg you will consult Lady R. about
politics," wrote Savile from Rufford. "It will prejudice me

much in favour of your measures when I come." Political
success, opined Sir George, would "come with exceeding
grace if not snatched prematurely by impatient ones." [44] On
March 31 the Marquis wrote to his wife:

> . . . in my letter wrote tonight to Sir George Savile, I have
> told him that *he* must come, for that now that I have not *my
> Minerva* at my elbow I must beg my *mentor* to come.
>   You do justice to the honour & integrity of those with whom
> I am most strictly united in the political matters, when you do
> not think that they would wish or recommend to me, that I
> should give up in any degree my own consistency.[45]

His firmness was put to the test again soon afterward. On
April 7 Meredith gave notice in the House that, if no plan
or proposition should be offered by administration with respect to the East India Company, after so prolonged a parliamentary inquiry, he would the following week move to end
the inquiry. Rockingham called this "our plan" and summoned friends to be present on April 14. The Easter recess
was to follow, and the Marquis thought it "right to press for
some decision in this matter while the house is full, as administration have always the advantage when the house is
thin." [46] Here, then, was to be another test of what the whole
opposition might be able to do. On April 10, however, the
Duke of Bedford moved an address to the crown to take
into consideration an act of the Massachusetts Assembly
which had usurped the pardoning power of the crown. The
Lord Chancellor told the peers that this affair was still *sub
judice* and Grafton moved the previous question. In the debate Halifax censured Conway's conduct in the previous administration and was answered by Richmond. Bedford's motion failed by 63 to 36, and Rockingham voted with the
majority, as did Richmond, Dartmouth, Monson, and Edgecumbe; but fourteen whig peers including Newcastle, Portland, Winchilsea, Scarborough, Albemarle, Bessborough, and
Grantham, went away to avoid voting against their leader.[47]
The Marquis told his wife that "upon the whole it rather
appeared to me somewhat unfair & uncandid to the Admin-

istration." Newcastle was aghast at this affront to the Duke
of Bedford, whose friends in the House of Commons were
expected to support Meredith's motion. Hardwicke on the
following day told Lyttelton that he had no engagement
with the Marquis' whigs which could prevent himself and
his brother Charles Yorke from taking office with Grenville
and Temple. It was Burke's opinion that his chief's conduct
hurt the support of Meredith on April 14 when the latter's
motion failed by 213 to 167: the Marquis "did right un-
questionably; but an impression was given that weakened the
whole body." [48]

His strategy unchanged, Rockingham went off to Newmarket for the spring meeting, after confiding to his wife
that he had been heartened by a speech Charles Townshend
had made in favor of "a solid connected & strong administration composed of men of abilities & of men whose principles & whose forefathers etc. had been supporters of the
true constitution of this country." [49] In the races his famous
horse "Bay Malton" won £15,000 and another named
"Steady" outran the Duke of Grafton's "Pancake." The
King congratulated him on the win by "Bay Malton," and
the Marquis moralized a little on the subject to the fretting
Newcastle: "I thought & expected success with my *Bay Malton* & had that confirmation of the opinion which in all
occurrences I like to adhere to, namely that of trying to form
a judgment on good grounds & then abiding by it." [50] Burke
wrote to Lady Rockingham:

> As to the old Duke—Well! My Lord R.'s temper is the first
> of *his* virtues; I really believe, the first of political virtues.
> For to bear with such persons, yet not to yield to them; and
> against their will to make them in the end subservient to your
> great ends, is a matter of some praise. Every engine has been
> used to bring the Grenvillian system into vogue among the
> Rockinghams; but it is as far from being the fashion as ever.[51]

The "Rockinghams"—this word was fast coming into general use to designate the main body of whigs.

After Easter the affairs of America were brought into

Parliament. This was an unhappy event for the Rockinghams, not only because it showed that their boasts of having
restored concord to the empire were vain, but because it
made the Marquis' political strategy unworkable. Conway
and Townshend took different directions, and the latter proposed measures which Rockingham could not support without breaking his prized consistency. That legislative proposals respecting the colonies would be introduced was
generally expected. Two scandals were common knowledge:
the Massachusetts act pardoning Stamp Act rioters, and the
New York Assembly's refusal to obey the Mutiny Act's re-
quirement for supplying the King's troops. Rockingham's information led him to expect that a general bill would be
brought in to prohibit colonial governors from assenting to
legislative measures until assemblies had complied with the
Mutiny Act.[52] He also knew that Conway had not only refused to sponsor what was to be proposed but would disagree
with it. The business fell to Townshend who was known to
hold strong views on the subject of strengthening executive
government in the colonies. The day was to be May 5.

A council of Rockinghams (the Marquis, Richmond,
Meredith, Savile, and Lord John Cavendish) took place on
May 4. Presumably they planned to take shelter with Conway, and Rockingham was gratified to find that such great
lawyers as Mansfield and Charles Yorke disapproved the
expected bill. On the next day, however, it was revealed that
Lord North, the Paymaster, would open the business,
Townshend having been disabled by cutting his eye. A motion by Rigby to postpone the matter until May 13, perhaps
as a courtesy to Townshend, was carried. That the Rockinghams may have suspected the Chancellor of the Exchequer of wishing to evade a task which Conway had refused,
is suggested by Burke's doubt that Townshend was much
obliged to Rigby.[53] In reality Townshend was balking in
order to obtain crown authority for proposing measures to
raise an American revenue.

While waiting for the American day in Parliament Rockingham wrote to his friend Joseph Harrison, whom he had

named collector of customs at Boston in the previous July. This man, a friend of Savile, had lived for many years in Connecticut, returned to England shortly before the change of administration in 1765, and assisted the Marquis with information and advice in the measures of colonial conciliation, actually living for a time in his house. Rockingham now deplored to him the exercise by Massachusetts of the pardoning power, as going "much beyond the limits of their constitution." He entrusted Harrison with a letter to the speaker of the Massachusetts Assembly and concluded: "Mr. Dowdeswell and Mr. Burke send their compliments to you, and are well. Our system of acting is, to be consistent. I don't think we have impaired the credit we were in when you last saw us, and I don't think we shall." [54] His letter to Speaker Timothy Pickering, although dated May 11, had been written the previous December in answer to a vote of compliments he had received from the Assembly in 1766. His words show the image of himself which he wished to have projected in America. He said that he hoped to continue in the favorable opinion of the Massachusetts Assembly "by acting consistently upon the principles which I have fixed in my own judgment"; whatever "warm and ill-founded ideas" might arise on either side of the water he would "always consider, that this country, as the parent, ought to be dutiful." Without mentioning the indemnity act which had stirred anger in England he gave a gentle warning that the minister of conciliation ought not to be misunderstood:

> A system of arbitrary rule over the Colonies I would not adopt on this side; neither would I do otherwise than strenuously resist when attempts were made to throw off that dependency to which the Colonies ought to submit, not only for the advantages of this Country, but for their own real happiness and safety.

On May 12 Rockingham conferred with Dowdeswell, Meridith, and Savile, and, as he told Newcastle, they "arranged matters for tomorrow in case the plan of administration comes out as expected. The chief point will be, to object to their proposed bill & Mr. Dowdeswell's idea will be thrown out for consideration & in which Mr. Yorke concurs." [55] Exactly what that idea was is not clear.

The next day Charles Townshend threw the Rockinghams into confusion. His tone was moderate; he disavowed violent measures. The offensive Massachusetts act, he said, had been annulled by the Privy Council, hence that much-agitated affair was disposed of; all the colonies were not culpable; he had fair words for several; only New York had "boldly and insolently" defied the supreme legislature, and he proposed a restraint of its legislature until obedience was rendered. Townshend also called for a "moderate and prudent" taxation of the colonies for the support of the army in America and for the salaries of civil officers so that these might be rendered independent of assemblies. His mode of obtaining this revenue was the imposition of certain port duties and a new, more efficient regulation of the customs. Not as Chancellor of the Exchequer speaking for ministry, he said, but as a mere member of Parliament did he ask for these revenue measures; which evidently meant that he never got the authorization he sought from the cabinet. Taken aback by the unexpected lenity of the proposed punishment of New York, Dowdeswell attacked it as inadequate and seems to have argued for an enforcement of the Mutiny Act in the colonies. Savile "thought strong measures were necessary as we were only carrying on acts of parliament against acts of assembly & making paper war," and Charles Yorke said that "the measures could scarce be too strong." [56] According to Horace Walpole, Burke "arraigned the idea of dissolving their assemblies" (which makes no sense) and "advised a new model of their police." [57] A full account of the debate cannot be constructed, but it is clear that the Rockinghams were disconcerted. Two days later they assumed an attitude more consistent with their reputation by supporting a motion to recommit Townshend's resolution (which had been made and passed in committee) in order, as Dowdeswell said, to come to "more just & less offensive resolutions." At

the same time the latter lamented that the subject of New
York had been brought into Parliament since "it ought to
have been settled by the King & Council with unanimity."
On this day Grenville moved for leave to bring in a bill to
impose on all colonial officials a kind of "loyalty oath" to
uphold the authority of the British legislature. The motion
was lost, 150 to 51, the Rockinghams voting comfortably in
the majority with Conway and Townshend.[58]

After that the Marquis' friends, so far as is known, contested no more against Townshend's American measures
which passed rapidly through a thin House in the end days
of the session. There is nothing to show that they had the
slightest glimpse of the portentous significance with which
later events would endow the New York Restraining Act,
the Revenue Act, and the act creating an American board
of customs at Boston—Charles Townshend's fateful legacy.
Political strategy seems to have made it inconvenient for
Rockingham to lead the whigs against a man they hoped to
reclaim for the party. Moreover, they had begun to play a
different North American game of politics in which prospects for success were brighter.

A concerted attack was planned against administration
for its failure to propose a plan of civil government in
Canada.[59] This was the subject on which, the previous year,
Lord Northington elected to quarrel with the cabinet and
precipitated the break-up of the Rockingham administration.
The attack was to open with a motion by the Duke of Richmond for papers relating to the previous year's plan, and
well in advance of this day (May 21) Rockingham had a
kind of political census made of the House of Lords. Forty-
three peers were listed as "Friends to the last Administration," seventeen as of the Bedford faction, fourteen as
Temple–Grenville peers; twenty were "doubtful" and 104
were classified as "Friends to the Court." [60] If Bedford and
Grenville forces supported Richmond and some of the
doubtful were gained, a good opportunity was promised for
vindicating the ministers of 1766. Administration, however,
avoided a confrontation by accepting Richmond's motion,

and when this was followed on June 2 by a second motion for the establishment of a civil government in Canada, 61 peers divided against a majority of 73.

In the meantime Grafton's forces in the House of Lords had been run even harder by two motions (May 22 and May 28) of implied censure upon administration for having merely disallowed the Massachusetts indemnity act instead of condemning it *ab initio*. The lead in this effort was taken by Lord Gower, a Bedfordite, but the Rockingham peers came into it. In these two divisions the ministerial majority fell to six and then to three. So weak was Chatham's administration under his *locum tenens* Grafton in the Lords. And as this was being dramatically demonstrated, the ministers in the House of Commons displayed an astonishing spectacle by withholding support from a measure which originated at Grafton's Treasury board. It was a bill to stop an increase in the dividend for proprietors of the East India Company, and was managed in the House by Jeremiah Dyson of the Board of Trade. Against a combined opposition —but dwindled in numbers because the end of the session was near—the bill became law. Such was the state of government and Parliament when Edmund Burke observed (with some rhetorical exaggeration) that

> The Ministry broken, divided, weak, and fluctuating, without mutual confidence, united interest, or common consultation, still holds. The Secretary of State and Chancellor of the Exchequer vote (on questions of state and finance) in a minority. . . . Sometimes an inferior member of a board, sometimes a person belonging to no board at all, conducts what used to be considered as the business of government. The great Officers of the Crown amuse themselves and the house, with jests on their own insignificance.[61]

From an interior view of administration, things did not look very different. Grafton and Northington on May 28 painted to the King the embarrassed state of his affairs, and then Grafton sent an appeal for counsel from the ailing and secluded prime minister. Since the beginning of the session, he said, Conway and Townshend had been acting "in direct contradiction to all cabinet decisions," while in the House of Lords administration was menaced by "the prevalence of faction." Without Chatham's assistance Grafton could see "no possibility of serving his Majesty with effect, honour or justice to him or the public." The King underscored the urgency of this appeal by writing (May 30) in his own hand to Chatham, saying that Secretary of State Shelburne was a secret and Charles Townshend an avowed enemy of Northington, Grafton, and Camden; that Conway was resolved to retire, and that Grafton might not remain "above a day" unless Chatham "would see him and give him encouragement." [62] Chatham mustered the ability to do that much and the discordant ministry staggered through the remaining days of the session.

The conduct of the Rockinghams, especially in the House of Lords during late May, had not been consistent with the Marquis' desire to demonstrate to the King that his friends were not like Bedfords and Grenvilles, were not a closet-storming faction. There had been exchanges with the Bedfords and concerting of forces for the Richmond and Gower motions. The Marquis, however, had been repeatedly unwell during these days and there are hints that Newcastle's influence got into the ascendant, and that Rockingham did not wholly approve what the old Duke was doing.[63] However, the Marquis concerted with the Bedfords in mid-June for a mobilization of peers against the East India dividend bill,[64] and there can be no doubt but that the Rockinghams gave the appearance of being part of what the King described to Chatham (May 30) as

that hydra faction, which has never appeared to the height it now does. Though your relations the Grenvilles, the Bedfords, and the Rockinghams are joined with intention to storm my closet, yet, if I was mean enough to submit, they own they would not join in forming an administration.

This was not the impression on the royal mind which the Rockingham strategy had aimed at making.

III

On June 20 Conway called on Rockingham and communicated (what many suspected and the King knew) his determination to resign. That the system formed by Chatham must now dissolve, seemed a certainty. From this moment until early July the Marquis retreated into quiet and inactivity either because or under cover of ill health, personally quitting the scene of combined opposition to the ministry. During these days—the last of the session—administration was run less hard and the King could tell Chatham on June 25 that the majority in both Houses was "now very handsome"; but the ailing prime minister was asked to sketch a plan for filling expected vacancies, since Conway was going after Parliament rose, Northington's health had failed, and Townshend was willing to remain only if stability could be secured. Chatham could do no more than advise Grafton to stay and to recruit men who might strengthen his own position.[65] So that, from an interior point of view, it was not a dissolution of the system which impended, but a negotiation to preserve it.

General Conway, not yet quit of his office, dined at Rockingham's on July 3 with Portland, Winchilsea, Albemarle, the Cavendish brothers, and Dowdeswell, and told them that Grafton was ready to negotiate with the Marquis but would insist on the retention of Lord Granby as commander-in-chief and Camden as Lord Chancellor. If the Rockinghams were unwilling to treat, the General hinted, offers would be made elsewhere. After much discussion, it was decided that no answer could be given without further information. Was "a general and solid plan" aimed at, or only a few changes? If the latter, the Marquis thought that "we would much prefer seeing any sets undertake administration on that foot, than be the undertakers ourselves." Later that night Rockingham learned from the Bedfordites,

Gower and Weymouth, that Grafton was making a similar overture in that direction. From all this he concluded "that the present Administration is at a loss how to turn themselves & that the Closet is much in that situation & that now they are sounding about by way of separate treaties & I own my opinion is, that *we* ought to be cautious & till more light is given, say as little as possible." [66]

Grafton having found the Bedfords "unreasonable" in their expectations and unwilling to cut loose from the Grenvilles, the overture to the Rockinghams was followed by more specific proposals. Conway pressed this upon the King, who despite misgivings authorized Grafton to open negotiations; and on July 7 the Marquis met with the Duke at Conway's house to receive a message from the King. Here is Rockingham's memoir of what transpired:

> His M[ajest]y's message by the Duke of Grafton, to know whether we would come into his M[ajest]y's service to carry on administration with the remains of the present administration & the *Treasury* offered to me—That we should prepare a plan—It was *understood* that we might propose the D[uke] of Bedford's friends along with our *own* but not to extend to G. Grenville etc. Lord Chatham understood to be no part. The D[uke] of Grafton would support either in or out of office. Memo: I took up the conversation first, in complimenting the D[uke] of Grafton on his handsome behaviour in this matter. Said, we had had last year *but one* difference & which only proceeded from his Grace's great confidence & opinion of the necessity of L[ord] Chatham etc. That I had attributed all that had passed since to the same motive. That I desired in case his Grace perceived symptoms of caution in us or in me that he would not attribute it to any diffidence in regard to his Grace, but merely from the desire of forming an administration that would not be too weak, from the same causes which had heretofore weakened all administration.[67]

Those "causes" were, of course, court-connected persons who refused to support or even opposed the measures of administration and yet were screened by the King against disciplinary removal. From several letters the Marquis wrote to friends on this day a little more can be known of what he understood to have passed at his meeting with Grafton. He had sought to know what was meant by "remains of the present administration" and been told that it related particularly to Camden, that others were not mentioned lest it appear that the King had already decided to give up this or that person.[68] Grafton's account of the meeting (written eleven days later to Northington) was as follows:

> . . . the conversation was long and very diffuse; many questions asked upon particulars which were answered by saying that the time was yet too early to go into them till his lordship offered his plan. On his enquiring whether the plan was to be confin'd to his own people or whether it was to comprehend the Bedfords and even the Grenvilles; my answer was that the King had particularized no one, but that if his lordship went to including both parties as well as his own, I could not make out, how it could possibly be consistent with His Majesty's most gracious opening to his lordship where the remainder of the present Administration together with the Chancellor was to be the foundation of it. After much conversation the words I was directed to report to his Majesty were these, *"That his lordship and his friends on considering the opening His Majesty had honoured them by making, were of opinion that they would not do right to come into Administration without it could be made to comprehend Lord Rockingham and his friends, the Duke of Bedford and his friends, such of Mr. Grenville's also as chose to come into office."* [69]

From the context of this passage it seems that Grafton subsumed into it more than had passed on July 7, and had included a statement made by Rockingham at their next meeting eight days later.

In the evening of July 7 the Marquis recorded, in a letter to Grafton which may or may not have been sent, a more specific statement of his resolution:

If it is his Majesty's intention that a general plan for an administration should be proposed, it should then be considered as a plan *de novo,* or if it is his Majesty's pleasure that it should not be so, it would be necessary to know with some precision what and who is meant by the *Remains of the Present Administration.* Indeed, my dear Lord, it is no easy matter to form an administration well composed in point of weight and abilities and well united from mutual confidence, but such a one is necessary and no consideration shall ever press me to act in an administration which in my opinion may be too weak effectually to serve the King and the country.[70]

Since there is no evidence to show that Grafton received such communication, presumably the Marquis' sober second thought withheld it. The Duke would hardly relish being pressed to answer a question he had already said he could not; besides, it might be better for the Marquis to hear first from Bedford—better to feel out his strength before probing the court. "I consider this," he told Newcastle, "only more of an opening than as yet any thing on which a judgment can be formed—the material matter is, how far his Majesty will incline to allow us to introduce a number sufficient to give real strength. If that can't be done, I own I shall have no desire to be a part." If only he could have ascertained that, how much agony and embarrassment he might have spared himself! But the true answer to that question could be found only in the strength of his bargaining position and in the measure of the court's exigency. Hence his initial move was to employ Albemarle, then at Woburn, to ascertain whether the Bedfords would "take a warm and confidential part with us in this matter." Newcastle was delighted by all this; at last the Marquis was doing what he ought to have done months earlier; the old Duke saw no hazards in the way but Rockingham's fastidious aversion to the Grenville brothers and excessive tenderness toward Conway and Grafton.[71]

On July 8 came Albemarle's word that Bedford was happy "to join with you in the great plan of removing the

Favourite and his friends from court." Had the Marquis an objection to treating with Grenville? Albemarle had ventured to say that he had not, "provided it was through his Grace as one of his [Bedford's] friends." Rigby would meet Rockingham that night at Arthur's. The Marquis characterized Albemarle's report as "an answer which in part I like." Presumably there was a part which he did not like. In soliciting Albemarle's service he had outlined a prospective union with the Bedfords and the remains of the existing administration for the purpose of making "a solid administration"; he had said nothing of "removing the Favourite and his friends from the court," nor had he so much as mentioned Grenville. That night, however, he told Rigby that, although he could not properly send any message to Grenville, he thought it not improper for Bedford to communicate with him and that "great good might arise, if thro' the D[uke] of Bedford etc. any insight might be got, on what plan & how a general junction of the three parties might be made." [72] These words are from his account to Newcastle and naturally they sent the old Duke into transports of delight. It might seem that the Marquis had run off the rails of his previous political strategy. But since he had no idea of abandoning old friends his conduct is intelligible as an attempt to fortify himself for negotiating with the court. If the Bedfords annexed the Grenvilles while he annexed the Bedfords, what with his old friends among "the remains" of Chatham's administration he could find himself at the head of a formidable whig union.

On setting out to visit Bedford at Woburn, however, he would admit no more than being "near the time of knowing with some certainty the material grounds on which we shall be able to judge & act." Perhaps in his heart he did not believe that he could succeed in what he was attempting. Lady Rockingham hoped, while her husband was at Woburn, that the next accounts would be "that all is at an end & we are setting out for Yorkshire." But all went smoothly at Bedford's. Rigby, after misrepresenting Rockingham to Grenville, brought from the brothers what Bedford called

"a most satisfactory answer." There was no discussion of
particular arrangements. It was agreed that the next step
was for the Marquis to obtain an audience with the King.[73]

On July 15 he told the Woburn story to Grafton, expressed desire for a "comprehensive" administration, and
asked if it was the King's intention that he prepare a plan
of that nature. Did that mean, Grafton asked, removing all
in office? Rockingham answered that removals would indeed
be necessary but that to remove all would be neither a prudent intention to declare nor a wise policy to adopt. The
Duke said the King could easily accept a less extensive plan,
but the Marquis insisted that his own and Bedford's friends
were unanimously of opinion "that a comprehensive plan of
administration was the only one which could effectually
serve his Majesty & this country." After putting Rockingham's question to the King the Duke sent an answer restat-
ing the original proposal of July 7: ". . . the King wishes
your Lordship to specify the plan on which you & your
friends would propose to come in in order to extend &
strengthen his administration, that his Majesty may be
enabled to judge how far the same may be advantageous to
his Majesty & the publick's service." [74] The Marquis then
requested Grafton to explain to the King that

> the principle on which I would proceed should be to consider
> the present Administration as at an end, notwithstanding the
> great regard which I have for some of those who compose it.
> If His Majesty thinks it for his service to form a new
> Administration on a comprehensive plan, the general idea of
> which has been opened to your Grace, I should then humbly
> hope to have his Majesty's permission to attend him, in order
> to receive his commands, it being impossible to enter into
> particulars till I have His Majesty's leave to proceed upon
> this plan.[75]

Some of his friends thought that he was acting in an
astute manner: that the court must now yield or take the
responsibility for breaking off a negotiation which it had
begun. Newcastle saw the court cornered and "never knew

a negotiation of this importance, more wisely conducted, or carried off with more prudence & steddiness than this has been by the Marquis." Bedford, kept *au courant* by copies of the exchanges with Grafton, thought "that the present negotiation is over unless His Majesty shall immediately send for you," and promised that he and his friends would give "the same answer as you shall have done, to any future offers that may be made to them." The Marquis reflected that his communication to Grafton would "go thro' all the fiery trials to see what to lay hold of," and longed "to be out of suspense." [76] When the next move was made he knew that he had been outmaneuvered.

I have laid your lordship's letter before His Majesty [wrote Grafton on July 17], and have the satisfaction of acquainting your lordship, that the King's most gracious sentiments concur with your lordship's in regard to forming a comprehensive plan of administration, and that His Majesty desirous of uniting the hearts of all his subjects, is most ready, and willing to appoint such a one as shall exclude no denomination of men attached to his person and government.

When your lordship is prepared to offer a plan of administration formed on these views His Majesty is willing that your lordship should yourself lay the same before him for His Majesty's consideration. [77]

Rockingham's position was now rendered very awkward. Without a commission from the King to form an administration he could not negotiate with authority, yet if he declined to proceed he must take the responsibility for ending the negotiation. As Lord Hardwicke said, he had "the ball laid at his feet & must take some steps towards carrying on the negotiation." There was a respectful duty to try to meet the expressed royal wish, to take it at face value. Hence, even before making another and futile effort for the prior audience, he wrote to Bedford that it was necessary to proceed: "If your Grace sees this affair in the same light as we do here, our next step must be to consider on a plan of arrangement." He hoped that Bedford would inform himself of the ideas of Grenville and Temple and ascertain what their wishes were for their friends. Bedford now abandoned the opinion that all would be over if the prior audience was denied, and agreed that the negotiation should proceed, expressing his confidence that "all the chicane which will certainly be employed against you in the construction of the word *comprehensive* . . . will with prudent management on our part turn against themselves." A meeting of principals was fixed for July 20.[78]

It is clear that Rockingham meant to go through with his task in deadly earnest, with candor to Bedford and fidelity to friends in office. He assumed that the King was not trifling with him and that his purpose was not unrealizable. He spelled it out to Charles Yorke on July 18:

> The task of arranging a comprehensive administration is a heavy one, but if my friends will lend me their assistance & advice, I shall hope to get through with it. The prevailing maxim which has occasioned all the turmoils of the last six years, has been, *divide & impera*. I desire to combat it, by conciliation, & as far as in me lies, to suppress my own & to stem in others, the passions of revenge & personal resentments. Those who have been fattened by the policy & effect of the *divide & impera* maxim deserve but little mercy & yet in wisdom it may be well not to go to the utmost extremity & perhaps in the end [that] may be the securest method of preventing the future rise of that power under which they have flourished.[79]

It was "that power" which had provoked Rockingham to resign from court in 1762 and had then struck at him in Yorkshire; "that power" which had forced out Newcastle and broken the whig connection to pieces; "that power" which had tried to thwart his own measures of conciliation with the colonies; "that power" which protected men in crown offices when they opposed the measures of ostensible ministers. It was the so-called party of Bute, the "king's friends," whose influence worked to dissolve the natural connection of men. On "that power" no administration could

rely; without it none could stand. Bedford, Temple, Grenville, Newcastle, and Rockingham, all believed that it was
a reality, that in office they had felt it. If they knew in their
hearts that "that power" was in truth one man, George III,
there was only folly in saying so. The King could do no
wrong, said the law of the constitution and the rules of
political prudence.

On the day before the meeting with Bedford, Rockingham met Grafton at Arthur's and was told that Conway's
resignation was due on Wednesday, July 23. This was good
news: so timely an event augured well for royal acceptance
of Rockingham's comprehensive plan of administration. He
wrote to Conway:

> I think I have tolerably digested in my own thoughts, the prin-
> ciples on which we should proceed in the arduous task of form-
> ing an Administration on a comprehensive plan.
> The great object is to restrain and put an end to that mis-
> chievous power, which had occasioned all the confusions and
> divisions, which have tore and perplexed this country for some
> years past. . . .
> By this time tomorrow I shall probably be well enabled to
> judge, and if upon the whole such a system and plan is adopted
> as will give content and satisfaction to those I esteem, and will
> bid fair for general approbation in the publick, I shall be very
> happy indeed.[80]

In reply Conway confirmed his intention to resign on July
23, but confessed that he was fearful of giving offense to
the King in doing so, that his situation was awkward, "the
more so as it has seem'd the desire and expectation of your
Lordship and others." Afterward he would give the Marquis his "full and fair opinion" on the plan to be offered to
the King. There was one plan, namely, that envisaged by
himself and Grafton on July 7, which he approved—"for
the rest I must suspend judgment." He agreed in restraining "that mischievous power" but was not sure that he and
the Marquis saw eye to eye with respect to the mode: "I
would do what was necessary for that purpose and no more;

and I wou'd take care the world shou'd see that alone was intended, and that other views and purposes were not substituted to it; for I think too much may be done, as well as too little, towards that right purpose, and may even succeed the less to that very end." [81]

Conway's gentle admonition must be read in the light of what Rockingham had no way of knowing, namely, the King's exertion of every means to induce the General to stay in office. His remaining and continuing as minister in the House of Commons was the *sine qua non* of Grafton's staying, even though the Duke was willing to vacate the Treasury to Rockingham if the latter's plan was acceptable to the King. Both Grafton and Conway disliked what the former called "the extension of Lord Rockingham's connections," and neither was likely to leave the sovereign at the mercy of a Rockingham–Bedford–Grenville coalition.[82] Moreover, neither was as sensible as former ministers of "that power," perhaps because the King's relations with Lord Bute had ended the previous year. It was unfortunate for Rockingham that he could not spell out in advance to Grafton and Conway the detail of his comprehensive plan. Not less than Grafton did he desire to have Conway as minister in Commons. He expected their trust without giving them his confidence, which he could not do until he had settled his plan with Bedford and given it to the King.

The Rockingham–Bedford conference took place at Newcastle's house in town. The Marquis had with him Portland, Richmond, Keppel, and Dowdeswell; Bedford brought Weymouth, Sandwich, and Rigby. Newcastle had forebodings because he knew of Rockingham's wishes with respect to Conway whom the Bedfords held in aversion, but hoped to play the role of moderating Nestor. Rockingham arrived in a state of displeasure over what Bedford had revealed to him earlier in the day, namely, that the Grenvilles had supplied no list of their friends and that their support would be dependent on Rockingham's agreeing to "a capital measure for asserting and establishing the sovereignty of Great Britain over the Colonies." Soon after the conference began the

Marquis denounced the Grenville brothers on this account.
According to Bedford he flew into "a violent passion" and
said "many outrageous things." [83] According to Dowdeswell, who recorded an account of the conference, Rockingham said "that upon the whole course of this matter, and
from the knowledge he had of those persons he cou'd not
but conclude that they meant to obstruct instead of facili-
tating, and did in his own mind foresee an unhappy event to
this great and important business." Much wrangling followed. Dowdeswell suggested that Grenville might be satisfied with an agreement to *maintain* and *support* instead of
assert and *establish*, but Rigby said that that would not satisfy Grenville and urged that Bedford moderate this difference. At length Bedford spelled out this: "That with regard
to the American colonies no new measure should be understood to be agreed upon at this meeting, unless new matter
arises, but if new matter should arise the sovereignty of this
country should be asserted and established with firmness and
temper." [84] (The "firmness" was for Grenville, the "temper" for Rockingham!) Rockingham accepted this and Bedford hoped that his absent allies would swallow it. Proceeding to talk of men and offices the Marquis proposed Grafton
and Conway. Bedford balked at the latter, was amazed, and
thought that the General intended to return to the army.
Deadlock followed and when the parties met again the following night it was tightened by Rockingham's insistence
that Conway must be the minister in the House of Commons:
"I thought it material to myself that the person who was
leader in the House of Commons should be a Person, in
whom I might confide." Nobody knew, of course, whether
Conway would, after going out, come in again under another Rockingham administration. Insisting on the minister
who had led the repeal of the Stamp Act was the Marquis'
real answer to the Grenvillian demand for a declaration on
the subject of America. Bedford remained adamant: he could
not assent without separating from Grenville and sinking his
party in Rockingham's. And so the negotiation ended, each
party setting the other free of engagement.

The next day the Marquis went to court to report the unsuccessful outcome of his effort to form a plan for a comprehensive administration. He began by apologizing to the King for having pressed a plan which went beyond what Majesty had at first intended, then explained why he had thought such a plan right and practical and why at the present it could not be arranged: the blame was put at the door of the Grenville brothers. In explaining why he had thought the comprehensive plan necessary he said that when he had been in the King's service "the Measures of Administration were obstructed by men in office acting like a corps"; that he flattered himself that this was not entirely with his Majesty's inclination, and was "very detrimental to his service." If the Marquis expected or hoped that the King would now commission him to form or reform administration, he was disappointed. Majesty had nothing to propose, and pointed out that in strict truth the Treasury had never been offered to him. Rockingham was taken aback, having understood differently from the royal message given to him by Grafton on July 7; whereupon the King said that the Treasury would have been his if a suitable plan had been formed. "As soon as I came out," he recorded, "I took the Duke of Grafton and General Conway aside & told them what had passed on the word *offer*. The Duke of Grafton & General Conway said it was nothing, for that from the beginning I had every right to consider & represent that matter as understood." [85] It was far from "nothing." The story of the royal denial of the offer was to wing its way in distorted version over town and country, to make Rockingham appear presumptuous and foolish.

Grafton and Conway displayed surprise that the King had made no further proposal to the Marquis, and urged him to meet with them that night. He said that "it could be to no purpose." This was the day the General was to resign, but he did not. The next day he sent to Rockingham asking for another meeting with Grafton who would bring a message from the King. This proved to be a restatement of the overture of July 7 and was rejected, the Marquis saying that he would rather see his old friends come out than himself go in, since they could not be strong enough to command the confidence and support of the court.[86] Yet another appeal to unite with administration was sent by Conway via Richmond that night and the Marquis replied that if the King summoned him, and asked him to form an administration, he would treat again with the Bedfords, making such offers as would put them in the wrong if they refused. Only then would he feel justified in coming in upon a narrower plan.[87] It was a safe answer. The King would not summon him to undertake as long as Conway, and therefore Grafton, stood by their sovereign to defend him against having his hand forced. Rockingham's hope for creating a strong and solid, or "comprehensive," administration had been founded on royal necessity arising out of the dissolution of the system Chatham had formed. Conway held the string to unwind it but did not pull that string. His brother Lord Hertford, successor to Portland as lord chamberlain, urged him not to desert the King, as did his cousin Horace Walpole; and there was his soldierly sense of a duty to stay at his post for his sovereign's sake. He liked Rockingham, however, and wished to work with him in office. On July 25 he made still another appeal:

> There is a moment left & I should be happy indeed if your Lordship could on reflexion use it to bring on what still depends absolutely on yourself & do reflect that if you & your friends don't come in, there is, as I think, no one good alternative. For surely that which you seem alone to have any taste for is impracticable: the Bedfords have shut the door to any junction with them to your Lordship & they have barred it to me. I dread any thing that looks like a separation, even a political one from your Lordship & your friends; but I have the misfortune to differ widely as to the present determination & have no plea or pretense to take the part you seem inclined to take.[88]

The Marquis could not justly hold that Conway had broken a promise since the latter had only declared an intention to resign, but he undoubtedly felt that he had been deceived, not very honorably. There is an unfinished draft of a reply to Conway:

> As far as my judgment can point out to me, both for my friends & for my own conduct I must even in doubtful occasions, prefer & recommend that decision which appears most for their honour as men, though neither in the moment nor perhaps in probable speculation most advantageous as politicians.[89]

IV

During the entire negotiation, Rockingham had been in constant touch with advising friends: Albemarle and Keppel, Newcastle, the Yorkes, Portland, the Cavendishes, Richmond, Dowdeswell, Burke. A stream of advice poured upon him from the old Duke, turning into bitter criticism when he broke off with Bedford. Dowdeswell, who was at Rockingham's side at both meetings with the Bedfords, may have been the friend who understood him best. A draft of Dowdeswell's opinions survives. The first part of it was written on July 23 (the day the Marquis talked to the King) and was addressed to the question whether he should consider joining with Grafton and Conway, after having failed to form a comprehensive plan. The conclusion was that he should not, lest doubt be thrown on the sincerity of his negotiations with Bedford. Instead, he should "stand still and leave it to chance to bring about those events which may possibly enable him to be useful to his king and Country." The second part of this paper was written on July 24 and discussed what the Marquis ought to do if, after rejecting junction with the existing administration, he should be asked to form another. The conditions on which he might accept were, first, a direct commission from the King "without the interposition of any of his ministers"; second, that the King was brought to understand "the real cause of all the public misfortunes," which was to be imputed not to the influence of "particular persons" but to the prevalence of a "political principle which says that the power of the Crown arises out of the weakness of the administration"; and finally, that Majesty be apprised of "a manly resolution not to maintain the pageantry of administration an hour after it is divested of its necessary weight in the Closet and its necessary power in other places." If, on these conditions, Rockingham were able to proceed he should again attempt a comprehensive administration with "a manifest superiority of his own friends" in "all offices of business." Bedford should be applied to again, and in order to ease a new negotiation Charles Townshend, instead of Conway, should be secretary of state and leader of the House of Commons; moreover, Bedford should be told that Rockingham would "pay all possible civility and attention" to George Grenville and "live in hopes . . . that they should in time get nearer to each other." Dowdeswell was an old friend of Charles Townshend and a great admirer of his talents; he was, too, less distant than the Marquis from the American politics of both Townshend and Grenville; and as a House of Commons man he had a more practical sense of their weight in that chamber. But Dowdeswell's paper shows that he did not believe that the King was then likely to give Rockingham an opportunity to put these recommendations to the test; nor did he favor a united opposition with Bedfords and Grenvilles:

> I confess that I see no fair prospect before us—standing still is the only thing we can do. This may possibly weaken us as a party. It depends upon the virtues of our friends whether it will or will not, but I am sure it will do us honour as individuals. In these unhappy times when we find ourselves well in the opinion of mankind the best thing we can do is to stand still and enjoy the reputation which we have, not resign it for something new, the chances of which are against us.[90]

Although Rockingham would later tell Dowdeswell that he had twice read the paper with "pleasure and approbation," there is nothing to indicate or suggest that it had governed his conduct. Nor can all views expressed in it be assigned to the Marquis. During the negotiation he had said nothing to Townshend and there was no hint of considering him for office in the comprehensive administration. That he had led the Marquis up the garden path while Parliament was in session, is clear. Burke was to say on August 3 that Townshend "has no regard for me and I have no confidence in him." [91] But there is a Rockingham record of silence on this mercurial man until death removed him early in September.

Although Albemarle, Dowdeswell, Portland, Burke, and to a lesser extent the Yorkes (who were partial to Grenville) approved in general of the Marquis' conduct during the negotiations, he had to face dissent from Richmond and the Cavendishes against the decision not to join Conway and Grafton, and Newcastle condemned his conduct toward the Bedfords as the extreme of folly. The last and greatest crisis in Rockingham–Newcastle relations arose out of the negotiation. From the beginning the old Duke was vexed at not being consulted before Rockingham met with Grafton on July 7, and although he applauded every step down to July 20 he suspected all along that the Marquis had too strong an inclination to Conway, which probably was the meaning of Lady Rockingham's telling him on July 15 that "we differ *a little* or perhaps *not a little* upon the present political affairs." [92]

When all was over Newcastle was unsparing of reproaches: the Bedfords should have been trusted to manage the Grenvilles; Conway should have been given up; nothing that Rockingham did was right except his telling Grafton and Conway at the end that he would approach the Bedfords again if called upon to form an administration. Mansfield, who knew him so well, said of Newcastle that "with respect to the late transactions, he was wholly and solely a Bedford." Charles Yorke recorded that the old Duke was "against Lord R[ockingham]'s returning to the Treasury & for taking Gre[nville] along in cordiality. . . . But he durst not speak out." In a long letter to the Marquis on July

25 Newcastle spelled out his case against the former's ill judgment, even condemning his setting free the Bedfords from engagement. The Marquis gave a patient answer: he had only acted in fairness—"a handsome & becoming part" which must improve, not hurt, cordiality with the Bedfords, with whom he wished to maintain cordiality. Newcastle's complaints were "much too captious." [93]

While Rockingham was in Yorkshire, whither he had gone by the end of July, Burke visited the Duke of Richmond. Admiral Keppel was there and Burke reported him as "very right, and the more laudibly so, as he is not without a strong feeling of the inconveniences attending a protracted opposition from the craving demands of friends and dependents." But Richmond was not "right," and did not understand the Marquis, who ought to write to humor that young Duke. Toward the end of August Burke was at Newcastle's Claremont for the first time in his life. He found his host still full of complaints against Rockingham and suspicious of a continued attachment to Conway who, as Burke had said, had "gone fairly to the devil." Newcastle had just heard from Albemarle (who had it from Rigby) that nothing barred the Bedfords from uniting with the Rockinghams but the want of a declaration from the latter against all connection with the ministry. The old Duke was for that and commissioned Burke, who was going soon to Wentworth, to carry the recommendation to his chief; and then, to be sure of an adequate hearing for his views, he spelled them out in a letter of nineteen folios to the Marquis.[94]

Meanwhile the master of Wentworth was taking a holiday from politics. He wrote to Dartmouth on August 15:

Since I came here I found so much real private business & so much amusement in riding about inspecting farming & other occupations, that I own I took up such an indolence of mind that I dreaded the idea of setting down to write on political matter. Indeed for the last ten days I have had company constantly with me. . . . I am to set out for York Races tomorrow.[95]

By early September he was a politician again. Alexander Wedderburn visited Wentworth, talked about American affairs, and found the Marquis "blaming exceedingly the indiscretion of the present Ministers, who had ventured upon strong measures without being prepared to support them, especially after the experience they had had that the powers of Government in that country were insufficient to execute the law." [96] Then Burke arrived with a cargo of reports of various conversations and refreshed his leader's grasp upon the map of politics. On September 11 the latter wrote to Dowdeswell a long political letter wherein he discussed the differences which had arisen among his friends and stressed the necessity of recurring to two principles which he could not think that any would abandon:

> Our first principle was, that Lord Bute's *power* was dangerous & therefore to be resisted.
> Our second arose from G. Grenville's conduct as a Minister, whose measures and opinions we opposed & afterwards corrected & therefore consistency requires that we should never aid to throw government into his hands, much less act the part of assistants in an administration so formed.

To go into administration on the Grafton–Conway basis would breach the first principle; allying with the Grenvilles and Bedfords in a closet-storming opposition would breach the other, since the Rockinghams had no man who could dispute the primacy of George Grenville in the House of Commons. Grenville was a menace to the peace and tranquillity of the empire. A union with the Bedfords remained desirable but not on Grenvillian terms. So the Marquis was resolved to stand, even though "time-serving politicians" might discern "no pleasing prospect."

> You know I never disguised to our Friends on trying occasions, that I considered them as a forlorn hope, but that the maintenance of character & credit was in honour incumbent upon them & would in the first place be a comfort to their own minds, &

though it might appear improbable in present, yet it was not impossible but that such conduct would prove the better policy.

Dowdeswell was asked to come to Wentworth:

Mr. Burke is here—Lord John Cavendish is within call if you can come. The Duke of Portland will be in the neighborhood in a few days. Old White is not at a great distance. We might form a good conciliabulum & from the state of politics in the present moment, material accounts may come from London, which will shew what turn the *Remains* of the present administration will now take.[97]

A few days later Rockingham told Portland that if he did not feel "the inward satisfaction of acting uniformly & up to our professions" he would sink under the anxieties of his own mind.[98]

Strong moral resolution is starkly evident in Rockingham. It is easy enough to understand why he could erect "No Bute, no Grenville" into principles of political negation. He saw the one as subversive of the proper way to work the constitution, and the other as a way to disordering the empire. But why this moral fervor for a "forlorn hope" and sinking under anxiety unless he felt an "inward satisfaction," etc.? He was a man of the world of whiggery, of White's and the Jockey Club, and a practicing politician who saw little in the world to moralize about or to try to reform. He had commanded militia, served a court, headed a Georgian government. He was not a man of sensibility cultivating a consciousness of rectitude. The truth is that the Marquis was a grandee who combined a strong sense of duty derivative from station with an intense relish for private life, for his stables and the turf, and lacked a taste for politics as a professional game. The endless labor of writing political letters, which never tired Newcastle, was a heavy burden on the Marquis. Constitutionally frail, that kind of work wore him down, and any sort of bustle ravaged him. He was not crafty enough to be a good negotiator, and made too generous an estimate of the measure of honor in political men. A great turmoil could be stirred in him when his inborn impetuosity struggled against practiced patience. He liked the straight fair courses. Intensely fond of friends, he drew about himself men of excellent character and delighted in political counseling with them; but although he naturally desired success in what he undertook he had neither ambition nor appetite for employing power.

NOTES

1. *The Public Advertiser*, 6 Aug. 1766.
2. These complimentary addresses are preserved in WWM R 58 and 59.
3. For 8/11 August.
4. WWM R 1: 675.
5. An estimate from Namier-Brooke, *Hist. Parl.*
6. WWM R 1: 679.
7. Add. MS 32976, ff. 488–489. The public was told in Edmund Burke's "Short Account of a Late Short Administration" (*St. James's Chronicle*, 7 August): "By the temper they [the retiring ministers] manifest they seem now to have no other wish, than that their successors may do the publick as real and faithful a service as they have done."
8. Portland MSS.
9. Add. MSS 32976, f. 489; 32977, ff. 91, 92, 201; WWM R 1: 696, 697.
10. Add. MS 32976, ff. 13, 14.
11. WWM Burke papers.
12. Add. MSS 32977, ff. 341, 343, 350; 35362, f. 44.
13. *Corr. Burke* I 277–279.
14. *Chatham* III 126–129; Add. MS 32977, ff. 415–417; WWM R 1: 709.
15. WWM R 1: 708.
16. Add. MS 32978, ff. 1–5, 11–12.
17. To Lord Scarborough 21 Nov. (printed in Albemarle II 19–24).
18. *Hist. Parl.* I 190–191. Another Rockingham list dated 20 Dec. 1766 shows a more detailed breakdown: Bute, 71; Chatham, 56; Swiss (supporters of any administration, "king's friends"), 100; "Bute tories," 36; tories, 47; doubtful, 54; Bedford, 35; Grenville, 18; absentees, 16; whigs (Rockingham's friends), 122.—WWM R 86.
19. Add. MS 32978, f. 9.
20. *Ibid.*, ff. 23–25
21. *Corr. Burke* I 283; *Grenville* III 389
22. Portland MSS.
23. Add. MSS 32978, f. 78; 35430, f. 61.
24. Add. MS 32476, ff. 106, 168.
25. *Grenville* III 394; Add. MS 32978, f. 166.
26. Portland MSS.
27. Add. MS 32978, f. 168

28. *Ibid.,* ff. 378, 404–407, 418.

29. WWM R 1: 742 (printed in Albemarle II 31–34). Dowdeswell answered: "I perfectly approve of your Lordship's discourse with Lord Lyttelton. It has that firmness & consistency & is so well founded in principle that every man of honour must approve it."—Dowdeswell MSS (Clements Library). At this conference with Newcastle and Bessborough 17 Dec. Rockingham was asked what advice should be given to friends in the House of Commons and how they should judge on points to be opposed or supported. He said that "they might be desired to go with Mr. Dowdeswell."

30. *Corr. Burke* I 285.

31. Dowdeswell to Burke 4 Jan. 1767 (Dowdeswell MSS); *Corr. Burke* I 289; WWM R 1: 743. That Dowdeswell feared being unable to write a party pamphlet shows in his letter of 10 Jan. to Rockingham: "I am a whimsical man & have some particular notions of my own. . . . I am afraid that I commit others with whom I have the honour of being well connected, & to whom malevolent men will impute every whimsical idea of mine."—Dowdeswell MSS.

32. Add. MS 32978, f. 468. These words point to Edmund Burke as the author. Burke was shy of Newcastle who had branded him as a papist to Rockingham in 1765. On more than one occasion afterward the Duke expressed to Rockingham a kind of envy of the latter's relationship with this man of genius. The letter in the *Public Advertiser* was signed "SULPITIUS," which may have been suggested by Sulpicius Rufus who served as legate to the Consul Pompeius Strabo in 89 B.C. and was soon after elected to the tribunate; he was a distinguished orator.

33. Add. MS 32979, f. 143.

34. WWM R 1: 747; cf. Savile to Portland 12 Jan.—Portland MSS.

35. *Corr. Burke* I 290.

36. Add. MS 35608, f. 1.

37. Add. MSS 32980, ff. 130, 144; 35362, ff. 65–66; Albemarle II 37–38; WWM R 81: 189.

38. John Brooke, *The Chatham Administration* (London, 1956), 96.

39. Grafton MS 491 (photocopy by courtesy of Rev. Cornelius Foster, O.P.).

40. Add. MS 32980, f. 108.

41. WWM R 1: 740, 741. Townshend assured Rockingham "that my love & honour for you will be pleased with any opportunity of maintaining the cause of those whom you protect & desire to assist"; and that "I hope the storm will rise, that I may have some share in smoothing the waters . . . for, such as I am, I shall ever be at your command. I would not have said this to other men in your situation; to excuse it, recollect how long we have lived in intimacy, & let your knowledge of me be my justification."

42. Add. MS 32980, f. 207

43. *Ibid.,* 440, 444, 454

44. WWM R 1: 767.

45. WWM R 156: 9

46. *Ibid.,* 12.

47. Add. MS 32981, ff. 112–113

48. WWM R 156: 13; *Grenville* III 223; *Corr. Burke* I 307.

49. WWM R 156: 14.

50. Add. MS 32981, f. 256.

51. *Corr. Burke* I 309–310.

52. Add. MS 35430, ff. 73–74.

53. Add. MS 32981, f. 295; *Corr. Burke* I 312.

54. Both letters are printed in *Grenville* IV 12–13. A number of Harrison's letters to Rockingham are preserved in WWM R 63. Vide Carl Bridenbaugh's study of Harrison's brother, *Peter Harrison, First American Architect* (Chapel Hill, 1942).

55. Add. MS 32981, f. 356.

56. *Ibid.*, 375–380.

57. *Memoirs* III 26.

58. Add. MS 32981, ff. 393–395.

59. *Ibid.*, ff. 365, 367, 389, 399; 32982, f. 48.

60. WWM R 1: 783.

61. *Corr. Burke* I 315.

62. *Chatham* II 257–258, 260–262.

63. Add. MSS 32981, f. 367; 32982, ff. 136, 279, 301–302, 334; 35430, ff. 75–77; Dartmouth MS D.1778.vi

64. Add. MS 32982, f. 280

65. *Chatham* III 295–296.

66. *Grafton*, 139; Add. MS 32983, ff. 55–57

67. WWM R 9: 4.

68. Add. MS 32983, ff. 125–127

69. *Grafton*, 146–147

70. WWM R 1: 807.

71. *Ibid.*, 808; Add. MS 32983, ff. 129, 136–140.

72. WWM R 1: 806, 810; Add. MS 32983, ff. 166–167.

73. *Ibid.*, f. 189; WWM R 147: 4. The Woburn meeting and Rigby's dealing with the Grenvilles are related in close detail in Brooke, *Chatham Administration*, 183–187.

74. Add. MS 32983, ff. 267–270; *Bedford* III 374–378; WWM R 1: 819; *Grafton*, 44.

75. WWM R 1: 820.

76. *Ibid.*, 827(a); R 9: 26; *Bedford* III 373; Add. MS 82983, f. 268.

77. WWM R 1: 827; *Grafton*, 144–145.

78. Add. MS 35362, ff. 135–136; *Bedford* III 376–378, 381–382; WWM R 1: 832.

79. Add. MS 35430, ff. 83–84.

80. WWM R 1: 824 (copy). Conway had written to Rockingham the night before that Grafton "has a great mind to see you & as I think his ideas come nearer to what you seemed to wish as to the method of proceeding, would you call on him for a moment in the morning."—*Ibid.*, 803.

81. *Ibid.*, 836.

82. *Grafton*, 148.

83. *Bedford* III 382–383.

84. WWM R 1: 838.

85. Rockingham's apologia to friends: a letter to Lord Hardwicke 26 July of which many copies were made.—*Ibid.*, 845 (partly printed under incorrect date in Albemarle II 50–54).

86. Add. MS 32984, f. 34

87. WWM R 1: 840.

88. WWM R 9: 21

89. *Ibid.,* 2

90. WWM R 1: 841, printed with an introduction by M. Francis de Sales Boran in *Crisis in the "Great Republic,"* ed. G. L. Vincitorio (New York, 1969), 1–13

91. *Corr. Burke* I 319

92. Add. MS 32983, f. 261

93. *Grenville* IV 139; WWM R 1: 843; Add. MSS 32984, ff. 36–37, 49–50; 35366, f. 137

94. *Ibid.,* 324–325; *Correspondence of the Right Honourable Edmund Burke,* edd. Earl Fitzwilliam and Sir Richard Bourke (4 vols.; London, 1844) I 144–146; WWM R 1: 681; Add. MS 32984, f. 358.

95. Dartmouth MS D.1778.vi

96. *Grenville* IV 161

97. WWM R 1: 556

98. Albemarle II 58.

6

"The *Enfans Perdus* of Politics"

WHEN ROCKINGHAM LEFT THE TREASURY in July 1766
there were about 170 members of the House of Commons
who can be discerned as supporters of the general direction
which he signified in politics.[1] This number does not include
many who had voted for the measures of his administration
merely because it was the administration; but it represents a
measure of potentiality for a revitalized whig party headed
by the Marquis. It included many who remained in place
under Chatham, old Pelhamite whigs faithful to Newcastle,
the Cavendish family and its connections, and such personal
friends of Rockingham as Grafton, Conway, and Charles
Townshend who might in certain circumstances be happy to
see him again as the Minister. It included too a good many
who prided themselves on independence of all party connection: country gentlemen who respected Savile and Dowdeswell and thought that the Rockingham administration had
served the country well. In November, when he broke with
Chatham, the Marquis estimated the "whigs" in Commons
at 121: a shrinkage which hardly surprises. Early in March

1767 Newcastle, who judged and counted men differently, saw only 101 whigs, of whom but 77 had been on Rockingham's November list.[2] Whatever this may mean it suggests a dwindling, which must have gone farther as a result of refusal to unite with the Bedford–Grenville party of 50-odd. Nothing fails like failure, and what with the abortive July negotiation and resultant differences among his principal friends, the wonder is that Rockingham did not quit the business of party.

In the latter part of September he held a *conciliabulum* at Wentworth with Dowdeswell, Burke, Portland, and Lord John Cavendish. They agreed to show cordiality to the Bedfords and all but Lord John were for giving up Conway. Then Rockingham went to town, to Newmarket, and toured about seeing other friends. He tried in vain to convince Newcastle that he had done the right thing in the late negotiation. He went to court and found the King "most abundantly gracious." [3] There he met Conway who seemed embarrassed yet desirous of conversation, and a rumor went about that Grafton made new proposals of the kind rejected in July. Richmond re-argued the case for formal treaty with Grafton and Conway, painting the alternative as desperate:

> If the support of Lord Bute's friends, which you would have, if you joined with the present Ministers, frightens you, I suppose you mean never to come in, but when you have them in opposition to you. If so, I would ask your Lordship if you think you can ever come in but by force? How long you may think it will take to bring that about. Whether when brought about you will not have the King in his heart your enemy, and hating you.[4]

The friends remained at sixes and sevens. The Marquis' horses, like the politicians, ran badly at Newmarket and there was a return of his "old complaint." Even a slight shadow fell upon his relations with Burke who considered an invitation to stand for Lancaster in the approaching election until the Marquis vetoed the enterprise in the interest of the Cavendishes. An anonymous writer in the

Public Advertiser depicted Burke as "Mr. Brazen" offering
himself for sale to administration, and a story circulated
that a joint-paymastership was offered to him. Was he
tempted to quit a hopeless cause for the emoluments of
office? Rockingham took the trouble to tell him that there
never was nor ever could be "a likeness to that picture." [5]

The Marquis returned from his tour with no lights but a
vague hope that the Bedfords might quit Grenville (since
the court appeared so averse to him) and unite with the
main body of the whigs, "which if once effected on our own
plan of consistency would carry a strong body of men, and
perhaps the whole publick without doors along with us."
In any event, he intended to continue the way he had gone:
no junction with ministers unless reinforced by a Bedford
alliance, and no junction with the Bedfords unless they were
quit of Grenville. He was sure that it was right and to the
honor of his friends that they stay on that course. And so
thought that stern political moralist, Lady Rockingham,
who cared nothing for Newcastle or Bedford and believed
that the latter's followers would come to terms with administration instead of allying with her lord. "As to your
political conduct," she wrote to him on November 17, "I
think it not likely to err, as I am sure uprightness will always be its foundation." [6]

Soon after the opening of Parliament (in late November)
the Bedfords treated with Grafton, broke from Grenville,
and fused with administration. The Marquis was dismayed
and yet quietly proud. "We wait with all patience for the
dénouement of all these political meanderings," he wrote
to Richmond on December 14, "& though they don't afford
matter of prospect to us as a party yet they please as they
seem to throw an honorary lustre on our own proceedings."
To Portland he described the Bedfords as "wallowing in
the mud." Newcastle's tactical notions being now obsolete,
the old Duke came around handsomely and told Rockingham: "My political conscience & my political conduct, I
entirely give up, to be directed by you; I am easy & happy
in so doing. I much approve your conduct; I know your

unshaken zeal for the true interest of your country." [7] With the accession of the Bedfords the Grafton administration was so strengthened that all hope of the King's turning to Rockingham was gone. The competent Lord North, who as a political man belonged to the King alone, now took over the leadership of the House of Commons from Conway, who to Rockingham's extreme disgust remained as a part of administration. Gone therefore was any basis for the kind of strategy the Marquis had followed in the previous session. The Rockinghams were fully an opposition party at last.

> We have nothing to do now [wrote the Marquis on December 22] but to look to our own friends, form our own plans for any matters of business which we may think proper to bring on & need not trouble our thoughts about what may suit this or that set of men, as there are none, as *sets,* with whom we can have any thing to do.[8]

There was something exhilarating in being on their own. Burke called his party at this time "the *enfans perdus* of politics . . . keeping a distance from all others, shunning and shunned by them." If they were dupes it was to their rectitude, and he confided to a private friend that he felt "inexpressible comfort" in being of "a set of men willing to go on all together on a plan of clear consistent conduct." [9] Sir William Meredith was optimistic for he had thought that in the past they had been too much beholden to Pitt, then too much obsessed by Conway and Townshend, and afterward too courting toward the Bedfords. He now told Rockingham that he hoped "your friends may look to themselves & themselves only" and that "if Mr. Dowdeswell, Sir George Savile, Lord John Cavendish & Burke act together & take up measures strongly without offering any personal consideration to divert them, they must lead the independent part of the house & absorb the attention of the public." [10]

From a practical point of view their prospects were hopeless. Without political patronage, without a royal duke or

prince to extend favor and protection, an opposition party
could hardly endure in that age when a strong public prejudice existed against "factions." The whigs of the Walpole–
Pelham–Newcastle era had been the court and Treasury
party. Without the court and Treasury, the Rockinghams
might claim the apostolic succession, but were likely to
shrink into a sect. The pride of grandees, the sense of personal dignity and honor, the spirit of friendship, mutual
admiration, constituted all the capital they had for remaining in a corporate state. And there was nothing to do but
to look out for an opportunity to move something of large
and recognizable benefit or to oppose something greatly
disliked by the public. But a revivified whig party—in opposition—so behaving as to persuade George III to make
its leaders his ministers, was only a dream. The principle of
party, thought Lord Hardwicke on December 27, was "extinct, at least so divided and filtered out, that it forms no
bond of union which has either consistence or solidity &
interest carries every body to the shop which distributes the
loaves and fishes." [11]

Nor was it auspicious for the Rockinghams that a new
storm was blowing up across the Atlantic to destroy what
remained of their boast that they had conciliated the Americans. The incorrigible Bostonians, hating the Townshend
Revenue Act and the lately arrived Customs Board, were
again boycotting British manufactures. On the first day of
Parliament mention of this stirred Grenville to deliver a
philippic against the Rockinghams for their past conduct
toward America. The Marquis inquired in London commercial houses for the latest intelligences. Barlow Trecothick
predicted (December 13) that the movement in Boston
"would not be so alarming as in appearance it might seem."
Rockingham wrote to him:

> I can hardly think that the *act* of combination or opposition
> against the sale of European commodities on the pretense of
> patriotism & economy, is or should be deemed criminal. Tho'
> I must say that the *intention* in those who have set it on foot in

Boston is deserving of the private censure of every man who means well either here or there.[12]

Two weeks later another merchant in the American trade, Moses Franks, told him that letters of November 4 from New York indicated that there too "the leven of that spirit which works strongly at Boston" was to be apprehended. Presumably the Marquis had by this time received a detailed account (dated November 1) from his friend Harrison, customs collector at Boston, who said that Pitt's famous praise of American resistance to the Stamp Act was the text of political harangues by a "set of wicked and abandoned incendiaries." As yet they went on in an orderly way, but Harrison dared not say how long that would continue although he trusted that "many of the best gentlemen in town" would exert themselves "against any outrage that might be attempted." [13] No violent disorders occurred at Boston until the following June. Ministers moved nothing on the subject of America for nearly a year, and the Rockinghams stayed shy of such an unprofitable cause for the party. The existence of a problem in British-American relations may have contributed importantly to justifying their existence as a party, but they would have been happy if the colonies had sunk politically into a deep sleep.

While in Yorkshire for the Christmas holiday Rockingham discovered some business more promising for his friends: a cause sure to gain favor with the country gentlemen in Parliament. Certain interested persons were inquiring into the validity of land titles in crown grants. The Surveyor General's office was naturally interested in accurate demarcation, and when allegations were made of illegal possession would recommend to the Treasury a lease to open the way for a determination in the courts. Among Rockingham's papers is a manuscript copy of a letter (dated November 11, 1766) to the printer of the *York Courant,* asserting that "frequent attacks" had been "made of late years on many Gentlemen in some of the Northern Counties, by certain adventurers, who somehow or other have ob-

tained Grants from the Crown to fish for such pretended
Concealments." [14] The Marquis' attention seems not to have
been drawn to this practice, however, until the Duke of
Portland was victimized. Part of the property in Cumber-
land County which William III had granted to the first
Lord Portland was leased (December 28, 1767) to Sir
James Lowther, whose family had long dominated elections
in Cumberland—and Lowther was a son-in-law of Lord
Bute! A new parliament would be elected in 1768, the
Lowther influence was being challenged by a party of gentry
whom Portland was supporting, and the votes of several
hundred electors were at stake in the disputed property.
"I have much curiosity to know all the maneuvres," wrote
Rockingham to the Duke on January 4, "in order (as Jack
White would say) to feed my indignation." [15] He went to
Welbeck, learned how Portland had tried to prevent the
lease, and hurried to town convinced that the whigs had a
good cause: the defense of property against dormant claims
of the crown. The prejudice against Bute could be exploited,
and also something which was then only beginning to be
felt—the rising influence of the crown. After conferring
with Dowdeswell, Meredith, Savile, and Burke, he put the
matter to Charles Yorke, whose legal talents would be required in preparing the motion. Yorke, who little relished
opposition politics, was shy of bringing Portland's cause into
Parliament (as was the Duke himself) and did not become
cooperative until the Marquis explained that

> the idea we have is not immediately arising out of the Duke of
> Portland's case, tho' in fact part of the zeal on the occasion
> may arise from feeling on his account. Our notion has been,
> that the proposition would be for the general good, quiet &
> ease of all persons possessed of property.[16]

After much canvassing and counseling the plan crystal-
lized in a motion to renew and amend an act passed in James
I's reign to prevent the crown from suing to recover lands
held in private possession for at least sixty years. The pro-

posed bill would abolish the legal maxim *nullum tempus occurrit regi*; it would, as Burke stated, "extend the principles of prescription and limitation of claims, which prevailed between subject and subject, to the Crown." Some delay in bringing on the business was caused by the Marquis' difficulty in persuading Savile to be the mover. Sir George's immense credit with country gentlemen and independent men in the House made him the indispensable man, but he had great doubt that his health and ability were equal to the undertaking. As the day for the motion (February 17) neared, Rockingham predicted "a very good show" and a "strong impression" which would "do us honour." [17]

> I take all the pains I can [he told Newcastle] to send & speak to all & everyone, where I have a chance of being persuasive, for really I am so fully convinced both of the propriety & of the necessity of this revival of the principles of the bill, that I am exceedingly anxious for its success, & I am persuaded that if we make a good figure upon it this year, in one or two years, this bill will be forced by the publick upon the Ministers.[18]

He was not to be disappointed. The battle fought by Savile, Dowdeswell, Meredith, Burke, Lord John Cavendish, and other whigs—with George Grenville also speaking for the motion and dividing with the Rockinghams—rallied 114 against administration's 134. The 114 may be compared with the miserable 41 mustered by the Rockinghams a few weeks before against a ministerial bill to continue limitation upon the East India Company's dividends. A convincing demonstration was thus made of what could be done if something of real interest to the independent part of the House were brought forward. The Marquis heard the debate from the peers gallery, and afterward entertained friends at his house until three in the morning. They all felt that something big had been achieved, that they had prevailed in the debate, and that the next parliament would enact the *nullum tempus* bill into law. Burke recorded:

About 6 out of our people had fallen ill, or rambled for want
of whipping in, or, you see, we should have run them very hard.
Conway had the decency to absent himself. The temper of the
house was such, that I have not the least doubt of our carrying
our point next Parliament; they will scarcely venture, I think,
to contest it.[19]

The debate took place behind closed doors, but the event
and all that had brought it on were ventilated in the press.
Notable were two long and prominently placed letters signed
"MEMNON" in the *Public Advertiser* which stated that a
"shock" had been given to "the whole landed property of
England." The motion for leave to bring in a bill to abolish
the *nullum tempus* rule had been made by "one of the ablest,
most virtuous and most temperate men in the Kingdom,
supported by a steady band of uniform patriots." "Memnon" insinuated the influence of Bute in the lease to his
son-in-law and related the practice thus exemplified to "the
growth of arbitrary and despotic principles in this country." [20]

The expectations of the Rockinghams that such a bill as
Savile had introduced would be passed in the next parliament proved well-founded, but that is not to say that the
Marquis, who shared the expectation, believed that the
ministry would thereby be overturned.

Don't mistake me [he wrote to a Yorkshire friend] & imagine
that I mean that in the next session of Parliament *we* shall
get the better of Administration. It is only from the goodness
of the question & the manner in which it has been conducted
which will make us in *this* successful. An Administration like
the present really supported & exerting the powerful influence
of the Crown will not be so soon dislodged.[21]

II

To what extent the *nullum tempus* question affected the elections for a new parliament in March–April 1768 it is not

possible to say. The historian[22] who knows most about the elections did not mention it as influencing any of them; yet it was the liveliest question of the day and almost a third (167) of the men returned at the polling had not been in the House of Commons before the dissolution. The number of contests was 83, or thirty more than in 1761.[23] There were eight of those dreaded expensive county contests, twice as many as in the previous election; and in four of these the Rockingham connection acted with varying degrees of successful effect. If, as does appear, parliamentary voting on the land-tax question had some influence on the electorate, it is hard to believe that the *nullum tempus* issue was without effect.

What with the nature of the electoral system, it need hardly be said that there was not a concerted whig election-strategy. Burke, to be sure, had suggested the previous summer that the moneyed men of the party go after the "venal boroughs"; and Newcastle had in December urged upon Rockingham "a general attention to all elections where there is any contest; your influence, at the head of us all, will operate in most places." [24] To a small extent such an exertion was made. The Marquis helped Sir Edward Astley who topped the poll in the Norfolkshire contest, and Peter Ludlow who gained a contested seat in Huntingdonshire. Robert Gregory owed his success at Maidstone to Rockingham's influence, as did William Weddell at Hull, and Beilby Thompson for his uncontested nomination at Hedon. At Malton the Marquis declined to recommend John Mostyn, his cousin who had held a seat from that borough for twenty-seven years, and brought in Lord Downe. Mostyn had voted against repeal of the Stamp Act and did not vote on either the land tax or *nullum tempus*. The other member for Malton, Savile Finch, was returned again. Rockingham brought in Frederick Montagu, a reliable party man, for the single-member borough of Higham Ferrers, Charles Yorke's election for Cambridge University having made it possible for John Yorke to give up Higham Ferrers and come in for the Yorke family borough of Reigate.[25]

Rockingham's major election activity was naturally in Yorkshire, where comparative quiet reigned. Savile and Lascelles were returned again for the county with his support and without contest. In the city of York a problem arose. Sir George Armytage, whom the Marquis had successfully backed in the previous election, decided not to be in the next parliament. Rockingham expressed great regret to the club at York, saying:

> I have strove to find a proper successor & I will say, what is well known to many who hear me, that I have taken infinite pains to persuade persons to offer themselves candidates whose principles & whose fortunes would make them most fitting for the honour & trust of representing this City. The determination of my own mind has long been the wish to see men of property & good principles, coming into Parl[iamen]t.[26]

One man of that description was eager to offer his services: Sir Charles Turner, who had threatened a contest in the county in 1761 and who prided himself on "constitutional" opposition to the influence of peers in parliamentary elections. Rockingham had no relish for Turner, and resented any suggestion that he meddled in elections, thinking it entirely proper that the weight of his interest and property, as part of the landed interest so much threatened by moneyed adventurers, should be asserted in the choice of a representative in Parliament. For all his misgivings Rockingham preferred supporting Turner, who had a good deal of popularity, to getting into a contest. So much was indicated to Turner in January when the Marquis also suggested that he join the Rockingham Club. Turner disapproved of that organization on account of its name which seemed to signify the practice which he condemned; yet he wished for the support of the club's members and the endorsement of its head as well. In the end Rockingham made a virtue of necessity and gave that endorsement. According to Lady Rockingham, "as soon as my Lord proposed him, Charles made his *appearance* & a *speech* at the Club. . . . I am extremely glad to find that he has acquiesced in certain

points & thereby enabled my Lord to propose him there." [27]
The Marquis had scarcely gotten back to Wentworth when
Lord John Cavendish arrived (March 14) bringing news
of his failure at Lancaster, and on the same day came word
from York that Fox-Lane, the other city nominee, had
chosen not to stand. Rockingham instantly mounted a horse
and rode to the city—forty miles—to propose Lord John.
In two days all was arranged:

> I called my friends together the next morning & warmly recom-
> mended Lord John Cavendish. It was received with the utmost
> joy & approbation. . . . Lord John & Sir Charles join & we
> shall have no opposition.[28]

When all was over throughout the county, he was much
gratified, telling Sir George Savile:

> Nothing ever was more fortunate than all the Yorkshire elec-
> tions have turned out, where we were interested. . . . The
> assistance we have been of in bringing Yorkshire men of large
> properties into Parliament, has given great satisfaction.[29]

Neither then nor at any other time in his life did Rockingham carry electioneering politics to the length of buying
nominations from venal boroughs or purchasing burgages in
order to control the choice of members of Parliament. Malton and Higham Ferrers, which he had inherited, remained
his only nomination boroughs. He thought that the main
difficulty in building the parliamentary party was not in ac-
quiring such boroughs but in finding enough prudent and
honorable men who were willing to serve in Parliament.
"The great expence of elections," he regretfully observed,
"have indeed too much in general deterr'd the prudent &
proper persons from attempting to come into Parliament."
Some months after the 1768 election he wrote to Burke of
"a very good *sort of man*—a Yorkshire man—with a
thumping landed property" who wished to get into Parliament: "I wish I knew of 20 more of the same disposition,

KING GEORGE III
Studio of Alan Ramsay
National Portrait Gallery
London

EDMUND BURKE
Studio of Sir Joshua Reynolds
National Portrait Gallery
London

WILLIAM PITT
FIRST EARL OF CHATHAM
Studio of William Hoare
National Portrait Gallery
London

THOMAS PELHAM–HOLLES
FIRST DUKE OF NEWCASTLE
William Hoare
National Portrait Gallery
London

there might perhaps come a day in which I could assist them." [30]

For the Rockinghams in 1768 the Duke of Portland was the electioneering hero. With the cooperation of Meredith he had in the previous years acquired an interest in Wigan, and both his candidates, George Byng and Beaumont Hotham, triumphed in a close contest. In Cumberland, where the election was one of the most famous of the century, the Portland-backed Henry Curwen led the poll and his ally, Henry Fletcher, put Sir James Lowther out of Parliament by reversal of the return through petition. Lowther-backed candidates lost too in Carlisle, and Portland's brother Edward Bentinck and George Musgrave were returned. And in Westmoreland county, still another clash of Portland and Lowther interests occurred, with the Duke's candidate Thomas Fenwick gaining a seat. In the borough of Leicester the intervention of Meredith and Portland was productive in the victory of a good whig, Booth Grey, the Duke's brother-in-law who led the poll. Portland also made an attempt at Callington in Cornwall, backing two candidates but without success probably because his great costs in the north prevented the sending of enough money.[31]

In London the Rockinghamite Barlow Trecothick was elected although with fewer votes than the other three members chosen. At Chichester in Sussex the Duke of Richmond brought in a Keppel and his relative Thomas Connolly without contest, while the Duke's brother Lord George Lennox and Newcastle's nephew Thomas Pelham shared unopposed the county representation. Newcastle carried on a large and varied electioneering activity with remarkable success in view of his declining health and influence. No doubt this was, in considerable measure, because many of his friends were less recognizable as opposition men and because Treasury electioneers were reluctant to disturb local patterns of interest. Owing to two "ungrateful nephews," he was attacked in Nottinghamshire boroughs long subservient to him and lost an old reliable—John White—at East Retford. In his home county he lost an election at Lewes. For many months in advance of the 1768 dissolution he had fussed and fretted over this kind of business, bitterly resenting the little treacheries an obsolescent politician must always suffer and hurting his failing health. Rockingham conjured him to stop torturing himself: "Believe me, I am much more of a friend than a politician & I don't weigh *ten* members of parliament, more or less, as in any degree comparable to my wish & desire to see your Grace perfectly reistablished in health." [32] After the heats were over the old Duke counted the men he had helped to return and wrote: "I think I can announce for every one of them, except perhaps one, that they will go with the Marquess of Rockingham in every thing." Newcastle thought too that of the men coming into Parliament "we shall have a good chance of having a great, if not the greatest part of them." This judgment, made before the elections were all over, was fairly sound. The new parliament was to show a substantial increase in the number of opposition whigs.[33] So that "the *enfans perdus* of politics" were now less hopelessly lost.

III

In the most turbulent of the elections, that for metropolitan Middlesex county, the Rockinghams had no direct interest although the Marquis seems to have regretted the defeat of a fairly steadfast whig. In Wilkes, the winner, they had nothing; and the spectacle of an outlaw, untouched by crown authorities, first standing for London and then for Middlesex, and firing an explosion of riots, was at once a negation of the politics of tranquillity and a demonstration of weakness in the ministry headed by the Duke of Grafton. Such a breach of the peace of civil society could not happen in Yorkshire, which Alexander Wedderburn at this time described as "a country of plenty, frugality, and sobriety . . . where the laws execute themselves, and where the name of Wilkes is never joined with liberty, nor mentioned but with detestation." [34]

That he would be expelled was a natural expectation, and when Rockingham heard in mid-April that ministers would have business of importance when the new parliament met on May 10, he suspected (but wrongly) that it would be Wilkes's expulsion. The Marquis did not know how such a motion could be opposed if Wilkes remained in the status of an outlaw, but his surrender to the court which had tried him and his lodgment in jail altered the aspect of the case. It would be wrong, Rockingham thought, for Parliament to act against him while he was in the hands of the law:

> If the business of importance should be Mr. Wilkes's case, there will be such an appearance of violence & precipitation . . . that it will give much cause for uneasiness, if it is moved, & I think if the friends we have in town make a stand upon that point, the weight of their arguments will distress more than the question of their numbers.[35]

Those arguments did not have to be spoken, however, because a ministry of divided counsels did not move against Wilkes that spring. Nevertheless this short session of Parliament—little more than a month—had some importance in the history of the Rockingham party.

It opened amid riots wide over the cities of London and Westminster. Peers and commoners gathering at St. Stephen's were jostled and insulted. A mob vainly wishing to escort Wilkes from jail to Parliament clashed with royal troops in what was exaggeratedly described as the "Massacre of St. George's fields." The Mansion House was attacked, a sawmill pulled down; weavers and coal-heavers were out against their oppressors, and a strike of sailors swelled the immense disturbance. What was the cause of civil government's failure to secure the peace and order of society? In the debate on the address (May 13) Dowdeswell called for a parliamentary inquiry to find out the cause. Burke, who would soon be writing a pamphlet on "the cause of the present discontents," supported Dowdeswell in a speech declaring the cause: a malign influence working to destroy the natural respect of the people for their natural leaders, by sowing discord among leading men and lowering them in the public estimation.

> Formerly [he said] these things were not so. The upper ranks were kept in order by a sense of their own importance, but now they will go part after part, until the whole shall fall to pieces. I appeal to the feelings of gentlemen whether this is not the case—whether . . . the class between the sovereign and the mob, has not disappeared: and if so does not such a state of things demand inquiry?

That the upper ranks might come again to a sense of their own importance through whig reunion under the leadership of Lord Rockingham, Burke plainly implied; when Conway interjected that no cause had contributed so much to the riots as "party divisions, and many potent factions," Burke answered: "Sir, this country will never be well governed until we see those who are connected by unanimity of sentiment hold the reins of power." Lord John Cavendish gave the House a more ample statement on the subject of party:

> With regard to party connexions, it is easy to imagine individuals associated with the worst designs; but men of honour will never unite together for unworthy purposes. This country can never be well governed, but by persons united in principle, concurring in sentiment, and bound together by affection.[36]

On May 16, by which time quiet was returning to the metropolis and the word was out that nothing would be moved against Wilkes, War Secretary Barrington brought in a bill to authorize the King to call out the militia against rioters in the event that regular troops were not available to support magistrates. Burke argued for inquiry to precede legislation, avowing that the cause of discontent was general and had inflamed people "from one end of the Kingdom to the other." That night he met with Savile, Dowdeswell, and the Marquis to discuss what they ought to do about Barrington's bill. Rockingham urged his friends to oppose it:

In the light it strikes me, I think it is a declaration that there
is no civil authority left in this country. . . . I also think it
will tend to create more & more remissness in the civil magistrates in every part of the country, whose fears may make them
too readily adopt the idea that the danger is so great that nothing but powder & ball must be had recourse to.

The next day Dowdeswell, Lord John, Savile, Burke, and
Frederick Montagu fought the bill and seemed to carry
the sense of the House, so that Barrington retreated and
agreed to put off the second reading to a day when, as all
knew, Parliament would not be in session. This was not a
ministerial defeat since North was undecided about the
bill and Barrington acknowledged that it was his own, not
administration's. Nevertheless the Rockinghams felt that
they had won a feather. Newcastle wrote to the Marquis
that Dowdeswell, Burke, Savile, and Lord John Cavendish
"have taken possession of this new House of Commons." [37]
In reality, members were impatient for the session's end
and no more wished for Barrington's bill than for the
Rockinghams' inquiry.

"Our people are almost gone into the country," Burke
told Charles O'Hara on June 9, "but we keep our union
and spirits, and are increased in numbers very considerably."
A few days later there was rejoicing over the return of a
lost sheep to the whig fold. Thomas ("Tommy") Townshend, who had sat on Rockingham's Treasury board and
continued under Grafton until raised to a joint paymaster-
ship, threw up his office. He had joined in the attack against
Barrington's militia bill and afterward resented being asked
to give over the Pay Office to Richard Rigby and to take an
Irish vice-treasurership. An admirer of Chatham, Townshend may have relished an opportunity to justify parting
from an administration which had lost its Chathamite character and become (in the language of the day) a system
of "Butes" and "Bedfords." Rockingham said of him: "I
have always had a partiality towards Tommy Townshend
& I do believe that the present warmth arises from his never

having been so satisfied in his mind, since he separated from us." [38] Townshend never became a solidly-connected Rockingham whig, but he stayed in opposition until 1782.

The short session ended in mid-June while rumors went about of royal dissatisfaction with ministers for not moving the expulsion of Wilkes, and of a likely change of administration—which, however, was remote from the King's intention. Rockingham departed for Wentworth on June 18, after telling Newcastle: "I think all our material friends are in the dispositions we could wish & I hope that when Parliament really meets that we shall set out with vigour & alertness. I am sure there will be some sufficient matters of importance." [39]

Even a Rockingham–Grenville cooperation in politics no longer seemed utterly impossible. Abandoned by the Bedfords and detested at court, George Grenville, with a knot of faithful supporters, was in a state of political isolation. More and more he seemed to affect the role of an elder statesman who would never again be the King's minister. His was a respectable but ineffective position and no man in the House of Commons was esteemed superior to him in knowledge of business, honesty, and parliamentary ability. He had supported Savile's motion to bring in the *nullum tempus* bill. Dowdeswell had written to Lady Rockingham on March 20: "I made a little attempt for G. G. not long ago, without much success indeed, for I own it was abrupt & G. G. must pave the way for me by *proper submission* before I can hope for success." [40]

Grenville's political agent, Whateley, told him (July 12) that Wedderburn had had "a long conversation with Mr. Burke, whose language with respect to you . . . was very different from any he had ever heard from that quarter." Burke was described as saying that Grenville was "an excellent party-man," that "it was pleasant to be connected with such a man, and the party would act with confidence who acted under him." [41] The source here is hearsay of hearsay, but there is no improbability about Burke's making compliments which he knew would reach Grenville's ears.

IV

"I imagine there is no great political matter stirring in London," wrote Rockingham to Newcastle on July 17; "at least I know of none. . . . I should not be sorry for a long vacation from politics." [42] Two days later intelligence reached the capital of mob violence against the customs commissioners at Boston; which was only a detail of the ominous picture now unveiling of an intercolonial combination to vindicate the proposition that the British legislature had no authority to lay a tax for revenue in America.

The Marquis ought not to have been much surprised. He may not have been aware of the Massachusetts Assembly's circular letter of the previous January to enlist the support of other colonial bodies for a constitutional position flatly opposed to the unlimited supremacy of Parliament, or of Lord Hillsborough's sending the royal command to governors to dissolve assemblies bold enough to affirm that position. But Rockingham had had it all spelled out in a private letter from the Speaker of the Massachusetts Assembly which he received in the late winter or early spring of 1768.[43] No doubt he trusted that common sense and material interests would prevent the forcible assertion of an abstract doctrine subversive of British authority. He had heard nothing from his confidential informant Harrison, the collector at Boston, since the early winter, but another friend, Governor John Wentworth of New Hampshire, had written (May 6) to communicate "the temper of the colonies" and had not painted an alarming picture: some "factious minds" were trying to stir up trouble, but they might "long write and declaim without the least hazard of propagating any ideas of independence, exclusive of that subordination to G[reat] Britain, which your Lordship has so powerfully recommended." [44] When news of the June riots in Boston reached England, Rockingham received an authoritative account from Harrison, a main target of the mob, who told of a "dangerous and seditious combination" to resist payment of duties of any kind and to drive the customs commissioners and all serving under them from the country unless assurance were given that all port duties would be repealed. News of the "Wilkes and Liberty riots" in the mother country had hastened similar proceedings of violence in Boston.[45]

All this was rudely disturbing to the Rockinghams. It blurred their outlook upon the future. They did not wish to be put again in the role of appeasers of misbehaving Americans; nor could they bring themselves to support British punitive measures. Savile thought it "a very melancholy story" but the Americans were "above our hands"; he feared that it was in the nature of things that colonies so situated must ultimately rebel. Burke wished that the colonies were "in a state of as much division" as the ministers. Newcastle said that the New Englanders "always were a refractory people, ever since & indeed in King William's time." Rockingham sent a copy of "poor Harrison's account" to Dowdeswell, and put upon him the assignment of thinking through the problem of what ought to be done in the event that what Newcastle called "the farce given out that the Ministers intend to act with vigour" proved not to be a farce.[46]

Dowdeswell thought it "the most difficult subject" he had ever tackled: the conduct of the Americans was indefensible. The Townshend duties were not a grievous burden upon them and they even opposed the "reduced duty on molasses meant now to be really collected & to say the truth for revenue not for commerce." Reducing that duty had been the beneficent work of the Rockingham administration. One might, thought Dowdeswell, argue for the repeal of Charles Townshend's duties as injudiciously laid, "being injurious to the manufactures of this country, & operating as bounties upon the like manufactures in America," but that would not meet the real question which was the principle asserted by the Americans: "It must either be admitted which is timidity, weakness, irresolution & inconsistency; or it must be resisted & the arms of this country must be asserted against her colonies." But "a contest with the colonies supported as they will be by the enemies of this country, must be destruction to us in the first place." The wiser course, therefore, was to try to induce the Americans to avoid violence, to stop their combinations, and to petition for repeal of parliamentary taxes for revenue; and to admit —if there were no acceptable alternative but to admit—that after all no real difference existed between external and internal taxes, that "port duties laid for revenue are in their nature the same as qualified stamp acts," and to renounce them as "Grenvillian." [47]

While Dowdeswell was spelling out his recommendations for the party, the Marquis talked with Savile and Portland at Welbeck. Afterward Sir George undertook a long letter to Harrison of the kind the Rockinghams desired to have widely read in America. He deplored the raising of the question of constitutional right and what seemed a fanatical madness capable of stirring a countermadness in Great Britain. He chided Americans for embarrassing their real friends in England. He recalled the repeal of the Stamp Act, said he thought that was right and thought so "yet"—"pray attend to that last word: Are they all determined not to have a friend in England, not a single friend?" [48]

A house full of guests, York Races, and an expected visit by the King of Denmark at Wentworth, kept Rockingham "in one uninterrupted series of occupation and hurry" until late September. Lord John and Lord Frederick Cavendish visited him. Newcastle, sounding in the south, wrote that ministers intended strong measures in America but he did not believe Parliament could be induced to "join in a measure that must totally dissolve all connection with the colonies." He was doubtful of some friends but strong for the principles acted on "when we repealed the Stamp Act." [49] In late September–October the Marquis went to town and to Newmarket, where he answered Harrison. Savile had already given the collector advice against returning to England for his health, the latter having expressed such a desire; now Rockingham told him that he would only be replaced and perhaps be made a scapegoat because of his connection with men in opposition. Besides, Harrison might do much good where he was "in bringing about peace & good order, whenever calm sense begins to bear up against the rashness & passions of a few, I hope, vain men." The Marquis avowed that he would ever adhere to the Declaratory Act of 1766, but the implied right of the British legislature to tax the colonies ought to be prudently restrained, for the good of the empire, and not exercised in such a way as to vex America.

> If the affairs in America go on with warmth, I have no doubt but that the restrictions of the Act of Navigation will be consider'd as a virtual taxation. I am sure I so far agree with them, that they have the same tendency as a tax & I always use it as an argument to those, who assert that the colonies pay nothing to the support of the mother country. If I tie my tenants to grind at the manor mill, I certainly raise money upon them *virtually* for I let my mill the better for their being tied to be its customers.[50]

From this premise it could be argued that the colonies were not a proper object of parliamentary taxation for revenue. In due course that would become a basic doctrine of Rockinghamite colonial policy.

The Marquis was apprehensive that the revival of rioting and combinations for non-importation in America might move the King to bring Grenville back into administration.[51] The latter's credit in the country seemed to rise since he was the only public man with a reputation for dealing firmly with the colonies. What his remedies for the ills of empire might be was set forth in a pamphlet which appeared early in October. Entitled *The Present State of the Nation*,[52] it was addressed "to the King and both Houses of Parliament." The author saw an impoverished and heavily-burdened public, declining trade, rising prices, a licentiousness despising all authority, government "relaxed in every sinew." He envisaged a more equitable distribution of the

costs in maintaining the enlarged establishment of government and bearing the swollen debt. He proposed to get
£100,000 from Ireland and £200,000 from the colonies in
America: offering in return, to Ireland the opening of colonial markets to her commerce on an equal footing with
Great Britain, and to the American colonies, representation
in Parliament and wider trading-opportunities. The American revenue was not to be raised by any such method as a
stamp tax, or by port duties (rejected as contrary to the
principles of the navigation laws), but by Parliament's assessing a specific sum from each colony and leaving the mode
of raising it to the several assemblies. With the colonies
thus performing "their parts as members of the British
empire," it would be incumbent upon the supreme legislature
to promote their interests in all ways not injurious to the
mother country. No longer should they be obliged to send
enumerated products to Britain solely for the advantage of
British re-exporters; only products required for consumption and manufactures in Britain should be kept on the
enumerated list. Other products should go wherever they
found a market, but only in exchange for bullion: "The
cheaper the products of the colonies can be sent to market,
the greater will be their consumption; and if a strict guard
is kept, that nothing be carried back but from Great Britain,
the advantage of an increased foreign demand for the com-
modities of the colonies, will be shared by Great Britain
with them." Thus, while colonial exports might move with
greater freedom, the screw of control over imports would
be turned to absolute monopoly. The argument of utility
was employed in support of colonial parliamentary constituencies: the supreme legislature should pay more attention to the colonies because of their vast growth in territorial extent, population, and wealth, but that could not be
expected unless they elected members of the House of
Commons.

The Present State of the Nation had plausibility and
there was something in it to appeal to all sorts of opinion.
The King was flattered, no politician was personally at-

tacked. The controversial peace of 1762 was justified by faint praise. Economic discontents were explained. The singling out of Wilkes for punishment when others were equally culpable was inferentially condemned, together with the incompetence of ministers who knew not how to uphold order against licentious mobs. The Rockinghams could hardly have been more explicit in denouncing "divided heterogeneous administration," but they saw that the pamphlet should be answered. And the necessity seemed heightened by the firing of Shelburne and resignation of Chatham which momentarily at least opened the door of administration for the apprehended coming in of the Grenvilles. If that took place (it did not) and Camden followed the example of Chatham, Rockingham was certain that the tempting prize of the Great Seal would be offered to Charles Yorke, who might be unable to resist it. The prospective appearance of *Observations* on the Grenvillian pamphlet was advertised in the press before the month was out. Burke undertook the task with Dowdeswell's help,[53] but the work did not reach the bookstalls until February; by which time the circumstances of the party were much altered.

V

The King's speech opening Parliament (November 8) deplored the outbreak of "the spirit of faction" in some of the American colonies and described Boston as "in a state of disobedience to all law and government." Every necessary measure, it was said, had been taken to induce "a due obedience to the authority of the legislature," and "to defeat the mischievous designs of those turbulent and seditious persons . . . whose practices, if suffered to prevail, cannot fail to produce the most fatal consequences." In the debate on the address Dowdeswell called for inquiry into causes, moving an amendment to take into immediate consideration the conduct of ministers in relation to the colonies. It was supported not only by the Rockinghams but by known friends of Chatham and Shelburne. Burke scored the dissolution of assemblies, denounced the Townshend Revenue Act as like the Stamp Act, and protested the sending of troops to Boston. The Chathamite William Beckford said that taxing America for revenue would never do: "Why do you stir up those waters? Let the nation return to its old good nature, and its old good humour." Colonel Isaac Barré said that the time had come for all to hold one doctrine—namely, that Parliament had no right to tax the Americans but should rely in times of emergency on the old practice of crown requisitions. Even George Grenville was for Dowdeswell's amendment, because he was not satisfied that ministers had taken all necessary measures to uphold the authority of the British legislature.[54]

A month passed before ministry's American resolutions were brought in, and during that time Rockinghams and Grenvilles voted together in important divisions: on Savile's motion for leave to bring in the *nullum tempus* bill (which ministry did not oppose), and on a motion for papers respecting the conduct of government in relation to the French aggrandizement in Corsica. Thus there appeared what the *Annual Register* called "a casual coincidence of opinion, in many public matters, of two formidable parties, whose leaders had filled the first offices of the state." Nor was this coincidental alignment disturbed by the report of a personal reconciliation between Temple and the convalescent Chatham which was said to include Grenville; and which started gossip that the King would again consult the Great Man who would recommend his brothers-in-law as ministers. Rockingham, who detested Temple and had concerted nothing with Grenville, adopted an attitude of detached curiosity and wrote to Lady Rockingham (November 29) that "To *us* indeed who are mighty indifferent about any of these gentry, these events only afford matter of entertainment."[55] The last thing the court desired was a Grenville family administration, and so Grenvilles and Rockinghams went on dividing together. Both groups voted for Beckford's motion of December 7 for American papers, and did the same nine days later against North's attempt to induce the House to take into consideration, without prior inquiry, a new seditious libel published by Wilkes from his prison. On this occasion Rockingham who attended in the peers gallery thought that Grenville "spoke exceeding well, took in some part Dowdeswell's line, & upon the whole did well." [56] On that same day the Grenvilles were in the majority for Henry Fletcher's petition to reverse the return of Sir James Lowther for Cumberland. By this time Dowdeswell and Grenville were consulting together on motions.[57]

Meanwhile, ministry's intentions with respect to the American crisis had been unfolded, December 15, in the House of Lords, where Hillsborough moved a series of strong resolutions. Rockingham's tactic in this business was to maintain consistency of position without opening a parliamentary battle for a cause likely to embarrass the whigs. He wrote to Dartmouth on December 12:

> The American papers have laid upon the table in the House of Lords some time. . . . Today we read on & tomorrow finish them but the resolutions to be proposed are not to be moved till Thursday. What the resolutions are, does not transpire, & yet there are expectations that they will be much too hot for our politics.
>
> The papers laid before the house are certainly very partial informations;—the present circumstances of the state of Boston which must make every information of the more or less consequence according to the date, should naturally incline a wise administration not to be precipitate, & yet possibly in these times the desire of gratifying resentment may overweigh all prudential considerations.[58]

The ministerial resolutions proved merely denunciatory and self-justifying. No new measures were proposed, no additional power was asked. They passed without division, as did even the Duke of Bedford's motion for bringing into use, if necessary, an act of Henry VIII's reign for punishing treasons committed outside the realm—a threat which few could imagine being carried out. When the resolutions were brought forward in the House of Commons, six weeks later,

Dowdeswell led an attack centering upon Bedford's motion and forced a division (February 8) in which only 65 voted against concurrence with the Lords.[59] George Grenville called the resolutions "waste paper" but declined to oppose them, not wishing to give "countenance to the wild doctrines now afloat." He wanted a wise and comprehensive plan of imperial government which would work beneficently for both the mother country and the colonies. This had been spelled out in *The Present State of the Nation*.

On the day of that division Burke's attack on the Grenvillian pamphlet was published.[60] He set forth what must be regarded as the Rockingham doctrine with respect to the American colonies. No revenue was to be got from them "but by their freest and most cheerful consent." There was something in the nature of such colonies which made them an unfit object of taxation: by submitting to Britain's monopoly of their imported manufactures at prices "enhanced by our taxes" they paid "a share of our impositions." An American representation in Parliament was out of the realm of the practicable. All reasoning about America should be drawn from actual circumstances: "People must be governed in a manner suited to their temper and dispositions; and men of free character and spirit must be ruled with, at least, some condescension to this spirit and character." The current disorders in America could be subdued only by a return to the healing principles of 1766.

Burke's pamphlet attacked opinions attributed to "a person who had been in the management of the highest affairs, and may soon be in the same situation," but it also carried an implied appeal from a Grenville ill-informed to a Grenville better-informed. The author of *The Present State of the Nation* had lamented the growth of disconnection and distrust among public men. Burke said, "we lament it together," but insisted that there nevertheless did exist a body of men of "unshaken adherence to principle, and attachment to connexion, against every allurement of interest." If they were the friends of Lord Rockingham it was because they knew him by personal experience "to have wise and enlarged ideas of the publick good, and an invincible constancy in adhering to it . . . and that, in or out of power, change of situation will make no alteration in his conduct." These men might be reproached "for want of ability in their political transactions" and for "not profiting of several brilliant opportunities of fortune," but they could endure that reproach because they could not acquire "the reputation of *that kind* of ability without losing all the other reputation they possess." If they were charged with a spirit of exclusion and proscription because they would not "mix in schemes of administration, which have no bond of union, or principle of confidence," they would suffer that charge too with patience; although it was not true that the idea of a united administration meant proscription of any other party. No such system could be formed which did not leave room for "healing coalitions," and the essential point was "having the great strongholds of government in well-united hands, in order to secure the predominance of right and uniform principles." Thus the banner of the Rockinghams was raised, inviting all good men to repair to it— even by "healing coalition."

According to Horace Walpole, Burke's *Observations* made all approach to Grenville by the Rockinghams impossible,[61] but this may be doubted. Dowdeswell continued to consult with him about motions in Parliament. And it seems fair to say that the Rockinghams generally had more relish for the sort of business in which Grenville concurred, even though all in opposition did not, than for the question of Wilkes and Middlesex which was to swell the minority as no other business could. Grenville's zealous support (February 24) of the *nullum tempus* bill was perhaps decisive in stopping an emasculating amendment moved by the attorney general. He spoke the Rockinghamite language in arguing not only for the merits of the measure but from the necessity of pleasing a public violently agitated by the Wilkes case: "Parliament does not stand well in the eyes of the people. . . . Unless some good measures are taken to restore Parliament to the good opinion of the people, our constitution is overturned." Administration gave up all effort to prevent Savile's bill from becoming a statute. Rockinghams and Grenvilles fought another battle in late February–early March against paying, without prior accounting, the huge debt incurred by the crown on the civil list fund. Their hope was to show that the arrears had accumulated very recently, that none had existed when Grenville and Rockingham were Treasury ministers, that the debt must have been incurred by the misuse of money to corrupt members of Parliament.[62]

> Mr. Dowdeswell & our friends are hurrying down [wrote the Marquis to Charles Yorke on February 28]. . . . We mean to try to force the administration to lay the Civil List debt before Parliament, specifying the particular periods & which if we succeed in, you know what I told you would happen—neither more nor less than honour where you wish it & disgrace where you can have no objection to its falling. Grenville and Dowdeswell have met, they agree perfectly.[63]

Here was a good question for winning support from independent members, and in the division minority rose to 135. The Marquis prized the civil list debt question so much that, in the House of Lords, where 28 peers voted against concurrence with Commons, he spoke for the first time in three years. Clearly he was determined that the party should take possession of this question. When it came on again in 1777 they would end a secession tactic against the American war, and the principle contested for would be vindicated in Burke's Civil Establishment Act of 1782. Of his vocal effort on March 3–4, 1769, he wrote to Portland: "I was from beginning to end, in a violent agitation & was obliged to speak notwithstanding, *three* times. I got a good draft of Madeira before I went to the house." [64]

It was not without some value to his own and his party's reputation that he conquered a nervous timidity unbecoming in a political leader. Horace Walpole, who had always thought him to be very dim, said that "being very civil and very gentle, he was well heard." [65] Richmond, a ready speaker, wrote to him: "Indeed my dear Lord you owe it to yourself, to your friends, and to the cause which you stand at the head of, to deliver those sentiments in public which have made you so many private friends. . . . you cannot speak too often; practice will make it easy for you, you will do yourself credit, the cause good, and take away the only objections your enemies can raise to you as a minister." [66] A year later Burke would testify that the Marquis "may be said to be now among the regular speakers—a matter of infinite consequence to himself and to all of us. It was obvious, that if he could conquer the difficulty of public utterance, he would show more substantial and extensive understanding of business than any of them." [67]

As the most-heated controversial question since the repeal of the Stamp Act was being opened, "the *enfans perdus* of politics" were in a stronger position than could have been expected when Burke had coined that description. They had lost Newcastle to the grave the previous fall, and the loss was the more serious because his heir belonged to the court. But no desertions from the inner councils of the party had occurred. A tactical cooperation with George Grenville had been developed in the House of Commons. [68] The public had been addressed in a brilliant political pamphlet, and in still other ways the press was being used to advantage. The hand of Rockingham may be detected in the letter from the sheriff and grand jury of Yorkshire to the county representatives thanking them for their conduct on the *nullum tempus* act. The practice of seizing upon well-selected occasions for recording cogent, splendidly-composed protests in the journal of the House of Lords had been started. These too would not only make their way into the press but provide a detailed and consistent series exposing the principles and positions of the party. Moreover, the Rockinghams had a commanding influence upon the recording of contemporary history as a result of Burke's connection with the *Annual Register*. [69] They were appealing to the mind of the country as well as to the interests of the country gentlemen and leading merchants, so that their instincts ran against the metropolitan radicalism then welling up. They did not wish to stir up the country but to quiet it: to persuade the King that they knew the way to keep kingdom and empire in tranquillity.

NOTES

1. An estimate based upon biographical sketches of members in *Hist. Parl.*

2. *Ibid.,* I 190–191.

3. WWM R 1: 869; 2: 56; Add. MSS 32985, ff. 306–307; 32986, f. 58; *Bedford* III 393.

4. Albemarle II 60.

5. WWM R 1: 867; 153: 1. Rockingham to Burke 6 Oct. (WWM Burke papers). *Corr. Burke* I 330; IX 392–393; H. S. Woodfall, *Junius* (3 vols.; London, 1812) II 492–496; *Hist. Parl.* I 316–317; Carl B. Cone, *Burke and the Nature of Politics* (2 vols.; Lexington, 1957, 1964) I 316–317.

6. WWM R 168: 117. Rockingham to Burke 4 Nov. (WWM Burke papers). "In such uncertain times, it may probably be the wisest rule to abide & content oneself with doing the thing that is right in the moment without looking much further."—Rockingham to Dowdeswell 24 Nov. (R 1 : 891).

7. *Ibid.,* R 9: 8; Rockingham to Portland 17 Dec.—Portland MSS; Add. MS 32987, f. 274.

8. Add. MS 32987, f. 393.

9. *Corr. Burke* I 340.

10. Albemarle II 64–65.

11. Add. MS 35362, ff. 172–173.

12. WWM R 1: 909, 912.

13. *Ibid.,* R 1: 921; R 63: 9.

14. *Ibid.,* R 1: 789.

15. Portland MSS. Copies of principal documents in this business are preserved in WWM R 5. Accounts of the Portland–Lowther conflict are given in A. S. Turberville, *A History of Welbeck Abbey* (2 vols.; London, 1939) II 101–135; *Hist. Parl.* I 242–244; and Brian Bonsall, *Sir James Lowther* (Manchester, 1960), 75–105.

16. Add. MSS 35362, f. 175; 35430, ff. 95–103. Rockingham to Portland 20 Jan.—Portland MSS.

17. *Corr. Burke* I 344; Add. MS 35430, ff. 110–111.

18. Add. MS 32988, ff. 308–309 (14 Feb.).

19. *Ibid.,* ff. 369–371; *Corr. Burke* I 344. "It was a most honourable day for *us*. Our friends exerted themselves, they moved the matter and conducted it ably. The credit of the day is ours—the public will reap the advantage. . . . I think I may also add that the landed interest in England highly approves our attempt."—Rockingham to Albemarle 23 Feb. (printed in Albemarle II 73–74).

20. 24 Feb./4 March. Burke's authorship seems probable.

21. WWM R 1: 982.

22. John Brooke, *Chatham Administration* Ch. 9, and *Hist. Parl.* I 67–73.

23. According to the *Annual Register* for 1768 the election "was carried on with much heat, and violent contests ensued in many parts of the Kingdom."

24. *Corr. Burke* I 322; Add. MS 32987, f. 378.

25. *Hist. Parl.* I 220, 310–311, 313, 339, 344, 387, 435–436.

26. WWM R 1: 984.

27. *Ibid.*, 882, 983, 991, 992; Collyer, "The Rockingham Connection," 224–225; *Hist. Parl.* I 443; Add. MS 32989, ff. 175, 187.

28. To Newcastle, 16 March.—*Ibid.*, ff. 187–190. When the candidates were chaired Rockingham told Portland that he got "as drunk as a man can be, who drinks wine and water."—Portland MSS.

29. *Foljambe Manuscripts* (Hist. MSS Comm. 15th *Report* App. v 145–146).

30. Add. MS 32986, f. 328; *Corr. Burke* II 13.

31. *Hist. Parl.* I 225–226, 242–247, 319–322, 403–404.

32. Add. MS 32988, f. 164.

33. Add. MS 32989, ff. 242–243. In WWM R 220 there is a list (dated Nov. 1768) of 94 members of Parliament upon whom Rockingham felt that he could rely.

34. *Grenville* IV 263–264.

35. Add. MS 32990, ff. 1–2.

36. *Sir Henry Cavendish's Debates of the House of Commons, 1768–1771,* ed. J. Wright (2 vols. [London, 1841–1843]; hereafter cited as *Cavendish's Debates*) I 14–15, 17.

37. *Ibid.*, 18–22; Add. MS 32990, ff. 83–85, 109.

38. *Corr. Burke* I 353; Add. MS 32990, f. 208.

39. Add. MS 32990, f. 216.

40. Dowdeswell MSS.

41. *Grenville* IV 311.

42. Add. MS 32990, f. 311.

43. WWM R 62.

44. *Ibid.*, R 1: 1047.

45. *Ibid.*, R 63: 1. Harrison's letter of 17 June was carried to England by Benjamin Hallowell, comptroller of customs at Boston, who had arrived by 23 July.—*Grenville* IV 319.

46. *Albemarle* II 76; *Corr. Burke* II 11; WWM R 1: 1083; Add. MS 32990, ff. 340, 389.

47. Dowdeswell to Rockingham 14 August.—Dowdeswell MSS.

48. WWM R 42: 1.

49. Rockingham to Portland 19 Sept.—Portland MSS; Add. MS 32991, ff. 94, 138; *Corr. Burke* II 11–13.

50. WWM R 1: 1100.

51. *Ibid.*, 1083.

52. London: J. Almon, 1768. The pamphlet was written by William Knox and approved by Grenville.—*Grenville* IV 297–299, 319–321, 335–337, 359–360, 363–364, 366–369, 394–396. Add. MS 42086, ff. 52–53, 70–71, 149.

53. Dowdeswell to Burke 4 Jan. 1769.—Dowdeswell MSS. Burke visited Dowdeswell at the latter's home (Pull Court) in Worcestershire just after *The Present State of the Nation* was published.—Rockingham to Portland

15 Oct. (Portland MSS).

54. *Cavendish's Debates* I 30–46.

55. WWM R 156: 17.

56. Add. MS 35430, ff. 131–139.

57. *Ibid.*, f. 140.

58. Dartmouth MS D.1778.vii.

59. *Cavendish's Debates* I 190–225.

60. *Observations on a Late Publication Intituled "The Present State of the Nation"* has been reprinted in various editions of Burke's works. Extracts were serialized in *The St. James's Chronicle* from 18/20 April to 23/25 May.

61. *Memoirs* III 222.

62. *Grenville* III 411–412; *Cavendish's Debates* I 240–251, 263–307.

63. Add. MS 35430, ff. 151–152.

64. Letter of 5 March.—Portland MSS.

65. *Memoirs* III 228, 230.

66. WWM R 1: 1169.

67. *Corr. Burke* II 139.

68. "I imagine some late appearances of G[eorge] G[renville] acting in a sort of concert with our friends, must be to a degree a matter of surprize & must occasion various speculations. It may be proper to remark that he adopts many of our points, not *we* his & it may also be to be remarked, that his language etc. of late has softened upon the subject of N[orth] America."—Rockingham to Joseph Harrison 19 May 1769 (WWM R 1: 1186.)

69. Vide Thomas W. Copeland, *Edmund Burke's Friends and the Annual Register* (London, 1963).

7

Whiggery Mobilized

WHEN PARLIAMENT WAS OPENED in the autumn of 1768 Wilkes petitioned the House of Commons for release from jail to attend in his seat as member for Middlesex. Soon afterward the hero of the metropolis published a new libel which the House of Lords condemned—a judgment Rockingham thought precipitate but not unfair. When Lord North asked Commons for immediate concurrence with the peers the House balked. Another heated election contest had just been concluded in Middlesex. Wilkites had triumphed in a fresh release of passions and disorders, and the nation was, in the words of one Rockinghamite member, "distracted, distempered, and feverish." Hence the libel question was put off until January 27 when Wilkes was to be heard before the bar of the House.[1]

The Rockingham leadership deplored every aspect of this business. They hated the disorders and wished to see Wilkes stripped of his martyr's role for the quiet of the country. On the first day of the session Dowdeswell spoke for his petition, and when the libel question emerged Lord John Cavendish said in the House: "I wish we were rid of this, anyhow. The manner in which it is set about, tends to increase the discontent now so prevalent." Two days before Wilkes was to be heard (January 25), Joseph Martin, a new member whom Burke later described as "of our corps," moved that Wilkes was entitled to the privilege of Parliament. Dowdeswell, Burke, Meredith, Savile, and Frederick Montague spoke in support of the motion, which would have reversed the 1763 resolution on privilege and undermined the ground for the expected motion to expel Wilkes from Parliament. Seventy-one divided in favor of Martin's motion;[2] these were the men who wished neither to favor nor to persecute Wilkes but to consign him to oblivion. The 71 may be compared with the 136 who voted against condemning his libel and the 137 who voted, February 3, against expelling him. When he was returned anew in an uncontested election and the House rejected him on the ground that the "fixed law of parliament" disqualified an expelled member from candidacy until a new parliament was chosen, Dowdeswell tried to get the rejection based on the rule against reversing a parliamentary vote in the same session. When Wilkes was again elected and the election voided for the same reason, the Rockingham leadership pleaded against taking any notice of the event and against issuing a new writ, and Dowdeswell argued for letting the Middlesex seat remain vacant until quieter times; while Burke charged that they were "the friends of Wilkes and the enemies of their country" who kept him constantly in the public eye. In that debate (March 17) the emerging constitutional question became more sharply defined: whether a resolution of the House of Commons alone or an act of the legislature was required to incapacitate a man from eligibility for Parliament. One member stated it thus: "You have a right to expel and reject him; but that by no means implies more than that he is not admissible into this house; not that he is ineligible. Nothing but positive law can enable you to circumscribe the electors in their choice." A month later Henry Lawes Luttrell contested with ministerial support against

Wilkes and received but a fourth of the votes. Against a minority of 143 the House (April 15) resolved that Luttrell, having got the majority of legal votes, ought to be returned as member for Middlesex.[3]

This event provoked the first of the many grievance petitions to the crown which were adopted wide over the country in the ensuing months. It originated from a mass meeting of Middlesex electors on April 17, and in the drafting swelled into a detailed indictment of ministers on a great variety of counts expressing all the grievances men felt or heard about.[4] In this activity the Rockinghams had no part. Instead, they promoted a petition in the prescribed parliamentary mode against seating one whom the electors manifestly did not wish to have as their representative. "I approve the idea of petitioning the H. of C. very much," wrote Dowdeswell to the Marquis. ". . . I very much wish it may be presented by one of our friends." [5] Rockingham wrote it, Burke supplied an addition, and Sir George Savile brought it before the House on April 29. He asked for a hearing by counsel in the next session (the House having thinned) but the day of May 8 was designated. A call of the House was moved and the whips brought members swarming back to town. Every element of the minority was represented in the front line of the battle. Luttrell was painted as a court hireling foisted upon county electors against their will, and it was said that what could be done in Middlesex could be done in other constituencies until Parliament no longer represented the people but was chosen by the court.[6] Minority swelled in the division of 152 against 221, and the *Annual Register* said that the seating of Luttrell raised more alarm and wider discontent than any event "since the accession of the present royal family."

Seventy-two of the minority dined together at the Thatched House Tavern (May 9) at Dowdeswell's invitation. Many toasts were drunk, the last "to our next meeting." The Rockinghams were there in large number, together with Grenville, Barré, Beckford, and various unconnected men who had put on the mantle of patriotism.

The doctrine that the House of Commons alone could "make, alter, suspend, abrogate, or annihilate the law of the land" was declared "damnable." Lord Temple affected to see "a band of brothers, united in one great constitutional cause." No one, however, had any idea how to vindicate that cause. The session was ended, Luttrell was seated, decision was made and could not be reversed. "We have all broke up," wrote Burke, "without any plan of action for the future." [7]

Rockingham's thoughts went no further than the idea of employing the press to enlighten the public on the violated rights of electors. He suggested to James Adair, a city lawyer who had aided the Marquis' friend John Lee as counsel for the petition against the return of Luttrell, that he publish a statement of the argument. Adair assented but stopped when he learned that Sir William Meredith was writing a pamphlet on the subject. The latter's manuscript was talked over in the Marquis' dining room on May 17, the guests being Dowdeswell, Burke, Savile, Meredith, Lord John Cavendish, Charles Cornwall, and Alexander Wedderburn.[8] The last was a Grenvillite, a great ornament of the bar, an oratorical hero on May 8, and a valuable link between the Rockinghams and Grenvilles. Meredith's pamphlet[9] was published on June 16, by which time the Marquis and his friends were dispersed over the country in blissful holiday from politics. They took no notice of the Middlesex freeholders' extravagant petition to the King which was presented on May 24. The Marquis, still in town, could write to Dowdeswell two days afterward: "Since you left London, nothing very material has happened."

Twenty miles away in Buckinghamshire, where Burke had recently become a country squire, he described himself (May 31) as "serene and quiet . . . still and calm as if debate, dissention, and the rage of party never had an existence." [10] A similar mood came upon the Marquis after getting back to Yorkshire where he wrote some words to the Duke of Richmond which stir one to wonder how such a man could force himself, year after year, to act in politics with-

out personal ambition as motive and with so little probability of ever again being a minister.

> I most perfectly agree with your Grace that the pleasures one
> enjoys at one's own place in the country very far exceed the
> scenes which we have been used to in public life. . . . I feel
> here, as your Grace does at Goodwood; I think, I have every-
> thing wherewithal to gratify my wishes within the bounds of
> reason and moderation. My time does not hang heavy upon me
> for want of matters to occupy & to entertain my mind with; I
> often think, that I could set down here, attend & watch on
> the wants & necessities of those who are near to me, be of
> use & assistance to many & finally secure to myself the com-
> fort of thinking, that I have done some good.[11]

Small wonder that the master of Wentworth had no relish
for the hot politics which boiled up that summer!

II

Their natural dislike of busy political agitators, scheming organizers, and demagogic proposals kept the Rockinghams wholly aloof from that Society of Supporters of the
Bill of Rights which was started early in 1769 by friends of
Wilkes to raise funds to pay his debts and then became the
organ of metropolitan radicalism. Early in May it had
created a committee of correspondence to circularize the
kingdom. By mid-May newspapers were reporting that "a
very extraordinary petition" was in preparation "to be sent
through every county in Great Britain, in order to be signed
by such Freeholders of the Kingdom as may approve its
contents." This model, evidently, was the petition of the
Middlesex freeholders to the King. A country-wide appeal
for money to support this activity was resolved upon by the
Bill of Rights society in early June. The idea of constituents'
instructing their representatives how to vote was being dis-
seminated along with that of electing a new parliament annually.[12]

On June 21 Sir Anthony Abdy, a Surrey freeholder who

sat for a Cavendish nomination borough in Yorkshire, sent
Rockingham an account of a meeting in a London tavern of
gentlemen who planned a county meeting of Surrey freeholders.

> Sir George Colebrooke tells me that the gentlemen for the most
> part agreed to confine themselves to the one great question, but
> that Bellas one of Wilkes's committeemen was among them &
> pressed them much to take up at the meeting in Surrey all the
> variety of matter contained in the Middlesex petition to the
> Crown.

George Bellas was of the Bill of Rights society and had had
a hand in that initial petition. Sir Anthony feared this in-
triguing interloper: "Mr. Bellas is no Surrey man & therefore improper to have been there, for the meeting should
have been of a few gentlemen who should have formed their
plan . . . cooly & calmly & have privately engaged all their
friends in the scheme before it had been declared." Instead
an opportunity had been given for getting "all the scum of
the county together," and many respectable men who ought
to attend would stay away. What was to be done? Sir Anthony asked for the Marquis' advice and said that he would
be "guided entirely" by it. While he waited for that the
London livery met and adopted a great petition, only a little
less wild than the Middlesex model, and the Surrey freeholders met with the Bill of Rights men in the ascendancy,
as Sir Anthony had feared. He did not like what had happened, did not see how petitioning the crown could vindicate
the violated rights of electors:

> How [he wrote, July 1] can the Crown take notice of the pro-
> ceedings of the house of commons? or if it should, how can
> the Crown constitutionally give the redress we wish for? I
> remember too well that Charles the 1st offended the constitu-
> tion more by his meddling with the house of commons where
> he had no business than for any thing else he did.[13]

The Middlesex petition had asked the King to fire his
ministers. The London livery beseeched him to use the

"great and extensive powers . . . intrusted to the Crown"
by the constitution, and Surrey freeholders asked for "an
exertion of that royal prerogative . . . so properly placed
in your majesty's hands." [14] The implication here is that the
King was asked to dissolve Parliament and call a new election, since there could be no other mode of royal redress of
the grievances of electors. But since the Hanoverian succession, dissolving before a parliament had run out of its seven-
year term had become almost as obsolete as the royal veto;
no King had appealed from Parliament to the electorate.
On the previous February 17 Lord North had even warned
members against having anything to do with petitioning for
a dissolution lest Parliament "think itself injured and insulted and punish the individuals who so injured and insulted them." [15] The idea of employing such a weapon for
any reason whatever was naturally abhorrent to all who
possessed a parliamentary interest and liked elections to be
as infrequent as possible.

While the Bill of Rights men were busy in the metropolis
Lord Rockingham had been journeying in a meandering way
—with much "entertainment and quiet"—home to Wentworth. Sir Anthony Abdy's first letter must have been await-
ing, or come soon after, his arrival on June 24. Burke sent a
detailed account of the London meeting and petition, and
newspapers brought reports of what took place in Surrey.
The Marquis relished all this as little as his attack of boils
which, he told Burke, "made sitting extremely unpleasant."
He wished that the London petition had been well modeled
but had not expected it to be; Surrey's, he feared, was "too
much in the general vague and wild manner of the other
two." He sensed a desire in Yorkshire to do something, but
not that sort of thing. He disliked the idea of calling a
county meeting which would "at once be known that it could
scarce be without my *actual desire* and suggestion." If Yorkshire were to be set in motion, general opinion must move it.
The assizes, he thought, would be a proper occasion for the
grand jury to address the county members (as in the spring
after the *nullum tempus* act), thanking them for their con-

duct in defense of the rights of the Middlesex electors and urging alertness against "the views of any minister who might wish to form a house of commons composed only of such on whose obsequiousness he could depend." In such an address the *nullum tempus* and the condemnation of general warrants might be recalled to public attention, the better to remind Yorkshiremen "to what party they were indebted for these services." He asked Burke what he thought of this tactic and may have been somewhat taken aback at discovering how far the latter was infected by the spirit in the metropolis. Burke answered quickly (July 2) that he liked the idea as far as it went, but cautioned against mention of general warrants lest George Grenville be affronted, and urged the mode of petitioning "because it carries more the air of uniformity and concurrence; and being more out of the common road, and yet I apprehend constitutional enough, it will be more striking, and more suitable to the magnitude of the occasion." [16]

This was not what Sir Anthony Abdy thought, nor was it in line with Cavendish views. Lord John thought such meetings as in Surrey were "mischievous" and that "to follow the lead of such people as have put themselves forward" was "ridiculous." He hoped nothing of that sort would occur in Derbyshire:

> I have no doubt, but the gentlemen of the county will be ready to do any thing; but we have been a great many years teaching them to acquiesce & be content with what their members do for them; if we encourage them, to take any thing into consideration, they may choose to interpose themselves much oftener than I am likely to think convenient.

Meanwhile, nothing was done at the Nottinghamshire assizes, Frederick Montagu telling Rockingham that "our friends are not too pushing"; and Sir Cecil Wray tried twice without success to have a county meeting called in Lincolnshire. By early July, however, Yorkshire was stirring and the Marquis expressed some apprehension to Lord John that there was more danger of doing too much than too little:

> I hear it is a favourite topick among the polititians in this county, that the constitution will be undone by the number of *placemen* in parliament & that a bill should be brought in to that purpose & that the crown should be told, that it is deceived by the ministers, who carry things in parl[iamen]t merely by the dint of placemen, against the general sense of the nation. . . . I like much better for *here* particularly, that if any thing is done, the time should be at the assizes & not by calling the county together.

And on July 11 he wrote to one of his political agents, Stephen Croft:

> I am confident that a letter or address or whatever you please to call it to the county members might be so worded & so full upon many points, that it would contain equally as much & would in my mind have a better appearance than the petition. . . . I may over think the matter, but really I feel such an anxiety for the honour & dignity of this county, that I fear the appearance of following the mode of petitioning, when indeed hitherto the petitions have not be so digested as to redound much to the honour of the petitioners.

If, the Marquis added, the address of the grand jury appeared inadequate to the necessities of the occasion, the matter could be canvassed further at York Races in August: "Some time should still run, that if the county does petition, the petition in every respect should be well consider'd & well form'd that it might do the fullest credit & honour to the county." [17]

At York on July 14 the sheriff and grand jury adopted an address of thanks to the county members for defending the rights of Middlesex electors with "uniform constitutional zeal." That the text was not first certified by the Marquis is shown by his calling it inadequate and deploring to the Duke of Portland a reference to "the best of Kings" which he thought was proper only if understood as "somewhat of a sarcastical compliment." [18]

Meanwhile Burke had re-argued the case for Yorkshire's petitioning: Chatham had recovered health and been to see the King, who might again summon him to reform administration, in which event he would surely "buttress it up with Grenvilles and the Shelburne people." Hence now was the time to act with strong effect and incite fear at court, which would never give the Marquis credit for his moderation but attribute his doing little to inability to do more. The court should be taught that "the people have their leaders too," and ought not to be comforted "by finding a slur cast upon the mode of petitioning." Rockingham in reply acknowledged that the northern parts of the kingdom were "warm" and ready with a little encouragement to show it; but he remained unwilling to approve a mode of action which he thought had been discredited by metropolitan politicians.[19] On July 30 Burke returned to his argument, pointing to scheduled county meetings in Cornwall, Wiltshire, Worcestershire, as well as Buckinghamshire, in spite of ministerial efforts to stop them. If the spirit which "extends and strengthens" were allowed to dissipate, ministry would proceed against petitioners "to make an example of terrour to all future attempts of expressing the will of the people, in any other way than by votes of the House of Commons."

> I assure your Lordship, by every thing I can find, that both friends and foes look with very anxious eyes towards Yorkshire, the one very eagerly expecting, the other very heartily dreading some motion of yours.

A few days later Dowdeswell visited Burke and wrote to the Marquis echoing this appeal.[20] Still Rockingham would not move.

Nor would the Cavendishes. Nor would Richmond in Sussex lest he appear "factious" and cause divisions in the county—instead he went to Paris! Savile agreed with Rockingham that Yorkshire opinion should crystallize without their directing it. Dowdeswell was disconcerted by the small attendance at the Worcestershire meeting on August 10, where an attempt was made by the secretary of the Bill of Rights society to color the petition; afterward, as it was carried through the county for additional signatures, great reluctance to sign was encountered, so that it was "amazing how in most places people of rank & fortune shrink from this measure, and with what deference all orders below them wait for their leaders." Dowdeswell became dispirited enough to give up "unless our friends take the determined part that becomes them." Even in Buckinghamshire there was great slowness in setting a date for a county meeting. The ardent Burke, ambitious and more eager than any man to serve his party, fretfully declined his chief's invitation to Wentworth and groaned to Charles O'Hara (August 28):

> There is a great spirit all over the northern part of the kingdom, which if improved, supported, and rightly directed, could not fail of being infinitely useful. But God has given different spirits to different men. The profligate and inconsiderate are bold, adventurous, and pushing; honest men slow, backward and irresolute.[21]

Not until York Races week, beginning August 21, did Rockingham satisfy himself that the gentlemen of the county desired a meeting on the great question. About forty prominent men including several members of Parliament requested the high sheriff to summon it for September 27. The Marquis then said that it should be a full one, that sufficient time must be allowed for all to attend; that the honor of the county required that what was done should be well weighed and considered, and that York should set an example instead of following one already given. He remained unconvinced of the wisdom of a petition to the crown. All his York friends, he thought, agreed that "the chief and principal and perhaps *only* matter on which the sense of the county should be shown" was "the great point of the rights of the freeholders." Some were for a petition to the

King, others for resolutions with instructions, still others
for a petition to the House of Commons. To settle what
lead was to be given, the Marquis called for the counsel of
his party associates.

Burke was sent to Sir Anthony Abdy, who preferred the
mode of petitioning Parliament, to collect his thoughts on
how that might be done. Wedderburn was invited to Wentworth, as was John Lee, a Yorkshireman who had just been
chosen in Rockingham's interest as recorder at Doncaster
and had been chief counsel for the petition against Luttrell's
return. Dowdeswell was invited, and Burke was asked to go
north after the Buckinghamshire county meeting in mid-
September. Until then Rockingham retained all his misgivings over petitioning the King, and not only because of
disagreeable precedents. To ask for a dissolution meant
invoking an exercise of royal prerogative just when the
whigs were complaining against the growing power of the
crown; and if the King refused where then was the next
step? Again, the Marquis must have been sensible of the
practical difficulties in the way of obtaining signers to a
petition in so large a county as York. There were 20,000
electors and only a fraction of these could be expected at the
meeting; but if a large number failed to sign, the partisans
of the court would represent a York petition as coming
from a small minority. One of his political agents told the
Marquis that if all who attended were to sign a paper the
meeting would "last longer than a county election for five
country men will give their votes more readily than one can
write his name." Manifestly, copies would have to be carried through the county, and timidity, which might be overcome in the excitement of a great meeting, could make many
shy of putting down their names. Moreover, many did not
know how to write their names. Much easier, therefore,
would be adopting resolutions or voting instructions to
members of Parliament. Early in September Wedderburn
wrote to Rockingham in favor of instructions as falling in
"with the sentiments of the moderates" without going
against "the inclinations of those who are more violent." [22]

A few days later Burke reported that Abdy had changed his mind and favored petitioning the King to dissolve, and Sir Anthony himself wrote to the Marquis:

> I now think a petition to the crown the only way of proceeding. Relief asked for can be nothing but a removal of ministers & a dissolution of parliament & I am bold to say that let who will succeed to the administration they cannot stand long, unless the present parliament is dissolved.

Burke had been assigned to consult too with such faithful Rockinghamites as Lord Albemarle, Admiral Keppel, and Sir Charles Saunders. Albemarle sent their collective opinion to Wentworth, which was for petitioning and throwing the book at the court after the fashion of metropolitan petitions.[23] Perhaps Burke had been evangelizing for hotter politics which his chief was likely to adopt.

Wedderburn and Lee were at Wentworth in mid-September and showed Rockingham an account of parliamentary proceedings in 1701 wherein a precedent was found for petitioning the crown to dissolve. The Marquis came round to supporting such a petition, grounded solely upon the violated rights of electors. To direct an appeal to the House of Commons to unseat Luttrell, he told Savile (with whom he had considered it), would strike at "a constitutional security which every member has when one has set the 14 days unmolested & unimpeached in his seat by petition." [24] Instructions by resolution compromised the independence of judgment of a member of Parliament. A petition distinguished by markedly respectful language and citation of constitutional precedent would at once answer to the feelings of Yorkshiremen while showing their aloofness from the wild ways of metropolitan radicals. His decision made, the Marquis displayed a relish for what was on foot, and even wished for some show of opposition at the meeting so that "a most triumphant victory" might be claimed. To Stephen Croft, who would help to manage things, he wrote on September 20:

I know it is urged by some that *tho* the matter in question is a great grievance, *yet* that it is wrong to inflame the public. I own I think that supineness & non-resistance is a most dangerous encouragement to those . . . who to gratify their immediate resentments stride over the barriers of the constitution. Had the judges in Charles yᵉ 1st's time not been courtly, but had declared to the King & his ministers in that day, that the ship money was illegal, it might have stopped an arbitrary system in its cradle, & the violence on both sides which afterwards ensued, might never have been.[25]

Rockingham chose to stay away from the meeting. The assembled freeholders, he explained to Dowdeswell, would "like the *appearance* of its being their own act & would think that *my* being present might so far lessen the weight of the proceeding, as that it would be attributed in part to personal friendship & opinion & not to the genuine spirit for the constitution with which those present were actuated." [26] His was the ruling will, however, through the instrument of the Rockingham Club, one of whose members told him that nothing could be done "without some Great Man being at the head. . . . not only our eyes, but those of the whole kingdom and her colonies look up to your Lordship as that Patron." And the same man said again: "The plan to be adopted will, let appearances at the meeting be what they may, take its rise from your Lordship, whose steady friends will form the principal part of the company, and consider themselves as under your banner." [27] A draft of the petition was made at Wentworth by Rockingham, Wedderburn, and Lee about two weeks in advance of the county meeting; a copy was sent to Dowdeswell who may have suggested alterations when he arrived. Burke on reaching Wentworth "found the petition determined on and prepared; a very manly and proper piece." Sir George Savile, although reluctant to tell his constituents what they should do, yet approved the petition, and just before the meeting opened at York it was he who ironed out final difficulties. According to Lord John Cavendish, "Some gentlemen that were showed the draft of the intended petition, made some objection to part of it. . . . They accordingly came to Sir G. Savile's lodging & presently settled it with a few trifling alterations." [28] So was the final sanctifying touch given by the most popular gentleman in the county.

Perhaps 800 electors attended the meeting.[29] Lord John, who was there, observed that there were "not so many of the common people, but almost all the gentlemen of fortune of the county, except those who were known to be against it." Burke was pleased by the "considerable number of the clergy" present and commented on the numerous young tories who were "very sanguine and earnest for the petition." Sir George Armytage chaired the assembly, called up the county members of Parliament to relate the history of the seating of a minority candidate for Middlesex, and moved the petition. One man wished to be heard against it, and he was answered by Wedderburn who, Burke said, was "whiggissimus." When the motion was put, only three hands were raised against it. The day was not long enough to collect all the signatures, and even if it had been, copies of the petition still had to be circulated through the county to get the largest possible number. Rockingham was confident that this laborious task could be done. By the time the petition was given to the King upwards of 10,000 signatures— about half the county electorate—were obtained.[30]

"After Yorkshire has marched out," wrote Savile on October 2, "the war may be said to begin in the north." [31] By the end of the year, Derbyshire, Northumberland, Cumberland, and Durham had petitioned after the fashion of York; as had the cities of Coventry, Newcastle, Berwick-upon-Tweed, Durham, and Liverpool. A movement which began in the metropolitan counties and then seemed to flag during mid-summer took on new dimensions; but however influential York's example was in the north, the Rockingham leadership could make no claim of eclipsing the Bill of Rights men or of drawing the movement under their own banner. A month before the York meeting the City of Westminster had adopted a petition limited to asking for a dissolution; it was a decided improvement over the first metropolitan

screeds and showed that the Bill of Rights men knew how
to mend their manners. In fact, Westminster first refired
the stalling engines of the movement. The Duke of Grafton
was so shaken by the great mass meeting in the city of
Parliament that he posed the question, "what are the
penalties these gentlemen who have been the promoters of
these steps may have made themselves liable to, or how far
they are criminal?" [32] In Buckinghamshire, Lord Temple
shaped the petition which showed some radical tinge, although Burke worked a little moderating influence. Before
the end of the year, Hereford, Somerset, Devon, Cornwall,
Dorset, Kent, and Essex were added to the list of petitioning counties: eighteen in all, in addition to thirteen cities and
boroughs. It has been estimated that the total number of
signers was about a fourth of the whole voting population
of England and larger than the number who signed loyal
counter-addresses. Rockingham's influence was exerted most
effectively in the counties (especially in the north), and the
Bill of Rights men exerted dominant influence in many of
the petitioning cities.[33] A majority of electors, as might be
expected, were too local-minded to take any interest in a
nation-wide movement; no doubt, too, many signed for
reasons having no connection with the cause of righting
electors' wrongs. Still, political consciousness was stirred.
The *Annual Register* recorded "a great ferment . . . the
like of which had scarcely been ever remembered"; and
"Junius" said it was "wonderful that the great cause, in
which the country is engaged, should have roused and en-
grossed the whole attention of the people." [34]

III

Friends of the Marquis wrote not only petitions but also
pamphlets in 1769. Meredith's *The Question Stated* being
attacked in a counter-pamphlet by Sir William Blackstone,
he wrote another in reply. His were party pamphlets. A
Rockingham council, as we have seen, deliberated upon the
first manuscript, and when the second was written it was sent

to Rockingham who read, approved "most exceedingly," and desired its early publication.[35] Dowdeswell too addressed the public in defense of the rights of electors, gave his manuscript to Burke to read, and then sent it to the Marquis, who also read it, as did Lord John and Wedderburn. As it slowly made the rounds of critics Dowdeswell became depressed and considered suppressing it, but after Yorkshire's marching out Rockingham said that Dowdeswell's "warmth" was justified by his arguments, and it was made ready for the press. In November *The Sentiments of an English Freeholder, on the Late Decision of the Middlesex Election* was published.[36]

Meanwhile, a more notable Rockingham party pamphlet was in genesis: Burke's *Thoughts on the Cause of the Present Discontents*. On June 29, when the Marquis was looking with disgust upon metropolitan petitions, he wrote to Burke:

> I am exceeding glad you have begun to look over the papers of the system of the last 9 years—that indeed would be at this time a most useful work and would do more good in giving right ideas to the publick—than all the proceedings have done hitherto of late.

On July 17, after being twice importuned by Burke to set Yorkshire on the road of petitioning, Rockingham suggested that he get on with his writing: "I do believe it would do great service. I am sure we never do ourselves much good but when we adhere strictly to our own line of conduct. I wish the publick had it laid before them." It is perfectly evident that Rockingham desired his political secretary to produce a treatise which would explain why so many disorders and discontents had arisen in the reign of George III. Burke was slow in getting on with it; at the end of July various business had hindered "a vigorous pursuit" of the object. Perhaps he was dilatory from want of relish for a task undertaken in service to a leader who seemed so reluctant to lead. By late September when he went into York-

shire he was able to submit a partial draft to his chief, who
urged that it be completed and published before the opening
of Parliament:

> I think it would take universally, and tend to form and to
> unite a party upon real and well founded principles—which
> would in the end prevail and re'establish order and govern-
> ment in this country.

Parliament was to meet in January, and the Marquis expected Burke to finish his composition and bring it to Wentworth in mid-November. He found himself unable to keep
to such a schedule, begged off from going north again, but
half-promised to send "something for your consideration."
The Marquis was expecting to have Dowdeswell, Meredith,
Savile, and Portland, and he wrote to Burke on November
4:

> . . . if the *work* was in such forwardness, that you could
> bring it—that our friends might see and *sanctify*—that would
> still be best. I know pretty well from the conversations I have
> had with several—that the idea totally corresponds as much
> with their *present sentiments,* as it does with all their *past con-
> duct.*

A few weeks later the major part of the manuscript reached
Wentworth. What the Marquis had seen in September was
now much revised and Burke said that the design of the
whole appeared distinctly:

> If you and your friends approve of it, you will be so good to
> send it back with your observations as soon as possible, that it
> may go to press; when I have got through the concluding part,
> you shall have that also; and on its return, it shall follow the
> rest.[37]

Burke's design was a plausible explanation of the "strange
distemper" afflicting the nation. The cause was discerned as
the rise of a court faction or party of "king's friends" which

interrupted and misused the favor of the crown for its own ends: frustrating ostensible ministers; separating court from administration and rendering the latter dependent for continuance on the former; dangerously expanding the influence of the crown while lowering the reputation of ministers; weakening government for the sake of its own power; preventing stability in royal councils by the frequent undoing of ministries; breaking by intent the connections formed by the natural leaders of the people; suborning Parliament to factional purposes by the distribution of court honors and places. This theory was refined from the experience of Rockingham and Grenville as the crown's first ministers, and Burke avowed that there was not a public man in or out of office who had not at one time or another testified to an infusion of court favoritism into government. Here was the basic reason why government had become at once odious and feeble; why colonies were alienated and alliances disrupted; why mobs clashed with soldiers; why a quarrel had been brought on between the House of Commons and its constituents. The remedy for the evil was not to be found in old, stale, popular notions of more frequent elections or a place bill to protect the representatives of the people from seduction by the executive part of the constitution. Bad men had combined; therefore the good must associate. The right medicine for the state was a firm combination of public-spirited men supported by the concurrence of the people at large, to break and crush the court faction; or, in other words, whig reunion on the principles of Lord Rockingham.

Burke had serious doubts that the men above him in the party would approve publishing this manuscript. Was it wise to tell the public of a court faction acting in the way he described? Was that a reality, or only a theory and not a very credible one at that? Richard, his brother, and Will Burke "thought some things a little too ludicrous," and Edmund admitted to Rockingham a want of confidence "that the doctrines avowed in this piece" (although clear to him as principles) would be "considered as well founded." If the pamphlet were supposed to express Rockingham's views he would be put on terms "irreconcilably bad with the court, and all its adherents" without reconciling all the opposition. Burke also feared being suspected of the authorship and was himself against publishing it unless his friends promised to defend him against the attacks he felt sure would be provoked.[38] The widespread suspicion that he was the writer of the "Junius" letters made this a point of special concern to him who of all the Rockinghams was the favorite target of the ministerial press.

Only Dowdeswell was with Rockingham when Burke's manuscript reached Wentworth. Of their first thoughts upon it there is no record. It was taken to Portland who thought Burke was not severe enough on Bute and had depicted the King as "a thing of straw" innocent of responsibility for the conduct of persons close to him. The Duke also thought that certain "hints and insinuations" against "other sets of people" in opposition ought to be dropped out.

> What real hurt the publication can do [Portland said] I can't foresee: it will make you enemies . . . but only those that, for your own sake, you would be ashamed to call your friends, except one, i.e. the King who never will like you till he sees he can't go on without you, and when that is the case, he will feel and own a pleasure he never as yet can have experienced.[39]

Savile reacted very differently, fearing the pamphlet would inflame without doing real service. He declined to advise publication because he could not give Burke a promise that he would be able to defend it. He thought it ill-timed in view of the many petitions to the King, and said that the distinction between the King thus appealed to and the idea of the court responsible for the wrong needing redress, was "fair enough in theory of the constitution but hard enough to keep up gravely in practice." Sir George disliked Burke's necessary fictions. If there existed a court faction such as Burke described, Savile knew that George III headed and directed it; but "the private parts of the constitution" could not be "treated decently," nor could the idea of a court

faction employing royal influence without the King's aware-
ness be reconciled "to the common ideas of royalty." [40]

In spite of Sir George's opinion Rockingham favored
publication after certain alterations were made. "The publick in general," he told Portland, "have never as yet had
a state of our principles laid before them. In my opinion
they will like them." [41] And yet he delayed. On the same day
he wrote the words just quoted (December 5), Burke wrote
to him expressing "some impatience" for the return of the
manuscript "with your observations and corrections." [42] Not
until December 23, however, did Rockingham respond and
then via Dowdeswell, saying:

> Along with this letter you will receive Mr. Burke's manuscript
> & the remarks, which I made, when you was here. I have wrote
> to him & enclosed the letter in this packet. I have told him,
> what is very true that I have not been able to add to my first
> remarks & that I think them hardly legible or intelligible with-
> out your assistance who was present when I made them. If he
> is in town, which I suppose he is I wish you would deliver him
> my letter & get him to look over the remarks etc. along with
> you as soon as he could. In my letter to him I have mentioned
> some other particulars. I wish it was possible that this work
> could soon make its appearance, I am only fearful that my own
> delay must have made it difficult.[43]

Neither Rockingham's "remarks" nor his letter sent to
Burke with the manuscript is extant. Hence no explanation
can be given for his dilatory conduct with a piece of writing
which he had wished to see published at an early date. Not
until April 1770 did the *Thoughts* reach the bookstalls.

IV

If a "firm combination" was to be formed against the alleged
court faction the principal leaders of parliamentary opposition would have to ally. No one seriously expected the
King to comply with the petitions for a new parliament, so
that what lay ahead was a struggle against administration

in the existing parliament. The Rockinghams had to chart a course which would not compromise their fastidiously-maintained principles. Already some friends thought that the Marquis was embarked upon a reckless line of conduct. Lord Dartmouth lamented doing anything to increase the "distractions & distresses, which we seem to be running ourselves into." [44] Charles Yorke had never given his opinion on the constitutional point raised by the seating of Luttrell, but was convinced that the opposition view was wrong; he had in fact no relish whatever for whig opposition and the Yorke family were growing shy of Lord Rockingham. [45]

Relations with the Grenvilles could hardly have been better in the petitioning activity, what with Wedderburn's role at York and the prominent part Burke had taken in cooperation with the Grenvilles in Buckinghamshire. How well this undeclared alliance of parties could go on working depended to a great extent upon Lord Temple, who had taken the lead in Buckinghamshire, and upon his great brother-in-law Chatham now recovered from his long illness. It was being put out in the press that Chatham held the seating of Luttrell to be an illegality which could be corrected only by a new parliament. [46] Temple was advertising to the world that he and his brother George were again united with Chatham in politics. Burke feared the ascendancy of the "three brothers" in a union of opposition ranks, saw "a very delicate game to play," and told Rockingham that he could neither refuse them his cooperation without advantaging the court nor engage without the risk of putting himself in their power. [47]

After touring about to see friends and attending Newmarket Races, Rockingham came to certain conclusions which he wrote out in a letter to Burke, of which copies were made for other friends. [48] He was for an appearance of union with the three brothers but did not believe that a closer connection could produce "any real agreement." If the King were driven to make a change of administration, it was probable that Chatham would be recalled to act as he had done in 1766, not to make a "family" administration; or the court might employ Lord Mansfield to recruit another administration. If a negotiation were thrown into Chatham's hands, the result would be another "court patched up administration"; if into Grenville's hands, "something a degree better" would result. Meanwhile Rockingham favored communication with Grenville when Parliament met, concerting plans of operation in a manner "very civil and good-humoured." If a negotiation were thrown into Rockingham's hands he thought that "notwithstanding all the difficulties we should probably have in forming an administration . . . we ought and should undertake." And he thought that George Grenville would "sacrifice *something,* to be really and confidentially united with us." Thus, in mid-October, Rockingham was building his hopes on the same straight line pursued since the winter of 1767–1768. This had led to the coincidental alignment with Grenville in the House of Commons; its continuation might win Grenville to the party. No man was more respected in the House, and no more differences with him over America seemed likely. "Our line of conduct is nice & requires much consideration," the Marquis wrote to Dowdeswell.

> I think as a general rule, we should constantly look back to what it has been & adhere to the same lines in future. I think, we & *we only* of all parts now in opposition, are so, on system & principle, that we ought to avail ourselves of other parties now in opposition, in order to effectuate our purposes, but that we should be cautious not even to throw the appearance of *leading* into hands whose principles we have no reason to think similar to our own & whose honour we have no reason to confide in.[49]

The Marquis remained in Yorkshire from mid-October until the first of the year and had no correspondence with Grenville or Temple, Chatham or Shelburne. He made no effort to contradict Temple's boasting of a united opposition with the three brothers at the head. Lord Fitzwilliam reported Chatham as declaring that he never again would sit in the King's council except to meet the friends of Lord

Rockingham; that old differences should be forgotten and private animosities laid aside; that the Marquis alone had "a knot of spotless friends, such as ought to govern this kingdom." To this sort of thing Rockingham made no gesture of response.

> I make no doubt [he wrote to Portland] when we all get to London we shall hear more of these matters. In the meantime & indeed at all times I wish to act on our own judgments & neither to be led by a little cajolery or drove by what some call great Authority.[50]

The King opened Parliament on January 9 with a speech which made no mention of the discontents blown up by the Middlesex election. The petitions, it was plain, were to be ignored. Rockingham was in town the previous ten days without concerting in any way with the three brothers. His summons had brought enough friends to town to form a majority of the ninety opposition men who dined again at the Thatched House the day before the opening. Grenville, who had just lost his wife, was not there. Chatham was eager for battle. According to Horace Walpole he had sent a message to Rockingham proposing that they meet to effect a union of the "friends of the public" and the Marquis answered that he lived in Grosvenor Square.[51] The Rockinghams formed the main part of opposition: who would treat must come to them.

Chatham, however, was in the more advantageous position for attacking the Grafton ministry. Having made it as it was before the accession of the Bedfords, he felt, as had Rockingham in the autumn of 1766, that he might unmake it by calling men out of it. Lord Chancellor Camden was prepared to play Chatham's game, as was Lord Granby, master general and commander-in-chief. Chatham wished Camden to keep the Great Seal the while Granby started a spate of resignations to show the King the necessity of his own recall. This most illustrious of Englishmen, after three years of absence from the parliamentary scene and now resurrected as it seemed to a new life, on the opening day moved an amendment to the address, to take into consideration "the causes of the discontents which prevail in so many of your Majesty's dominions, and particularly the late proceedings of the House of Commons, touching the incapacity of John Wilkes . . . and depriving the electors of Middlesex of their free choice of their representative." Thirty-six peers, including Rockingham and his allies, were in the minority for the amendment; although the Marquis had intended to move a similar amendment without mentioning the name of Wilkes. This was moved by Dowdeswell in Commons where the minority counted 138.[52]

These numbers were of less significance than the revelation of a crisis within the ministry, for Camden declared his agreement with Chatham, and Granby voted with the minority in Commons. Neither man resigned. Camden knew that he was marked for dismissal, but he did not expect to go until the crown had secured his successor, who in the circumstances might not be easily available. On this same day, however, the King directed Grafton to offer the Great Seal to Charles Yorke, who met the Minister three days later and asked if the offer meant that a negotiation was intended to extend administration to include those with whom he had long been connected, namely, the Rockingham whigs. Grafton answered that he wished for a system as comprehensive as possible which could be brought about only by the reunion of the whigs, and that he would be happy to have Yorke's assistance to effect that. "Mr. Yorke appeared to be pleased with this answer," Grafton wrote, "and after many civilities on both sides we parted." [53] A little time was allowed him to consider, but he was given to understand that the King would resent a refusal. Yorke consulted his brothers and conferred with Rockingham, who strained every effort to fix him in a determination to refuse an offer that looked like a temptor's enticement.[54]

The son of the great Hardwicke, Yorke had entered into and acted in public life as a whig of the party of Newcastle, Rockingham, and the Cavendishes. He was bound to it by the kind of obligation which the age recognized as natural and honorable. A man of party might differ with his friends on particular questions, as Yorke differed on the Middlesex election question, but he could not desert for private advantage or to satisfy ambition—in circumstances hurtful to friends—without breaching the rule of honor in friendship. There was, against this, the common sentiment that a man's first duty was to the King; but the Rockingham view was that no man could serve his King well who began by deserting his friends. There was too the Yorke family interest, long centered upon getting the Great Seal back into it; but even Charles's brothers did not see how, in the circumstances, he could accept it—much though they desired him to realize his brightest ambition, and fearful though they were that refusal would so offend Majesty as to close the door against another opportunity. On January 15 Yorke went to Grafton and declined, but out of respect for Majesty attended in audience the next day to thank and explain. Unwilling to accept the decision as final, the King commanded Yorke to attend his levée the following day; on which day (January 17) Granby, Solicitor General Dunning, two bed-chamber lords, the groom of the stole, the master of horse to the queen, and a vice-treasurer for Ireland threw up their places. Thus Chatham, with Rockingham's unwitting assistance, played out his trumps—but George III gained Yorke. Three days later the new Lord Chancellor was mysteriously dead, whereupon Grafton elected to resign; but the King was adamant against giving in to what he imagined was a united opposition of Rockinghams, Grenvilles, Chathamites, and city radicals, all committed to a dissolution of Parliament. Rather than yield to that, he told General Conway, he would abdicate his crown.

He was, of course, mistaken in thinking that leaders of opposition were engaged one with another to force a dissolution. Rockingham had no engagement whatever with any politician; nor was he even committed to vindicate the Yorkshire petition, which was only a means toward correcting a wrong which might be righted without a dissolution.

Burke told Horace Walpole at this time that his friends
"would be content without a dissolution, provided an Act
of Parliament were passed to take from the House of Commons the power of incapacitation." [55] Given the natural inclinations of the Marquis and the strong distaste of his
friends for elections, it seems a certainty that they at heart
preferred this mode of closing the breach made in the constitution. As a minister in 1765 Rockingham had not urged
a new parliament, and if he had become minister again in
1770 he could not have forced Majesty to do what Majesty
would not. The King ought to have understood that the
Marquis was chalking out his own line of conduct, moderate
and respectful to Majesty.

On the other hand, Rockingham may have blundered by
not employing the offer of the Great Seal to Yorke as a
means of proving himself to the King. A wholly unanswer-
able question emerges here. Why did he not advise Yorke
to accept on the condition that whig reunion, which Grafton
had said was so much to be desired, begin by putting a
negotiation into his, Rockingham's, hands? He had already
told friends that if such were tendered it ought this time
to be accepted. Why, in other words, did he see the approach
to Yorke as designed to hurt his party instead of as an
opening to it? Perhaps Yorke was less than candid with
Rockingham and never passed on what Grafton had said
about whig reunion. Perhaps the Marquis thought Yorke
hardly the kind of man to state conditions to Majesty. Or
it may have been that Rockingham thought that the better
strategy was to hold off Yorke in the expectation that the
impending resignations would ripen the court's necessity.
But pressing him to refuse could hardly fail to strengthen
the King's belief in Rockingham's wish to force the royal
hand. The Marquis lost whatever chance there may have
been to correct the King's mistaken notion. He also lost the
Yorkes whose final alienation from the party was occasioned
by their brother's tragedy.

V

On January 22—the day George III talked to Conway of
abdication—Lord Chatham called on Rockingham. So began
a political cooperation of the principal leaders of opposition
who had little in common but the desire to complete the rout
of the Grafton administration. Chatham strongly supported
Rockingham's motion of that day for taking into consideration the state of the nation. Four days later the minority in
Commons swelled to 180 for Dowdeswell's motion that the
House in judging election questions was bound by the law
of the land. On January 30 it was public knowledge that
Lord North had succeeded Grafton at the Treasury. The
Duke, it appeared, had been driven to resign and North
could be but a stop-gap. The minority on the following day
rose to 181 for Dowdeswell's motion that only an act of
Parliament could incapacitate a candidate for Parliament.
The same resolution was moved by Rockingham in the Lords
on February 2 and the largest minority since the spring of
1767—forty-seven—divided for it. Chatham, who had been
ill, returned to take his part on that day and even was of
the 41 who signed the protest which Rockingham had prepared. Burke said on February 8 that "our minority gets
strength daily," and four days later it soared to 188 for
Dowdeswell's motion to bring in a bill to reduce the influence
of the crown in elections by disfranchising revenue officers.[56]

This was the crest of opposition's wave, even the start of
the ebb, for North had been very industrious in getting
regular supporters of government to attend the House. He
had 263 against Dowdeswell's motion and the King complimented him on "a very handsome majority." Moreover,
opposition in Commons had now all but exhausted the possible modes for framing resolutions on the Middlesex election which could be moved without breaching the rule of
Parliament. The great constitutional question was lost.
Chatham was for continuing to agitate it. Burke urged that
the opposition secede, but was overruled. By February 19

Temple was complaining that the Rockinghams gave themselves "too many airs of taking the lead." Failure was, as
always, breeding discord. In late February and March
Grenville in Commons and Rockingham in the Lords revived
the civil-list debt question by moving, unsuccessfully, for accounts of the previous year's expenditures; and the Rockinghams were in concert with Grenville on the latter's bill to
reform the mode of deciding election questions in Commons
—a bill which became law.[57]

The month of March witnessed a development which put
a strain upon relations between Rockinghams and Chathamites. London electors produced a "remonstrance" to the
King. It alleged a "secret and malign influence" working
through successive administrations to defeat every good and
to suggest every bad intention; it avowed that the seating
of Luttrell had been "a deed more ruinous . . . than the
levying of ship-money by Charles the First, or the dispensing
power assumed by James II"; it questioned the legality of
the acts of the legislature which could "no more be valid
without a legal House of Commons, than without a legal
prince upon the throne." [58] This was the extreme and wild
spirit in the metropolis which had disgusted Rockingham
ten months before and caused his reluctance to forward the
petitioning movement. His taste in politics had not changed;
yet Chatham, Temple, and Shelburne appeared to encourage
this. A ministerial motion (March 15) to ask the King to
lay the remonstrance before Parliament hinted at punitive
action against alleged libelers in the House of Commons.
The minority sank to 108 after a debate in which Lord
Mayor Beckford and the radical aldermen Townsend and
Sawbridge defended the remonstrance and avowed their own
leading part in producing and presenting it to the King.
Rockinghams and Grenvilles opposed the motion while
ostentatiously refusing to defend the remonstrance. That
some of the Rockinghams had shied off from voting in the
minority is suggested by the Marquis' telling Portland
(March 17) that it would not be unlucky "if the administration should be very violent, as they would drive back to us

the more moderate men who at present seem alarmed, *as if we* were violent." [59] That the Rockinghams were determined not to let the ministry force a split in opposition ranks was shown two days later when they voted against a motion to censure the London remonstrance; and on March 22 they attended *en corps* the Lord Mayor's banquet for the opposition at the Guildhall.

It was one thing, however, for the Marquis' friends to oppose ministerial motions calculated to inflame the city and to frighten moderate men from voting in opposition, but another thing altogether to give the slightest encouragement to a movement now under way for sending up remonstrances to the crown. On March 29 Sawbridge told John Calcraft who relayed it to Chatham that a Middlesex remonstrance would not be adopted because the movers of it were offended by half-hearted support given in Parliament to London's, and laid "the whole of the mischief to the Rockingham party." Calcraft said too that he feared that "the City warmth" against that party "would break out at last"; and that Lord Mansfield was trying what he could do "in Grosvenor Square." Chatham refused to believe, however, that Rockingham was playing a double game. He gave notice, before the Easter holiday, of intention to bring in a bill to reverse the decision of the House of Commons on the Middlesex election, and although Rockingham must have thought this futile, he urged his friends to be on hand to give support. [60] Nor did Chatham take any offense at Burke's *Thoughts on the Cause of the Present Discontents* which at last appeared during the Easter holiday. Later he would say that it had done harm to the cause of united opposition, but there is no record of his taking any notice of it in the spring of 1770. Burke said in May that the pamphlet was received by partisans of the court as "a piece of gentlemanlike hostility" but encountered its "fiercest enemies . . . in the republican faction." Its professed aim was to embody all whigs in an opposition party but it marked out a line which metropolitan radicals never could be expected to follow. One can only speculate on why this pamphlet was delayed until the day before Parliament reconvened after Easter. Perhaps the remarkable quiet of the metropolis, despite the release of Wilkes from prison and a Westminster by-election, made the moment seem right for addressing the public. That Rockingham had sought wider counsel on the wisdom of publishing it is suggested by Cornwall's writing to him on April 5 that it was "a very masterly performance" and that he saw "no sort of objection to the immediate publication of it." [61] Eighteen days later it was in the book-stalls.

In spite of his weariness with the futile question Rockingham went through the business of Chatham's bill to reverse the Commons adjudication on the Middlesex election. Chatham sent a draft of the bill to him on April 27. It would extend the reversal all the way to Wilkes's expulsion, and the Marquis proposed that it be turned into a declaratory bill against the doctrine that expulsion created incapacity. "We are indeed very sure of being beat," he told Chatham, "but we have an option on what grounds we shall be beat." A compromise was worked out at a meeting of peers in Rockingham's house two days later, and on May 1 Chatham moved the bill which failed by a great majority. Again on May 4 he had the support of Rockingham peers for his motion to censure the advice which had led the King to answer the London remonstrance with strong words of condemnation.[62] A week later Chatham notified Rockingham that he would move an address to the crown for a dissolution. He said that they had previously talked of such a motion but that the Marquis had doubted of its expediency— now, in the last days of the session, it must be done. "A surmise begins to spread," Chatham wrote, "that zeal for this indispensable measure is slackening every hour, and that symptoms appear of a tendency to waive this great object of the people." He never could wish a friend of his to go into the King's service unless a new parliament were called, and he said that if he and Rockingham finally differed on this object his "pain and distress" would be great. Rocking-ham answered that a motion of this sort would not be generally favored by the opposition lords; it was not that they did not adhere to the measure of dissolution but thought it futile to ask the King to do what the King would not do. The Marquis also implied that Chatham was influenced by certain people who threw out "suspicions or reflections" of lukewarmness for the popular cause, and added that it was neither to Chatham's honor "nor for ours to suffer ourselves to be sworn every day to keep our word." When Chatham retorted that the idea of the motion was his own and not the suggestion of others, Rockingham graciously answered:

> . . . putting the matter entirely on your Lordship's own opin-
> ion of the propriety of *now* moving the address, is, I assure your
> Lordship, of more weight with me, and may be with the others,
> than the argument of the former letter, where your Lordship,
> in part, put it on the necessity of clearing up doubts, which
> some have spread, or attempted to propagate among the peo-
> ple.[63]

The Marquis secured as many supporters as he could for May 14 when Chatham moved the address, which was rejected without a division. Five days later the parliamentary session which had opened so auspiciously for the opposition ended with their abject failure.

For the Rockinghams nothing had been gained but a cultivated cordiality between their head and Lord Chatham, whose influence was in decline, who never could be a Rockinghamite. Despite his resolution against being drawn in Chatham's train the Marquis had not been able to resist its suction without being accused of betraying the popular cause. That cause failed because the country was not angry enough over the violated rights of Middlesex electors, and in a sense it was unfortunate for the Rockinghams that the cause arose. They could not refuse to support it, but in doing that they were driven from their natural course, which was to build public reputation without appearing to the King as men who would storm his closet. Such men as Chatham, Temple, and Shelburne had connections with metropolitan politicians and were far less reluctant than Rockingham to stir up remonstrances and to play what Burke called "the popular engines." It was, Burke said, "the great calamity of the times" that those who could play them with the best temper and skill had "a great reluctance to meddling with them at all," while those who did play them were "by no means our wisest, or perhaps our best man."[64] It could not have been otherwise. The calamity arose from the incompatibility of the popular cause with the nature of the Rockingham leadership.

One small fruit of the Rockingham–Chatham cooperation was the agreement in June between Trecothick and Lord Mayor Beckford[65] which led to the election of two Rockinghamite sheriffs in London and Middlesex and to Trecothick's succession (on Beckford's death that month) to the lord mayoralty by defeating the Wilkite Brass Crosby in a close election. These elections evidenced a quieter temper in the city and gave the Rockinghams, for a short time, a larger influence in the city than they had ever possessed.

Chatham saw Rockingham in town on July 25 and it is probable that they talked of the movement showing in a few places to adopt remonstrances to the crown after the fashion of London, which had sent up a second one after Parliament had risen. The movement had nothing like the scope of the petitioning in 1769. After their meeting Chatham wrote to John Calcraft that he had

> learnt nothing more than what I knew before; namely, that the Marquis is an honest and honourable man, but that "moderation, moderation!" is the burden of the song among the body. For myself, I am resolved to be in earnest for the public, and shall be a *scarecrow of violence* to the gentle warblers of the grove, moderate Whigs and temperate statesmen.[66]

Rockingham discovered at York Races in August that the spirit of 1769 was still very much alive in the county. Gentlemen desired another county meeting which the Marquis, al-

though he knew his friends could control it, did not relish.
It was fixed for September 25. The advertisement, signed by
many recognizable county friends and members of the Rockingham Club, went out early that month. The Marquis wrote
to Burke on the 5th:

> A remonstrance was not at all liked in general and even of a
> warm meeting of about—18—*four only* were at all inclined to
> it. . . . The intention therefore is—to do something which may
> shew the adherence here to the former measure, and the scheme
> now is—to thank the members for the County etc. for their
> conduct, to recommend and inforce their perseverance to take
> every means of redressing the grievance and to watch and guard
> the constitution against the dangers it is under from evil minis-
> ters and evil counsellors.

Once again Burke tried to push his leader farther than
he was prepared to go. He urged that the county members
be instructed to move a bill to reverse the adjudication of
the House of Commons on the Middlesex election and to
decline further attendance if such a bill were rejected. He
also pressed for a communication of the Yorkshire plan to
other opposition leaders, who "would think that they had
little less than an actual right, to expect communication in
all steps relative to the Middlesex decision." [67] Rockingham
neither answered this letter nor adopted the advice it contained.

About 300 men—less than half the gathering of the
previous year—met at York, with Sir George Armytage
again in the chair. He said that the King had received their
petition of 1769 with a smile, "but we were soon taught,
that the smile of a King was like the chaff which the wind
scattereth. . . . Shall we again kneel at that altar, where
our most ardent prayers have been ineffectual? For my part,
I shall not vote for a remonstrance." The only eligible
mode, he continued, was to address "our worthy representatives" to exert their vigilance and ascertain the causes of
discontent which prevented "the rays of royal justice and

paternal affection from diffusing their healing influence on the minds of a generous people." The text of such an address was ready, and, after they heard Sir George Savile tell of what had been tried in Parliament, it was adopted. Sir Charles Turner, seconded by Sir Cecil Wray, proposed naming a committee to draft a remonstrance to be presented if the wrong done to Middlesex electors were not righted in the next session. Sir John Cavendish spoke against this proposal and it was rejected.[68] The Marquis wrote afterward to Dowdeswell:

> It appeared to me very plainly for a long time that the general sense of the county was not for a remonstrance, but the doubt was, whether forbearance would not be considered as acquiescence. This indeed determined that there should be a meeting, in order to shew that the county did firmly adhere to their sentiments of last year & therefore the object was, so to manage what should be done, as to shew their adherence, & yet not to adopt the measure of a remonstrance. I think the mode is in all respects proper. I think there is expressed sufficient warmth without passion.[69]

To Burke he said that this was "the properest and best mode that could be proceeded in here." And he sent a copy of the address for Burke to show to Trecothick in advance of its publication. The Lord Mayor was considering a meeting of the livery at which an attempt to follow Yorkshire's example might be made. Rumors were about of a break-up of the Bill of Rights society and the Marquis hoped to collect "the most valuable men amongst them" for political association with "those who make it a rule not to raise the expectations without a certainty in their own judgments, of the propriety and possibility of fulfilling them." [70]

Meanwhile, Chatham was telling Shelburne that he waited "anxiously to learn the result of the meeting at York." He hoped that it would "aim right" but expected that nothing would "hit the mark full but the city of London . . . where the modern dictionary does not yet prevail enough to proscribe the word *remonstrance*." [71]

The "gentle warblers of the grove" and the "scarecrow
of violence" were moving toward the parting of their ways.

NOTES

1. Add. MS 35430, f. 136; *Cavendish's Debates* I 106–111.
2. *Corr. Burke* II 222; *Cavendish's Debates* I 115–120.
3. *Ibid.,* 139, 222–237, 366–386.
4. *Annual Register* (1769), 197–200.
5. WWM R 87: 1, 2.
6. *Cavendish's Debates* I 404–405, 413–433.
7. *Chatham* III 359–361; *Corr. Burke* II 26.
8. WWM R 1: 1184, 1185; *Corr. Burke* II 25. Meredith told Portland
(9 June) that Savile, Lord John Cavendish, Burke, and Wedderburn read
it and made small alterations.—Portland MSS.
9. *The Question Stated, whether the Freeholders of Middlesex lost their
Right by Voting for Mr. Wilkes in the last Election? In a Letter from a
Member of Parliament to one of his Constituents* (London: G. Woodfall,
1769).
10. *Corr. Burke* II 26.
11. WWM R 1: 1199.
12. *St. James's Chronicle,* 3/6, 13/16 May, 29 June/1 July.
13. WWM R 1: 1200, 1204. Sir Anthony Abdy was a lawyer who sat in
Parliament for the Cavendish family borough of Knaresborough, Yorkshire,
and was a Rockingham whig.
14. *Annual Register* (1769), 199, 202–203.
15. *Cavendish's Debates* I 229. The offense, North said, would be a
breach of the privilege of Parliament, "the most culpable, the most punish-
able, that the annals of the country can produce."
16. *Corr. Burke* II 31–39, 40–41.
17. WWM R 1: 1205, 1206, 1209, 1210, 1212.
18. *Annual Register* (1769), 121; *Corr. Burke* II 47–49; Rockingham to
Portland 12 July.—Portland MSS.
19. *Corr. Burke* II 47.
20. *Ibid.,* 50–52; Dowdeswell to Rockingham 5 August.—Dowdeswell MSS.
21. *Corr. Burke* II 57–59, 69–70, 82–83; Add. MS 35362, ff. 259–262.
22. WWM R 10: 3; R 1: 1216.
23. *Corr. Burke* II 75–76; Abdy to Portland 9 Sept.—Portland MSS; WWM
R 1: 1226, 1227.
24. WWM R 1: 1230, 1234.
25. *Ibid.,* 1231.
26. *Ibid.,* 1230.
27. *Ibid.,* 1223m, 1225.
28. *Ibid.,* 1230; *Corr. Burke* II 86; Lord John Cavendish to Portland 28
Sept.—Portland MSS.
29. Savile's estimate, made by Burke too. A deprecating report from "XY"

in the *Public Advertiser* (2 Oct.) stated that only "a tenth part of the County" assembled at York "notwithstanding the united Efforts of a noble Marquis and of the two County Members."

30. *Corr. Burke* II 96–97; *Foljambe Manuscripts* (Hist. MSS Comm.), 146–148; WWM R 1: 1235.

31. Albemarle II 137.

32. *Grafton,* 238–239.

33. George Rudé, *Wilkes and Liberty* (Oxford, 1962), 135–136; L. S. Sutherland, *The City of London and the Opposition to Government* (London, 1959), 25–32.

34. Woodfall, *Junius* II 35.

35. *A Letter to Dr. Blackstone* (London: Woodfall, Jan. 1770); Rockingham to Portland 17 Dec.—Portland MSS.

36. London: Dodsley, 1769. Dowdeswell to Burke 20 July.—WWM Burke papers; Dowdeswell to Rockingham 3 Aug., 5 Sept.—Dowdeswell MSS; *Corr. Burke* II 69–70; WWM R 1: 1230.

37. *Corr. Burke* II 39–40, 49, 52, 92, 101, 104, 108–109.

38. *Ibid.,* 107–109.

39. WWM R 1: 1250.

40. *Corr. Burke* II 118–121.

41. Portland MSS (5 Dec.).

42. *Corr. Burke* II 114. Two weeks later Burke wrote to the Marquis that "I have abated something of my zeal, on finding by your delay in sending the copy, that something either in the scheme or the execution requires a more mature consideration."—*Ibid.,* 122.

43. WWM R 1: 1254.

44. Dartmouth MS D.1778.vii.

45. In October when Lord Hardwicke told his brother that Rockingham was coming in hope of seeing him, Charles answered: "The materials in his budget from *Newmarket* and *Yorkshire* I can guess. But I do not admire the *petitioning* plan, nor see the good sense of such work to any party. . . . I can not persuade myself that I shall be a loser of what tends to edification, tho' I value and esteem his friendship."—Add. MS 35362, ff. 261–262.

46. "The Earl of Chatham has publicly declared within this Fortnight, that certain Proceedings, with Regard to Mr. Luttrell's Election are illegal, in toto & in parte. But it is an Illegality of that Kind, which cannot be remedied in the present P———t, and no Redress can be obtained but by another."—*St. James's Chronicle,* 21/23 Sept.

47. *Corr. Burke* II 88–89.

48. *Ibid.,* 89–95.

49. WWM R 1: 1238.

50. R 1217: 85; Portland MSS.

51. Rockingham expected "a very numerous & respectable" meeting, larger than that of 9 May.—Add. MS 34728, f. 200. The names of those who attended are listed in WWM R 1: 1259. Walpole, *Memoirs* IV 22–23.

52. *Chatham* III 387, 390; Walpole, *Memoirs* IV 23.

53. *Grafton,* 245–247.

54. For a full account of Yorke and the offer of the Great Seal, see D. A. Winstanley, *Lord Chatham and the Whig Opposition* (Cambridge, 1912), 296–315.

55. Walpole, *Memoirs* IV 41–42.

56. *Chatham* III 414–416; *Corr. Burke* II 123. Although Rockingham was on record as favoring such a measure, it seems to have been Grenvillian pressure that induced Dowdeswell to make the motion.—Add. MS 42087, ff. 126–127.

57. *Corr. Burke* II 138; Winstanley, *Chatham and Whig Opposition,* 341; Albemarle II 167; *Cavendish's Debates* I 505–514.

58. Text in *Annual Register* (1769), 199–201.

59. Portland MSS.

60. *Chatham* III 431, 436, 438–439; Albemarle II 171–172.

61. *Corr. Burke* II 139–140; WWM R 1: 1291.

62. *Chatham* III 445–449; Albemarle II 176–177.

63. *Ibid.,* 180–185; *Chatham* III 455–457.

64. *Corr. Burke* II 138.

65. WWM R 1: 1304.

66. *Chatham* III 469.

67. *Corr. Burke* III 151–154, 158.

68. Christopher Wyvill, *Political Papers* (3 vols.; York, 1794–1802) I xxii–xxxv.

69. WWM R 1: 1314.

70. *Corr. Burke* II 162–163.

71. *Chatham* III 471.

8

The Rout of the Whigs

By 1770 THE MYTH OF BUTE as minister behind the curtain was fading and imagination was projecting another evil genius of the court: Lord Mansfield. He was Scotch. Early in the reign he had deserted the Pelhamites. He was Lord Chief Justice, and a popular reaction against the law courts was stirring. He had presided at the conviction and sentencing of Wilkes. Since the easy-going North was not convincing as a prime minister (in the language of the age, "the Minister"), another's potent influence in the royal closet had to be supposed. "I consider him [Mansfield] as the King's Minister," wrote Chatham that autumn. An opportunity for attacking the Justice was provided in the trial that year of the printer[1] of the letter by "Junius" to the King. Mansfield had directed the jury to confine its deliberations to the facts of printing and publishing and leave to the bench the decision whether the writing was a seditious libel. However consistent his opinion may have been with the current practice of the courts, his unpopularity combined with the notoriety of the case and the angry frustration of the partisans of the lost cause of the Middlesex electors to provide a new cause for opposition to exploit. It was not relished, however, by the inner corps of the Rockinghams because it was charged with personal animus against the Lord Chief Justice, who was the Marquis' uncle.

Burke early warned Lord Mayor Trecothick against encouraging a city demonstration against Mansfield, and reported to Rockingham:

> This is I dare say by far the most favourite point with Lord Chatham; partly from political views, and partly from personal animosity to Lord Mansfield. . . . I did all in my power to possess our friend with the absolute necessity, of declining to engage in any matter of law, however specious, until we should have an opportunity of consulting those of the profession, who act with your Lordship.[2]

Although separated in politics, the Marquis and his uncle were on amicable terms, and the improved relations between the Rockinghams and George Grenville, whom Mansfield admired, may have brought the latter to view his nephew's conduct with less disfavor. They had met at York Races in August. "Nothing very material in politics passed between us," Rockingham told Burke. But Horace Walpole was to allege that the subsequent moderation of the York county meeting was the result of Mansfield's having proposed that Rockingham enter into coalition with the North administration. It is likely enough that the court did employ the Justice to take soundings of the Marquis' disposition. Another story then current had Lord Holland dangling the Irish viceroyalty before his brother-in-law, the Duke of Richmond. These were common tricks for loosening the cement of opposition. Walpole perhaps saw further evidence of an approach to Rockingham in the visit of the Duke and Duchess of Northumberland at Wentworth in early September, and in the Marquis' going to town after the York meeting. Walpole said that he went to conclude a treaty with administration only to find that he could not have the Treasury. An unfounded tale: his own testimony is that he went to see his friend Lord Albemarle before the ailing Albemarle went abroad for the sake of his health.[3]

With respect to political action in the oncoming session of Parliament, Rockingham was naturally influenced by the war scare blowing up in late September as a result of the Spanish seizure of the British Port Egmont in the Falkland Islands. It reminded him that ministry had in the previous March rejected a Rockinghamite motion for an augmentation of seamen. He wrote to Dowdeswell (September 28) that this should be "a heavy charge against the Ministers at the opening of the session." Whether it was to be peace or war, he said, ministry must be attacked for derelictions in the national defense. Lord Chatham, on the other hand, was resolved that the danger of war should not be allowed to divert opposition's efforts to vindicate the rights of the people. He concerted with Shelburne in promoting another London remonstrance which listed "juries forbid to judge of the whole matter before them" along with "electors not suffered to elect" as grievances calling for redress.[4] Rockingham did not despair of cooperating with Chatham, however, and visited him on the eve of Parliament's opening. Since the latter said of the Marquis afterward that "my esteem and confidence in his Lordship's upright intentions grow from every conversation with him," it seems improbable that they talked about the rights of jurors. Probably the Marquis communicated the text of an amendment to be moved on the address, since Dowdeswell had prepared one which aimed at ascertaining if ministers had been alert and diligent timely enough to meet the Spanish threat. It stated also that nothing could so surely restore respect for government at home or abroad as "removing all doubts . . . concerning the exercise of the rights of electors." This amendment was not moved on the opening day because of George Grenville's death and the resultant absence of many, but the speeches of Dowdeswell, Meredith, and Burke in Commons and of Rockingham and Richmond in the Lords revealed a party tactic: indictment of ministers for neglecting national defense, along with lip service for the defeated cause of the previous session.[5]

After a decent two-day interval of respect for Chatham's mourning, Rockingham wrote to him that it was "much to be wished that a plan should soon be formed, so that in both houses of parliament the proceedings should go hand in hand. I imagine the object should be to point out the neglect of administration in not having prepared earlier." Chatham answered that he wished "to have opportunities of communicating sentiments with your Lordship at all times, and more particularly in the present, when public dangers of every sort are imminent." In the body of opposition there were inevitably various opinions but he would always "recommend *vigour* as the best *prudence,* and consider *relaxation* as the worst *policy.*" He could hardly have been plainer in pointing the contrast between Yorkshire's rejection of a remonstrance and London's sending up another with his blessing. The public dangers, Chatham held, were not only from foreign menace but from unconstitutional exercise of power at home; wherefore did he press upon the Marquis "large and comprehensive views" and deplore that Burke's pamphlet of 1770, "however well intended," had done "much hurt to the cause."

> In the wide and extensive public, the *whole* alone can save the *whole* against the desperate designs of the Court. Let us, for God's sake, employ our efforts to remove all the just obstacles to a true and public-spirited union of *all* who will not be slaves.[6]

Reflecting that this was exactly the purpose of Burke's *Thoughts,* Rockingham began a defensive answer to the effect that the offending parts of the pamphlet related to "merely speculative points of amendment in the constitution" and expressed doubts that these could have the effect "which their begetters imagine." Then he appears to have thought it idle to dispute with Chatham over a pamphlet, and instead sent notice of motions to be offered by Dowdeswell and Richmond on the origins of the quarrel with Spain. Chatham supported them in the Lords (November 22) in the manner of a man convinced that war was inevitable and offering himself again as the nation's savior. He called for an administration capable not only of defeating foreign enemies but of restoring the rights of electors. He denounced city magistrates who had obstructed the impressing of seamen; complimented Trecothick who had supported the impressment; praised the late Grenville (whose friends he courted) ; sneered at Mansfield, and avowed his respect for the Rockinghams—"that honourable connection which arises from a disinterested concurrence in opinion upon public purposes." [7]

The Rockinghamite opening tactic met with inevitable reverses in both Houses, whereupon Chatham and Shelburne concerted to bring on motions more popular with their own natural followers. Finding that Dowdeswell objected to anything relating to the Middlesex election until after the Christmas recess, the great patrons of city politicians began to feel their way toward getting the question of jury rights before the House of Commons. Cornwall was asked to move for leave to bring in a bill to prevent the starting of libel prosecutions by the attorney-general's filing of *ex-officio* informations in the courts. He backed off, however, when Shelburne objected to advance communication with the Rockinghams, and Constantine Phipps, an unconnected man, was cast for the part. Just before the appointed day (November 27) Chatham spelled out the aim of this maneuver in plain words:

> It is fortunate that the pulse of the house will be felt without an air of personality from any particular quarter; but should that pulse be found faint and uncertain, it seems to me indispensable, that the lukewarm, the wavering, and the treacherous should be brought to the test, and the discrimination made between the votaries of the constitution and the pretended patriots. My opinion is that all *will* follow, because they *must*.[8]

The day did not bear out Chatham's expectation. Cornwall endeavored, with Dowdeswell's silent approval, to have Phipps's motion so amended as to aim for an inquiry into the administration of justice. After John Glynn had spoken of juries as "cramped, mangled, restricted in their powers" —an implied thrust at Mansfield—Burke supported Cornwall with an argument which ran the opposite way. An inquiry, he said, was necessary to find out why so many libel prosecutions failed to get convictions from juries: why "the whole band of booksellers have defeated the whole body of the law." He blamed the prosecuting part of judicature but held the "judicial" to be "untainted." The proposed inquiry should ascertain why juries could not be "prevailed upon to find any thing a libel," and why the liberty of the press had run into a licentiousness "too strong for government." Phipps, who refused Cornwall's amendment, lost his motion by 72 to 164. Wedderburn, primate of the decapitated Grenville knot, had refused to support either the motion or the amendment; and the Rockinghams had sabotaged Chatham's parliamentary strategy. The latter's reaction may be read in what he wrote the next day to Shelburne:

> Matters are hastening to some crisis in the interior of the thing called opposition. I think all is ruined. . . . I will bring matters, before it is too long, to an explanation; and if Burke's picture of juries, and of that mode of justice is to be adopted, I shall separate from so unorthodox a congregation.[9]

He was "much satisfied," however, by conversation with Rockingham (November 29) who had by now formed the opinion that, although Mansfield's doctrine on the rights of juries in libel cases was legally correct, the law ought to be changed to secure for jurors competence over the whole matter of such cases. Either at this time or soon after, Chatham and Rockingham agreed upon motions against incapacitation by mere resolution of the Commons and for inquiry into the administration of justice with particular reference to rights of juries. Chatham would undertake the first and Glynn the second, with assurance to the Marquis that the latter would not take a personal turn but, as Chatham stated, "go to the doctrines, and the dangerous consequences that flow from them." [10]

Chatham's motion failed (December 5) against the usual majority. In his speech he made a divagation on the subject of juries which drew a defensive response from Mansfield. Two days later while supporting Glynn's motion, Burke avowed "the best opinion of our courts of justice" and venerated Mansfield who, if erring, erred in the best of company and with authoritative precedents; but Parliament should "teach him better doctrine" by enacting better law. Burke was complimented by the attorney general who suggested that opposition forgo inquiry and bring in a bill; which must have sounded like a hint of administration support. Only 75 voted for Glynn's motion; whereupon Dowdeswell gave notice that after Christmas he would move for leave to bring in a bill to resolve doubts and controversies over the rights of juries. Rockingham was beforehand in communicating this intention to Chatham who, aware that the Rockinghams had been laggard in supporting Glynn, said that the matter should be left to Lord Camden, and that if any bill were brought in it should be declaratory of what the law was and ever had been[11]—in other words, a bill of implied censure upon Mansfield, who, in Chatham's language, was afflicted with "political leprosy." Camden having put certain questions of law to the Lord Chief Justice, a great debate between these luminaries of the bench was expected, and Chatham was confident that Camden would have the better of the argument; which might obviate the need even for a declaratory bill.

At this moment Rockingham had to rush posthaste to Bath where his wife lay seriously ill. There he read Camden's questions and wrote (December 15) to Burke: "I still persist in the opinion that our *idea* of a bill is the right and proper step; I would not have us either cajoled or intimidated out of it by any great politicians." He wished his friends to spread the word that to leave the question of jury rights to disputing lawyers would be "spinning a fine web instead of twisting a stout cable to hold the constitution firm and tight." He advised counseling with James Adair, a city lawyer who might be useful in winning support for the measure "from some at least of the warm gentry," and urged getting to him soon because efforts would be made to persuade the public "that any who were not for a *declaratory bill* in the teeth of all authorities etc. are betrayers of their country etc." Dowdeswell did as the Marquis advised and also gave a copy of his bill to Dunning, who recommended putting it off until after the expected Camden–Mansfield juridical duel. Dowdeswell assented on condition that this take place soon after the holidays, and Burke justified the accommodation to Rockingham: "He was certainly right; it might look as if we were running races; and making the discussion, rather a contention for popular applause, than a ground of serious relief to the subject." Soon the candor of the Rockinghams was rewarded by unauthorized publication of the text of the bill in the press with the comment that it would "effectually skreen" Lord Mansfield. Rockingham at Bath thought it not hard to guess where this leak was, and now advised his lieutenants to spread the notion that "*the Bill* would not be agreeable to either of the Law Champions," but that if either would assist in confirming "the rights of juries to judge of both law and fact" such an one would be the "better friend to posterity." [12]

During the parliamentary adjournment the Rockinghams' political prospect, however dim, darkened still more. Burke painted it (December 29) for his chief:

> The Corporation of London (whatever it may be) possessed much more entirely by the Shelburne faction; Lord Chatham endeavoring to discredit you with the people, and what is worse, to weaken you within yourselves; the Court irreconcileable to you . . . and the sober large-acred part of the nation, whom you have most studied to please, and whom it is most reputable to please, entirely indifferent about us, or of no considerable weight in the public scale.[13]

Meredith was loosening his connection with the party and Dartmouth was drifting away. Credible rumor (vindicated before Parliament reconvened) said that the decapitated Grenvilles were coming to terms with administration, so that Wedderburn whom Rockingham greatly valued would be lost to opposition.[14] And to cap these distresses Rockingham was detained through the winter at the bedside of his wife, so that in the last phase of the nemesis of the "united opposition" of 1770 there were no shadow cabinets in Grosvenor Square, no opportunities for the Marquis to smooth and conciliate Chatham. Richmond deputized for his leader but knew his own inadequacy and wrote to Rockingham:

> . . . the want of you to keep people together particularly the H[ouse] of C[ommons] gentlemen is too apparent. There are many of them who will upon most occasions vote with us, but want to be spoke to. . . . The thing that influences them is the personal regard they have for you which will make them do for your speaking what they will not do for another man's.[15]

Richmond was ardent but a little giddy and uncomprehending as was shown in the idea he advanced for winning over Camden to the party. The latter was balking at Chatham's course, had no intention to contend with Mansfield who had all the judges on his side, and told the Duke that he was a single man detached from connection and that the Rockinghams were "the most respectable men in the Kingdom." Richmond wrote to Rockingham that the party "must have a lawyer," Yorke being dead, Wedderburn gone to the court, Dunning of "another sett," and Mansfield "our enemy"; that Camden was not only the "ablest lawyer in England" but was "high in repute with the people"; that to "get him" Rockingham had only to "see us clear of Lord Mansfield" and join in attacking him "upon the matter of libels." [16] In other words the Marquis had only to give up his measure, his judgment, and his character.

On February 1 Chatham said to Richmond that a bill was

after all necessary but that Dowdeswell's bill would not do because it was *enacting*, whereas it should be *declaratory*: a bill to explain and render more effectual Edward I's Second Statute of Westminster.[17] There was force in the argument that such a bill would be more receptive to the general temper and spirit of men and their ways of acting because it appealed to ancient rules and rights. Moreover, as Richmond told Rockingham, press libels abounded so widely that Chatham could fairly contend that parliamentary opposition was more likely to win support by maintaining the rights of juries as "part of the old constitution, than to admit of any doubts & desire people now to make the law, for that many people with the cry that it is against the abuse of the press would not be for adding any thing now in favour of the press, but might be induced to support the old right in juries." On hearing what had passed between the two peers, Burke urged Dowdeswell not to yield "an iota" of the bill, saying that the aim of Chatham was that the Rockinghams "should do nothing that is useful." Dowdeswell "perfectly agreed." On February 3 Richmond, Savile, Keppel, Burke, Montagu, and Dowdeswell met to consider what might be done to conciliate Chatham. Their decision was to retain the enacting principle of their bill but to yield any language that might, as Dowdeswell stated, appear "to give something to the jury that it ought not to have had before." [18] Richmond's subsequent conversations with Chatham failed to win him over and revealed a depth of difference going far beyond the question of the rights of jurors.

Chatham reproached the Rockinghams for making "a man" their object: their "great defect" was their resolution (in the event of a whig administration) to place the Marquis at the head of the Treasury. He acknowledged that Rockingham had "a very good judgment, abilities sufficient, and the most agreeable, affable, and gentlemanlike manners"; that he was "a considerable man in the country," but still it would not be improper (if the whigs came in) for the King to choose Lord Temple for Treasury minister. Richmond denied that his friends identified their aim with a man; their

object was to unite the opponents of the court and "by acting on true whig principles, to recover the weight and party
of the whigs." He contended for the Rockinghams that
"reduced as we are, we are still the most numerous corps in
either house of parliament and in the nation, indeed we are
the *only* party now left." Their principles, he contended,
required that in taking office their leader should become the
Minister, and if Rockingham were to do "so wrong a thing"
as to give way for another, that would be "the single point"
on which his friends would not support him. Chatham countered that "as the oldest whig in England" he was willing
to recognize the Marquis as head of the whigs but that did
not mean that a party could impose a Treasury minister
upon the King. In view of the fact that nothing was more
remote from the King's intention than a whig administration, these disputants seem to have gotten rather high and
abstracted. In relating what passed to Rockingham, the
Duke said that he was keeping it from Dowdeswell who was
"devilish sulky at Lord Chatham already," and from Burke
who was "combustible." Dowdeswell was indeed so angry
at the failure to obtain an opposition concert on the jury bill
that he branded Chatham as "malicious" and wished never
again to consult "those who desert us." He feared that Richmond "from nothing but an anxiety to keep the opposition
together" would go too far in conceding. "Neither Burke
nor I," he wrote to Rockingham, "can see the least possibility of further concessions without giving up our principle.
If our friends should relax so as to give up any part of the
principle, I should think myself bound to move the bill as it
stands . . . & probably be silent & inactive for the rest of
my life." If only Lady Rockingham were well enough, he
groaned, to allow the Marquis to come to town.[19]

Rockingham attempted to guide his friends by letters
urging both adherence to the bill and making concessions
designed to blend the declaratory with the enacting principle.
He suggested striking out reference in the preamble to
doubts and controversies and stating the actual facts:

Namely, that now & heretofore the judges have by their charges etc. to juries, shown plainly, that in law, they thought the jurymen were scarce competent to judge on the matter contained in the libel, writing etc., but that the jurymen should rather restrain themselves & judge only on whether the fact of publication, the authorship etc. was proved. That, on the other hand, both now & heretofore the jurymen have happily assumed to themselves a right to judge on both parts & that your bill is to secure to juries that right, which they either have by law or custom, & which is too essential to the constitution now to remain undecided.[20]

Was it possible, the Marquis asked, that Chatham would listen to such an idea? Or that Camden could dispute these facts? These questions went unanswered because Rockingham's friends in town ignored his counsel. Richmond notified Chatham (February 20) that the bill would be moved the following week, and that "we are unwilling to admit of any words that . . . may involve us in questions upon what is past, and which are not necessary for our purposes." Chatham answered that he would resist the measure, and to men close to him he blamed Dowdeswell's "inflexibility" in which he saw "a melancholy proof of the spirit of *connection.*" He even uttered a suspicion that the Rockinghams were in collusion with the court. A further attempt at composing differences was made at a meeting at Savile's house but proved futile and provoked Chatham to sneer at "Lord Chief Justice Dowdeswell." Presumably, Rockingham's advice to his friends had foundered on the intransigency of their leader in the House of Commons. The following week he was able to go to town to make a new effort to harmonize differences. The motion for leave to bring in the bill was put off, and the Marquis talked to Chatham in what the latter described as "his candid and temperate manner." A promise appears to have been exacted from the great Earl not to urge his friends to oppose the motion for leave, since after the meeting Chatham told Shelburne: "The *wrong* bill, it seems to me, should be admitted to be brought in, in order

to make it *right*: that is, *declaratory*, in the committee." [21]
It would seem that Chatham did imagine that Rockingham
was in collusion with the administration on this bill as otherwise there could be no likelihood of its ever reaching the
committee stage; but the Marquis was not in collusion and
did not expect the motion for leave to be passed; he was
only trying to prevent an open and ostentatious breach in
opposition ranks. Presumably, he brought Dowdeswell too
around to a more conciliatory disposition, which the latter
revealed on the day (March 7) of his motion.

In offering it he employed historical argument reaching
back to the reign of Edward I, said his aim was to bring
Parliament back to the maintenance of "that right of the
jury, which they were constitutionally in possession of"—
very Chathamite language! A right which was truly part of
the constitution, he pleaded, had gone out of sight during
the previous century, as could be seen in a multitude of
precedents since 1663, yet he would not impute misconduct
to living judges who had but followed the practices of their
predecessors. Many had asked him if his bill was a declaratory or enacting measure, but he professed not to understand
the distinction: "I call it a remedial bill; a bill asserting and
confirming the right of the juries to try the whole matter."
What exactly the bill would be was a question to be decided
in committee; when it reached that stage the gentlemen
would speak their views and he would speak his. The bill in
his hand, he said, presupposed the ancient rights of juries,
asserted that doubts and controversies had arisen over
jurors' rights "to try the whole matter laid in indictments
and informations for seditious libels," and enacted that
juries "be held and reputed competent" in the whole matter.
After Savile seconded, Barré, Dunning, and Calcraft spoke
the Chathamite line for committing the bill to make it
declaratory. Tommy Townshend was not sure that any bill
was necessary, but made the unwelcome suggestion to
Dowdeswell that the latter would "perhaps consent that the
bill should be declaratory." The leader of the Rockinghams
reached to his limits in responding: "If I enact that such and

such things shall be held and respected, is not that a declaratory bill?" Burke made a powerful speech, citing precedents in which the enactment of statutes had been required to reinforce the common law and the constitution, and asked the House to see two things: that a bad doctrine respecting jury rights had taken possession of the courts, and that it ought to be rooted out. It was not the error of one judge but of the profession, and he warned that a bill on the declaratory principle only would be thrown "upon its back" by the judges in the House of Lords. Ministerial voices were silent as the men of opposition displayed chaos in their ranks, and a motion to adjourn was opposed by only 72 against 218.[22]

So ended, ignominiously, the last serious attempt by the Rockinghams until 1775 to obtain a positive legislative measure for the public good. The Marquis had conceived the jury bill in the same way he had envisaged the Stamp Act repeal, condemnation of general warrants, revision of the Grenville Revenue Act, and *nullum tempus*: as necessary to the quieting of controversy, to the liberty of the subject, and to the tranquillity of the kingdom. If the King's ministers could not be induced to accept a good measure but preferred to let the question of jury rights hang fire—as it was to do until 1792—and if the Chatham–Shelburne wing of opposition could sabotage such a measure because it was not pointed at the disgrace of the nation's most eminent jurist, there was no use in attempting anything. The weakness and incompetence of opposition shown over the jury bill contrasted so strikingly with the strength displayed during this session on other questions. Thus when Savile had moved for leave to bring in a bill, prepared by Dowdeswell, to strip the House of Commons of the authority to incapacitate a candidate, 105 had divided for it; and against the convention for peace with Spain Dowdeswell had led (February 15) an opposition of 157, while in the Lords the number rose to 38. But potential strength was useless if leaders could not concert.

The Rockinghams could, of course, play little games of politics at which they were not very competent. One such game was going on as the jury bill flopped. During the winter a quarrel had split the men of the Bill of Rights society. Once faction headed by Aldermen James Townshend and John Sawbridge was patronized by Shelburne and stigmatized by Burke as "the republican faction." They had turned against Wilkes, an alderman now and the most formidable city politician. Rockingham expressed the hope early in February that each side would ruin the other and thus provide an opportunity "for Trecothick and our other friends to take the good men there may be in either party." Soon afterward certain printers in the city were charged in Commons with violating privilege by printing speeches of members and libelous reflections upon them. Wilkes, Lord Mayor Crosby, and Alderman Oliver invoked the chartered immunities of the city to obstruct parliamentary prosecution of the printers; no printer was punished but Crosby and Oliver, members of Parliament, were sent to the Tower for the duration of the session. Most of the Rockinghams opposed this attempted persecution of the press but as a corps they were in great disarray. Immediately after the magistrates were punished the Marquis told Dowdeswell: "It strikes me that consistently with the objection made by Sir G. Savile and you . . . we are to consider the Lord Mayor and Alderman as sent to the Tower by the prevalence of power, and not in consequence of a fair and just trial." Wherefore did Rockingham gather a party of friends for a popularity stunt in the city. He, the dukes of Portland and Manchester, Dowdeswell, Burke, and Aldermen Martin and Baker, proceeded ostentatiously through the city to the Tower to demonstrate their championship of magistrates who suffered in defense of the freedom of the press and the ancient privileges of London. This stunt may have had some influence in shaping the outcome of an election of sheriffs a few months later for London and Middlesex. Wilkes and an ally, with the support of the Trecothick–Martin–Baker forces, prevailed over both the Shelburne faction and the court. Rockingham, who pledged a contribution to Wilkes, told Dowdeswell that he rejoiced in

his success; but there was little in this for a party which
never could adopt into itself that great demagogue. "These
small games of politics," observed Burke, "amuse us a
little in this entire stagnation of the greater." [23]

Meanwhile the session of Parliament had ended with
the North administration more firmly than ever in easy
control. Dowdeswell had consulted no more with the faction which had let him down so badly, but in the last days
Chatham renewed contact with Rockingham on a proposed
motion to address the throne for a dissolution of the parliament which would not reverse itself on the Middlesex election. The Marquis pleaded preoccupation with his wife's
health and turned the business over to Richmond.[24] Two
motions, perhaps inspired by the contest brewing in the
city, probed the scabbed-over sore and met their easily
predictable fate.

II

The plight of the party was now desperate and never had
the Rockinghams been so near to quitting the business of
politics. With the remains of the Grenvilles and Bedfords
incorporated in the system which North headed, and North
appearing more and more to the King as the man Majesty
had been searching for since the beginning of the reign,
opposition could do nothing in Parliament. Even opposing
merely displayed the poverty of numbers. The Duke of
Grafton's acceptance of the privy seal in June showed a
former Treasury minister's judgment on the durability of
the ruling system. Burke, Keppel, and Saunders were at
Goodwood in July whence Richmond wrote to the Marquis:
"I say nothing on so unpromising a subject as politics. We
have scarcely talked of it here." Rockingham attended York
Races and described "a very quiet meeting" with scarcely
a word about politics. Not until December did he answer
a summer letter from Dowdeswell on that miserable topic.
In September, musing on follies and vanities, Burke wrote
to Charles O'Hara that "Politics, one of the worst of them,

I almost as completely forgot as if I never had any share in them; and most assuredly if the thing were to be done again I never should meddle with them." Soon afterward Trecothick told him: "I never have meant . . . more than to do any little good I can to my country collectively and to commerce in which I have spent my life—it will be too much to give up the remainder of my short life to fruitless efforts after what the degeneracy of mankind renders hopeless." [25] In October the Rockinghamites in the city were reduced to supporting, along with the Wilkes, the ministerial candidate against the Shelburne faction. That autumn Savile was nearly killed by falling from a horse.

In only one respect were circumstances somewhat less unfavorable for men in opposition. After the contest between the House of Commons and printers and city magistrates, the newspapers were less fearful of printing what was said in Parliament. It became easier, therefore, to reach the ear of the public. From this time, the protests of peers appeared in the papers and the Rockinghams were to make of them more effective means of stating their case to the nation. But their lassitude bred by despair even dried up their pamphleteering. Dowdeswell meditated writing something in the summer of 1771 and the Marquis told him that Burke would "be ready to attend you when you could wish him." [26] But there were no Rockinghamite pamphlets until 1775.

Until December there is hardly a record of Rockingham's political thinking or acting. For six months he wrote neither to his political secretary nor to his leader in Commons. His wife's slow convalescence and the want of materials to write about no doubt explain his silence. Newmarket saw him, inevitably, in October, when he also went to town and talked to Burke. By Christmas he had seen Portland, Savile, Saunders, Keppel, and Lord John. "The public & opposition seems at present asleep," he wrote to Dowdeswell (December 19), "but yet I don't find the least variation among any of those we call our friends." All concurred (as did Dowdeswell) that they "should act entirely upon their own judge-

ments & not suffer themselves to be hurried on by any of
the precipitate rash & ill designing men, who I think have
now fortunately lost all possible credit with the publick." [27]
Sorry was the state of that political party which could relish
the discrediting of potential allies. The Marquis was against
attempts to engage Chatham by putting questions to him,
and believed that nothing positive could be attempted without courting disaster; although the corps ought to stand
ready to resist wrong measures. To Burke he wrote on
December 27:

> I don't expect much satisfaction in the state of politicks except
> that satisfaction I have often experienced of finding all the
> friends I love and honour much in the same sentiments and
> dispositions as they were in when last we parted. . . . tho' the
> fruit is not always on the tree, I shall choose to continue to
> cultivate the vine rather than the thorn, in expectation of
> grapes.[28]

Off in Somerset Chatham was writing to Shelburne that
he could not see "the smallest good" for the public in going
up to the meeting of Parliament in January. He saw the
city as "sunk to nothing" while in another quarter "the
narrow genius of old-corps connection" had so weakened
whiggism that "national union on Revolution principles"
had become impossible. Not until the spring of 1774 did
this great man appear again in the House of Lords. Shelburne, who would attend as a sort of *locum tenens* for
Chatham, fancied that "a secret influence" (i.e. Mansfield's) like that so much complained of at St. James's had
penetrated opposition.[29]

Rockingham urged friends to be in town for the opening
of Parliament (January 22) but they were lackadaisical in
coming up. There might be nothing to do but, as he told
Portland, inactivity might be of less consequence "if the
publick nevertheless see every appearance of our continuance
in union, friendship etc." [30] Burke knew by mid-November
that a bill to regulate marriages in the royal family was
likely, but his chief had no foresight of a new and major

parliamentary contest over it. Richmond was typical: he started for town, turned back from heavy snow, and sent word that if any business came on—which he did not expect—Rockingham should send for him; otherwise his motions would be guided by his own convenience. When the address was moved, all parts of opposition were silent, which Will Burke said was "a thing not heard of even when opposition scarce existed." [31]

Early in February an event occurred which showed how the Rockinghams could scatter on a subject relating to church and religion. Meredith, separated and soon to receive a court place, introduced a petition from certain Church of England parsons and professional men who desired freedom from having to subscribe to the canon of Anglican doctrine, the Thirty-nine Articles. The petitioners had first applied to Savile and Lord John Cavendish who had declined from a characteristic whiggish dislike of subjects prone to agitate religious consciences and the susceptibilities of churchmen to alarm. And Burke had told a correspondent that although "nearly all" of his party were friendly to the petition, he would take "a determined opposition to it." [32] Historically, the whigs were identified with the principle of religious toleration and courted the Dissenters at elections. Therefore, they were likely to favor another latitudinarian advance in the established church; but the Rockinghams could not relish the question raised by the petition. The Marquis attended, as he often did, in the peers gallery and wrote an account of the debate which offers a glimpse, very rare, into his own church principles.

> . . . Many of our friends were divided in opinion. Several held the opinion that the petition which *seemed* to go against *subscribing* any articles, ought to be rejected. Others held, that the petition might be received & laid on the table, (tho' not to be proceeded on) as they thought other *relief* (which was part of the prayer of the petition) might afford & might serve future consideration.
>
> Much stress was laid on the impropriety etc. of requiring (as at Oxford) that all *young* persons coming to the University,

should be obliged immediately to subscribe the 39 Articles,
when neither their time of life nor the course of their studys
could probably have enabled them to have formed any clear
judgment of what they signed.

It was also urged, that at Cambridge, no person can receive
any degree, whether he is intended for physick, law etc. without
subscribing the articles. This is also held by many to be a hard-
ship. Tho' from the time of life, they may or ought to be
informed & capable of some judgment.

Lord John Cavendish, Sir George Savile etc. were for receiving the petition. Dowdeswell & Burke were against it, tho'
I think the former not quite so strenuous as the latter &
yet both of them in *parts* think some relief might be given.

These *"parts"* related to compulsory subscriptions by stu-
dents entering the university and by candidates for degrees
who entered lay professions. Rockingham's view was that
such relief was proper, but he did not approve relaxation
of fixed doctrine for clergymen of the Anglican Church: "I
imagine that few will chuse to leave the clergy . . . free
of all controul & trust their interpretations of the abstruse
& difficult points which occur in the Scriptures." He thought
too that the ministry's letting Sir Roger Newdigate, tory
member for Oxford, take a principal part in opposing the
motion (thrown out 217 to 71) "upon the highest flown
doctrines of High Church" would cause "great disgust in
the nation." [33] Toward the end of this session the Rockinghams were able to vote *en corps* and *whiggissime* for a bill
to relieve Dissenters from the obligation under the Toleration Act of 1689 of subscribing to most of the Thirty-nine
Articles. The Rockinghams were in a minority of 117 for
a bill (not their own) to apply the principle of the *nullum
tempus* act to the security of property against dormant
claims by the church.

Meanwhile, they fought a parliamentary battle of major
dimensions against the royal marriage bill in which they
saw further aggrandizement of the power of the crown.
Two of the King's brothers having lately married without
his approval, his Majesty asked for a new law to make it

illegal for a member of the royal family to wed without the consent of the crown. The business was opened (February 20) with a royal message to Parliament which received a rather cool reception. That night Rockingham informed the Duke of Portland: "I find in the House of Commons there is a great dislike to this bill & by what I collect in the House of Lords there are many who object there." [34] An auspicious feature of the moment was the resignation from the Admiralty board of the brilliant young Charles Fox, Lord Holland's son; he had already voted with the minority for the church *nullum tempus* bill and would now oppose the royal marriage bill; moreover, he had a host of friends. The Rockinghams began a general mobilization.

The bill brought into the Lords (February 21) declared the existence of a long-established if undefined royal right of approving marriages in the King's family, and enacted that no member under twenty-five could contract a lawful marriage without the King's approval; also, that none older might marry, Majesty not consenting, unless a year's notice was given to the Privy Council and Parliament raised no objection. All descendants of George II, save the issue of princesses married into other royal families, were placed within the scope of the bill, which vested this new authority not only in George III but in his successors.

Rockingham was able to have the judges interrogated in the Lords and to extract from them an opinion that royal authority over the marriages in the King's family had never in the past reached beyond his own children, grandchildren, and heir presumptive. The final vote of the peers showed 26 non-contents, although on two divisions opposition had mustered 32 and 35—without Chatham! Rockingham led the fight and according to Will Burke "spoke in every stage with clearness, perspicacity and address." [35] A protest signed upon the journal by fourteen Rockinghamite peers stated the position they had defended. It condemned the declaratory part of the bill as unhistorical, prophesied that with the passing of time it would make many families in the kingdom dependent upon the pleasure of the crown, that it

would drive princes of the blood into "a disorderly way of
life," and branded it as incompatible with religion and
natural law, and of a tendency to produce a disputed title
to the throne.

> If those who may be affected by it, are in power, they will easily
> procure a repeal of this act, and the confirmation of a marriage
> made contrary to it: and if they are not, it will at least be the
> source of the most dangerous party that can exist in any coun-
> try, a party attached to a pretender to the throne, whose claim,
> he may assert, has been set aside by no other authority than
> an act to which the legislature was not competent, as being con-
> trary to the common rights of mankind.

Rumor that Mansfield had drafted the bill helped to
produce an even stronger prejudice against it in Commons.
The strategy of Dowdeswell, however, was not to oppose
committing the measure, but to try to transform it in committee of the whole House into a bill narrowing royal
prerogative by parliamentary regulation in this sphere.
Some confusion resulted from Charles Fox's declared intention to oppose commitment.[36] A published division list
shows such men as George Byng, Cornwall, Weddell, and
Savile voting with Fox, Meredith, Barré, Dunning, Tommy
Townshend, and Sawbridge against commitment. Another
list printed in the press[37] gave the names of 31 members
of "the Rockingham Party who voted with the Ministry in
support of the Royal Marriage Bill," an insinuation, characteristic of the Shelburne faction, that the Marquis' principal friends were in collusion with the court. Here appear
the Burkes, Baker and Martin, the three Cavendish brothers, the Keppels, Saunders, Dowdeswell, and other recognizable regulars. On March 13 Dowdeswell's attack in
committee against the declaratory part of the bill was supported by 164 against 200. The minority approached the
dimensions to which opposition had swelled in 1770. It
prompted Horace Walpole to say that "the court, by new
intemperance and folly, raised from the dead a departed opposition." Rockingham wrote exultantly to Portland:

Conway, the Walpoles & various others were with us in the division & we have great hopes, that we shall keep up a general shake among the ministerial gentry in the further progress.[38]

The Marquis felt an elixir and busied himself writing to press for attendance. He kept a careful account of division lists, noted that "on very strong points" more than 200 had voted at one time or another against administration, and speculated on March 19 that if men wished to preserve "any consistency of conduct" about 190 would oppose the bill when it emerged from committee.[39] The last division in committee (on a motion to limit the measure to the King's life and three years after) was lost by only eighteen. "Eight of our people returning from dinner were locked out," testified William Burke, "and had we pressed an attendance we should have carried it, as many of their country gentlemen were weary of the business, and fairly came over to us." By this time Rockingham had fallen ill. Had he been able to sustain his campaign, Will Burke thought, his friends would have prevailed.[40] It had been, Horace Walpole observed, "A considerable struggle," and Edmund Burke judged that opposition had not been stronger "since the Middlesex election."

Some Rockinghamite peers did not relish a hot contest to alter a measure known to be so strongly desired by the King, and Portland saw an inconsistency with what he had understood as a party plan of inactivity and standing alone instead of getting caught up with others who never could be won to the party. Reflecting upon "the characters who wish to ally themselves with us on the present occasion," he thought it strange "that there could be a wish for such an appearance as might induce the world to suspect an union amongst us." [41] The Marquis was less fastidious and thought a bad bill ought to be opposed or improved and that the personal authority of the sovereign should be diminished. Moreover, the party he led—perhaps sponsored would be the better word—was pre-eminently a Commons party which naturally liked to swell with all who would vote against ad-

ministration; and the royal marriage bill which touched the
King's family, morals, and religion was of lively interest to
the public.

The Marquis was afflicted now with protracted illness. He
was well enough in April to go to Newmarket but kept ailing on and off through spring and summer. The "old complaint" acted up, with complications. By June 12 he reported
himself "mended very much tho' not without frequent and
considerable interruptions." At the end of the month Burke
thought that he gained strength "very slowly." Instead of
going into Yorkshire he spent the summer on an estate he
had bought at Wimbledon, and from June to October he
seems not to have written to anyone. Burke found him in
mid-August "recovered surprisingly considering the length
and heaviness of his disorder"; but before that month was
out Horace Walpole heard that he was dying. Not until
October do we find him again, first at Newmarket and then
at Wentworth, writing again to political friends and de-
scribing himself and his wife as "tolerably well." [42]

If he had not recovered it seems doubtful that the party
could have survived. Neither Portland nor Richmond had
his gift for holding men together and exerting strong influence over men of the House of Commons. Dowdeswell
was disgusted with politics.[43] Savile never did really believe
in party. While Rockingham was ill, Burke seriously considered accepting an offer (glittering to so poor a man) to
go as a member of a supervising commission to India to
put the affairs of the company in order; the prospect was
for a long absence from England. His brother Richard had
acquired doubtful title to a large tract of land in the West
Indies, which looked like a possible fortune for the Burkes;
but help from the Treasury was needed to secure it. Moreover, Edmund Burke was now agent for the colonial assembly of New York; which kept him in frequent contact with
the Board of Trade where his usefulness to his principals
was related to his personal standing at that government
office.[44] It was, therefore, very agreeable to him to have a
former political friend, Lord Dartmouth, succeed Lord

Hillsborough that summer as American Secretary and head of the Board of Trade. Frederick Montagu, who owed his seat in Parliament to Rockingham, commended Dartmouth's acceptance and was himself offered a seat on the board, which he declined. Nor did the Rockinghamite Duke of Manchester hesitate to ask from Dartmouth the kind of favors which conferred obligations.[45] The country was quiet, the spirit of party almost extinct, and the temper of the times was against whig politics. The year 1771 had witnessed a viceroyal revolution in Irish politics which humbled an oligarchy before the power of the crown, and in 1772 occurred a royalist coup in Sweden and the first partition of Poland by neighboring rulers. The easy supremacy of the kingly influence in the British Isles seemed to exemplify a trend against which resistance was vain.

Convalescing at Wentworth that autumn Rockingham reflected much upon the general susceptibility of corruptible men to the potent influence exerted by the crown through its swelling patronage, and lamented the great dearth of good men willing and able to contest against it in elections. To one of his friends, a Scotch member disposed to retire from Parliament because of financial inability to keep up an interest among his constituents, the Marquis wrote that he could not "wonder that you and others should be tired out with the drudgery of parliament and in continuing a system of politics which affords little prospect of success."

The expensiveness of elections will I am sure in the end occasion that few but those who mean to make a profit of their seats & must vote accordingly, will henceforth chuse to become members of Parlia[men]t. Some there will always be, who from principle of conscience considering their situations & stations of life will think it incumbent upon them to get into Parl[iamen]t & throw their mite to prevent bad measures & oppose bad men. The publick at large are languid at present & afford but little encouragement to such men, either to give themselves much trouble or much expence. In time there may & I hope will arise a more general patriotick spirit, & that both the men of rank & fortune & the actual constituents will cooperate together. The race now is, whether the men of rank etc. or the constituents are the *most* corrupt. The race must be which shall be the least corrupt.[46]

III

Rockingham's physical condition in the autumn of 1772 no doubt deepened his feeling of utter impotence in politics, and he was low enough in spirit to feel no inclination to mobilize friends even on an issue which he had long seen as of paramount importance—namely, that of the crown and the East India Company. As early as 1763 he had taken up voting qualification as a shareholder and had opposed government influence in the company. In 1767–1768 he had defended it against the overreaching hand of ministers, and had been active in the same direction in 1769.[47] Company directors friendly to Rockingham had tried in 1772 to obtain legislation which might enable them to curb abuses in India which were being ventilated in the press; but instead the House of Commons named a select committee to inquire into the affairs of the company. Rockingham's apprehensions were then spelled out:

The Ministry will proceed to shew the inability, or even perhaps the iniquity of some of the E[ast] I[ndia] Directors at home & then will expatiate on the necessity of some thing being done, to remedy the grievance & to save so important an object to this country. The result will naturally be, that Parliament i.e. the *Ministry* must take the super direction of the E. I. Company's affairs. The lucrative offices, & appointments relative to the E. I. Company's affairs, will naturally fall into the patronage of the Crown. Such addition to all the appointments of the Crown—in army, navy & revenue, Church etc. must be felt, when already what the Crown possesses in patronage has nearly over-ballanced the boasted equipoise of this constitution.

Charles the 1st & his ministers had not the advantage of a diffusive patronage to create *influence* & therefore strove to create a high undefined prerogative in the Crown, which might operate in terrorem & tend men's minds towards obedience,

whose affections they had not the ways & means of influencing.
. . . I pay due honour & credit to the men, who made the noble
struggle & who warded that mischief from this country. The
task at present is a much severer trial of men's virtues. There
is some thing so mild & alluring in coming under the benign
influence of the Crown & it not only gratifies the individual, but
also affords him the opportunity of exerting one of the best
principles of the human heart—his social love in behalf of his
friends & relations etc. So that one ought not to wonder that
many men either won't see the danger, or are not of such stuff as
can withstand the temptation.[48]

During the summer and autumn of 1772 a serious credit
crisis culminated in the East India Company's inability to
meet its obligations and turning to government for help.
Parliament was called early to deliberate upon this mo-
mentous business. With full grasp upon what portended
Rockingham opened a canvass of opinion among his friends
on the question "whether we should be very alert or not in
attending parliament." From such friends as Sir George
Colebrooke, then head of the East India direction, and
another director, Robert Gregory, whom the Marquis had
helped to come into Parliament, he knew enough to form a
sound judgment on what the directors ought to do but he
did not believe that they would do it. Payment of dividends
ought to be suspended, thus evading the obligation since
1767 to pay a large share of profits to the Exchequer; but
the prevailing view in the direction was for seeking a loan
from government, which would inevitably dictate the terms.[49]

Burke, Dowdeswell, and Richmond were for non-attend-
ance in Parliament on questions in which their activity would
be futile. All his friends urged the Marquis to mind his
health and stay in Yorkshire until it was mended. But no
consensus was reached on either the question he had posed
or the East India business. Such men as Savile, the Cavendish brothers, Frederick Montagu, and many others thought
that they should not be derelict in representing their constituents; so that most of the Rockinghams came laggardly
to town when Parliament was opened (November 26).

Some influence was exerted over them by Lord George Germain who since Grenville's death had seemed to approach Rockingham. He was a member of the select committee on Indian affairs, and the Marquis asked Burke to get his views too on the question of an indifferent attendance in Parliament. They were, according to Burke, that "we might rather run the risque of being forgotten by the public than of exciting in them the spirit that we wish to raise." [50] Rockingham remained at Wentworth and deputized Portland for the task of getting men together. The Duke said that "as we are not encumbered by numbers we might act as an army of observation" to the "advantage of the country & credit to ourselves," although the grand object was the Marquis' recovery if the party were to be kept in being:

> The only hope of ever seeing the credit & character of this country restored to its ancient lustre consists . . . in preserving the small remains of that party to which we have steadily adhered. . . . you are the centre of our union. Without you I think & fear we should become a rope of sand.[51]

Parliament was opened with a poor attendance by the opposition, Dowdeswell not putting in an appearance until more than a week passed. No amendment to the address was moved, and a motion passed without division for a committee to consider in secrecy what ought to be done with respect to the East India Company. Out of this body there quickly came a bill to restrain the directors from sending a commission of supervisors to India; which seemed to prove that reform was to be the work of the legislature, even though Ministry naturally desired the cooperation of the company's governors. Against the motion to bring in the restraining bill Dowdeswell divided with a pitiful 45 to 117. "Your Lordship will not wonder at it," he wrote to his chief; "you know the feeling of men with respect to the E. I. Company." The final vote on the bill came in what Dowdeswell called "a very mortifying division: 151 to 28," and he groaned: "In this state, what can we do?" [52]

In the Lords, Portland and Richmond mobilized a mere 6 against the measure, although an elegant Rockinghamite protest was entered upon the journal and published in the newspapers.

At Wentworth the Marquis read the dismal accounts from friends as he recruited his health. By early January he found himself "prodigiously better" and wrote: "I have long known that a winter's soiling was an excellent thing for a worn out horse, and I have found it a good thing for a politician." [53] Portland now implored him to come to town when Parliament met (January 19) after the holidays

> to consider differences & moderate opinions which the strictest honesty in some & vanity may have suggested in others, but which . . . ought to be modelled if possible to such a shape as may enable us to exert all our power. . . . There is no other person capable of undertaking it but yourself; & I therefore would most earnestly exhort you to it, if I was not convinced of your being equally sensible of the necessity of doing it.[54]

Burke painted to his chief a picture of the party in utter-disarray and said that it would be much better to stay away from the House "than to dispute among ourselves, divert the Ministry, and divide twenty-eight."

> We fall into confusion the moment you turn your back; and though you have the happiness of many friends of very great ability and industry, and of unshakeable fidelity to the cause, nobody but yourself has the means of rightly managing the different characters, and reconciling the different interests, that make up the corps of opposition.[55]

Nevertheless, the reopening of Parliament found Burke visiting his son in France. He would not return until March. And not until January 29 did the Marquis get to town.

Some life was now to stir in the opposition. Rockingham urged East India proprietors to sabotage negotiations then going on between government and directors, and the Duke of Richmond astonished the City of London by appearing in person to lead an opposition in the Court of Proprietors. On February 12 he gave what Horace Walpole called a "signal defeat" to the measures of government by carrying a large majority against proposals agreed upon by directors and government. This event stirred lively public interest and won metropolitan popularity for a Duke who could play so unducal a role. Next, Rockingham rallied supporters in defense of a new application by Dissenters for relief from the Thirty-nine Articles. Lord North had let their last application pass Commons to die in the Lords, but this time administration opposed it (March 17) in the lower House. Sixty-seven—a far better showing than 28—voted in the minority. Afterward Burke wrote that "we have nothing to do unless we make business for ourselves." [56] But soon something was concocted to raise again the spirit of 1770 which was already stirring in the city where the Common Council in March adopted another remonstrance to the King, repeating the call for dissolution of the House which had violated the rights of Middlesex electors. A month later Wilkes kicked up more fuss by trying through a legal technicality to obtain his seat in Parliament; which brought on a motion favorable to him which was supported by 124 against 227. The Rockinghams could not have instigated this, but it cannot be doubted that they exploited the moment and that a motion by Savile which followed immediately (April 26) had its origins in the Marquis' councils. Sir George, who had refused to contest against ministers in the East India business (to the great vexation of Burke), moved for leave to bring in a bill for more effectually securing the rights of electors in choosing members of Parliament. Dowdeswell seconded and the minority swelled to 151 against 200,[57] showing that when the cause was whiggish enough opposition could come alive.

Five days later Richmond induced a majority of East India proprietors to petition against arbitrary resolutions of Parliament. He was to keep up these tactical forays at India House on into 1774 in order to invigorate resistance to the power and influence of government in the great imperial company. "My cousin the Duke of Richmond who I regard most truly," wrote Admiral Keppel to Rockingham, "has diverted himself among the mob very much." Perhaps the Duke relished this role the more from the fact that Portland had eclipsed him as Rockingham's deputy. He was creating a popular image of himself which would have great importance to the party in later years. There are a few evidential hints that the Marquis was not very happy over Richmond's conduct; that he doubted that the effect was worth the sustained effort, and distrusted the Duke's ability to moderate between "men of much natural warmth" and "men of cooler passions." Moreover, Rockingham, who always prized having a reliable friend in an influential place, could not have been pleased by Richmond's refusal to vote for the Rockinghamite George Monson to be commander-in-chief in India lest that be "imputed to private partialities." [58]

The dwindled, discordant, and defeated Rockinghamites scattered for the summer and more or less forgot about politics. Off in Worcestershire Dowdeswell could envisage no business in the next session of Parliament except more East India legislation, and he was convinced that his friends should stay away.[59] The Marquis confessed to Portland in mid-summer that he grew "less & less fond of publick life & business" and could only hope that the principles he and his friends had acted on might have "good effects on the rising generation" and prevent "the constitution being over-run by the present abject & corrupt servility." [60] Some Rockinghamites so far forgot opposition politics as to court a little favor from government. Thus Burke, who had gotten his New York agency through the influence of men friendly to his chief, obtained a favor for them, a nomination to the council at New York, from Lord Dartmouth.[61] Also, Burke was an affectionate friend of Charles Fox who had returned to administration with a seat on North's Treasury board. A few years before, Burke's brother Richard had bought extensive lands from the Carib Indians on the West Indies island of St. Vincent, only to have the purchase invalidated by the council at Grenada. Richard's interest—indeed a Burke family interest—required Treasury support and Edmund pressed for this through Fox, who did all that he could in a cause which was ultimately to fail.[62] The Marquis himself plunged into a cause which could not be vindicated without the favor of ministers. His friend and perhaps kinsman, Governor John Wentworth of New Hampshire, had been accused of illegal conduct by a member of his own council and the case came before the Board of Trade, over which Dartmouth presided. In the latter's absence a report adverse to Wentworth was approved and sent to the Privy Council in May 1773. Convinced that the report was prejudiced and unjust and that the Governor had not been adequately represented by his counsel, Rockingham obtained Lord Chief Justice Mansfield's opinion that Wentworth was right and the Board's report wrong, and engaged John Lee to draft a memorial to the Privy Council (July 1773) asking for a re-hearing. "The more I look into the matter, the eagerer I grow in Gov[erno]r Wentworth's behalf," he told Lee. "The construction put upon Gov[erno]r Wentworth's conduct, & stamping it as illegal—arbitrary etc. etc. are deep wounds to a man's private character." Moreover, a condemnation in Privy Council must surely lead to Wentworth's recall, in which event the Marquis would lose a valuable connection in America. John Wentworth revered Lord Rockingham, had built a house in New Hampshire which he named after Wentworth Woodhouse, and his connection with the Marquis seemed not unlikely to damage his case in ministerial minds. Rockingham tried repeatedly to see Lord Dartmouth in behalf of Wentworth and perhaps did reach the secretary of state shortly before the Governor was exonerated (October 8).[63]

While this case hung fire Rockingham heard from Lord Bessborough of a bill to be brought forward in the Irish Parliament to lay a discriminatory tax upon the rent rolls of absentee landlords.[64] Here was something to raise whig blood pressures. Given the existing constitutional relations between Great Britain and Ireland it was impossible for such a measure to be enacted without prior consent of the British Privy Council. Heads of bill might be moved and passed at Dublin but the enacting process required that such be sent over to England, there to die if not returned by the crown in Privy Council. However, five years before British government had sent back a bill to limit the duration of Parliament in Ireland: a reform long desired by Irish patriots who resented the subordination of their legislature to that of Great Britain. Followed in 1771 the overthrow of the old whiggish "undertaker" politicians (whose chief was Bessborough's brother John Ponsonby) to the delight of patriots. The outlines of a viceroyal strategy aimed at courting patriots in order to fortify the power of the crown in Ireland had become discernible. A tax to retain a portion of absentee landlords' Irish income was a long-standing patriot project, and now it appeared, if Bessborough's information was true, that the thing would be done. Rockingham, who got part of his income from estates in the counties of Wicklow and Wexford, was at first incredulous. He could not bring himself to believe that "an *English* privy council" would tolerate such legislation in Ireland. The King's revenue in Ireland attacking the fortunes of his subjects in England! A minister who advised it might be "impeachable."

> We have a right to protection [he replied to Bessborough] we have committed no crime; our property is our own; we have a right to spend it where we please.

And recollecting what had appeared to him as a court tactic in England of sowing dissension among all parties in order to destroy them, he continued:

> I can't help suspecting that there is a little degree of trick in its having been so strongly stated to your Lordship; for, undoubtedly, the Ministry will wish that, if it is proposed in Ireland, it may be objected to by your Lordship's friends; and it will sufficiently answer the good purposes of the Ministers here, if they can create confusion among all parties in Ireland.[65]

By the end of September, however, he knew that the tax was
not opposed by ministry and would be passed if a strong
resistance were not offered. The viceroyal administration
at Dublin had proposed it and obtained Lord North's assent.
Burke told his chief:

> It would be ridiculous to understand it as any thing other than
> a measure of British administration. . . . It will come to pass
> in Ireland; it will be tolerated in England; it will not be op-
> posed in Council by any great Law Lord in this kingdom.

Irish though he was, Burke had the strongest constitutional
aversion to such a measure and recommended an early and
direct confrontation with ministry by men of great weight
and property before the Dublin Parliament (scheduled to
be opened in mid-October), become possessed of the bill.
If British ministers could be frightened enough Burke
thought that Lord Mansfield ("your Lordship's great
friend") might feel able and willing to go into the royal
closet and caution against a measure which must inevitably
be disliked in England.[66]

The Marquis now quit the pleasant life of Wentworth
and went to town, not to rally his party but to organize a
pressure group of men who had Irish property to defend
and any others who could be induced, irrespective of party
connections, to protest the dreaded tax on constitutional
grounds. He had to identify, canvass, persuade, and mobilize; and he was resolved if necessary to fight the bill in
Privy Council. Parliament not being in session it was not
easy to reach men scattered wide over the country, and it
was not until October 16—significantly, after the exonera-
tion of Governor Wentworth—that a paper which was at
once a remonstrance and an interrogation went to North
over the signatures of Rockingham, Devonshire, Milton,
Bessborough, and Upper Ossory. North grudgingly admitted the truth while half-disavowing British government's
responsibility for the expected measure. Whereupon Rockingham had copies of this exchange and a circular letter sent

to all absentee owners of Irish property whom he was able to list. Eight clerks were employed and by the end of the month more than 200 communications had gone out. With Burke as his right hand Rockingham assumed sole direction of the campaign. A wave of hostility to North began to rise. The Marquis grew confident "that the city of London & all the parties" were likely to concur with the protest; that North "had got into a bobble"; and that the confessed intention of government would "do them more harm in any reasonable person's mind than any thing that has yet been done." Half-panicked, North wrote to the Irish Viceroy: "The cry against it is universal. Friend and foe, those who have and those who have not estates in Ireland, join in condemning and abusing it." A sensitive nerve in the English nation had been touched, for this was the kind of question which could make James II and Ireland reverberate in English memories. Mansfield told ministers that they were in a "scrape" and ought to get out of it, and perhaps passed this to his nephew who wrote to Portland on November 4: "Lord North is in a scrape—I trust." [67]

Rockingham did not know, of course, that North had never liked the absentee tax but had accepted it from Dublin Castle as a detail of a comprehensive fiscal policy directed toward strengthening the royal hereditary revenue in Ireland; and it was agreeable to the King only if moved by an independent member of Irish Commons and then acquiesced in by the Castle. Now Majesty and Minister directed government in Ireland to stop the measure. Rumors to this effect were set afloat in England, but Rockingham's campaign to bring landlord pressure to bear upon members of Parliament in Ireland was sustained until he knew (November 29) that the bill had failed.

He sought, of course, to keep that campaign upon a higher level than mere protests in behalf of his and others' private interest. Burke's famous letter to Sir Charles Bingham, a member of the Irish Parliament, exemplified and perhaps served as a model for the mode of argument; it put the case

against the tax on such high principles of imperial states-
manship that Irish opponents of the measure were surprised
to discover the lofty virtues of their cause.[68] Rockingham's
best effort may be seen in his letter of November 19 to Sir
William Mayne, wherein he said that good government
should try "to conciliate the affections mutually between
G[rea]t Britain & all parts which compose this empire."
Did the absentee tax tend to conciliate? On the contrary,
it would create differences and animosities. If and when (he
hoped soon) a measure favorable to Irish interests should
be moved in British Parliament there would be "a lurking
desire of retaliating injuries." He had long thought that
British policy was "too close & niggardly" toward Ireland,
but that could not justify such "narrow and confined politicks" as a discriminatory tax. "This great empire rose to
its zenith on solid principles & more liberal ideas," and it
would crumble if politicians resorted to obstructing the intercourse between its different parts and the capital center.[69]

He was immensely elated by the success of his campaign.
His initiative had launched and his energy had sustained a
movement which reversed an intent of government. Letters
of congratulation poured in upon him containing, as he said,
"a considerable portion of myrrh and francinsense." To his
wife he reported himself as "in high favour with all concerned in this business & in general with the publick. . . ." [70]
To show this bright feather to the world and to let all
know who had carried a major point against the ministers,
he now gave his exchanges with North and his circular letters to the newspapers, for doing which he was both attacked
and defended in the press. He even meditated a resolution
in Parliament to commend the Irish House of Commons
"for rejecting a proposition injurious to the welfare of both
countries and the whole empire." Such a resolution might
not only quicken the near-dead opposition in England but
suggest to the King that his ministers had poorly advised
him.[71] But when Parliament was opened in January not
Ireland but America dominated the public attention.

1. H. S. Woodfall, in whose *Public Advertiser* had first appeared No. 35 of the famous Junius letters, a libelous affront to the King.

2. *Corr. Burke* II 160.

3. *Ibid.*, 153, 164; Walpole, *Memoirs* IV 126–127.

4. WWM R 1: 1314; *Chatham* III 480–481.

5. *Ibid.*, 487; *Cavendish's Debates* II 37–54.

6. *Chatham* III 489–491; WWM R 1: 1326, 1327; Albemarle II 193–195.

7. WWM R 1: 1328; *Chatham* IV 2–18.

8. *Ibid.*, 24.

9. *Ibid.*, 31–32; *Cavendish's Debates* II 88–116.

10. Chatham to Rockingham 3 Dec.—WWM R 1: 1335a.

11. *Cavendish's Debates* II 121–140; *Corr. Burke* II 170.

12. *Ibid.*, 171–173, "I wish Lord Mansfield might have such an idea & I am sure if he had, the publick would be benefitted, whether personal animosities were gratified or not."—Rockingham to Dowdeswell 13 Jan. 1771 (WWM R 1: 1348).

13. *Corr. Burke* II 174–176.

14. Just before the reopening of Parliament in January Richmond wrote to the Marquis: "The desertions we have had will stagger people."—WWM R 1: 1348.

15. R 1: 1363 (printed in Olson, *Radical Duke,* 146–147). Rockingham seemed to fade from politics; the newspapers of this period depict Richmond as leading the party.

16. WWM R 1: 1352.

17. *Ibid.*, 1354.

18. *Ibid.*, 1356; *Corr. Burke* II 189–190.

19. WWM R 1: 1356, 1358.

20. *Ibid.*, 1360.

21. *Chatham* IV 98–100, 103–105, 107–108; Albemarle II 204.

22. *Cavendish's Debates* II 352–377.

23. *Corr. Burke* II 192, 204–205, 222; Albemarle II 207–209; WWM R 1: 778, 1463a.

24. *Chatham* IV 165–168.

25. WWM R 1: 1382; *Corr. Burke* II 237–238, 246.

26. R 1: 778.

27. *Ibid.*, 1389.

28. *Corr. Burke* II 297.

29. *Chatham* IV 186–189.

30. Portland MSS (2 Jan. 1772).

31. WWM R 1: 1393; Hoffman, *Burke,* 513.

32. Horace Walpole, *Last Journals* (2 vols; 2nd ed. London, 1846) I 9; *Corr. Burke* II 299.

33. To Lady Rockingham 7 Feb.—Ramsden MSS. Horace Walpole described Burke's speech (printed in various editions of his works) as "popish" but Lady Rockingham thought it "incomparable."

34. Portland MSS.

35. Hoffman, *Burke*, 517. *The Public Advertiser* (5 Mar.) reported that he spoke four times and "spoke well." The same newspaper for 21 Mar. stated: "During this Day's Debate, the Marquis of Rockingham spoke twice. *Quere*, Which of the Two is most difficult—to make the Marquis SPEAK, or to make Edmund HOLD HIS TONGUE?"

36. Walpole, *Last Journals* I 47; Lord John Cavendish to Portland 14 Mar.—Portland MSS.

37. *The Public Advertiser*, 17 Mar.

38. Portland MSS (14 Mar.).

39. *Ibid.* (19 Mar.).

40. W. Burke to John Ridge 24 Mar.—Hoffman, *Burke*, 522. According to Horace Walpole, 14 were shut out of whom 12 would have divided against administration.—*Last Journals* I 70. James Scawen, who was against the act, stayed away and explained to Rockingham that he had been ordered to by his father who wished to please the Lord Chancellor.—WWM R 1: 1399.

41. Albemarle II 222–223.

42. *Corr. Burke* II 320, 326; Walpole, *Last Journals* I 133.

43. "I am inclined to leave business now to Lord North."—Dowdeswell to Burke 20 May (Dowdeswell MSS).

44. Public rumor now made a placeman of Burke. The New York agency was said to be worth £1,000 a year (twice the actual salary), and Burke was said to aim at a secretaryship of the Treasury.—*Public Advertiser* 24, 28 Oct.

45. *Manuscripts . . . Dartmouth* (Hist. MSS Comm.) II 87, 104.

46. WWM R 1: 1430.

47. L. S. Sutherland, *East India Company in Eighteenth-century Politics* (Oxford, 1952), 103, 175, 193–194.

48. To Charles Turner 7 April 1772 (WWM R 1: 1410).

49. *Corr. Burke* II 342–347.

50. *Ibid.*, 360–369; WWM R 1: 1409, 1411, 1412; Dowdeswell to Rockingham 8 and 19 Nov.—Dowdeswell MSS.

51. WWM R 1: 1413.

52. *Ibid.*, 1419.

53. *Corr. Burke* II 402.

54. WWM R 1: 1422a.

55. *Corr. Burke* II 408.

56. *Ibid.*, 423, 426; Walpole, *Last Journals* I 181; WWM R 1: 1425.

57. Walpole, *Last Journals* I 188–189.

58. *Ibid.*, 200; WWM R 1: 1428, 1435; *Corr. Burke* II 459, 487.

59. Dowdeswell to Rockingham 18 July 1773.—Dowdeswell MSS.

60. Portland to Rockingham 18 Aug.—Portland MSS.

61. Hoffman, *Burke*, 121–122.

62. Philip Magnus, *Edmund Burke* (London, 1939), 44–45; *Corr. Burke* II 370, 450, 453, 461–463.

63. *Journal of the Board of Trade, 1765–1775* (London, 1937), 357; Rockingham to John Lee 1 June, 5 July 1773.—Lee Papers (Clements Library); Rockingham to Portland 29 Sept.—Portland MSS.

64. WWM R 1: 1442. The history of this affair has been told by many but the best account, based largely upon the Rockingham papers, is that

of Samuel J. Fanning, "The Irish Absentee Landowner" (University of California dissertation, 1952).

65. WWM R 1: 1446 (printed in Albemarle II 228–229).

66. *Corr. Burke* II 464–470.

67. WWM R 1: 1453, 1454, 1458; R 156: 26, 27; Fanning, "Irish Absentee Landowner," 113; Rockingham to Portland 4 Nov. (Portland MSS).

68. *Works of the Right Honourable Edmund Burke* (Rivington edition; London, 1826) IX 134–147.

69. Published with a commentary by J. E. Tyler in *Irish Historical Studies* 8 No. 32 (Sept. 1953), 362–369.

70. WWM R 156: 36.

71. *Corr. Burke* II 498–499.

9

Peace with America

IN THE HALF-DOZEN YEARS before the re-emergence of the American question in Parliament in 1774 Rockingham had used what influence he had to prevent agitation of differences with the colonies. He had deplored the hot ministerial resolutions in the session of 1768–1769, and, even though his friend Trecothick tried at that time to start petitions from London and Bristol merchants for repeal of the Townshend Revenue Act, the Marquis did not encourage support for the motion (April 19) that the House go into committee to reconsider that act. However desirable repeal was, it could not then be obtained, so that Burke spoke the opinion of his leader that day when he said: "Why go on with the parade of parliamentary debates? . . . What is done must be done silently, and in the closet." [1]

During the winter Rockingham had received illuminating letters from three American friends, Joseph Harrison the customs collector at Boston, James Delancey who led the majority in the New York Assembly, and Governor Wentworth of New Hampshire.[2] The impression they conveyed

was that most of the trouble in North America was the
result of an arrogant and haughty spirit in royal officials,
especially the members of the recently established American
board of customs commissioners. Governor Wentworth,
whose province was tranquil, had visited Boston in November and found "that more obstructions had arisen to the
service in this country from the servants of government than
from any other cause." He denounced, as did Harrison,
those customs commissioners whose "superciliousness &
publickly expressed hatred to the country excited disrespect
and apprehensions." Wentworth blamed the reaction against
the Townshend duties upon the odious demeanor of these
officials: "In other hands I have no doubt but this act would
have obtained without even a petition against it, but now
it is impracticable to any good effect." By the time of the
motion to reconsider it, not only had another account come
from Wentworth, but Harrison's son who witnessed the
disorders in Massachusetts had visited Rockingham and
given a more detailed report. Intelligence of this sort goes
far to explain Burke's words in the House on April 19, and
how faithfully he had echoed the opinion of the Marquis
may be seen in what the latter wrote afterward to Joseph
Harrison:

> If you was now amongst us, you would find our sentiments on
> the subject of America, just the same as when you left us. We
> still abide by that opinion that the idea of making America a
> *revenue mine* is absurd, & I think so far that I perceive with
> pleasure that doctrine gains ground. . . .
> The tax upon certain imports to N[orth] America, which
> was laid two years ago & which we call C. Townshend's tax,
> has been in general here condemned, as contrary to the first
> principles of commerce. . . . The tumultuous proceedings at
> Boston were in fact the only arguments which could have been
> & which were used against the repeal. No actual motion was
> made for the repeal & indeed I tryed all I could & perhaps was
> very instrumental in preventing its being moved. My reasons
> were that it was evident in the *then* disposition of administra-
> tion & of many others in the House of Commons, that the at-

tempt to repeal it, would not be attended with the least chance
of success, but that it would only afford an opportunity of many
violent & hot speeches on the subject of N[orth] American disobedience & that the report of those speeches going to America
would only tend to add fresh fuel to the fire. My opinion
strongly was that, that we should give men's minds time to cool
on this & the other side of the water.[3]

When he wrote the above he had learned that ministry had
decided to propose repeal of the Townshend duties in the
next session and he so informed Harrison, although not
quite accurately since he did not know of the intention to
retain the duty on tea. On such a pleasing expectation he
rested a hope that the American question would again
vanish from Parliament.

Multiplying reports of American combinations, like those
of 1765–1766, to force an end to British taxation for
revenue fused with the Middlesex-election crisis to swell the
public discontents. "The misconduct of administration in
respect to North America," wrote Rockingham to Burke on
July 17, "will be felt and when it is, and comes in addition
to the home jealousies etc. it will become a very serious topic,
and will add fuel to the fire." [4] Many of the petitions then
being adopted and sent up to the throne cited the grievances
of the colonists as among the many reasons why the King
should turn out the ministry; but Rockingham had no inclination to exploit the colonial question for the ends of
party. Nor did he relish the current notion that some great
new plan was needed to improve Anglo-American relations.
One such scheme, devised by an unidentified West Indian
merchant, was sent to him by Lord Dartmouth. It envisaged
a North American union under a constitution resembling
Ireland's with a parliament and lord lieutenant. The Marquis doubted the practicability and effect. If it were practicable it might lead to the colonies' erecting themselves into
"a state independent of the mother country." But the circumstances of Ireland were totally unlike those of America.
British government had great influence in the Irish Parlia-

ment where "the honours & emoluments from the crown to the families of Ireland, have their effect"; English peerages were sometimes given to Irishmen; many of the first families in that country were united with English families and had sons in the army, navy, and places of government; the same church was established in both countries; many Irishmen of great property spent their lives in England, and many Englishmen had large estates in Ireland; moreover, the Irish revenue, pension list, and political patronage fortified the British influence. The weight and influence of England in an American parliament "would fall very short" of the measure prevailing in Ireland. Nor was the Marquis sure that he wished British government to have a comparable influence in America, since "it would add exceedingly to the weight of the Crown etc. at home" to which he did not think any increase "at all necessary." If Americans were to ask for a constitutional status like that of Ireland, Rockingham said that "it would be a tempting proposal & yet the better policy for this nation would be, not to accept." [5]

Soon afterward Joseph Harrison arrived from Boston and visited Rockingham, bringing along the fruits of a six-months effort in gathering accounts from all of the American colonies. These materials, the Marquis told Dowdeswell, would "give us more insight into the interior trade etc. of all the colonies, than is in the hands of either administration or any one else." [6] To what extent Harrison's researches helped to make the Rockinghams more knowledgeable of America it is impossible to say; but it is certain that they never thought of a better way to get along with the colonies than not to lay objectionable taxes on them, not to dispute with them, not to impede their growth or interfere in their own management of their own affairs. To the Marquis and his friends, who prized the empire but were not imperialists, the colonies were an expanding market and a nourishment of naval power: the means of strengthening Great Britain that she might the better hold her place in the system of Europe. This, they thought, was the wisdom of whiggery.

When Lord North in March 1770 moved to amend the

Townshend Act by striking out all colonial port duties on imports from Great Britain save that on tea (which was not a British manufacture but a re-export), his motion was grounded upon the inutility of such duties, their inconsistency with the navigation laws, their stimulus to manufactures in the colonies. His argument thus wore some resemblance to the case of the Rockingham administration for repealing the Stamp Act; and the Marquis' friends attacked only the inadequacy of the proposal, Trecothick and Meredith urging removal of the tea tax, too. Neither Burke nor Dowdeswell, however, took part in the debate, perhaps to avoid differing with Grenville who called North's motion weak and chided government for not bringing forward a plan of effective government in America. But the Rockinghams favored getting rid of the tea duty, and in the Lords the Marquis tried to obtain its elimination.[7] The party tactic appears to have been an attempt at complete repeal without appearing as champions of misbehaving Americans. It was about this time that Rockingham wrote to James Delancey:

> There is too much heat both on this side & on your side. I believe both sides are beginning to tire of quarrelling, but when your assemblys meet, you put into your resolves etc. sharp & passionate expressions beyond what is at all necessary on the matter & indeed in some assert matters not tenable in argument & beyond what I am sure is your intention to persist in. . . . This conduct on your side draws on violent language from here & also harsh resolves in terrorem & which I scarce believe there is any man rash enough to wish to see carried into execution. I preached moderation here, so it is but fair in me to preach it on both sides.[8]

Once again in the session of 1770—and for the last time until 1774—there was an American day in Parliament although the North ministry did not bring it on. It resulted from the exigencies of the concert in opposition of the Rockinghams and Grenvilles and there is no evidence that the Marquis himself had any heart for it or saw any wisdom in what was done. When the so-called Boston Massacre became known Trecothick moved for papers relating to all clashes of soldiery with citizens in America during the previous year. North agreed and Burke gave notice that he would give the House "a more ample view of the government of America for the three years past." George Grenville, eager for a better plan of British government in the colonies, desired to attack administration for failing to keep faith with what he interpreted as a commitment in the King's speech to produce such a plan. On May 9 Burke moved a series of resolutions as a foundation for an inquiry into the causes of American disorders. He charged ministers with first provoking and then appeasing the colonists with the result that British government in the colonies had been "shaken to the foundation, by the entire absence of common sense." He toured from Massachusetts to the Middlesex election, came round in the end to the thesis of his *Discontents* pamphlet, and placed responsibility upon bad ministers serving a court faction which worked a corrupt influence on Parliament: "Restore Parliament to its native dignity, and you will then restore repose to America." The speech was not one of his best. Grenville, acknowledging previous communication of Burke's resolutions, spoke for them, praised the Rockinghams for their "consistency and integrity," and said that Lord North would be "criminal in the highest degree" if he failed to produce a plan for stronger civil government in the colonies. North asked wittily which plan it should be, theirs who proposed the Stamp Act or theirs who repealed it, and easily disposed of a business which had been hardly more than a tactic of desperation by the sinking opposition.[9]

The Rockinghams as a party seem hardly to have thought much about America during the next four years. The Marquis, as has been noted, came to the defense of Governor Wentworth against his attackers in 1773, and Burke had the business of his New York agency. He owed this nomination to Rockingham's friend Delancey, who wrote to the Marquis: "I was happy to see when I proposed him to the house, that it passed without one dissenting voice. . . . My friends and I would receive great pleasure in having one of your Lordship's party for their agent as I consider you the only real friends of the colonies." He hoped that Rockingham would prevail upon Burke to accept, and it is clear from this letter that the New Yorkers aimed at receiving and not conferring an obligation. Delancey venerated the Marquis, and his party in the Assembly exemplified a political spirit rather like that of the Rockingham whigs.[10]

At the time Burke undertook the agency Lord Hillsborough, Secretary of State for the Colonies and head of the Board of Trade, was enforcing a rule that colonial agents must be chosen by the whole legislature of a colony —assembly, council, and governor—not merely by the assembly. The rule tended to convert agents into placemen. Burke was strictly the Assembly's agent and would not have served on any other terms; yet Hillsborough's rule, which was enforced against such a man as Benjamin Franklin, never barred Burke from transacting his principals' business at the Board of Trade—perhaps because his party had become so inactive as an opposition. When Dartmouth succeeded Hillsborough in 1772 Burke got along well with him and the Rockinghams seem to have assumed that government relations with the colonies were in safe hands.[11] Such ominous events as the attack on H.M.S. *Gaspée* in the Narragansett and the revival of hot differences between governor and Assembly in Massachusetts in 1772–1773 hardly produced a recorded apprehension among the Rockinghams. To the speaker of the New York Assembly Burke expressed regret "that the Ministers could be so ill advised as to order the persons guilty of the outrage on the King's vessel in America to England for trial"; and his sorrow "that the indiscretions of both sides in one of your neighbouring colonies has introduced discussions that ought forever to be buried in silence." [12] This was the Rockinghamite manner. The comparatively calm period (1771–1773) in Anglo-American relations undoubtedly nourished the hope of the Rockinghams that they would never again be forced to consider that subject; which hope may have contributed to blinding them in the spring of 1773 to the likely consequences of Lord North's Tea Act.

II

For the opening of Parliament (January 20, 1774) the disheartened Rockinghams came straggling to town. Their head, suffering a minor malady, remained at Wentworth until after the beginning of February, although three weeks earlier he told Burke that he believed there were "*points* on which *we* might take up to advantage, and be of some service in." He was still thinking of censure motions for the attempted absentee tax in Ireland. In advance of the opening there were several opposition dinners at the Thatched House, and Richmond, whose thoughts were at India House, wrote to Rockingham that "our friends have agreed to be very silent in parliament till some matter of great importance calls them forth which seems to me to be very wise." No amendment to the address was moved. Lord John Cavendish thought the state of the opposition "comical" but inaction was "better than bustle." It seemed almost symbolic of the plight of the Rockinghams that Trecothick was dying of the palsy and Dowdeswell growing very deaf. Even after news arrived of the Boston Tea Party and the humiliation of Dr. Franklin at the Privy Council hearing on the Massachusetts Assembly's petition for removal of the governor, Burke could write: "Here, as we have met, so we continue, in the most perfect repose." When a motion was made (February 1) in the Lords for papers relating to what looked like a new crisis in America, Richmond, Dowdeswell, Lord Fitzwilliam, and Lord John Cavendish thought that their friends should stay away from Parliament and not countenance, as Burke phrased it to Rockingham, "the interested petulance of those paltry disconnected people who . . . think to make use of your weight to give consequence to every occasional spurt of opposition they think proper to make, in order to put the Ministry in mind, that they are to be bought by private contract. . . ."

The Marquis' first words on the violence at Boston were:

> The conduct of the Americans can not be justified; but the folly and impolicy of the provocation deserves the fullest arraignment; and notwithstanding all that has passed, I can never give consent to proceeding with actual force against the colonies.

When the bill to close the port of Boston was brought in, the disposition of the House of Commons was to support it overwhelmingly. Horace Walpole thought that even "the Rockingham party was cold," and the fact was that the inner corps split: Lord John Cavendish favored and Dowdeswell disapproved the measure.[13] Not until the final reading did Dowdeswell and Burke raise warning voices, the latter fearing that punishment of Boston would lead to blocking of other ports in other colonies and eventually draw "a foreign force upon you." The bill was passed by both Houses without a division. Richmond spoke against it and Rockingham, still unwell, at least planned a speech. Extant notes give the substance of it:

> This Bill inflicts pain & penalties on subjects of this kingdom *without* a charge specifically stated, without direct evidence of guilt against any individual or body corporate & *without* affording to the parties affected an opportunity of making their defence separately or collectively, which is contrary to all principles of substantial justice & therefore can not be agreeable to any rule of sound policy. . . . The mode adopted by this bill does not exclusively affect the rioters at Boston but every merchant, whether friend or foe to British government whose property & residence is at Boston, is included & punished under this extraordinary measure.

Since the bill required Boston to make reparation to the East India Company for the loss of the tea without stating the sum, and since the port was to remain closed not only until unspecified reparation was paid but until the crown judged that conditions were suitable to reopening, the fate of the city would be left to the arbitrary will of ministers. Therefore, the Marquis continued:

> To support parliamentary authority over the colonies surely Parliament should prescribe the specific terms which it requires should be complied with and not that Parliament should say to the Colonies—*Obey* the Ministers in what they require & we shall be contented. It is a power of authority & punishment much too great for the Ministers of the crown to ask.[14]

The subsequent ministerial measures to replace the quasi-republican charter of Massachusetts with a stiff royalist constitution and to alter that colony's administration of justice met with substantial resistance in Parliament. The Rockinghamites were more of one mind and the Marquis was for a vigorous show of opposition. To the Duke of Manchester who dreaded the party's going against "the high spirit of the people of England" Rockingham spelled out his case. Admitting the futility of making a stand until the public saw and felt the consequences of such wrong measures, he contended

> If, in the times of passing those measures, we do not show any disapprobation, we shall subject ourselves to blame, and the argument which will hereafter be drawn from our silence, or total inactivity, will be either, that we did not dissent, or that we did not foresee the possibility of the inconveniences which may arise.[15]

The largest number in the divisions against these bills was 64, mostly Rockinghams but including the city members, Lord Shelburne's followers (Isaac Barré and John Dunning), and even a few late supporters of administration, notably General Conway and Charles Fox. Many had hoped or even expected that after the punitive Boston Port Bill a

measure of lenity would be moved. Conway called for a
repeal of the tea tax and Rose Fuller, who was on the rim
of the Rockingham corps, resolved to move it. The Marquis
rallied his friends for the motion[16] but only 49 members of
the House could be brought to vote for it. On this occasion
(April 19) Burke made his famous speech on American
taxation which later was issued as a party pamphlet. In the
House of Lords Rockinghamite peers contested with energy
against the Massachusetts bills, the Marquis himself speaking at great length and well enough to win the praise even
of Horace Walpole.[17] Two protests entered upon the Lords'
journal against these measures show the signatures of the
dukes of Richmond, Portland, Manchester, and Leinster,
and lords Abingdon, King, Effingham, Ponsonby, Aber-
gavenny, Craven, Fitzwilliam, and Rockingham.[18] These
protests spell out in splendid prose the Rockinghamite doctrine respecting America. Abrogation of the Massachusetts
charter in the mode adopted was denounced as a violation
of substantial justice; before the peers of Great Britain an-
nihilated chartered rights, the specific legal offense ought to
have been clearly stated and proved, and the parties affected
ought to have been heard in their own defense. All the proceedings against Massachusetts were intended "for the support of that inadvised scheme of taxing the colonies." That
the authority of the British legislature was "supreme and
unlimited over all members of the British empire" provided
no argument for "an unwarrantable use of it."

> . . . this kingdom ought to satisfy itself with the advantages to
> be derived from a flourishing and increasing trade, and with the
> free grants of the American assemblies, as being more beneficial,
> far more easily obtained, and more likely to be lasting, than any
> revenue to be acquired by parliamentary taxes, accompanied by
> a total alienation of the affections of those who are to pay
> them. . . . To render the colonies permanently advantageous,
> they must be satisfied with their condition. That satisfaction
> we see no chance of restoring, whatever measures may be pur-
> sued, except by recurring, in the whole, to the wise and salutary
> principles on which the stamp act was repealed.

As the protests against the Massachusetts bills were being composed, a bill to establish (at last!) a civil constitution for the province of Canada was moving rapidly through the House of Lords with what the *Annual Register* recorded as "very little if any observation." To the extent that it secured the existing French civil law for *les habitants* of the former New France, that it avoided discriminating against them and confirmed the pre-1763 establishment of their Catholic religion, this measure was consistent with what Rockingham and most of his friends had long approved. Perhaps they were so much preoccupied with Massachusetts that they did not immediately notice that the territorial clauses of the bill ran the boundary of Canada south to the Ohio and west to the Mississippi without exact delimitation. In the House of Commons, however, opposition quickly stirred, in spite of the lateness of the session. The so-called Quebec bill was hotly attacked by whigs as popish and despotic (no elective assembly being provided for the province) and the territorial dimensions were denounced as a blockade and encroachment against the western growth of the older colonies. In the debate on committing the bill such Rockinghamites as Tommy Townshend and Lord John Cavendish joined with Barré and Dunning in condemning favor to popery and other despotic features in a reconstituted New France under the British crown. Dowdeswell was too ill to attend and Burke was out of town. In committee the Rockinghamite William Baker presented a petition from the Pennsylvania proprietors who wished to be secured against encroachment upon their western claims; and Burke acted on the assumption that his New York principals would wish him to defend their interests. Lord North was open to amendments and disavowed any intention to narrow the territory of other provinces; which enabled Burke and Baker to obtain a definite instead of a constructive Canada boundary along the 45th parallel, the St. Lawrence river, lakes Ontario and Erie, and a line from the lakes to the Ohio. Burke knew that he had not demolished what he

called "a line of circumvallation about our older colonies
. . . to establish a siege of arbitrary power." The concession did not overcome his objections to the bill which he
attacked on other grounds, although without pandering to
the anti-Catholic prejudices which the bill excited in press
and public. With nineteen others he divided against it on the
last reading. When it was returned to the Lords, Chatham
condemned the indulgence to popery in the strongest language, but there is no record of Rockingham's saying anything. There is Burke's testimony that the Marquis "objected to the idea of restraining the colonies from spreading
into the back country, even if such restraint were practicable; for by stopping the extent of agriculture they necessitated manufactures, contrary to the standing policy of colo-
nization." No other opinion in this respect would have been
consistent with the general Rockingham policy of letting
nature take its course in North America under the indulgent
sovereignty of the British legislature; but the Quebec Act
could hardly be said to hamper the growth of British coloni-
zation and Rockingham may have felt no great dislike of
that measure after the Commons had amended it. Burke
certainly believed that he had achieved something to render
it less offensive to New Yorkers to whom he reported that
he had gotten "a tolerable bargain." [19]

In view of Rockingham's strategic policy in the use of
peers' protests to spell out the record of his friends there is
probably some significance in the fact that none was entered
against the Quebec Act. Whatever its inflammatory effect
on American sensibilities might be—and there is no evidence
that he foresaw that—there was in it no breach of substantial justice, no punitive stroke against the older colonies. In
the wild imaginations of hot partisans on both sides of the
Atlantic a popish intrigue was suspected, but the Marquis
could not believe that. To single out the Quebec Act for one
of those stately protests on the Lords' journal would not
have been consistent conduct in a party which prided itself
upon its seriousness and respectability. In any event they

had protested enough to make clear a record of uncompromising opposition to rash and ill-considered acts likely to worsen Great Britain's relations with her colonies.

No more than Lord North did Rockingham believe, as the session of 1774 ended, that its acts would provoke a rebellion in North America. "I trust & believe," he wrote on June 25, "that the Americans will not break out into actual resistance & oppose by force." He feared instead a serious slump in trade with America because of the apprehensions of exporters that the colonists would again reject cargoes or refuse payments.[20] The summer passed without any disturbance of tranquillity at Wentworth by alarming news from over the Atlantic. At the Sheffield Cutlers Feast (September 8) he was told that no decline had occurred in their American business although such was expected. A week later Burke, with whom he had been out of touch since June, sent him the opinion that American affairs would not come to any crisis during the next session of Parliament or even for some years to come; that the dispute would "draw out to great length"; that it was "next to impossible, that the present temper and unanimity of America" could be kept up; and that if non-importation was again adopted "we should be in as much haste to negotiate ourselves out of our commercial, as they out of their constitutional difficulties."[21] Such weak judgments were the result partly of summer lassitude and inattention to a subject always unprofitable to the party, partly of preoccupation with what was to the Marquis and his friends a more pressing business—namely, preparing for parliamentary elections which were sure to take place not later than the following March.

Never had their outlook been so bleak. Dowdeswell was seriously ill with tuberculosis and Sir George Savile, also ailing and weary of futile politics, was resolved to retire from Parliament. The loss of two vastly respected and incorruptible county representatives would be bad enough, but Dowdeswell was irreplaceable as a leader of the corps in Commons and Savile was a main pillar of Rockingham's structure of influence in Yorkshire, the party's strongest territorial base.

After a summer of physical deterioration Dowdeswell early in the autumn went to Nice,[22] there to die and thus to end an era in the history of the Rockinghamites. Moreover, their remnant of interest in the City of London withered away with Trecothick's physical inability to continue in Parliament and Lord Edgecombe's refusal to provide again for the return of Alderman William Baker for a Devon borough. But perhaps nothing of a political nature ever alarmed Rockingham so much as Savile's threat. As early as May 1774 he began to appeal to Sir George on both public and personal grounds but with no more effect than to keep him from a public announcement of his intention. In August he wrote to Savile in near-desperation:

> I have an absolute horror of the approach of York races lest any thing should tempt you . . . to make any declaration . . . for assuredly if you give up the county, and I must add the public, I have nothing further to do but fairly to retire and relinquish all late ideas relative to Yorkshire, or of being of any service to the public.

Lady Rockingham too employed all her arts of persuasion and by early October, when it was known that Parliament had been dissolved, Savile was brought to submit to the wishes of friends.[23] The promising candidacy of his friend David Hartley at Hull also contributed to his decision, because Hartley was a busy and energetic man who could help much in the task of serving Yorkshire constituents. Savile and Edwin Lascelles were returned again for the county without a contest.

Rockingham had no problem in his borough of Higham Ferrers where Frederick Montagu was again returned, but he experienced some perplexity at Malton. His cousin, Savile Finch, would be continued, but Lord Downe was dying and the Marquis offered that seat to Nathaniel Cholmley who had fallen out with his patron at Boroughbridge. Then Rockingham learned that Lord Verney could not back Burke again at Wendover and that a speculative enterprise of Burke's to stand for Westminster with the support of

Wilkes had collapsed. It being absolutely necessary to provide for Burke, Cholmley (perhaps under gentle pressure) withdrew his acceptance of the Malton seat, and the voters were asked to elect Burke, which they obediently did, only to have their new member dash away to fight a contest at Bristol. Previous overtures to him from that city had not looked like a practical undertaking but a change in the aspect sent him into that famous and successful effort; which enabled Rockingham to give the second Malton seat to William Weddell, who had fallen out with the voters at Hull and been replaced by Hartley as the Rockingham–Savile candidate. The Marquis tried without success to persuade Lord Galway to bring in William Baker for Pontefract, and the latter fought a losing contest in London; he did not get back into Parliament until 1777. Borough elections in Yorkshire were less quiet than in 1768, four being contested. Charles Fox and a friend tried to raise the householders to overwhelm the burgage electors at Pontefract. They lacked whig magnate support and the attempt fizzled. In a warm contest at Beverley Rockingham supported Sir James Pennyman who led the poll. Hartley won by a narrow margin at Hull. In the city of York Charles Turner, who was a vexation to Rockingham's friends without ceasing to be one, and Lord John Cavendish had a contest forced upon them by a third candidate who however failed. The Rockingham interest in Yorkshire was secured in the elections, although the death of the old Duke of Newcastle was felt in two boroughs which had passed to his heir who had gone over to the court.[24]

It was generally true of whig magnates that they showed little zeal for electioneering in 1774. On learning of the dissolution Rockingham wrote to Portland: "I confess indeed that I think *all politics* are now in so low a state and so little likely to revive, that I should feel a hesitation in giving encouragement to an expectation that we can continue long to drudge on in such unsatisfactory and so unthanked a laborious occupation." [25] Portland compromised with Sir James Lowther (who was turning toward the opposition)

in Cumberland and retreated from Carlisle. His son had
been chosen there in 1768 and now lost a contest in Nottingham. The Duke of Richmond showed no relish for electioneering. Radical whigs were far more active, Wilkes and
Glynn carrying Middlesex without any one daring a contest;
and Wilkites won three of London's four seats. At Bristol
the American-born radical, Henry Cruger, raised the voters
against a long-standing whig–tory joint interest, and con-
servative whigs, dissatisfied with their old member, craftily
exploited this upsurge to make a practical proposition to
Burke—namely, to ride to victory on Cruger's coattails.
The latter, who ran far ahead in a month-long poll, was
little pleased by this stratagem, and many who voted for
Cruger voted for him alone. Had Burke contested for Westminster the tactic of riding a radical crest would have been
the same. It was not a game at which most of Lord Rockingham's friends were very adept. Apart from the metropolis Bristol was the largest city in England. Predominantly
commercial with an electorate of 5,000, it was deeply concerned with the American trade and its election was one of
perhaps ten contests in which it is known that the dispute
with the American colonies was brought into partisan politics.[26] Cruger was pro-American but Burke in addressing the
voters stressed the difficulty and delicacy of the crisis, blamed
no ministers, and said that he wished to maintain "unim-
paired and undiminished" the just, wise, and necessary constitutional superiority of Great Britain for the sake of
America "as well as for us." That superiority was "consistent with all the liberties a sober and spirited American
ought to desire"; his great object would be to "reconcile
British superiority with American liberty" and he was "far
from thinking that both, even yet, may not be preserved."

Burke's nosing-out of a tory who was supported by Treasury money was the only clear gain made by the Rockinghams
in the elections of 1774. No doubt it raised his weight in
their councils and his stature as a public man, but his party's
state was not significantly altered in the new parliament.
Despite an unusually large number of contested elections

(12 more than in 1768) fewer new members were chosen than in any other election from 1754 to 1790. The North administration was to be supported in Commons as well as ever.

III

Rockingham came to town for the opening of the new parliament (November 30) and was eager for a test of its disposition. The royal speech dwelt upon the "most daring spirit of resistance and disobedience to the law" in Massachusetts which was "countenanced and encouraged" in other colonies, and upon "unwarrantable attempts" to obstruct the commerce of the kingdom. Parliament was requested to support his Majesty's resolution "to withstand every attempt to weaken or impair the supreme authority of this legislature over all the dominions of my crown." When loyal addresses promising this support were offered in both Houses, Richmond in the Lords and Lord John Cavendish (*locum tenens* for Dowdeswell) in Commons moved an amendment to withhold such a commitment until the fullest information was had on the state of America. Not yet were the resolves of the Philadelphia Congress known in England. How much the new parliament resembled the former one was shown in the divisions. The address was carried in Commons 264 to 73 and in the Lords 63 to 13. The Marquis and his friends chose this occasion for entering another stately protest upon the Lords' journal. Significantly, Camden and Shelburne were among the nine signers who "wished to be known as persons who have ever disapproved of measures so pernicious in past effects, and their future tendency, and who are not in haste, without enquiry or information, to commit members to declarations which may precipitate our country into all the calamities of a civil war."

There was then sufficient public information to show that a very grave crisis existed in North America, but ministers alone knew that they actually hung upon the brink of an imperial civil war, from which such men as Dartmouth,

North, Barrington, and others shrank in fear. No hint did
they give of what they intended, and the fact was that they
were of divided counsels, not knowing how to retreat or
how to advance without going over the brink. Nor did the
papers from the American Congress clear away their per-
plexities or compose their differences. In this situation the
Rockingham tactic was to avoid appearing in any way as
defenders of American conduct. Thus Burke, although one
of the five colonial agents whom the Congress asked to present its petition to the throne, declined to serve on the
scrupulous ground that his employer, the Assembly of New
York, had not sent delegates to the Congress.[27] Yet that
petition was respectful, moderate, loyal, and neither contradicted outright the supreme authority of the British legislature nor asked for any new right. Indeed if that document had been the only work of the Congress Rockingham
and his friends could have contended plausibly that the
Americans were asking for nothing but a return to the
policy exemplified by the repeal of the Stamp Act. The petition did not get into the newspapers until late January, but
the Address to the People of Great Britain, the Address to
the Inhabitants of the Province of Quebec, and the Act of
Association for non-importation were quickly published.
The temper they displayed was in striking contrast with that
of the petition.

Everything, in this pregnant moment, depended upon the
King. He could go on with the ministers who with his strong
approval had advised the measures of the last session, or
he could effect a change in favor of men who might advise
a conciliatory direction of policy. Rumors of impending
change circulated: that a severe line would be followed with
the Bedfordite Lord Gower at the Treasury and Charles
Jenkinson at the Exchequer with the lead in Commons; and
conversely, that Chatham would be called to placate America.[28] Until the King's intention was known and ministers
moved for new measures, Rockingham saw nothing to do
but wait.

Others were less patient. Burke, for example, thought

that he could detect some rise of public spirit against administration and longed for party heads to do something to stimulate this. They should at least meet and rally forces well in advance of the reopening of Parliament on January 19. Lord John, whom Burke thought a poor replacement for Dowdeswell, should limit his fox-hunting and "shew a regular attendance on business." The Marquis ought if possible to find out what Chatham intended and "if possible to fall in with him." Something ought to be learned of the court's determination which Burke fancied would be influenced by Lord Bute and Lord Mansfield; therefore a spy might be put upon the movements of Jenkinson, their imagined confidant. Except for writing letters to bring men back early to town—which he must have done anyway—Rockingham let this advice roll over him without comment; nor did he need Burke's advice to convert a courtesy call by Chatham (January 7) into an hour's conversation which was not at all satisfactory. The Great Man blamed the Declaratory Act of 1766 for the revival of American discontents and stated his resolve to move an amendment of it so that authority might remain without the right of Parliament to tax the colonies. Rockingham demurred, dwelling upon the point that parliamentary taxes were the means of regulating the commerce of the empire which the Americans assented to from expediency, and citing the absence from their petition of any protest against the Declaratory Act.[29] He was not weakened in his conviction that it was not the avowal but the abuse of the supreme authority which had raised the crisis in America.

Soon afterward (January 10) Burke's speech of the previous April 19 appeared as a pamphlet on *American Taxation* in the bookstalls. It was a thoroughly Rockinghamite survey of the history of ministerial handling of relations with the colonies since 1766, and its moral was:

Again and again, revert to your old principles—seek peace and ensue it—leave America, if she has taxable matter in her, to tax herself. . . . Be content to bind America by laws of trade;

you have always done it. Let this be your reason for binding
their trade. Do not burden them with taxes; you were not
used to do so from the beginning. Let this be your reason for
not taxing. These are the arguments of states and kingdoms.

Meanwhile, Burke and Baker were exerting themselves to
stimulate petitions from the mercantile community although
with meager results, since the merchants showed "nothing
like the sentiments of honest, free, and constitutional resentments, which Englishmen used to feel, against the authors
of many public mischiefs." [30] The same men who had been
zealous a decade earlier to send up petitions which ministers
were eager to have now displayed little inclination to adopt
petitions which other ministers did not welcome.

When Parliament met again (January 19) a selection of
reports from America (designed to show rather the necessity than the practicality of forceful coercion) was laid before it. On the next day Chatham made his first appearance
of the session to move an address to the throne asking for
the withdrawal of royal troops from Boston "as soon as the
rigour of the season, and other circumstances indispensable
to the safety and accommodation of the said troops may
render the same possible." He declared himself for maintaining the authority of Great Britain over the colonies, disavowed a "naked, unconditional repeal" of the Declaratory
Act, but represented his motion as the first step in a plan to
secure an American's "right of not having his property
taken from him but by his own consent." No advance notice
of the motion was given to Rockinghamite peers, who nevertheless were in the minority of 18 who divided against rejecting it. The Marquis' support which included speaking
was nevertheless perfunctory. He still preferred waiting for
administration to show its hand and not, as Richmond put
it, "to get the start of Lord Chatham or run races with him
as to motions." Not liking this "plan of inaction," Burke
told his leader that the question was whether he chose to
lead or to be led: "to lay down proper ground for yourself,
or stand in an awkward and distressing situation on the

ground which will be prepared for you, and which, you can neither remain upon or quit, without great inconvenience and discredit." [31] Rockingham was unmoved by this. He could not know that ministry was not going to beat a retreat. It was hardly credible that Lord Dartmouth, who had been silent on Chatham's motion, would support military coercion in America. During the next week Dartmouth gave notice of a motion for January 31 but when the day came it was put off, and that night Chatham sent word to various peers, including Rockingham and Richmond, that he would on the next day—if his gout permitted—offer the House his "poor thoughts for preventing a civil war." To Rockingham he said that "a doom" was about to be "pronounced against America" and not a moment should be lost by "whoever has any thing to propose"; hence he lamented the "necessity" which precluded him from "collecting more particularly the lights and purposes of your Lordship, in this weighty matter." After trying without success to find out from Shelburne what specifically Chatham had in mind, the Marquis sent a coldly polite answer stating that he would attend and form the best judgment he could "on what your Lordship may then propose." [32]

Chatham moved to bring in a bill for "settling the troubles in America, and for asserting the supreme legislative authority and superintending power of Great Britain over the colonies." Here at last was a new plan of government for the older colonies of British North America, and some members of Parliament must have sighed with regret that George Grenville had not lived to see it. In language taken from the Declaratory Act of 1766 it asserted the "full power and authority" of the British legislature "to bind the people of the British colonies in North America" not *in all cases whatsoever* but "in all matters touching the general weal of the whole dominion of the imperial crown of Great Britain, and beyond the competency of the local representative of a distant colony; and most especially an indubitable right to make and ordain laws for regulating trade and navigation throughout the complicated system of British com-

merce." The bill met the American complaint against
maintaining an army in a colony without consent of its legis-
latures by stating that the King might send his forces wherever they were necessary to the safety of his subjects, but
that they must never be employed to violate or destroy "the
just rights of the people." Parliament would not lay any tax
or charge for revenue upon any colony of "British freemen
in America" without the common consent by act of provincial assembly. Since the American Congress had resolved to
meet again in May, Chatham proposed that it become a lawful assembly "to take into consideration the making due recognition of the supreme authority and superintending power
of parliament." After it had done that, but not before, the
Congress would be empowered to raise a perpetual revenue
to be placed at the disposition of Parliament for relieving
the national debt. The Congress would raise this fund by
fixing proportions and quotas among the several colonies
"in such fair and equitable measure as may best suit the
abilities and due convenience of all." [33] Thus an *ad hoc* body
of men come together to vindicate a common cause against
the British legislature would be converted by that legislature into a new piece of imperial machinery to raise a revenue for that legislature's disposition. Until this wizardry
was accomplished, all measures which had produced fiery
opposition in America should be suspended; afterward they
would be annulled.

Chatham's vision was splendid but madly impractical.
How could the supreme authority be limited to "matters
touching the general weal" of the whole empire? Who could
say precisely what these were? In any particular case strong
arguments pro and con might be advanced, and then pruden-
tial judgment, the already existing but unwritten law of empire, must take over. Moreover, the proposed erection of
an American Congress as a taxing power, in substitution for
the British Parliament, was totally unfitted to the actualities
in America. Rockingham listened to Chatham's fervent
effort, did not speak, and it was evident that he thought the
measure ill-conceived. Lord Dartmouth was prepared to let

the bill lie on the table for consideration, but other ministerial peers wishing to show no disposition to appease
America were for outright rejection. This was unusual procedure in the House of Lords and swelled the minority, 32
to 68. Rockingham, Richmond (who spoke strongly for
Chatham's motion), and other Rockinghamite peers were
in that minority, which was composed of virtually all who
favored some kind of conciliatory policy.

The next day North opened the intentions of administration to the House of Commons: resistance was to be called
rebellion and punished; more troops were to be sent and the
trade of colonies which would not trade with the mother
country was to be stopped entirely; but redress of grievances
would be offered to any colony which acknowledged the
supreme authority of the British legislature and made due
submission to the King. This plan was started with a motion
to address the crown to proclaim that a rebellion existed in
the Province of Massachusetts Bay. Thus Parliament was
asked to sanction military execution upon a British colony,
since to name rebellion was to authorize suppression. All
parts of opposition including Charles Fox and a coterie of
his friends opposed the address along with some regular
supporters of ministry who at last caught a vision of the
abyss which lay ahead. Fox made his first bid for leadership
of opposition in Commons by a motion to amend the address: to convert it into a declaration that the measures
taken by ministers "tended rather to widen than to heal the
unhappy differences between Great Britain and America."
The minority for the amendment swelled to 105 and against
the address to 106. Here was a little encouragement, and a
Rockinghamite tactic of dragging out the business—since
any hour might bring better news from over the sea—was
revealed in Lord John Cavendish's motion to recommit the
address, which brought on what the *Annual Register* called
"the longest and most interesting debate that had taken
place in the present parliament." In the Lords too a tactic of
delay was tried by Rockingham, who contested for taking
up petitions from London and West India merchants before

considering the address. He succeeded at least in putting off the fatal vote of concurrence, 104 to 29, until the small hours of the morning (February 8). Chatham had promised to take part in this effort but did not appear.[34] Two Rockinghamite protests against the refusal to consider the petitions before the address and against the address were signed on the journal by eighteen peers. The address was characterized as "amounting to a declaration of war . . . founded on no proper parliamentary information," and as promising "support to those ministers who had inflamed America, and grossly misconducted the affairs of Great Britain."

Opposition to North's bill for restraining the trade and fisheries of New England passed Commons against a minority diminishing from despair. Rockingham spoke twice against it and yet another protest drafted at his direction was recorded and signed by sixteen lords. As this was being done there was preparing in his councils a positive plan for peace and conciliation, not with hope for its acceptance but again for the record and in honorable discharge of responsibilities. Since North had admitted at least the idea of conciliation and even offered his bill to enable any colony to bargain its way to an accommodation, the Rockinghams thought it right to propose something genuinely conciliatory. Burke drafted the plan in the form of a series of resolutions. David Hartley showed them to Lord Camden who agreed to support, but with some uneasiness because, unlike Chatham's bill, they raised no prospect of a revenue from America. They were discussed at Rockingham's house the night of March 7. Lord John Cavendish went to Goodwood to inform Richmond. The Duke, who had shortly before been urging the Marquis to go to Chatham and settle on something to be done, now advised that the Rockingham plan be "very explicit in disclaiming any wish for a revenue, as an unwise measure, not only from the difficulty of obtaining it, but as not founded on sound policy." [35] How widely the consultation on the resolutions may have been extended does not appear; but it is evident from their nature as well as from Burke's famous speech on March 22 that an effort was made to comprehend and reconcile all opposition opinion.

The ground taken was pragmatic: America should be dealt with according to its nature. The question was not one of abstract right, not whether the spirit of America was blameworthy, but "what in the name of God, we shall do about it." To conquer the colonies was to destroy what it was desired to preserve. The argument was "not whether you have a right to render your people miserable, but whether it is not your interest to make them happy." Burke grounded his resolutions on precedents running back five centuries, and taken together they constituted the Rockingham plan for peace with America. This plan was for Parliament to exercise its authority in conferring upon the recalcitrant colonies an exemption from parliamentary taxation (except customs duties) and to leave to their assemblies the voluntary granting of aids and subsidies when circumstances dictated such request. Experience had shown that this way was "more agreeable to the inhabitants of the said colonies, and more beneficial and conducive to the public service, than the mode of giving and granting aids and subsidies in parliament to be raised and paid in the said colonies." The resolutions declared the propriety of repealing the Townshend Revenue Act, the Boston Port Act, and the acts altering the Massachusetts charter and administration of justice; and of explaining and amending the act of Henry VIII's reign for punishing treasons committed outside the realm. It was further proposed that colonial judges, once their salaries were fixed by act of assembly, have tenure during good behavior and be removable by the King only after a hearing in Privy Council of a complaint from some part of the colonial legislature. Finally, Burke proposed to modify the courts of Admiralty toward elimination of causes of colonial complaint with them. A comparison of these resolutions with the petition of the First American Congress shows that the Rockingham plan for peace went toward redress of all colonial complaints but two—namely, maintenance of a standing army in a colony without permission of its legislature, and the allegedly despotic and popish Quebec Act. The plan, therefore, was not for an appeasing surrender but for generous and practical conciliation, for the sake of peace within the empire. Rockingham heard Burke from the peers gallery and afterward told him: "The matter and the manner were equally perfect, and in spite of envy and malice and in spite of all politics, I will venture to prognosticate, that there will be but one opinion, in regard to the wonderful ability of the performance." [36] Three months later the famous speech appeared in pamphlet form and has ever since been judged as a masterpiece of political thought.

The Rockingham plan for peace was of course rejected overwhelmingly (278 to 78) by the House of Commons. Some historians[37] have called it inadequate since it did not squarely confront and propound a solution for the disputed question of authority; because it did not envisage a federal principle for the empire but looked backward instead of forward, vindicating a system which time had passed by, and not creating for the future. Such a view appears to take little account of the fact that the purpose of the plan was to resolve an existing crisis pregnant with the peril of war. No American revolution had yet occurred, only a resistance in Massachusetts to a new order fashioned by Parliament—a resistance aided by various persons throughout New England and supported by a patriotic movement of continental dimensions, even though New York, according to the latest intelligence, as yet remained aloof from that movement. General Gage had not yet taken an initiative against "rebellion"; nor could any one foretell that when he did he would be driven back to Boston, or that his action would topple colonial governments and provoke the rise of an American army.

Furthermore, it is not exactly true that Burke evaded the question of authority. Instead of discussing it or attempting to define its boundary, he proposed using it to confer a privileged enfranchisement upon the colonies. The Rockinghamite conviction was that the supreme authority had never been disputed except when it was misused; that if it was exerted with prudence and magnanimity for the common benefit of all the King's subjects, disputing about it would die away. It is true that the plan was offered too late to stop Gage, who had been ordered to cease standing on the defensive even before Parliament gave sanction to the proposition that a rebellion existed in Massachusetts. But a Rockingham party peace plan could hardly have been moved earlier. Poor though the state of that party had been before 1774, its plight was worsened by the American crisis, for which many actually blamed the Marquis and his friends: if they had only stood firm and never repealed the Stamp Act the Americans would not have been emboldened to defy supreme authority again—such was a widespread common opinion. They appeared as the appeasers shown to have been wrong. Whatever popularity they had once obtained was utterly lost and the last thing they now wished for was to be cast in the role of defenders of misbehaving American colonists. Since the opening of the new parliament they had hoped for the kind of news over the Atlantic which might either tell of American submission or sober ministers to a more prudent course. So that it was not until ministry started more rash measures—rash enough to shake some of its own supporters—that the Rockingham plan could be offered without further damaging the party's small ability to be heard. Late though the plan was moved, it cannot be said that its purpose would have been realized if George III had now fired his ministers and reversed the course of policy. A spirit was moving in America which perhaps no British government could quiet. However, the Rockingham plan was more generous than North's and less impractical than Chatham's. It squared with the best British understanding of American reality. There was nothing pro-American about it. The men who conceived it were not greatly interested in America but concerned solely for the peace, security, and prosperity of their own country. It was their last effort of the session, as a party, to arrest the drift to disaster, although perfunctory support was given to the Savile–Camden motions for repeal of the Quebec Act and to Burke's attempt in mid-May to obtain consideration for a remonstrance from the New York Assembly.

Rockingham was glad that Parliament was prorogued before news came of Concord and Lexington, since he thought that the ministers would have fired it with a still angrier spirit and striven to raise the pride of the nation "against giving way in any respect to the Americans." He saw nothing whatever for his friends to do after the sluice was opened. Politics, he told Burke, "must in great measure be left to their own time and their own turns." He discounted the value of half-hearted and timid activity on the part of persons promoting petitions: "Nothing but a *general sense* in this country of the impolicy of the late measures, can form a good foundation for any restoration of wisdom and policy in the government of this country. Time, & that only, can ripen it." Richmond, sunk in melancholy, sighed that "we are not fit to govern ourselves and much less distant provinces"; if the Americans gained emancipation it would be of "some good to humanity that so many millions of brave men should be free and happy as I hope in God they will be." Less disposed by nature to despair or inactivity, even Burke fell in the early summer into what he called "a kind of calm and tranquil despair." [38] In late July Rockingham had from Sir James Lowther an account of Bunker Hill and answered it in a manner which displayed both sagacity of judgment and a generous respect for his misled countrymen:

What effect this event may have upon the minds of the people of G[rea]t Britain, remains to be seen, it surely should awaken them. I rejoice that it is generally believed that Gen[era]l Gage and Gen[era]l Howe in their private letters, have fairly acknowledged that the Americans behaved with great bravery & I can conceive that the people of England will be more ready to be moved towards conciliatory measures, *now,* when convinced that it is to a brave people to whom concession may be to be made, than they would have been to such a dastardly people, as L[or]d Sandwich, & many of his Majesty's councillors represented them.

His Majesty's ministers, I hear, still propose to send more & more troops, & declare their determination of subduing the Americans by force.

It is indeed no longer a choice from judgment in them. Rash, dangerous, wicked, as the plan may be, *they* can adopt no other.

The action at Lexington—the proclamation against Adams & Hancock etc. & ultimately the last battle, must have imbittered matters to that high degree, that the present ministers can have no idea of any prospect of conciliation through them with the colonies. The ministers must therefore either continue in a plan of enforcing, or they must abandon the reins of government.

His Majesty, it must be supposed, is still persuaded that the scheme of conquering America, is both practicable in execution, & wise in policy.

Experience should already have convinced him that the practicability is not quite so certain, & if the attempt totally fails, his Majesty will have but little consolation from the support of an opinion that it was a wise attempt, when the consequences will be, the loss & dismemberment of so considerable a part of the strength, & source of wealth, of this once great united empire.[39]

IV

By early August Burke was fighting off despair and urging his chief to sound political dispositions at York Races. He put the question "whether honest men will make one last effort to give peace to their country." All illusions about New York had been exploded, and when Parliament met (in October) its sanction would be needed by ministers for carrying on a North American war. Burke did not agree with Rockingham's view that nothing could be done until the people began to feel the effect of what they had passively approved. He talked with Lord John Cavendish (who would carry the suggestion to Wentworth) of a scheme for reviving the party's interest in the City of London. Chatham had again faded from the scene; the time was opportune for the Rockinghamites to raise a banner to gain the better city politicians and to set them in motion for peace with America. William Baker would undertake the business. There was an influential Quaker merchant, Burke said, who might "feel the pulse of the people of Leeds and the adjacent country." John Lee, a Yorkshireman and lawyer much consulted by Rockingham, could help in such a cause and "if Sir George Savile could be persuaded to come forward"— Burke broke off, well knowing that Savile would not so act. After sending off these thoughts Burke went to Bristol where he found the Dissenters "well disposed" along with "nine tenths of the Quakers," and he was instrumental in forming "a trusty secret committee" to correspond with other towns. Bristol's example, he believed, would be followed by twenty or thirty other places once Lord Rockingham gave the signal.[40]

To Burke's dismay the Marquis had no desire to encourage another outdoor political movement in the counties and towns of the country. The general public was too lethargic and the royal proclamation (August 23) against rebellion and sedition made men very disinclined to manifest resentment against inconveniences not yet "felt." Rash and imprudent it would have been for a Yorkshire grandee who headed a large political interest and organization to risk all in an enterprise such as Burke favored. Already businessmen at Leeds—where Savile long enjoyed a great popularity —had adopted an address in support of the administration's American policy. Something similar was preparing at Hull, where Savile's interest had brought Hartley into Parliament. In mid-September the Recorder at York proposed that the city corporation adopt a loyal address to the crown. Rockingham's friends managed to smother it,[41] but here was another sign that the political system he and Savile had built up could not in such a moment be safely employed in behalf of a movement to stir country against court. The Marquis of course agreed that men who saw the calamities into which the country was being led should "exert every possible means to avert the mischief, or at least to bear such testimony of their disapprobation, as may clear them in futurity from having been negligent on so important an occasion"; but they should do this only within the confines of legislature. He, Sir George Savile, and Lord John hit upon the idea of "a joint memorial or remonstrance," so drafted as to accommodate the views of all parts of opposition and signed by all members in both Houses of Parliament, to be presented to the King. This could not be done until after the meeting of Parliament since only then could the necessary consultations take place; and because, too, proper timing would require that Parliament first give sanction (as none doubted it would) to a general war in America. The Marquis desired that, after presenting this memorial, his friends would "abstain from going to either house of parliament when American affairs were the subject of debate." [42] He told Lord John:

> I should like to retire back here & wait the issue. . . . Nothing but repeated disappointments & the feelings of real distress will either change the sentiments of those who rule, or will give that turn to the minds of the people in general in this country, which ultimately will be necessary to save this whole empire from perdition.[43]

Burke was asked to lay his leader's idea before Portland and Richmond and to get the latter to discuss them with Lord Camden. Answering, Burke said that if something was not done before Parliament met, nothing afterward would "avail in the smallest degree." Rockingham then extended his consultations and reiterated the party line to the secretary:

> I am indeed more and more convinced, that it behooves us, as honest and honourable men, to take the step of a protestation after parliament has met. . . . it must *have some effect* upon the publick at large, when they see men of high rank and fortune, of known principles and of undoubted abilities, stepping forward in so extraordinary a manner to face a torrent, not merely of ministerial or court power, but also of *almost general* opinion. . . . if hereafter we should call upon our friends in

the different counties etc. to express an opinion concurrent with
our own, we shall do it with the better grace, when we have
been the first to face the torrent.[44]

Burke now bent the knee, assuring the Marquis that the
latter's determination was sufficient to satisfy his mind "most
perfectly on the prudence and propriety of the plan to which
you adhere." If he had known that it was thought advisable
"to rest on our arms, and let the Court get out of the wind,"
he would never have "suffered any motions repugnant to
that arrangement in Bristol, nor made any in London." His
submission was merely verbal. He advised his Bristol friends
to keep up their local activity and correspondence while
taking care to act covertly and make certain that their communications were not betrayed. He also pressed Richmond
to urge his relatives in Ireland, the Duke of Leinster and
Thomas Connolly, into an activity aimed at blocking crown
measures in the Irish Parliament. He wished Ireland to
offer a mediation in the Anglo-American quarrel and argued
that Ireland held "the ballance of the empire, and perhaps
its own fate forever, in her hands." To stop the war the
Irish Parliament should refuse to vote supplies. Had Ireland so acted, Burke believed (several months later) that
British ministers must have retreated to conciliation.[45] There
is, however, no evidence that Richmond was tempted to play
so dangerous a game as scheming to set Ireland against
Great Britain with all America in rebellion. Nor does it appear that Rockingham knew of Burke's appeal to Richmond.
As in 1769 Burke shows himself at this time as a much
bolder politician than the Marquis, much less fearful of
getting the party entangled with Chathamites and radicals.
He was also less aware of the near-impossibility of making
the general public understand the Rockinghamite position
which combined maintenance of legislative supremacy with
peaceful conciliation in a system of policy aimed at serving
equally and reciprocally the interests of Great Britain and
America.

As Burke sought to nudge his leader in one direction Sir

George Savile—indispensable to Rockingham in Yorkshire —was for the exact opposite. He wished to stay away from Parliament and implored for "a melancholy silence" lest ministers be provoked to new extremes: "I know I feel . . . a temptation to encrease their damnation in proportion to the warnings they have had, & lay in a claim for the 'Didn't I tell you so' but I reject this as an unworthy wish. The situation of men who prophesy bad is always odious; for no man will believe they don't wish their words may come true." Nevertheless, the Marquis prevailed upon him to come to town for the opening of the session (October 26). During the previous ten days there were conferences in Grosvenor Square and efforts to collect the views of all elements in the minority. Rockingham had sent out his summonses for the strongest possible showing.

> I am very anxious [he wrote] that our friends should come to town as soon as possible that we may know their opinions, & that we may weigh & consult in what manner & what mode we should try to express our sentiments: our efforts too probably will be of little avail in stopping the career of the violent measures but we may at least secure to ourselves the conscientious satisfaction that we have not neglected our duty, & that we have done our utmost endeavours to warn both the King & the People of the horrors & ruin which must ensue from the continuance of this Civil War.[46]

The first Rockinghamite maneuver was Lord John Cavendish's motion to amend the address by converting a parliamentary commitment to support the crown in an American war into a promise to review past measures toward the end of stopping the "dreadful calamity, of shedding British blood by British arms." The largest minority (108) yet mobilized on the American question divided for the amendment. The address was not carried until North promised an indemnity bill to cover the admitted illegality of employing Hanoverians at Gibraltar and Port Mahon (as announced in the royal speech) in order to free the British garrisons for service elsewhere. There were signs of weakness and discord within administration, which seemed to waver. In the Lords Rockingham moved the same amendment offered by Lord John, and among the 29 who supported was the Lord Privy Seal, the Duke of Grafton, who then gave up his office. Want of harmony among ministers was matched, however, by differences in the ranks of the minority. Shelburne had answered Rockingham's previous communication of the amendment by declaring for a mere negative against the address since "so many different opinions may appear in the course of the debate." Camden, he said, was of the same opinion. Nor did Grafton yet swing toward collaboration with Rockingham. So that the old jealousies reappeared, stimulated perhaps by the apparent possibility that the King might change his ministers. Only 17 of the 29 who opposed the address in the peers put their names to the statesmanlike Rockinghamite protest entered on the journal. Camden withheld his, quibbling over the word *unconstitutional* in reference to the use of Hanoverian troops within the British empire, although he acknowledged that he thought it illegal. Nor did Shelburne sign, or Grafton, or any other peer of Chathamite connection. "The times are very, very interesting," wrote Rockingham on November 2; "it behoves us to be wary, and neither to be too precipitate in giving too much confidence to the professions of various men, nor on the other hand, to be over cautious, in taking umbrage and entertaining suspicions *too generally,* and I confess in my judgment, I would even overlook and not resent, tho' I had proof of *tricks* being played." [47] His grand design was massive minority voting which might show the King, who had always dreaded division in Parliament on great questions, that he had been ill-advised and should call to his service men who would strive to restore peace in the empire.

During November intensive Rockinghamite efforts were made again in the Lords: the Duke of Manchester's motion for censure of the employment of Hanoverians without prior consent of Parliament, and Richmond's attempt to have the "Olive Branch" petition from the Second American Congress recognized as ground for conciliation. The greatest and most memorable move by the Rockinghams was the preparation of a bill to compose the quarrel with the colonies which Burke opened on November 16. It proposed to new-model Anglo-American constitutional relations upon the principle of a statute of Edward I's reign whereby it was believed that the King, without abating his sovereignty, had given up the right to tax his subjects without their consent. The supreme legislative authority would confer upon the American colonies the privilege of exemption from parliamentary taxation. All aids from them, even customs duties, would in future come only by the free grant of their assemblies. The fateful tea tax would be repealed and a general amnesty would be offered to all Americans who had taken up arms. With this bill the Rockinghams came at last to accept Lord Chatham's doctrine that the right to legislate did not necessarily imply the right to tax—provided, of course, that the British legislature, with its illimitable authority, so enacted. Notice of Burke's motion for leave to bring in this bill was well advertised in advance. The Marquis sent out the usual calls to friends to attend, and conferred on the measure with both Shelburne and Camden who were displeased by its omission of any mention of the Quebec Act. The whole minority, minus Shelburne's men (Dunning and Barré), turned out for the occasion and divided 105 against ministry's 210.

Four days later North brought in the Prohibitory Bill, in effect a declaration of war against the colonies. Rockingham attempted another full mobilization but despair sank the minority to 62 against the motion for leave and to a mere 16 on the last reading. "In the House of Commons," wrote Richmond to Rockingham (November 25), "our friends will scarcely think it worth while to divide 60 after having been 105." [48] Only 19 bothered to vote against the bill in the Lords. Their bolt had been shot; the nation was committed by the supreme legislature to crush the American rebellion. The great protestation, which Rockingham on the eve of the session had envisaged as the minority's next step after failing in Parliament, was never achieved, presumably from want of concord among leading men. At his leader's request Burke worked during the Christmas holiday on some sort of paper which may have been intended as a draft of the stillborn protestation. He had little heart for the task, "now that all is cold and dead, and the evils it was wished as a means of averting have actually happened." [49] He promised to press on with it, but nothing more is heard of the protestation. While he worked Admiral Keppel visited Shelburne and reported to Rockingham that he could make little or nothing of that Earl's politics, having heard only compliments to the Rockingham party mixed with sighs that they did not speak out. Shelburne professed himself "a single person" who "had done with meddling," and regretted that "no sound system was adopted that could bring good about." [50]

Never had circumstances been less favorable to the cause of conciliating the North Americans, who seemed at the close of 1775 to sweep all before them. A British army was besieged at Boston, and the loss of both Quebec and Nova Scotia appeared probable. Small wonder that the British nation was resolved upon a great campaign to reverse this immense misfortune. Rockingham pressed for no further motions in Parliament, and that scene of futile effort was left to the initiatives of others. Into the void left by Lord John Cavendish's inactivity stepped Charles Fox, laying a claim to leadership of an active Commons minority. He dazzled Burke and stimulated the flagging spirit of his uncle, the Duke of Richmond, who in December had confessed himself "very languid about this American business." [51] Fox's natural talents, his recent desertion of North, and the admiration always evoked by an "independent" member standing bravely for conscience' sake against the court combined to make him the glittering star of the minority—its most gifted acquisition, youthful, without taint of Pelhamite old guard, full of the convert's zeal and of promise for the future. On February 20 he moved for an inquiry into the poor showing of the King's forces in America, and 104 supported—the largest minority division after Burke's bill.

Two weeks later Richmond, Camden, and Shelburne carried the brunt for opposition in support of Grafton's motion for peace. Rockinghamites formed a majority of the 31 who voted for the motion. But the Marquis' role was perfunctory; nothing, he was sure, could be done until an opportune time which could hardly come until after the 1776 campaign in America.

Inevitably murmurs arose from many against the seeming half-heartedness in the leader of the main body of the whigs. He had always wished his friends to avoid being reputed as a pro-American party, and saw no prudence in exposing them as partisans of what now seemed to most men the cause of the enemy. He had no natural sympathy with the American rebellion, but only a detestation of the follies and ministerial imbecilities which had provoked it. The Rockinghamite public record of opposing the measures which led to war, and of seeking to stop it for the sake of nation and empire, had been made. The Marquis was for standing upon this and not trying anything until time and circumstances ripened a moment for practical effort toward pacification. He neither spelled out this strategy at the end of 1775 nor sought to impose it upon friends, which he never could have done; but it was implicit in his conduct.

NOTES

1. Add. MS 42087, f. 2; *Cavendish's Debates* I 401.
2. WWM R 1: 1111, 1118, 1156, 1159; R 63: 12.
3. R 1: 1186.
4. *Corr. Burke* II 47.
5. WWM R 1: 1240; Rockingham to Dartmouth 8 Nov.—Dartmouth MS D.1778.viii. With respect to practicability he pointed to the same problem faced later by the makers of the United States Constitution: "The separate colonies would all value their own pretensions highly, in point of numbers of representatives from each & would be reciprocally jealous of each other, least any or some particular colonies should gain too much weight by having a larger number of representatives setting in a parliament so formed."
6. WWM R 1: 1254; the materials from Harrison are in R 61.

7. *Cavendish's Debates* I 483–509; Rockingham to Dartmouth 9 April.—Dartmouth MS D.1778.

8. WWM R 1: 1292.

9. *Cavendish's Debates* II 12–37.

10. Delancey to Rockingham 21 Dec. 1770.—WWM R 1: 1343.

11. Hoffman, *Burke,* 21–22, 105–107.

12. *Corr. Burke* II 430.

13. *Ibid.,* 516, 523; Walpole, *Last Journals* I 330; *Chatham* IV 335.

14. WWM R 49: 1.

15. R 1: 1428 (22 April 1774), printed by Albemarle II 244–245, under mistaken date.

16. Rockingham to Portland 17 April.—Portland MSS.

17. *Last Journals* I 365. "I hope you feel satisfied with yourself today; I am sure all your friends must be so for you spoke as they could wish you to do often."—Richmond to Rockingham 18 May (WWM R 1: 1490).

18. Chatham's excuse was his being unwell. His wife wrote to Rockingham of his regret "not to have the honour of his name, enrolled among those, who have signed them."—WWM R 1: 1491. Soon afterward he appeared in the House for the first time since 1771, to urge lenient measures to lure Americans "to their duty"; but said too that if their turbulence persisted after "proffered terms of forgiveness" he would be among the foremost to make them feel the consequences of provoking "a fond and forgiving parent."—*Chatham* IV 447.

19. Hoffman, *Burke,* 142–149, 260–267; John Wright, ed., *Sir Henry Cavendish's Debates of the House of Commons in the Year 1774 on the Bill for Making a More Effective Provision for the Government of the Province of Quebec* (London, 1839), 189–197; *Corr. Burke* III 13–21.

20. Ramsden MS (Leeds) 1, f. 57.

21. *Corr. Burke* III 25–26, 30–31.

22. WWM R 158: 57.

23. R 1: 1492, 1497–1505; *Corr. Burke* III 21–26, 28–36.

24. *Hist. Parl.* I 427–443.

25. Portland MSS (1 Oct.).

26. *Hist. Parl.* I 75. Another estimate is 16.—Bernard Donoughue, *British Politics and the American Revolution* (London, 1964), 197.

27. *Hist. Parl.* I 80–81; Hoffman, *Burke,* 167.

28. W. Burke to C. O'Hara Dec. 1774 (printed *ibid.,* 575).

29. *Corr. Burke* III 88–90, 90–92.

30. *Ibid.,* 94–99, 101–103, 106–109.

31. *Ibid.,* 107; WWM R 1: 1540.

32. R 1: 1543; Albemarle II 270; Rockingham to Shelburne 31 Jan.—Shelburne–Lacaita MSS (Clements Library). First drafts of these notes to Chatham and Shelburne (R 1: 1544, 1545) show hardly concealed vexation, suppressed in what was sent. Rockingham told Portland that Chatham's conduct was "very strange . . . not such as it ought to be."—Portland MSS. Lady Rockingham wrote ironically of "the *greatest* of all *Earls.*"—*Corr. Burke* III 109.

33. The text of the bill is in *Chatham* IV 533–536.

34. WWM R 1: 1548, 1549. Rockingham sent a short account to Chatham expressing hope that his gout would abate and that his "presence and

assistance may not long be withdrawn." Chatham did not appear in the Lords again that session.

35. R 1: 1554, 1558, 1559.

36. *Corr. Burke* III 139.

37. For example, C. S. Ritcheson in *British Politics and the American Revolution* (Norman, 1954), 189–190; also Bernard Donoughue, *British Politics,* 256–263.

38. *Corr. Burke* III 170, 172–173, 183; WWM R 1: 1569.

39. R 1: 1572, 1573. The latter is a copy by Lady Rockingham of the original letter now in the possession of the American Philosophical Society.

40. *Corr. Burke* III 182–184.

41. Jerome Dring to Rockingham 9 Oct.—WWM R 1: 1668.

42. *Corr. Burke* III 203–206. Rockingham sent sobering words to Richard Champion (Burke's principal Bristol friend) on 2 Sept. when he believed Burke to be still there: "By every thing which I can hear & by what many judge by the *Proclamation* . . . I think there is no doubt but that Ministers & Court are obstinately determined to run every risk. . . . The first idea, which has brought on this state of calamity, undoubtedly originated in the inmost recesses & probably will be pursued with the same perseverance with which the Object of that System has always been."—WWM R 158: 82.

43. R 1: 1601.

44. *Corr. Burke* III 211, 214–217.

45. *Ibid.,* 217–221, 244–245.

46. WWM R 1: 1612 (printed in Albemarle II 282–287); R 153: 12; R 1: 1610.

47. R 1: 1614, 1615, 1616, 1617, 1623, 1624, 1625; *Corr. Burke* III 235.

48. R 1: 1630.

49. *Corr. Burke* III 242–243.

50. WWM R 1: 1651.

51. R 1: 1637.

10

The Reversion

THERE IS AN UNDATED MEMORIAL which Burke prepared (probably in 1780) for Rockingham's use in explaining himself to the King. Since 1767, the Marquis appears to say,

> I have contented myself with doing my duty as a Member of Parliament. Even any considerable exertion in that line I should probably in great measure have discontinued and should have been happy in becoming very much a private man, if I had not seen undertakings of great boldness taken in hand, much above the powers of those who engaged in them, that there seemed to me hardly one day in the course of several years past in which the kingdom was not in imminent danger. I was besides made to believe that my continuing in business was in some degree conducive towards keeping together a set of valuable men, such as your Majesty might entirely rely upon in any trying exigencies of your government.[1]

This was a fair statement of his reason for continuing as a political leader at least since the outbreak of the American war. To maintain a consistent stand of disapproval of men and measures, while trying to avoid an aggressive conduct certain to offend national sensibilities and scandalize the King, was the delicate line he sought to follow during the war years. Even when the tide of public sentiment began to flow against the North administration, no man was more averse than Rockingham to disorderly manifestations against government. He refused to disallow the possibility, however remote, that Majesty might come to see a need for putting government into the hands of wiser and more prudent men; but no man was less likely to "storm the closet"; or more disinclined to head an administration without a convincing promise from the King to support its measures.

The full strength of the minority for peace with America in the session of 1775–1776 was 30-odd in the Lords and a few more than 100 in the House of Commons. A majority of the opposition to the war were the almost habitual followers of Rockingham and Richmond in the peers and of Lord John Cavendish in the lower House, although this is not to say that all these were conscious of belonging to a party; many, perhaps most, thought of themselves as perfectly independent members of Parliament. A great many other consciously independent men were influenced in varying degrees by such men as the Earl of Chatham, the Duke of Grafton, lords Shelburne and Camden, Charles Fox, General Conway, and Wilkes. Leading men were riven by distrusts dating back to 1766–1767 when the Chatham–Grafton ministry had succeeded Rockingham's. Shelburne, Camden, and Grafton were more or less disciples of Chatham, who though now ill and retired from the scene was destined to reappear upon it in the last year of his life. Chathamites were stoutly whig but disinclined to act as a party, and only Shelburne had a small group in Commons who reflected his views. There had never been cordiality between the Marquis and Shelburne who were in fact little known to each other. Camden had once shown a disposition to act with the Rockinghams but he was not without some shyness of the nephew of Lord Mansfield. Grafton had been part of the Rockingham administration until he struck it the near-fatal blow of throwing up his office. He had succeeded the Marquis as Treasury minister, had not been very candid with him in the negotiations of 1767, and since 1771 had held the privy seal. He recorded many years later that after quitting that office in the autumn of 1775 "Lord Rockingham's difference from me, with that also of his friends, having been only on political points; we renewed our intimacy, when the cause of misunderstanding was removed." On the other hand, Shelburne began to court Grafton, as did Fox who even declared himself willing to act with the Duke "with more pleasure, in any possible situation, than with any one I have been acquainted with." [2] Fox had a host of friends but not a party. Long-standing personal friendship with Burke drew him toward the Rockinghams as did his being nephew to the Duke of Richmond, but several years were to pass before he could be said to have linked himself as a party man with the main body of the whigs. Conway, the ministerial leader in Parliament who had carried the repeal of the Stamp Act, had not ceased to be a servant of the crown. A secretary of state until 1768, he had then held the office of Lieutenant General of the Ordnance until 1772 when he was given for life the governorship of the Isle of Jersey. This illustrious man, always reputed an uncompromising independent, possessed an influence growing out of the admiration he commanded, and he was in opposition only to the extent that he opposed the armed coercion of the American colonies. He had long been close to Grafton to whom he owed his seat in the House. The old intimacy between Rockingham and Conway when both were attached to the Duke of Cumberland and served together in office in 1765–1766 was broken in 1767 and had never been renewed. As for Wilkes, the leading radical in Parliament (member for Middlesex since 1774): all efforts to make a Rockingham whig of him had proved fruitless.[3]

In time of war a political opposition cannot flourish, and this disorganized minority of peace advocates was doomed to futility until failure in war made possible a reversion to the chiefs of whiggery. The leading men had been ministers, knew the King's hatred of party, and knew too that only he could make them ministers again; so that the less they acted in combination the less they incurred the displeasure of their sovereign. What Rockingham called "keeping together a set of valuable men" George III called party.

In the summer of 1776, when it was not yet known that Canada was safely held or even that General Howe's army was moving upon New York, Rockingham thought that the tendency of the news showed that the Americans "appear every day, to have more and more powers of resistance." He knew that a massive stroke was soon to fall somewhere upon them but expected that the event would be indecisive.

> Men's minds in this country are hung up [he observed to Burke on July 12] in the suspense of expectation, the end of the campaign is the *settling day,* and I confess that I am strongly of the opinion, that they will find and will feel so much disappointment in the expectations they had formed of success etc. that they will be more ready to adopt and probably more ready to join with those, who have always warned against the danger.[4]

A month later—as Howe was driving Washington from Long Island—news of the American Declaration of Independence reached England. Rockingham was at York Races, Burke en route to Bristol, Richmond in France for an extended stay. Portland, who was in town, was pressed by Fox to urge upon Rockingham a council at Wentworth of principal friends in order to settle upon something to do. Fox would bring the views of Grafton. Late in August this council took place. Who attended other than Portland, Fox, Lord John Cavendish, and Burke is not certain, but it was agreed that an amendment for peace would be moved against the address and that this would be followed by some sort of minority manifesto to justify a secession from Parliament by men opposed to war. The Marquis, however, did not deceive himself into thinking that anything of practical effect could be accomplished if the right kind of news—namely, of indecisive war—did not come from over the Atlantic. Soon afterward Admiral Keppel wrote to him in favor of trying anew to see "what a whole combined opposition could do when parliament opened." [5] But no concert of the whole was possible. There was no communication from Shelburne, and Rockingham was shy of treating with reckless metropolitan politicians.

One of these, Stephen Sayre, an American-born radical who had been arrested the previous autumn on a false charge of treason, approached Portland (among others) in early September with a proposal from an unnamed group. If "unfavourable news" arrived from America, Lord Mayor Sawbridge should assemble the London livery in Common Hall for a dramatic demonstration, to which should come a number of noble lords and respectable commoners "as though they were brought together by a common impulse of impending danger." Then a committee should be formed to send circular letters "to the several counties requesting of them to do the same that the sense of the nation may be known through their declarations." After consulting with Rockingham, who had had his fill of this sort of thing in 1769–1770, Portland gave Sayre a sympathetic but noncommittal answer. The Marquis had advised that this answer

> should be very civil & at the same time to be so contrived as not to be a handle for Mr. Sayre etc. to say, that your Grace *throws cold water,* or that you recommended that Mr. Sayre etc. should proceed with all the precipitation & wildness, which usually characterize every business in which the warm gentry in the City take the lead.

He suspected that Shelburne's influence with city politicians, which had so often worked against his own friends there, might be detected in Sayre's proposal. If the time were near when some sort of national manifestation against the administration were possible, Rockingham said that it could have a "weighty effect" only if it originated from "men of rank, character & fortune in this country." No doubt the concurrence of the city would then be useful and necessary but "the mode & manner of their doing it, must be planned & pointed out to them by abler and more discreet men than themselves." [6]

Three weeks before the opening of Parliament Howe's victory in lower New York was known in England. Painted by ministry as the most auspicious triumph, it was so widely acclaimed throughout the country that even the mayor and corporation of the city of York, Rockinghamite citadel and headquarters of the Rockingham Club, voted an address of congratulation to the King. Not only were the Marquis' hopes for some event to bring the country to its senses blasted but a blow was struck at his prestige in his own county. Fox wrote to him now urging a conduct "somewhat different from that which was projected at Wentworth": a secession would look too much like "running away from the conquerors" and Fox wished it to be "a point of honour among us all to support the American pretensions in adversity as much as we did in their prosperity." [7] The Marquis let this frantic letter go unanswered. When, he must have asked himself, had he ever supported American pretensions who had only condemned the measures which had provoked them? He told Burke (to whom Fox had sent a similar appeal) that the line of conduct for his friends to follow was not a difficult one:

> Our object has always been to try to preserve a friendly union between the colonies and the Mother Country. . . . We thought more highly of the interior force & strength of America, than the Ministers pretended to do, and notwithstanding what has happened in Long Island the various events have proved that we were right. . . . I have but little doubt, that the stile of the speech and address will afford us full opportunity of declaring the same sentiments, which we have held from the commencement, and I think we may do it, with dignity and solemnity.

As he set out from Wentworth to go again to Parliament he reflected upon the vanity of imagining "that this country

can or will be served by any thing like honesty, integrity—
or policy." The public was like "a silly echo" of what the
court sounded, while "the still voice of reason" was lost as
in a vacuum.[8]

Once again a verbal battle was fought hopelessly for an
amendment to the address, Lord John moving it in Commons and the Marquis in the Lords. In addition to indicting
ministers for misunderstanding America and misleading
Parliament, the amendment urged that "a wise and moderate use" be made of the advantage gained in New York
by "laying down, on our part, real permanent grounds of
connection between Great Britain and the Colonies, on principles of liberty and terms of mutual advantage." In a
Parliament better attended than usual in the early days of
a session, only 87 supported the amendment in Commons
and 26 in the Lords, where the whole text was entered as a
protest upon the journal. Soon afterward the planned "secession" took place. It meant that men absented themselves
from all parliamentary business relating to the American
war in the hope (how vain!) that if enough of the minority
followed the example of the Rockinghams a strong sobering
impression would be made upon both the King and the
public. So ill-executed was this policy that not even all of
Rockingham's friends fell in with it.

The Marquis departed in late November for Wentworth,
staying there until mid-January. Burke drafted the address
to the King which was to explain and justify the secession
of the minority. What with the alterations by others and
the need to satisfy a variety of whiggish views it turned out
to be one of his least-distinguished productions. Between
December 8 and January 6 it was in circulation among such
friends as Richmond, Frederick Montagu, and Portland,
and a copy was then sent to Rockingham. It restated the
now familiar arguments against armed coercion of the colonies, laid all responsibility for this upon the ministers, and
justified the secession on the ground that, "All our endeavours having proved fruitless, we are fearful at this time of
irritating by contention, those passions, which we have found

it impractical to compose by reason." Through the whole
ran the implication that in spite of the American Declaration
of Independence his Majesty might yet compose the quarrel
in the empire by employing wiser men as his ministers. Burke
was envisaging his party as the grand mediators who might
yet restore peace to British dominions. Hence he composed
also at this time an "Address to the British Colonists in
North America" for the purpose of convincing them that
they had many real friends in Great Britain, "well wishers
of the liberty and union of this empire" who abhorred the
war and longed for Anglo-American unity with such alterations in the constitution of the empire as would secure the
firmest guarantee of colonial liberties "under the paternal
care and nurture of a protecting parliament." [9] He considered going to Paris to deliver this paper into the hands
of his old friend Benjamin Franklin, lately arrived in the
French capital as emissary of the still unrecognized United
States of America. Burke was then interpreting the reports
of General Howe's "successes" as proof of the Americans'
inability to vindicate their cause. Unable to "look standing
armies in the face," they might delay but could not evade
defeat since they had little foreign aid and were unlikely to
obtain more. Franklin, thought Burke, would not gain a
French alliance and, failing that, might have authority to
negotiate with a British representative "on the basis of dependence upon this crown." Had his political friends approved Burke's proposed course they would indeed have
been playing with fire. He did not go to Franklin. "When I
had conversed with the very few of your Lordship's friends
who were in town," he told Rockingham, "and considered a
little more maturely the constant temper and standing max-
ims of the party, I laid aside the design." [10] He was to lay
aside too his address to the colonists of which nothing was
heard until his literary executors printed it a half-century
later.

While Burke was setting forth his thoughts in a long
letter (January 6) to the Marquis the latter was spelling
out some of his own in a missive which crossed Burke's. [11]

Very differently did Rockingham assess the actualities. Franklin's reaching Versailles was "much more than a ballance for the few additional acres" recovered by British arms, and the Marquis was far from believing that the colonists' resistance was hopeless:

> Further news we must expect to hear, and very important it will be, if it is true, that the latest accounts were, that General Howe and his army were at Brunswick—advancing towards Philadelphia, and that General Washington with considerable force was at Trenton ferry to obstruct General Howe's army and prevent their getting to Philadelphia. [Actually, Washington had already inflicted severe blows upon his enemy at Trenton and Princeton.]

Rockingham judged it only a "supposition" that the campaign of 1776 had ended fortunately for what he was pleased to call "the ministerial army." Nor did he believe that the colonies would not receive massive help from the Bourbon powers, since even if these states did not go to war with Great Britain "no one in his senses" could doubt "of their assisting, privately, the Americans to the utmost degree." So far apart were the Marquis and the "Secretary" in assessing probabilities at the beginning of 1777. Before starting back to town Rockingham confessed to Portland that he felt "no spring, no alertness" and longed only for "quietness & retirement." The sentiments of the public, he thought, were so strongly for the war that the friends of peace with America were fewer than ever. Savile summed up the position of Rockinghamites neatly: "We are not only patriots out of place, but patriots *out of the opinion of the public*." [12] The planned address to the King in justification of the secession was quashed. Burke was not himself sure that if presented it would not provoke ministers to impeachments or bills of pains and penalties against signers. We have only Horace Walpole's statement that consultations upon it were limited to the Marquis' chief friends and that they differed.[13] It seems safe to conclude that Rockingham saw no wisdom in offending the court without any prospect of support from the public.

Not until May was the public given, in Burke's *Letter to the Sheriffs of Bristol,* a much better explanation to justify the Rockinghamite secession. Formally addressing constituents who had not been much pleased by their representative's abstaining from representing them in great matters of state, he said that in giving up a futile contention which "rather inflamed than lessened the distemper of public counsels" he had acted with "prudent and well-intentioned persons" who could see no other way of demonstrating to the nation their abhorrence of the war. The pamphlet restated eloquently the Rockinghamite principles set forth in so many protests, speeches, and pamphlets. The Marquis was that man of "wisdom and temper" whose "mediatorial spirit and talents" had in 1766 warded off what less prudent men had afterward provoked. He and his friends had hoped to maintain the unlimited authority of the British legislature over all colonies by employing it for their benefit and that of all the empire. To effect conciliation after America was in arms they had moved "not only for a repeal of all the late coercive acts but for mutilating by a positive law, the entireness of the legislative authority of parliament, and cutting off from it the right of taxation." To critics who alleged that he was a man of faction he offered a brilliantly colored defense of his party:

> The only method which has ever been found effectual to preserve any man against corruption of nature and example, is an habit of life and communication of councils with the most virtuous and public-spirited men of the age you live in. . . . In the way which they call party, I worship the constitution of your fathers; and I shall never blush for my political company. All reverence to honour, all idea of what it is, will be lost out of the world, before it can be imputed as a fault to any man, that he has been closely connected with those incomparable persons, living and dead, with whom for eleven years I have constantly thought and acted. If I have wandered out of the paths of rectitude into those of interested faction, it has been

in company with the Saviles, the Dowdeswells, the Wentworths, the Bentincks; with the Lennoxes, the Manchesters,
the Keppels, the Saunders's; with the temperate, permanent,
hereditary virtue of the whole house of Cavendish.

And then, remembering those other whig patriots in the
minority who were not of this splendid company, Burke
continued:

> Those who perhaps have the same intentions, but are separated
> by some little political animosities, will I hope discern at last,
> how little conducive it is to any rational purpose, to lower its
> reputation. For my part, Gentlemen, from much experience,
> from no little thinking, and from comparing a great variety
> of things, I am thoroughly persuaded, that the last hopes of
> preserving the spirit of the English constitution, or of re-uniting
> the dissipated members of the English race upon a common plan
> of tranquility and liberty, does entirely depend on their firm and
> lasting union.

By the time this justly famous pamphlet reached the bookstalls the secession it defended was no more. A question had
arisen in Parliament of exactly the right sort to mobilize
the minority and provide the best possible opportunity for
the Rockinghamites not only to display their principled consistency but to exploit the doctrine brilliantly elaborated by
Burke in his party pamphlet of 1770—namely, that the
crown (or a court cabal) exerted a corrupting influence upon
Parliament. A royal message (April 9) asked for more than
£600,000 to pay debts incurred by the crown upon the civil
list. Unlike the procedure followed in 1769, accounts explanatory (in a general way) of the deficit were provided
by Lord North, who now asked also for an increase in the
fund annually appropriated for the civil list. Lord John
Cavendish moved for an inquiry into the causes of the debt,
and the minority supporting him swelled to 114 after a
protracted debate in which many ventilated the idea of an
excessive crown influence upon Parliament to hold it in support of bad ministers. In the Lords Rockingham moved a
hostile amendment to a compliant address in reply to the

royal message. Twenty peers voted for the amendment which afterward was entered upon the journal as a protest signed by fourteen Rockinghamites. They beheld "with astonishment and indignation, a profusion in his Majesty's ministers, which the greatest prosperity of our affairs could scarcely excuse," and concluded

> that a further increase of the present overgrown influence of the crown would be a treacherous gift from parliament, even to the crown itself; as it will enable the ministers to carry on those delusive systems which have been fatally adopted, and which, if pursued, must lead to the ruin as they have already produced the distraction, of this once great empire.

Another small elixir for the minority was given by Chatham's reappearance at the end of May to move for a cessation of hostilities and complete redress of all American grievances. He sent prior notice to Rockingham who with all his allies were of the 28 peers who supported the motion. Soon afterward Parliament rose and the impotent minority scattered as General Howe, leaving some of his forces under Clinton's command at New York, sailed for the Delaware and Philadelphia while Burgoyne moved from Canada toward the Hudson valley in the great double action to effect a military decision and end the war. The *Annual Register* recorded of the period from June to November when Parliament met again:

> No equal space of time for several years past, afforded so little domestic matter worthy of observation, as that part of the year 1777 which elapsed during the recess of parliament. Neither the town nor the country presented any new object of party contention. The American war, and many of its consequences, were now scarcely objects of curiosity, much less of surprise.

II

"With respect to public affairs," wrote Fox to Burke on September 8, "it seems to be the opinion of every body, that one must wait for events, to form a plan of operations." It was hard for this hot-spirited man to accept the political facts of life. He was then in pleasant whig company—"amiable people . . . unfit to storm a citadel"—at the Duke of Devonshire's Chatsworth, which was barely thirty miles from Wentworth House. Perhaps Rockingham too paid a visit there, for he had been in Yorkshire since mid-July. When Burke wrote to his chief on September 27 it was his first communication since they had parted nearly three months before, and he said that he had tried to banish public affairs from his mind, not reading "so much as a newspaper for near a month past." In answering Fox (a month after Fox had written to him), Burke joined in deploring the inactivity of the heads of his party (he was courting Fox for the party), and at the same time contended that any plan of action was "absolutely impractical." There was, he said, "some thing so weighty and decisive in the events of war, some thing that so completely overpowers the imagination of the vulgar, that all counsels must in a great degree be subordinate to and attendant upon them." This was exactly the Marquis' opinion with which Burke had previously differed. Burke's was an odd state of mind. He told William Baker that he did not know how to push others to resolution when he himself was unresolved. Still hankering for a plan of action which he admitted to be impractical, he yet sighed over the unwillingness of such men as Rockingham, Savile, and the Cavendishes—whose indolence was "connected with their disinterested intentions, plentiful fortunes, assured rank, and quiet homes"—to try the impossible.[14]

Meanwhile, Rockingham was watching the barometer of feeling and opinion in Yorkshire and cautioning friends against antagonizing the prevailing disposition to support King and country at war. At York Races he received graciously the new Archbishop of York, William Markham, whose recent elevation in succession to the Marquis' friend Dr. Drummond had been another blow to his interest.[15] Toward the end of October he judged that there was (as he wrote to Burke) "some dawn of light breaking in" at least to the extent that "those who have always abominated the violent measures against America, are not looked upon with quite so angry eyes, as they were some time ago." If what the public called "good news" came from America there would no doubt be a relapse into delusive expectations, but such news would have to be "really decisive" to meet with "greedy swallowers." He wished for a change in general sentiments to come without agitation by his friends; whose aim, after all, should not be for a triumph over the court or a vindication of their own opinions, but to be in a position to serve King and country if and when the opportunity came. Their opinions were copiously on record. No practical politician could wisely play the Cassandra role. Convinced as he was that British arms could not subdue America, Rockingham could see no termination of the war but in giving way to what the Americans desired, in order to re-establish friendly, fruitful relations with them. Until the mind of the public came to this view there was nothing to be done; attempts to hurry it up would backfire upon those who made them.

His Majesty may by events be necessitated *seemingly* to be willing to adopt wiser measures and even wiser *counsellors,* but that alone would be but a slender foundation to rely on. To restore peace and tranquility, to reconciliate in any degree the affections of America must require what would be deemed great *sacrifices* for this country to make.

Nothing but a strong and united administration could probably effect any thing, which would give a chance for so desireable an event—the public must see and feel the necessity, or no such event would have a probability of success, nor would there be any solid foundation on which any *man* or any *men* could attempt it.[16]

As the meeting of Parliament neared, Richmond was zealous for active opposition and even urged Rockingham to move the repeal of the 1766 Declaratory Act: "You are the man I should wish to see move the repeal. If you will not, pray consent to my moving it. . . . The passing it was a weakness, necessary I grant in the moment, but it is a most dangerous weapon in other hands, would now be useless to ours, and had therefore better be broken." [17] The Marquis did not reply. No proposal could have been more distasteful than that he make, as it were, a sort of public confession of an error he never could admit, and therefore of partial responsibility for the Anglo-American breach which he had striven first to prevent and then to heal. When he came to town in mid-November there were reports of Howe's successes in the Delaware campaign but rising fears for the fate of Burgoyne, whose position the Marquis thought "precarious and nearly a balance to the supposed advantage said to be obtained over Washington." In counseling with friends and allies he was more disposed than usual to let others take the initiative and to content himself with rallying support. Chatham was on the scene again and communicated to Rockingham a motion he intended for the opening day: to end hostilities and open a treaty "for the final settlement of the tranquillity of those valuable provinces . . . and fixing forever the respective rights of Great Britain and her colonies." The Marquis responded by welcoming every opportunity for cooperation "to the desireable end of saving this country from utter ruin." It was at his suggestion that young Lord Granby, of Chathamite political ancestry, was induced to offer the same motion in Commons.[18]

Divisions in both Houses showed no gains for the minority—only 28 in the Lords and 89 in Commons; but some encouragement was felt from the apparent revival of Rockingham–Chatham cooperation. On November 27 Richmond, Grafton, Fox, Camden, and Shelburne met at Rockingham's to consider a motion to name a day for taking into consideration the state of the nation. To resolve differences over tactical procedure the Marquis sought the advice of Chatham and concurred with it.[19] Ministry could not properly oppose a state-of-the-nation motion. The plan was to name the day of February 2 and in the meanwhile to offer a series of motions for papers, accounts, information of various kinds. Meetings of whig leaders to settle these motions would be held at the Duke of Richmond's house and Richmond and Fox would open this minority effort on December 2. In the plan of campaign it is easy to detect Rockingham's tactic of keeping himself in the background. There Savile and the Cavendishes also preferred to be.

Intelligence of the Saratoga disaster instantly transformed the whole picture before the eyes of both ministers and minority. All recognized the imminent probability of a French alliance with the Americans. A week later North promised to bring in after Christmas a plan for treating with the Americans for peace, and then carried an adjournment of Parliament for six weeks—time enough for the revived Rockingham–Chatham alliance to sunder on the question of how to end one war before getting into another. Richmond, Fox, Rockingham, and his principal friends were for simply stopping the war and if necessary giving up all claim to sovereignty over the warring colonies. Chatham and Shelburne did not go that far, believing that the Americans if rightly treated would annul their Declaration of Independence and return to being British subjects. To Chatham the Marquis explained himself as follows:

> My line in politics has ever been, not to hold out flattering expectations to the public, when I was not able to see the probability of their being accomplished. I conceive that America will never again assent to this country's having actual power within that continent. I cannot, therefore, so betray my trust to the public, as to act as if that was practicable, which I thought otherwise.[20]

In February came the Franco-American treaty and North's belated plan for sending commissioners to America to offer perfectly Chathamite concessions. In March British and French ambassadors were recalled. In April the peace commissioners sailed. Meanwhile the state-of-the-nation inquiry proved only that the minority in Parliament was swelling somewhat. The impending war with France turned the eyes of many expectantly toward Chatham, whose name had been honored in America and feared in France. Since he had declared in the Lords against giving up the colonies North advised summoning him, but the King would neither let North go nor have Chatham in any capacity but as a member of the North administration. In any event he was too old and ill. On May 11 he died. Shortly before Parliament rose in early June ministerial feelers were put out to sound the dispositions of other opposition leaders toward coalition. North would have been glad to go if the King had let him and the Bedfords wanted the Treasury. On May 29 Secretary of State Weymouth made an approach to Fox authorizing him to communicate with Rockingham, Richmond, and Portland. Fox had not yet come to the Marquis' opinion that no friend of his should take office except as part of a united body strong enough to engage the King's support for measures. Earlier that month indeed Fox had told Rockingham that if a strong whig party could not be made there was "nothing to do but to give the thing up fairly and see who can make his court best at St. James's." Richmond was now willing to compromise but the Marquis was not.[21] Nothing came of the Weymouth overture for which he had had no authority from the King, who held fast to North and kept the same set of ministers.

In June hostilities against France began with the nation united against the traditional enemy and hopeful that the Americans would, when the choice had to be made, opt for the generous British peace terms instead of ratifying the alliance with France. Partisan politics went into a state of suspended animation, and if coalition had not come about in the ministry something faintly like it was to be seen in the navy. Admiral Keppel, most faithful of Rockinghamites, who had refused to serve against the Americans, accepted command of the Channel fleet against the ancient foe. There was no opposition to a French war. The Marquis remained in town or at his estate at Wimbledon until August, thirsting for good news from Keppel's fleet which engaged the French forces out of Brest in the battle off Ushant (July 23–27) but failed to prevent their escape. At Wentworth during October Rockingham heard the first whispers of a suspected Admiralty plot to make Keppel a scapegoat for the navy's

want of victories at sea. Six days before Parliament opened
(November 25) he returned to town. The national outlook
was bleak. The American peace commissioners had returned
empty-handed. The army which had captured Philadelphia
had given it up and gone back to New York. Nevertheless
Burke judged the public to be "much as usual." The King's
speech deplored the want of success in ending hostilities
across the Atlantic, abstained from repeating a resolve to
suppress the rebellion, and applauded "that public spirit,
that steady order, and that love of their country, which
animate and unite all ranks of my faithful subjects." There
was no evident Rockinghamite strategy, no amendment to
the address in the Lords (although 31 peers simply voted
against an address flattering the ministers). In Commons
Tommy Townshend moved an amendment for inquiring into
the counsels and policy which had reduced the country "from
that splendid situation, which, in the early part of his Majesty's reign, made her the envy of all Europe." Fox, whom
Burke thought closer than ever to the Rockingham party,
spoke strongly for the amendment, but the address was
carried 220 to 107.

Soon afterward portions of a manifesto issued in America
by the frustrated peace commissioners appeared in the press
and motions in both Houses brought forth the whole text
of a wicked and foolish document. The peace commissioners
had threatened that the colonies, for rejecting a British
peace and accepting a French alliance, would have to suffer
a war of desolation and destruction and thus be rendered
useless to the ancient enemy of Great Britain. Thomas Coke,
an independent member, moved an address to the crown for
disavowal of the savage threat and was supported by 122.
Rockingham brought the matter before the Lords (December 4), moving a similar address in a speech of an hour-
and-a-half. There is no evidence of a prior effort to mobilize
friends and allies though that seems likely since Shelburne,
Camden, and Grafton were on hand to support. Thirty-
seven peers voted for the motion and 31 signed an eloquent
Rockinghamite protest which declared that

. . . the public law of nations, in affirmance of the dictates of nature, and the precepts of revealed religion, forbids us to resort to the extremes of war upon our own opinion of their expediency, or in any case to carry on war for the purpose of desolation. We know that the rights of war are odious, and instead of being extended upon loose constructions and speculations of danger, ought to be bound up and limited by all the restraints of the most rigorous construction. We are shocked to see the first law of nature, self-preservation, perverted and abused into a principle destructive of all the other laws; and a rule laid down, by which our own safety is rendered incompatible with the prosperity of mankind. Those objects of war, which cannot be compassed by fair and honourable hostility, ought not to be compassed at all. An end that has no means, but such as are unlawful, is an unlawful end.

The attack on the manifesto had at least the effect of producing in both Houses of Parliament ministerial disavowals of its expressed policy.

During the next two months the Marquis' attention was almost totally absorbed by the case of Admiral Keppel who was notified (December 11) by the Admiralty that he must face a court martial to answer capital charges arising from the battle of Ushant. This wore the appearance of a political plot hatched by court and Admiralty against an officer who had long enjoyed great public respect and favor. The parliamentary opposition sprang to his defense. The trial was held (January 7 to February 11) at Portsmouth which became a sort of temporary headquarters for the minority politicians, Rockingham taking a house in which Keppel lived during his ordeal. The Admiral's acquittal with honor was the occasion for something like a national celebration which was accompanied in the metropolis by an upsurge of vindictive and violent hostility toward all who were fancied to have been Keppel's enemies. Nothing like this had happened since the "Wilkes and Liberty" riots, and it was the first sign that massive discontent was rising in the country. The flagging spirits of the minority revived. Fox's two motions in early March, to censure the head of the Admiralty, Lord

Sandwich, and to convict ministry of deceiving the country with respect to the state of the navy on outbreak of war with France, produced minority votes of 170 and 174—the largest since early 1770. They only marked, however, the crest of a wave which receded.

As it surged new overtures were made by ministers, split by differing opinions and interests, toward coalition with some opposition leaders. At first an attempt was made to recover Grafton and Camden but failed. Then Fox was sounded, who asked Rockingham if it were not true that the Marquis never would have any part in a ministry not entirely of his own choosing. Envisaging a possible junction with the Bedfordite elements in administration, Fox asked further if Rockingham would at least countenance this by agreeing to some of his friends' taking employment. Admitting to Burke that the country could never be upon the best footing unless the Rockinghams held the reins of government, Fox judged that next to impossible and asked what others were to do who did not agree with their adamant stand.[22] If the Marquis answered Fox he probably did so orally at Portsmouth. On February 3 the chief Bedfordites, Lord President Gower, Lord Chancellor Thurlow, and Secretary of State Weymouth, met with Grafton, said that North was willing to yield up his office, and, professing to speak in the King's name, proposed coalition with the Duke, Camden, and Shelburne. After consultation the three said that no answer could be given until they learned the sentiments of Rockingham and the Duke of Richmond. So ended this negotiation. That the Marquis was informed of it seems to be implied in what Grafton, who is the sole source of information, recorded in his memoirs:

> We derived, however, one essential advantage from the opportunity it gave of shewing to Lord Rockingham, the Cavendishes, Mr. Fox, and their principal friends, that we would not stir, except in conjunction with them. This circumstance cemented the Opposition into a more solid body and furnished the means that Lord Camden and I improved by persuading Lord Shel-

burne not to contest with Lord Rockingham the Treasury, in case a new administration was to be formed.[23]

The Duke of Grafton may have had more confidence in Shelburne's word than the Earl himself had, but from this time there was, for more than a year, a greater measure of concord among the heads of opposition.

Rockingham had their full support when he brought before the Lords (May 11) the state of Ireland, where economic distresses allegedly caused by restraints upon trade were finding expression in associations and boycotting reminiscent of movements in the American colonies before the rebellion. For reasons obvious enough he had an audience with the King six days before his motion, in order to communicate his intention. Evidently he wished to persuade Majesty that he was not acting in a factious manner, and to give his sovereign (into whose closet he had not come since 1767) an opportunity to judge of the loyal spirit animating him. He spoke of commercial concessions, of allowing Ireland to send grain to England and to export some of her woolens (completely prohibited since the reign of William III).[24] The King would not suffer him to speak at length but interrupted to say that such business should come before the House of Commons, although in February the ministry had there refused to take the state of Ireland into consideration. It has been said that his Majesty played a "cat and mouse game" with the Marquis, and that the latter "had his revenge and seemed determined to play with fire" [25] when he moved an address to the crown to lay before Parliament "information concerning the relative state of the trade and manufactures of Great Britain and Ireland," in order that such regulation of commerce might be made "as shall be mutually advantageous to all his Majesty's dominions." He compared the grievances of Ireland with those of America, and warned that Ireland was in a "situation, which if not speedily remedied, would, in the opinion of many, justify resistance." It is certainly true that Rockingham's speech and motion, together with the words of many others spoken on this occasion—indeed the very fact that the affairs of Ireland were brought before the Lords—was interpreted by Irish patriots as a signal that their demands for commercial freedom would be met by British government; but it may be doubted that the Marquis was vengefully employing Irish discontents as a club to beat the King's ministers. His motion, amended by Lord Gower, was carried. It committed administration to lay the information requested before Parliament early in the next session. Fifteen days later, when North in effect repudiated his own supporters in the Lords by denouncing Irish demands as unwarranted, the Marquis spoke of ministerial "duplicity and neglect" which might stir Ireland to a "civil convulsion which would shake the government of these Kingdoms to its foundations." Other peers echoed his indignation, Lord Shelburne even charging that "the American war had commenced upon less provocation than this country had given Ireland." It is not to be doubted that leaders of opposition relished this opportunity to indict the North administration with fresh evidence of its incompetence, and that they were vexed when North in December stole their thunder by giving the Irish what they wanted; but it seems certain that Rockingham in initiating the question had intended nothing more than to get something done to quiet Irish discontents, to heal a wound before it festered. Having never wished to encourage the American colonists along the road to rebellion, he could hardly have desired to do that in Ireland. He was the least likely man in the opposition to play with fire.

As the session ended, although prospects had brightened in America by the successful launching of a campaign in the southern colonies, the national outlook was darkened by Spain's becoming the belligerent ally of France. With American privateers swarming about her coasts and a joint Franco-Spanish naval superiority in the Channel, Great Britain moved into a period of the gravest national peril.[26]

III

Rockingham remained in town or at Wimbledon until August, then went into Yorkshire. Many of the opposition were, like Savile, serving with the territorial militia which was called out by the fear of invasion. During August–September Burke busied himself in the politics of choosing a Buckinghamshire county candidate for an impending by-election. He also took time to tour about. He found that ministers were "universally detested and despised" but sensed no "proportionable desire for a change of men" since opposition did not stand well "with the people at large." Grafton told him that, there being no possibility of a complete change, any opposition leader who received an offer for himself and a few of his principal friends should accept, although not without conditions. "You see," Burke told Rockingham, "that you have the man as long as the Court makes him no offer." Both Fox and Rockingham were to reject this estimate of Grafton, although the Duke seems to have said the same to Camden, whose view at this time was for reducing opposition to a sort of quiet and polite disagreement with administration in order to show the public that they "mean really the good of the whole." So little cement was there among the great leaders that Camden saw no likelihood of "cooperation upon a system." In early October Burke, while admitting that "in the present state of things general county meetings did not seem practical," speculated to his chief on what he thought the very real possibility of setting the City of London in motion "in concurrence with and under the direction of a body of such weight of property and character as was included in the present minority." If that failed "our retreat of any kind would be honourable." Two weeks later Burke reported to Rockingham that he had seen Fox, who had been with Rigby, who had said that the ministry could not hold and that before Parliament met the King "would deliver all things, without any reserve whatever" into the Marquis' hands; but it was impossible, Burke thought, that such a change could occur at such a time. Distrustful as ever of the Chathamites, he urged Rockingham not to plan for the session in concert with them but to settle a plan of his own with his principal friends— "upon grounds and principles, which all opposition profess at least in commons"; this, he said, would either "force concurrence, or oblige those who refuse it to renounce the opinions they have so often declared." [27]

Meanwhile, the Marquis had remained in Yorkshire. From August to November he did not even write to Burke, but he was near to the Cavendishes and appears to have talked over the state of the nation with many Yorkshire friends. Late in September he dashed to Hull which seemed menaced by the appearance of John Paul Jones, but the latter did not attack and the Marquis' purpose was perhaps more political than military; although he was High Steward of Hull his influence there was sagging, and before setting out he planned to be back for the Doncaster Races. He made a speech, offered a battery at his own expense to the ill-defended town, and was much pleased when a secretary of state and the commander-in-chief informed him that the King expressed satisfaction with what he had done. He took a lively interest the next month in the stirring of Middlesex caused by administration's refusal to allow Rockinghamite George Byng to give up his seat for Wigan in order to stand for the vacancy resulting from the death of the Wilkite John Glynn. Byng, who was closely connected with the Duke of Portland, had much support among metropolitan radicals; so that again it could be said that Middlesex electors were denied their choice of representative. "I think a little riot in Middlesex," wrote Rockingham to Portland, "might be near enough his Majesty to wake him in a *flurry*." But not even the opening of the Irish Parliament (October 12) without a government measure decided upon to quiet a country on the brink of revolt from its imperial suzerain could "wake" the King, although it provoked the resignation of Lord President Gower whose example was quickly followed by Secretary of State Weymouth. A successor to the latter was found quickly in Lord Stormont who (like Rockingham) was a nephew of Lord Mansfield; but on the eve of the opening of Parliament the North ministry was nearer to breaking up than ever before. While still in Yorkshire Rockingham thought that its disruption would come soon, and he speculated that perhaps "in a short time" Stormont and Mansfield would advise the King that his ministers lacked public confidence, "that the nation is ruin'd, that there must be a change of men and measures." But the Marquis, like his Majesty, did not believe that the public was yet ready to "acknowledge that those who had so early advised them, and who have so long and so earnestly pressed them, to abandon folly and to reason, have much, or are entitled to much merit." Nor did he see any possible means of restoring "the happiness, the power, and dignity of Great Britain." The colonies were lost beyond redemption, but he dared to hope that "America, cruelly and wickedly as she has been treated, might be calm and cool enough to weigh, whether, in good policy, for *herself,* as *an independent state,* the annihilation of England, as a great European power, was advisable." He was convinced now that the general opinion of the country, although not yet "declared at the market cross of every town," was that "the corrupt influence of the Crown has enabled the Ministers to carry into execution the measures by which this country has been ruined." [28] What the Rockinghamites had for years tried to convince the public of was at last believed. When Parliament met they would exploit as never before this devil-theory of why the nation had been brought to so sorry a state during the reign of George III. The Marquis expected a united opposition and did his best to get a large attendance for the opening on November 25.

An economical reform of court and civil establishment, purging out sinecure places, to reduce at once public expenditures and the corrupting influence of the crown in Parliament, was dictated by the logic of this plausible theory. On such a measure the whole opposition could unite and make a strong appeal to independent men in the House of Commons. Other reforms long favored by radicals, such as more frequent elections, place bills, altering the representation (however abstractly desirable), could only sow divisions among men. Rockingham understood, as would any practical strategist of party, that the right measure at the right time is the one on which all can unite, and he remained steady in this conviction.

Never had administration, since the start of the reign, been so excoriated by so many voices in so formidable an opposition at the very start of a session, as at the opening of Parliament in November 1779. Lord John in Commons and Rockingham in the Lords led off with motions to amend the address by a request to the King to seek new counsels and new ministers. The *Annual Register* described the debates as "masculine, bold, serious, and awful," the attack being against "the pernicious system of government . . . calculated to destroy all principle, and to dissolve the bands of opinion which unite mankind . . . subversive of the national honour and character." One-hundred-thirty-four commoners and 41 peers—extraordinary numbers for so early a day—supported these amendments. And as they were debated the King was suffering his strongest doubts about being able to carry on with the North administration; while in the North Riding of Yorkshire a group of propertied and independent men was taking initial steps toward launching exactly the kind of outdoor movement among exactly the right kind of people which Lord Rockingham had long wished to appear.

Christopher Wyvill, leader of what was to grow into the Yorkshire Association, was a parson turned country squire imbued with zeal for cutting government costs, and for a Parliament less subservient to the crown and more representative of the interests of electors. With a few associates he opened a canvass of Yorkshire freeholders toward obtaining a county meeting of freeholders. He had no connection with Rockingham and wished to keep the enterprise free of the influence of peers, politicians, and members of Parliament; but it was soon evident that he could accomplish little without support from the Rockingham–Savile connection. The Marquis by mid-December was exerting himself to limit the purpose of the movement to economical reform for reducing the influence of the crown, since what he called "speculative propositions" would bring on discord and "the plain and direct road of doing essential because practicable good" would be lost. Tactically conciliatory, Wyvill accepted this limitation in a petition which was almost unanimously adopted by more than 600 men of weight and property gathered at York on December 30. Also agreed upon was the naming of a committee to canvass the county for additional signatures and to promote the same or similar petitions in other counties. Events in Parliament and the metropolis gave a spur to what was done at York. Notable motions for economy measures had been made by Richmond and Shelburne who were publicly thanked by the London Common Council in language which attributed the woeful state of the nation to the swollen influence of the crown. Burke, vividly aware of what was stirring in Yorkshire as well as in the city, gave notice to the House (December 15) that after the holidays he would bring in a specific plan of reform. Rockingham with a corps of friends attended the York meeting. After it he confided to his wife: *"my determination* not to interrupt unanimity among those, who at least have got hold of one right, essential measure for reform, made me most exceedingly inclined to acquiesce in everything." To Burke he wrote, "The generality of those who composed it were persons who I knew and with whom I have long acted and with whom I have long lived in friendship." Even the members of the committee to promote the petition were "almost all gentlemen of weight and character (and I may add that if the nomination of them had been left to me, I should have scarce made an alteration)." [29]

As county after county together with cities and towns were following the model set by Yorkshire, Sir George Savile brought his county's petition with more than 5,000 signatures before the House on February 8. On the same day Shelburne moved in the Lords for a committee, chosen from both Houses and composed of men not in crown employment, to examine into all public accounts. Rockingham spoke at great length in support of the motion and the full strength of peers in opposition was shown in a vote of 55 against ministry's 101. The protest entered upon the journal against the rejection was the first ever signed by all the leading Chathamite and Rockinghamite lords. Three days later Burke moved for leave to bring in a series of bills in which was framed a general plan of economic reform. Horace Walpole, who never liked Burke, said of his famous speech that it was "temperate, moderate, sprinkled with wit and humour, and had such a universal effect on the house, that it was thought he could that day have carried any point he had proposed." [30] It was designed neither to inflame opposition nor to disgrace ministers, but to please and conciliate; and the plan set forth was artful and persuasive, aiming rather at introducing principles of economy into the procedures of government than at a crude hacking away of places. North dared not attempt to mobilize his forces against the motion for leave. When Isaac Barré a few days later offered the same motion which the Lords had rejected from Shelburne, the ministry instead of objecting adopted the measure as its own. In the face of what was occurring in the country, administration dared not then set itself adamantly against economic reform. How narrowly the lines were drawn was shown (February 21) when Savile, going beyond Burke, moved for an account of all crown pensions and North stopped the motion in a large House with a majority of only 2.

Already, however, the seeds of disunion were burgeoning in the reform movement. Wyvill, working through a small Yorkshire subcommittee, was bent on forming a national association to back not only economic reform but shorter parliaments, a "more equal" representation of the people, and "tests" or pledges to be exacted from candidates in the general election due to take place not later than 1781. He went to town early in February and with the zealous collaboration of radicals planned a convention of delegates from the committees of petitioning counties and towns. Hearing of what was under way, Rockingham wrote to a West Riding magistrate who was a member of the Yorkshire committee that he rejoiced in "the spirit which now seems rising in all parts of the country." His native county had done itself honor in taking the lead with "much *sense* and *discretion*" but he declared himself uneasy with respect to rumors of "vague and crude propositions" which now seemed likely to be advanced. How, he asked, could men of honor submit themselves to the bondage of tests or commit themselves in any manner to "propositions . . . loosely and generally worded"? Who could say what "more equal representation" meant as a specifically defined reform? He did not object in principle to fixing the duration of Parliament at five or three years instead of the existing septennate, but annual elections could produce only "confusion and weakness."

> The grievances we feel, and the cause of our misfortune, arise from the *corruption of men chosen into Parliament.* Cut off the ways and means of corruption, and the effect must and will naturally cease. Mr. Burke's plan cuts off thirty-nine offices tenable and now held by members of the House of Commons. It also cuts off eleven now held by peers in the House of Lords. This indeed is *striking in earnest* at the influence of the Crown over persons in Parliament. . . . I think most seriously that if this county of York, at their next proceedings, adhere to the great objects of enforcing frugal expenditure, and striking at the root of corruption, by reducing the ways and means of influence in the Crown, success will attend their endeavors; but if various speculations are gone into . . . I fear, nay, *I am certain,* that there are so many visionary schemes and expedients *by way of reforms on float* that a *general* confusion and disagreement will ensue.[31]

The convention of delegates, which met (March 11 to 20) at St. Alban's Tavern in Westminster, bore out these apprehensions. Many petitioning counties shunned so bold a gathering under the very nose of Parliament, and the men who attended were far from unanimous on the several points in the Plan of Association adopted for submission to the various county and municipal meetings. This program or "platform" went beyond economy in government and reduction of crown influence to embrace the addition to Parliament of a hundred county members, annual elections, tests for candidates, and a law to lower costs and influence in elections. For the sake of opposition unity in Parliament, Rockingham, Richmond, and Shelburne tried jointly to steer the convention away from annual elections, tests, and altering representation,[32] but the apple of discord had been thrown and a "backlash" favorable to administration had set in. On the last day of the convention Burke's bill to reform the court and civil establishments was disemboweled in committee of the whole House and he gave it up, putting off all his bills to a more auspicious time. Yorkshire was first to accept the Plan of Association, although adopting triennial instead of annual parliaments—a Wyvillite concession to the Rockingham interest. The Marquis employed every available means to limit the object of association in his home county to the cause of achieving economical reform, but without the help of Savile who was now very much a Wyvillite. The meeting at York on March 28 rejected the counsel of the master of Wentworth Park. Elsewhere the Plan of Association met a mixed reception. The metropolitan counties and cities quickly followed the example of York. Some counties merely reiterated support for economical reform. Others endorsed the program of the association without taking steps to associate; still others shied away from a movement tinged with radicalism. In Parliament the force of inertia revived and all that opposition could accomplish when the many petitions were brought up for consideration was the passing of several abstract propositions: that "the influence of the crown has increased, is increasing, and ought to be diminished" (carried 233 to 215); that the House of Commons was competent to look into and to correct abuses in civil list expenditures (no division); and that it was the duty of the House to provide "an immediate and

effective redress of the abuses complained of in the petitions"
(no division). No specific reform measure passed Commons except a bill to exclude government contractors from
Parliament. It was thrown out by the Lords. As the session
wore away and attendance dwindled, Rockingham wrote
sadly in mid-May to a Yorkshire friend:

> Abstract principles, theoretically right, will furnish matter for
> disputation in the schools of Utopia, till time is no more. But
> poor old England may pine away and die for want of medicines,
> deemed *slight* ones, and which nevertheless may check her dis-
> order, and may give time for wisdom, sobriety, and attention
> to re-establish her miserable broken constitution.[33]

As the session wore toward its end no visible breach had
opened in the "united" opposition, although the radicalizing
of the petitioning and associating movement certainly started
a disintegrative tendency. Fox, whose most devoted friends
would follow wherever he led, headed the Westminster committee of the association, endorsed radical opinions, spoke
as the "voice of the people," and would be rewarded for his
conduct by a parliamentary seat for Westminster that autumn. This magnetic man exerted a strong seductive influence
on many Rockinghamites although not upon their nominal
leader, Lord John, or upon Burke. Shelburne and his small
party of Chathamites with their long-standing radical connections supported the association's program. So too did
Richmond who had, the previous autumn, concocted his own
half-mad scheme for recasting the administrative, electoral,
and representative system, and on June 2 moved a reform
bill which included annual parliamentary elections, a hundred additional county members, equal electoral districts,
and votes for all over eighteen years of age. On this same
day Parliament was rudely reminded that the metropolitan
populace, instead of blaming the excessive influence of the
crown for the woes of the country, had been persuaded that
the papists were the root of the evil. Ever since the Quebec
Act and Sir George Savile's partial Catholic Relief Act of

1778 Scotch and English dissenters had been simmering or boiling with suspicion and fear of popery, and the principal spokesman for this fanaticism (fed by unsuccessful war against the Catholic Bourbon powers) was Lord George Gordon, a Scotch M.P. for a Wiltshire borough and president of the Protestant Association in London–Westminster. After teasing the House with his eccentric opinions through the 1780 session, he brought in a petition (June 2) for repeal of the Savile act. A mob of many thousands who had assembled in St. George's Fields in support of this petition marched upon Parliament, surged about St. Stephen's, and invaded the lobbies and galleries of both Houses. The freedom of Parliament was assaulted, many lives were endangered, and a week of intermittent criminal disorders followed until royal troops were employed to suppress them. The Rockingham leadership and Fox too rallied to the cause of law and order, but Shelburne did not and ugly rumors arose which unjustly involved him and his connections in the instigation of the criminal violence. He went away resolving to go no more to Parliament, and the hinge of the united opposition was broken. Richmond went to the brink of doing the same until coaxed back by the Marquis. All parts of opposition suffered much discredit with the public, as did the Wyvillite association; while the administration, however battered, discordant, and disgraced, drew profit from the discomfiture of its opponents.

Soon after the riots the long gloomy aspect of the war in America was suddenly brightened by news of the fall of Charleston to General Clinton's forces. What with this auspicious event and the backlash of opinion against all outdoor political activity, North meditated an early dissolution of Parliament; and to strengthen government in the elections he opened negotiations with opposition leaders. At the end of June, he employed his Rockinghamite nephew Frederick Montagu to ask the Marquis on what terms he and his friends would make part of and support a coalition ministry. Complying with this request, Rockingham specified nothing for himself but proposed Fox and Richmond as secretaries of state, the dismissal of Germain and Sandwich, the placing of Keppel at the head of the Admiralty, and lesser places for several other Rockinghamites. Further, he stipulated for the King's acceptance of economic reform plus certain cognate measures and the recognition of American independence if peace could not be obtained without it. These terms were objectionable to his Majesty and North's subsequent counterproposal to compromise them met with no response from the Marquis.[34]

When he was first approached by North, it is probable that Rockingham considered requesting an audience with the King. The undated draft in Burke's hand (quoted at the start of this chapter) fits this historical moment better than any other. It was prepared to serve as a memorandum (to be left with the King) of substantially what Rockingham intended to communicate in the royal closet. It was never communicated because no audience took place, but the document is a perfect mirror of what he and his intimates wished the King to believe of them. Avowing that his own inclinations were "as cordial to your service as possible," the Marquis wished to "know from your Majesty yourself, and not from any one else, your own real sentiments, and the real extent of your intentions with regard to a change of your administration." He was apprehensive lest some misinformed persons had told the King "that I meant to distress you, or to use compulsory, or other disagreeable ways of coming into your service." Nothing was farther from the truth: he had ever had "all the imaginable regard and reverence" for his sovereign whose honor was as dear to him as his own.

> . . . nothing, but the very unusual exigency of your affairs, could prevail upon me to accept of any employment whatever; and certainly there are no circumstances in which I shall accept of it unless I have reason to understand, that on the part of your Majesty my appointment is one of the freest; and a thing which you not only consent to but actually command.

If Rockingham were so commanded his Majesty must not

expect, still less fear, that "a violent revolution in all establishments" would result. For some men now in office the Marquis professed a high regard, and "if others are pleasing to you Sir, it is reason enough for me to fall in with any moderate wish of theirs," for he represented no "persecuting party principle." But some changes of the first importance would have to be made: none of the present ministers should "take the lead" or all benefits from the change would be lost. If he and some of his friends were merely to take office in the present system

Nobody would consider me, or any of those who do me the honour to concur with me, in any other light, than that of venal men who wanted places—and this would, at the very first step, take away all heart and confidence from your people, at the time when they want most to be encouraged. . . . The revolted colonies would see no new inducements for reconciliation upon any plan which could be offered; and the courts of Europe would see no new grounds for forming fresh engagements or for renewing the old. So that the present system, instead of being changed and amended, would seem only to be strengthened by the accession of those men who, by a subordinate junction with those whom they opposed, had . . . thereby renounced their principles, and justly forfeited every degree of public confidence. . . . Indeed Sir dissentions must inevitably arise in such a system which would suffer nothing to prosper, and that unanimity of measures from whence we must derive all our hopes of salvation, instead of being promoted, would I greatly fear be effectually destroyed; and there is this further evil in it, that if that scheme should fail your Majesty would have no longer any men of character and reputation for probity to whom you could apply yourself and this is a very serious consideration.

. . . That in all these considerations, and many more which must occur to your Majesty's own penetration, it will be necessary, if your Majesty wishes any change, (and all I say is on a supposition that you do freely and entirely wish it) that your New Ministry may set out with every possible mark of your confidence and support, which they will want in the utmost extent it can be given in the arduous and dreadful undertaking they are to engage in.[35]

The memorandum indicated in the most general fashion the
measures which would have to be adopted by the kind of
new ministry which the Marquis and his friends could share
in and support, but it made no allusion to recognizing American independence if "reconciliation" proved unattainable.
Such was the picture drawn for the royal eyes (which never
were to see it) of what Rockingham and his allies would
be and do if they consented to take office.

IV

He was at Wentworth when he got the startling news (September 1) that Parliament was dissolved. This had been
expected but not so soon, not in the midst of the harvest
season. He had been with Lord John Cavendish at York
Races the previous week and had not even assembled the
Rockingham Club, so that he was unprepared for the elections which must now come on and therefore was very angry.
The court, he wrote to Portland on hearing the news, wishes
"to secure as many tools to be elected as possible, in order
to have a large body of Banditti to controul, thwart &
betray any *Men* who venture to undertake administration
when the present ministers perhaps flye their country." He
was in near-panic over county politics and "could scarcely
guess what may happen" at the county meeting called for
September 15 to choose candidates. Sir George Savile would
of course be adopted again unanimously, but Rockingham
did not wish to see the return of Edwin Lascelles who supported the American war, and the possibility of a contest
at the poll was a dreadful thought. Yet there was no acceptable successor to Lascelles in sight. Difficulty was compounded by the Marquis' being somewhat out of step with
Savile who had endorsed the program of the association, a
formidable new force in county politics. "The Associating
Gentlemen," he told Portland, "are quite wild." Not until
September 8 did an old and trusted friend, Henry Duncombe, who was of the association but not "wild," come forward as a candidate and thus save the master of Wentworth

from a humiliating failure. Duncombe was adopted by the county meeting and Lascelles' threat of a contest soon faded. The influence of the association was strong too in York city where there was a threat of what the Marquis called a "hurly burly." Charles Turner, always rather acceptable than pleasing to Rockingham, bowed to the association but Lord John defied it. Both were returned again without a contest. In his own nomination boroughs the Marquis routinely secured the return of the old members. The only clear setback to the Rockingham–Savile interest was at Hull where David Hartley failed to hold the seat he had narrowly won six years before. The Marquis had little regard for Hartley but Sir George prized him and was afterward vexed at his old friend's refusal to try to find another seat for him.[36]

The 1780 elections were in no sense a national contest between administration and opposition. There were fewer contests than in 1774 and the number of new men coming into Parliament was not unusually large; but time was to show that the 1780 House of Commons, though under North's control, was less safely so. There was a considerable increase of members who *might* desert administration if its affairs went very badly. Rockingham could not know this in the early autumn, could not form any judgment on the complexion of Parliament until it met. Fox's victory in Westminster (although a government candidate headed the poll) was a hopeful sign. Still more pleasing to Rockingham was Keppel's triumph in contesting the metropolitan county of Surrey after being turned out of his former seat for Windsor by a court-backed candidate. On the other hand Burke's loss of his Bristol seat was a severe reverse confronting the Marquis with the problem how to get this indispensable man back into Parliament. Love had long been dying between Burke and his Bristol constituents. He had no relish for the sort of electioneering required in a city of 5,000 electors. His voting for trade concessions to Ireland and setting his face against anti-popery, together with his inability as a member of Parliament in opposition to nurse his constituency with favors from government, had turned large numbers against him. If Rockingham knew this, as it is hard to believe that he did not, the question arises why he never said a word to Burke about providing another seat if Bristol were lost. Perhaps he hoped that Burke would try the harder to overcome his difficulties. "We are vastly hurt at the failure of Bristol," wrote Lady Rockingham to Keppel (September 17) ; "but our good and *wonderful* friend stands in a high and amiable light in that business." The Marquis was resolved that Burke must be in Parliament, if necessary for one of his own nomination boroughs; but the elections at both Malton and Higham Ferrers were over by the time the bad news from Bristol was known at Wentworth. No vacancy could be created until the new House met. Since Frederick Montagu, member for Higham, was of considerable stature in Parliament, one of the Malton members would have to be persuaded to give up his seat. Ultimately Savile Finch, who had never cut a figure in the House, was induced to make way for Burke.[37]

During all his years as a politician seeking to hold men together in a parliamentary opposition Rockingham had never advanced a single step toward promoting any sort of national organization of electors to support whig candidates. This was not only because such an effort would have been impractical, so great a part of the representation in Parliament being of property rather than of persons, and electors being far too attached to local interests and too ignorant of national affairs. It was also because he believed that men were more important than measures. The recruiting of strength for his party was mainly the work of finding men who were willing and able to act upon right principles, and helping them to get into Parliament. More often than not men of that sort had little relish or ability for contesting the so-called open constituencies wherein electors had to be flattered and bribed. Rockinghamites never could have become a popular party. In boroughs of large electorates (more than 1,000 voters), friends of the Marquis contested in only 4 (Bristol, Hull, Liverpool, Lincoln) and failed in all. Rockingham encouraged William Baker to stand in London but the vacancy expected there did not appear, and Baker contested instead for the borough of Hertford, winning by a narrow majority—but reputably, since that borough was regarded as one of the least corrupt in England. Rockinghamites were far better suited to the representation of nomination boroughs—what Burke called the "little sally ports of the constitution"—and to county seats for which rival interests arranged compromises in order to avoid contests at the polls. The only great Rockinghamite popular triumph in 1780 was Keppel's in Surrey (4,000 electors), and that was largely a metropolitan tribute to the brave sailor who had been so nearly martyred the year before. Most of the electioneering done by the Marquis and his friends consisted in writing letters wide over the country to enlist the influence of friends in behalf of particular candidates. The Marquis was able to bring 3 friends into Parliament for Cornish boroughs because the proprietor of them, Edward Elliot, having turned against administration, invited him to supply the nominations.[38]

Before the opening (October 30) of the new parliament, the temper of which no one could yet know, Rockingham formed an idea "that the majority of those who are not chose by actual ministerial influence" were "more likely to join in destroying the ruinous system . . . than to become supporters of it."[39] He wished economic reform to be brought forward again, and saw, or thought that he saw, many signs not only in Yorkshire but in other counties of a disposition to keep that measure from being mixed with radical reforms. The pre-Christmas part of the session was too short (only 5 weeks) for ministry or opposition to judge accurately how the new House of Commons would act. It was ill-attended by country gentlemen favorable to cutting the costs of court and government; so that the great Rockinghamite measure was put off until after the holidays. Not Lord John but Fox and his friends were the main voices of futile opposition. Shelburne stayed away, Camden saw the new parliament as "more devoted to the court than the former," and Richmond thought that the nation was still afflicted by "a general stupidity and indolence." The Marquis was perfectly inactive as a politician in these weeks and naturally many complained of this; but it is easy enough to understand. He was publicly committed to three great purposes, not to an unremitting opposition for opposition's sake. He stood for an end to the war in America, a general economic reform of court and administration, and a reduction of the influence of the crown in Parliament. There never had been a worse time for opponents of military suppression of American rebellion to open their mouths on the subject. The royal forces appeared to be advancing triumphantly in the southern colonies. A recent president of the American Congress, Henry Laurens of South Carolina, had been taken at sea and was a state prisoner in the Tower; and before Parliament rose for the holidays it was known that General Arnold, reputed in England to be the ablest of American officers, had deserted an apparently hopeless cause. Rockingham's other public commitments were the twin aims of Burke's bill, but even if there had been an adequate attendance before Christmas the moving of that measure had to be delayed until Burke got back into Parliament.

After a call of the House to secure maximum attendance Burke opened the business on February 15. North was still too uncertain of his strength to oppose the motion for leave which Burke had again asked in a speech designed to conciliate and win favor. When the bill came to second reading on February 26, however, it met a stunning reversal: instead of being sent to committee it was put off for six months, i.e., disposed of for the session, by 233 to 190. Many members would have voted for commitment had not North made it clear to all his friends that such a vote would have been a vote against the King's administration. Two truths were now evident, first, that the Parliament of 1780 favored the reform, and second, that it could not be passed until administration was in the hands of men resolved to carry it.

From this time all efforts of opposition were easily repulsed by the ministerial forces, and the 1781 session of Parliament ended without any serious public uneasiness over

the fortunes of war. Cornwallis' conquests were indeed withering as his army suffered maiming losses in North Carolina,
but little that was ominous could be read in the intelligences
published in England. A few days before Parliament rose
(July 18) his junction with Arnold in Virginia was reported.
That this army might be on its way to the trap at Yorktown
was unsuspected in England until mid-October. In comparison with the panic fright of 1779 the year 1781, until the
autumn, was marked by a revival of public confidence in the
King's fleets and armies.

V

The Yorktown surrender, known in England on the eve
of the opening of Parliament (November 27), was the
prime cause of the reversion of administration to the whigs,
but it took almost five months to work this effect. Slowly
and reluctantly North's supporters in Parliament fell away
until by mid-March 1782 he knew that he had lost beyond
hope of recovery the power to manage the King's business
in the House of Commons. The disintegrating process was
in no sense a progressive conversion of members to the
political views of Rockingham, Burke, Fox, and others
identified as men of a party who had long foreseen and
warned against the resort to arms in North America. Men
who prophesy failure are far more likely to be blamed for
the failure than applauded for sagacious foresight; the
Rockinghamites experienced that painfully. What took place
was only a negative recoil against an administration which
seemed unable to contrive a way to extricate the country
from its troubles. Ministers decided against further effort
to subdue the colonies well in advance of the motion offered
by General Conway (February 22) and carried by 234 to
215 against "the further prosecution of offensive warfare on
the continent of America." On this point there was virtual
unanimity but that did not mean that the Atlantic bases at
New York, Charleston, and Savannah should now be given
up, still less that the independence of the former colonies

should necessarily be recognized by Great Britain. It meant only that the armed contest with the Bourbon powers must no longer be embarrassed by an attempt to reconquer America. Many, including Rockingham, Fox, and Richmond, favored the earliest possible recognition of the independence of the colonies in order to extinguish their interest in continuing an alliance with France. Some ministers—certainly North—held the same opinion but dared not so advise the King who was implacably opposed to surrendering British sovereignty. Shelburne was reputed to be against according American independence prior to negotiations from which he hoped that an independent America in some sort of permanent special relationship with Great Britain might emerge. Thus, neither on this great matter nor on any other was there, as North sank, any agreement among whig leaders; and even if there had been there was no certainty that chiefs of opposition in union would be supported by all who now looked to the King to change his administration. Many dreaded the coming into great office of Fox, a notorious gambler who had so recently endorsed radical constitutional reform. If North had been able to envisage another set of ministers acceptable to the King and capable of carrying on his business, he might have resigned earlier than March 20.

The general sentiments were not for a party administration but for a national coalition of leaders irrespective of party. In the debate of March 15 on a motion to declare no confidence in the ministry Lord John Cavendish said that to pass it would mean not to place the opposition in power but only "to take the executive government from the present hands, and leave it to His Majesty to frame the new administration as His Majesty should think most proper." That Majesty's choice of men for the new administration must inevitably be limited to those who were not only willing but able to serve him, went without saying.

The King had already begun to change the ministry. Germain, on whom so great a share of responsibility for disaster in America was laid, had been replaced in January; and a month later an attempt was made to coax back Gower,

Weymouth, and Grafton but without success. Nor could Shelburne, Richmond, and Fox be persuaded to coalesce with the existing administration. Not until he had found "every description of men unwilling to stand forth" did the King authorize Lord Chancellor Thurlow to sound the heads of opposition on a proposal for a national coalition. The Chancellor asked Rockingham on March 11 if he could propose a plan for a "broad bottom" ministry. The Marquis declared himself willing to serve his sovereign but said that no good could be done "unless his Majesty's mind was open to receive a plan of measures, widely differing from those by which this country has been undone." Since no ministry could have sufficient strength without the King's support, Rockingham said further that he could not open to anyone on a plan of administration until he knew "his Majesty's disposition towards me" and until he was assured of the King's agreement to "certain propositions as necessary to be assented to." These were: no veto on American independence, assent to the economical reform bill, and acceptance of certain cognate measures for disfranchising revenue officers and excluding government contractors from Parliament. Should his Majesty be agreeable to these measures the Marquis, upon being so informed, would ask to be admitted to the royal closet "to enter with his Majesty, into a plan for an arrangement of such men in high offices, as would carry on the Administration of this country, with honour, dignity, and I hoped, with advantage." He also told Thurlow that he hoped the expression "broad bottom" did not signify a royal desire to retain in a new administration "any of the persons who had been considered as obnoxious ministers, or any of those who were deemed as belonging to a sort of secret system, from which many attributed all the evils of the present reign." [40] If a cat-and-mouse game was being tried with him the Marquis was putting up his guard.

After reporting back to the King the Chancellor sent a rather evasive note to Rockingham in which he seemed to make his opening to the latter a mere detail in carrying out Majesty's commission "to ask of those, whose situation might enable them . . . whether they could hold out to his Majesty any plan for quieting our intestine divisions, and forming an Administration, on such broad foundation as might give satisfaction, and promise permanency." He said he had told the King that Rockingham had "wished to be excused from entering upon the subject of the arrangement" which was a "final answer to my mission." With respect to the Marquis' specific propositions which were the conditions of his willingness to do what the King had been told that he would not do, Thurlow said that he had mentioned these in a general way as "sentiments" in favor of an early peace and a rigid economy in the spending of public money; which sentiments, the Chancellor added, were naturally shared by the King who rightly regarded them as "rather objects to be pursued by an administration when formed, than a basis to form it upon." Manifestly the hour of the reversion was not yet, but the exchanges between Thurlow and Rockingham were the occasion for the latter to affirm orally and then in writing:

> I could not with prudence and propriety enter a plan of arrangement until I was first personally assured of his Majesty's confidence, and of his gracious disposition to attend to my ideas on that subject. I must confess that I do not think it an advisable measure, first to attempt to form a Ministry by arrangement of office—afterwards to decide upon what principles or measures they are to act.[41]

To George III these opinions were an affront upon kingship, tantamount to saying that he who was over all men, and had a responsibility to seek the good of all, should contract with some men to help them to rule his kingdom; that he should as it were place himself in their hands. Not so did he understand the duty of the hereditary executive in that British constitution which he venerated. George III's fear of the "Great Party," his fallacious idea that his grandfather had been enslaved by the politicians, and the dislike of politicians which was in him even before his accession to the throne, appear to have incapacitated him for understand-

ing that Rockingham and his friends had no idea of placing their sovereign in a state of subjection to themselves.
They did indeed desire to restrict what they regarded as an
excessive influence of crown and court in Parliament, so that
Parliament might become more responsive to the great,
varied natural interests of the kingdom. They were resolved
too upon bringing civil list expenditures under parliamentary regulation, but they equaled the King in reverence for
that half-sacred structure, the "constitution as settled by the
Revolution." Long experience as a principal minister and in
opposition had taught the Marquis what the King knew
from the beginning of his reign—namely, that firm closet
support was necessary to ministers for the management of
the King's business in Parliament. He had learned too from
experience that ministers needed to be bound together in
mutual trust in order to prevent rivalry among themselves
for the royal favor, and to stop the attempts of others to
undermine the sovereign's confidence in his ostensible servants. If Majesty came to an opinion from a judgment of the
state of the nation that ministers had mismanaged government and produced widespread discontents among subjects,
Rockingham would have been the last man to dispute the
royal right and duty to dismiss them. For how many years
had he wished King George to fire North, Sandwich, Germain, Hillsborough, Jenkinson! The Marquis desired neither to dispute the sovereign's right of choice in employing
ministers nor to force his hand in any way. But British subjects, however devoted to their sovereign, were free to refuse
the employments of the crown or to accept on terms they
judged proper.

At the time of the Rockingham–Thurlow exchanges the
King was still resolved against a whig administration, still
determined never to treat with the heads of opposition. Less
than a week later he was confronted with the alternatives
of treating with them or abdicating. On North's advice he
reluctantly sent for Shelburne and soon discovered that he
still had cards to play in his imaginary game of saving his
royal person from enslavement by the magnates of whiggery.

Lord Shelburne, who had entered the political scene in the service of Bute and Fox and then attached himself to Chatham, relished administrative responsibilities but detested acting with men in party. Preferring power to friendships, he liked to work with subordinates instead of colleagues, and therefore he had never developed much regard for Rockingham. The King knew this when he now invited him to form a "broad bottom" system of Bedfordites (Thurlow, Gower, Weymouth), Chathamites (Camden and Grafton), and the Rockinghamites. He said that he could not, that the Rockinghamites would not take part in it, and that in the existing circumstances Lord Rockingham was the only man who could form an administration because only he had a large and loyal body of friends. After an unsuccessful attempt to induce Lord Gower to do the impossible, Majesty faced the inevitable, yet managed to use Shelburne as a go-between in treating with the Marquis.

The latter was now, in a certain sense, cornered—placed in the awkward position of being the only man able to form an administration in the dangerous hour when North had resigned and the ministry was in dissolution. Seventeen years before he had taken a great part in helping to rescue his sovereign from a disagreeable situation, but he had not then a program of measures to which he was publicly committed. Now he met Shelburne on the ground he had taken with Thurlow. A cabinet should be formed, he said, which would be suitable for carrying out "the very important measures" which he had submitted to the King through the Lord Chancellor:

> Upon Lord Rockingham being assured that his Majesty consents to these measures, and that he shall have their consent confirmed by his Majesty himself, Lord Rockingham is willing to state to Lord Shelburne his ideas of a Cabinet likely to concur in the principles of those measures, and therefore fit for the execution of them; upon which, if Lord Shelburne agrees, Lord Rockingham will proceed to talk with Lord Shelburne on the subject of other arrangements.

The Marquis had of course been consulting constantly with friends for many days and had prepared a plan for a new cabinet. It placed him at the Treasury with Lord John as Chancellor of the Exchequer; Fox and Shelburne were to be secretaries of state; Richmond was assigned to the Ordnance and Conway named commander-in-chief; the lord president would be Camden and the privy seal was for Grafton; Keppel would head the Admiralty. The Great Seal was left open. What happened between 6:30 P.M., March 24, when the above communication to Shelburne was written, and 2 hours later when Shelburne answered it, is not clear.[42] That the cabinet plan had been given to him is evident from what he said: "The names his Lordship has been pleased to enclose are so respectable that it is unnecessary for Lord Shelburne to give any opinions upon them." But he made no allusion to the Marquis' measures and insistence that assent to these be first confirmed *by his Majesty himself*. He said that he would that night see Camden and Grafton "whom it will be necessary to consult so far as regards themselves, as well as in regard to the formation of the whole," and that he would be ready the next morning to meet with Rockingham "for the purpose of considering further." They met and completed the plan, adding Dunning to the cabinet in the office of chancellor of the Duchy of Lancashire and leaving the Great Seal to Thurlow, and sketched out a list of removals and nominations. Burke was named Paymaster and Isaac Barré Treasurer of the navy. But this list was not completed until after the cabinet plan was presented by Shelburne to the King, who accepted it.

There is no evidence that Rockingham entered the closet to hear from the royal lips a promise to support his "very important measures," or that he received an assurance of that in any other way. Instead he gave way to the urgent necessities of the hour, counseled by friends and by his own understanding. To maintain his stand, and thus hold up the installation of a cabinet containing all the leading whigs of the opposition, could only have infuriated the King and incurred disapproval by many. It was widely believed, however, that he had exacted the necessary assurances from George III. Horace Walpole, who had always deprecated him, wrote on March 26 that the Marquis "triumphed without the shadow of compromise of any sort, this is most religiously true, he deserves all praise and all support." [43] The *Annual Register* for 1782 alluded to the public measures he "was said" to have stipulated "with the court" before consenting to form an administration.

VI

So began the second "Rockingham administration"—flawed from the start by the long-enduring jealousies of Rockinghamites and Chathamites, weakened by lack of royal confidence, facing the same Parliament which had so reluctantly withdrawn its support from North, and facing too the prospect of having to do many disagreeable and unpopular things in the liquidation of an unsuccessful war. Before he was confronted with the necessity of treating with the King through Shelburne, the Marquis seems to have envisaged a cabinet on what Burke called "a new system" in which every branch of the state would be in his own hands and those he could perfectly trust: a cabinet of great collective strength which would be the sole source of advice to the throne. Such a cabinet might wear the appearance of being "broad bottom" but Rockingham and his closest friends should be in command of it.[44] In the circumstances this could not be. No doubt Rockingham hoped for a greater coherence than the event proved since he did not know until after he had kissed hands as First Lord of the Treasury that the King expected him to share with Shelburne in recommending appointments in the various offices. His Majesty saw the new administration as what in truth it was—a coalition of rival politicians—and Shelburne enjoyed a favor with the King which Rockingham never was able to gain. Thus a duel over patronage and peerages started even before all members of the new cabinet were in office. Shelburne, having few personal followers in Parliament, showed a great desire to gain more by conferring obligations through patronage; while Rockingham had more friends than he could decently take care of, and moreover thought it unwise to carry out a wholesale turnover in all the lower offices.

The economic reform bill was now a measure for deliberation in cabinet. There it ran into unforeseen difficulties. The whole aspect of the business underwent a change when its sponsors were no longer opposition men zealous to reduce the influence of the crown but ministers needing that influence. That they were in office was proof in itself that this influence was not as malignant as they had contended. The scope of the measure inevitably contracted. The King wished to reserve to himself whatever reforms might be made in the royal household, leaving the rest of the civil list to Parliament. This would have emasculated the measure. His Majesty also was disinclined to initiate the business by a royal message to Parliament, the usual manner in which an important piece of legislation was started. After much wrangling in cabinet the ministers were brought to an agreement which enabled Rockingham to point out to the King that to exclude the household from the parliamentary bill would "prevent the display of your Majesty's bounty to the public . . . make it look diminutive, and raise doubts and suspicions on a matter which is undertaken to produce quiet and satisfaction." Rockingham promised that "not a single article of the expense to be retrenched touches any thing whatsoever which is personal to your Majesty, or to your Majesty's royal family, or which in the least contributes to the splendour of your Court." No offices were to be abolished, he said, except those "which may answer the purposes of us, or of those who may hereafter be your Majesty's Ministers, and which may serve to carry points and support interests of theirs, and not of yours." Sacrificing the opportunity to keep and fill these places with his friends was "the greatest act of self-denial" in the Treasury Minister's life. How useful these would be for "what is called strengthening political interest and connexion"—but the Marquis could not in conscience try to make himself "considerable" at his sovereign's expense! One would hardly suspect from this unusual paper that the grand argument for economic reform had previously been to reduce the influence of the crown. It was even contended that the places slated for abolition had been a source of weakness to "the administration of your late servants" because the holders of them

> did not attend as they ought to your Majesty's honour and service, so as to prevent by their diligence and foresight the disagreeable things that, without due care, will happen in Parliament, as well as those greater calamities which have happened to the nation.

It is not easy to envisage Rockingham as disingenuous enough to write this appeal to the King.[45] Probably someone else—very likely Burke—drafted it for him. It concluded by stating that if the reform of the whole civil list were not brought into Parliament by "those who have been the proposers and supporters of this salutary measure" disgrace would fall deservedly upon them, and that it would be introduced any way by "the country gentlemen, and the many persons in the House of Commons, who so highly approve of the principle of the bill." On April 15 the royal message was read in Parliament and Paymaster Burke brought in the bill, along with a second for the economic reform of his own office. These measures, as well as two others to which Rockingham was publicly committed—excluding government contractors from Parliament and disfranchising revenue officers—made their way with little difficulty to the statute book. Thus did Rockingham, who would be in his grave before the enacting process was completed, keep faith with the public.

To keep such faith—so to act in office that public trust in public men was not destroyed—had long been to the Marquis not only the preferred role of his friends but a dictate of personal honor. Obeying it, he became the first head of a British cabinet to come into office with a program of measures—a sort of platform!—and carry it into law. It has been common among historians to point out that the principal law, Burke's Civil Establishment Act, had smaller results than were expected and even some ill-effects not foreseen. So it has been with most legislative reforms, but at least Burke's bill secured in the British constitution the principle of parliamentary regulation of all executive expenditures.[46] For this Rockingham and his friends had contended in 1769 and 1777, so that also in this respect they vindicated the consistency of their public conduct.

Winning the royal assent to abandoning British sovereignty over the United States was a task which never fell upon Rockingham. He would indeed have liked the earliest possible opening of negotiations with them as independent states, but Shelburne and other ministers too—even Fox for a time—were for making such recognition a bargaining point. The practical business of terminating what was nothing less than a world war was certain to be a long and complicated work. It was in the hands of the secretaries of state who soon found themselves in conflict with each other over the strategy of peacemaking. If Rockingham had not been repeatedly ill during these months his arts of conciliation and compromise might have prevented the head-on collision of Fox and Shelburne in late June, when the Treasury Minister lay dying.

On July 1 the Marquis expired and with him his short-lived administration which none thought glorious. Ministers had not made peace, had even underestimated the capacity of Great Britain to withstand her enemies in what remained of the hostilities. Their coming into office and quick recall of one viceroyal administration in Ireland in order to name another headed by the Duke of Portland had raised apparently irresistible expectations and demands in the Irish Parliament for independence, with the result that British ministers felt themselves compelled to surrender the authority of the British legislature over that kingdom. The Rockingham administration had divided on parliamentary

reform, leaving it an open question in Parliament where
young William Pitt's motion to bring on consideration of
it was defeated. So that the hopes and expectations raised
among radicals by the coming into office of such men as
Fox, Richmond, and Shelburne were blasted.

Many words of praise for the dead Minister were uttered
in Parliament, but the almost instant royal appointment of
Shelburne to succeed him captured the attention of all. The
nation did not mourn his death. Not until his body was
carried into Yorkshire were great public honors accorded.
In York Minster he lies in an unmarked space within the
tomb of his parents.

His estates passed to his nephew Earl Fitzwilliam, but not
the marquisate. That peerage became extinct and never was
revived. Burke wrote to Fitzwilliam on July 3: "You are
Lord Rockingham in every thing. . . . I have no doubt
that you will take it in good part, that his old friends, who
were attached to him by every tie of affection, and of principle, and among others myself, should look to you, and
should not think it an act of forwardness and intrusion to
offer you their services." But this young lord could not,
knew that he could not, and dared not even try to, play the
role of his uncle in whig politics. There was no one but the
Duke of Portland to qualify for the honor of being head of
the whigs. Richmond was too eccentric, too much "the radical Duke," to lead a party. If Fox and Lord John Cavendish had been able to prevail upon the King, not Shelburne
but Portland would have been placed at the head of the
ministry. Lord John declined to remain in an administration
headed by Shelburne, who appeared to many of the Rockinghamites as likely to re-establish, with court backing, the
kind of administration associated in their minds with Bute,
Grenville, and North. Fox, whose peacemaking strategy had
been blocked by Shelburne in the cabinet, cordially detested
the new first Minister and quickly resigned. Burke too, but
with some misgivings, gave up the Pay Office. A majority

of some hundred and fifty supporters of the deceased Marquis who met at his, now Fitzwilliam's, house on July 7 were for a mass desertion of Shelburne,[47] but Richmond did not agree and stayed at the Ordnance. Keppel retained the Admiralty for six months before resigning, although two Rockinghamites quit his board. A half-dozen others gave up sub-ministerial places. The party thus found itself in a state rather like that of the friends of Rockingham and Newcastle in 1766, partly in and partly out.

Men would go on talking about the "Rockingham party" for a good many years, even though it now was led by Fox and the Duke of Portland. In 1783 these leaders startled the political world by forming a coalition with North to drive out Shelburne and, almost literally, to storm the royal closet. This course scandalized many, and both elements in the coalition lost strength on that account. It is not easy to imagine Rockingham being enticed along this fatal path. He had resisted similar temptations in 1767, 1778, and 1780, thinking it not right conduct to risk weakening the public faith in the sincerity of public men. At his first opportunity the King turned out the coalition ministers and gave strong closet support to young Pitt at the head of an administration which lasted almost as long as Sir Robert Walpole's. The Rockingham party with the name still in current language was now almost lost in the much diminished band of "coalition" whigs headed by Portland and captained by Fox. They had severe reverses in the 1784 elections. Sir George Savile died that year and Fitzwilliam failed to prevent the collapse of the Rockingham system of politics in Yorkshire, Lord John Cavendish losing his seat and going out of Parliament for a decade. As the years passed, death levied a heavier toll upon the older Rockinghamites than upon the younger generation of whigs who adored Fox. His friends virtually expelled Burke from the party in 1791 for differing with them over the French Revolution. After three years of attempting to prevent the divisive issues arising out of that political earthquake from splitting the whig party, Portland separated from Fox and led a section of the shrunken corps into wartime coalition with Pitt. At the same time Burke, who rejoiced in this junction, retired from Parliament; at 65 he had a slow but mortal disease upon him. Fitzwilliam entered the new coalition and presently went as viceroy to Ireland where he so acted as to come to an irreparable rupture with Portland. "As to our old friends," wrote the dying Burke to Fitzwilliam on January 4, 1797, "they are so many individuals, not a jot more seperated from your Lordship, than they are from one another. There is no mutual affection, communication, or concert between them." [48] The epilogue to the Rockingham story had ended.

NOTES

1. WWM R 155: 1–2.

2. *Grafton*, 275–278.

3. The varied positions of leading whigs in relation to the American war are described in G. H. Guttridge, *English Whiggism and the American Revolution* (rev. ed.; Berkeley, 1966), Ch. 3; and in A. S. Foord, *His Majesty's Opposition, 1714–1830* (Oxford, 1964), 321–362. The character of the Chathamites has been drawn by Peter Browne in *The Chathamites* (London–New York, 1967), esp. 34–108. The parliamentary conduct of Conway, Fox, and Wilkes has been accurately and succinctly described by John Brooke in *Hist. Parl.* II 244–246, 455–461; III 639–640.

4. WWM R 1: 1668; *Corr. Burke* III 282.

5. *Ibid.*, 291; WWM R 1: 1676, 1680.

6. Portland MSS: Sayre to Portland 7 Sept; Rockingham to Portland 10 Sept; Portland to Sayre n.d.

7. WWM R 1: 1686; Albemarle II 297–298.

8. *Corr. Burke* III 295–297.

9. Both addresses were first printed in Burke's *Works* (Rivington ed.) IX 173–215.

10. *Corr. Burke* III 309–315; Olson, *Radical Duke*, 171–172. The Duke of Manchester had recommended to Rockingham (15 Dec.) that someone be sent to Franklin.—WWM R 1: 1696. In an undated draft of a letter to an unidentified person the Marquis praised "the vigour, magnanimity & determined resolution" of Franklin and predicted that he would "plead forcibly" at the French court and that the Bourbon courts would not pass up an opportunity "to deal a deadly blow to this country."—R 78: 15.

11. *Corr. Burke* III 315–317.

12. WWM R 1: 1692; Albemarle II 304–307.

13. *Last Journals* II 93.

14. *Correspondence of the Right Honourable Edmund Burke* (1844) II 181–182; *Corr. Burke* III 378–389.

15. WWM R 1: 1695b and 1715 are drafts of letters showing Rockingham's aversion to Markham, with whom Burke had quarreled bitterly some years before.

16. *Corr. Burke* III 392–393

17. WWM R 1: 1739.

18. *Chatham* IV 450–456

19. *Ibid.,* 457–464

20. *Ibid.,* 491.

21. Albemarle II 353–356

22. Fox to Rockingham, 24 Jan.—*Ibid.,* 371–374.

23. *Grafton,* 307–308.

24. His notes for the audience are extant: WWM R 91: 31.

25. H. Butterfield, *George III, Lord North, and the People, 1779–1780* (London, 1949), 88–89.

26. Cf. J. E. Bunce, "The Whigs and the Invasion Crisis," in *Crisis in the "Great Republic,"* ed. G. L. Vincitorio (New York, 1969), 131–154.

27. *Corr. Burke* IV 139–145; Camden to Grafton, 21 Oct. in *Grafton,* 308–309.

28. *Corr. Burke* IV 159–164; Rockingham to Portland, 21 Oct.—Portland MSS; Rockingham to wife 23 Sept. and to Keppel ante 3 Nov.—Albemarle II 381–390.

29. WWM R 145: 45; *Corr. Burke* IV 185–187. Rockingham stated his wishes for the meeting in a letter to Stephen Croft 12 Dec.—WWM R 1: 1869.

30. *Last Journals* II 367.

31. To Pemberton Milnes 28 Oct.—Albemarle II 295–400.

32. Cf. J. E. Bunce, "Rockingham, Shelburne, and the Politics of Reform," in *Studies in Modern History,* ed. G. L. Vincitorio (New York, 1968), 172–173.

33. Albemarle III 409.

34. Ian Christie, "The Marquis of Rockingham and Lord North's Offer of a Coalition," *English Historical Review,* 69 (1954), and *The End of the North Administration* (London, 1958), 26–29.

35. WWM R 155: 1–2.

36. Rockingham to Portland 1, 15, 22 Sept.—Portland MSS; to the Duke of Rutland 12 Sept. (*Manuscripts of the Duke of Rutland* [Hist. MSS Comm. 14th *Report* App. I] III 343; WWM R 155; *Hist. Parl.* I 435–444).

37. *Corr. Burke* IV 266–280, 282–302; Rockingham to Portland 12 Sept., 14 Oct.—Portland MSS; *Hist. Parl.* I 307; II 42.

38. Rockingham to Portland 17 Aug., 1 Sept.—Portland MSS; Eliot to Rockingham 14 Sept.—WWM R 139: 29; *Hist. Parl.* I 307; II 42.

39. To Edward Eliot 8 Oct.—WWM R 140: 92; also Rockingham to Savile 17 Sept.—R 1: 1928.

40. Albemarle II 451–453.

41. *Ibid.,* 458–459.

42. The Rockingham–Shelburne exchange is printed *ibid.,* 463–464.

43. To William Mason.—*Horace Walpole's Correspondence* XXIX, edd.

W. S. Lewis, G. Cronin, C. H. Bennett (New Haven: Yale University Press, 1955), 209.

44. *Corr. Burke* IV 422–423.

45. Albemarle II 477–480.

46. E. A. Reitan, "The Civil List in Eighteenth-century Politics," *The Historical Journal,* 9, No. 3 (1966), 318–337.

47. *Corr. Burke* V 6, 9.

48. *Ibid.,* IX 220. The eclipse of the Rockingham whigs by Fox's party— through death, resignation, separation, and absorption—has been well described by L. G. Mitchell in *Charles Fox and the Disintegration of the Whig Party* (Oxford, 1971), esp. Ch. 7.

Index